Great Hatred, Little Room

Making Peace in Northern Ireland

JONATHAN POWELL

THE BODLEY HEAD
LONDON

Published by The Bodley Head 2008

2 4 6 8 10 9 7 5 3

First published in Great Britain in 2008 by
The Bodley Head
Random House, 20 Vauxhall Bridge Road,
London SW1V 2SA

www.rbooks.co.uk

Addresses for companies within The Random House Group Limited can be found at:
www.randomhouse.co.uk/offices.htm

The Random House Group Limited Reg. No. 954009

A CIP catalogue record for this book
is available from the British Library

ISBN 9781847920324

The Random House Group Limited supports The Forest Stewardship
Council (FSC), the leading international forest certification organisation. All our titles that are printed
on Greenpeace approved FSC certified paper carry the FSC logo. Our paper procurement policy can be
found at www.rbooks.co.uk/environment

Typeset in Dante MT by Palimpsest Book Production Limited,
Grangemouth, Stirlingshire

Printed and bound in Great Britain by
Clays Ltd, St Ives plc

Great Hatred,
Little Room

Making Peace in Northern Ireland

To the people of Northern Ireland
who have suffered so much

I ranted to the knave and fool,
But outgrew that school,
Would transform the part,
Fit audience found, but cannot rule
My fanatic heart.

I sought my betters: though in each
Fine manners, liberal speech,
Turn hatred into sport,
Nothing said or done can reach
My fanatic heart.

Out of Ireland have we come.
Great hatred, little room,
Maimed us at the start.
I carry from my mother's womb
A fanatic heart.

W. B. Yeats, 'Remorse for Intemperate Speech' (1931)

Contents

Preface

This book is not supposed to be an impartial account of the Northern Ireland peace process nor a comprehensive history of the conflict and its origins. It is probably too early for anyone to write such a history and I am far too close to events to be impartial. Instead, it is the story of the peace process from my perspective as Tony Blair's Chief of Staff and chief negotiator. What I hope makes it interesting is the unique vantage point I bring to it. For a decade I was at the centre of things, able to observe at close hand the panorama of different interests and parties. I have tried to be as honest and frank about our position in No. 10 as I am about everyone else's, and I hope I have been as even-handed as my perspective allows. Still, for me, the heroes of this story are Tony Blair, Bertie Ahern and the party leaders in Northern Ireland, all of whom had the courage to try to make peace work at some risk to themselves. But there are many other, unsung participants who had a crucial role to play.

I am very conscious that my position as narrator of this book, and the personal perspective on events I use, might suggest that I think Tony and I did everything on the British side. That is very far from the truth. Much of the hard work was carried out by the teams in No. 10 and the Northern Ireland Office who, over ten years, gave huge amounts of time and effort to the process, and their contribution should be recognised. To have named them all in the book would have been difficult, but I am profoundly grateful to them. The same goes for the remarkably able team of Irish officials with whom we worked, who were prepared to sacrifice thousands of hours of their time, and demonstrated enormous patience with our annoying ways. A large contribution was also made by the backroom teams from the political parties, some of whom have asked not to be mentioned by name.

To write the book, I have drawn on my memories, my personal
diaries and on the No. 10 files for the period 1997 to 2007. From 1997
onwards, pretty much every entry in my diary has some reference to
Northern Ireland, and I have been able to use it not only to map the
progress of the negotiations, but also to remind me of some of the
anecdotes that surrounded events. I am very grateful to the Cabinet
Office for allowing me to go back over the papers relating to my time
at No. 10. I wouldn't have been able to give such a full account without
doing so. Where the papers were particularly useful was in letting me
understand what our intent was at each stage. I have tried to write
this book without the benefit of hindsight, describing our feelings at
each step of the way without reference to what then ensued. Books
that justify everything that was done at the time by talking about the
outcome seem to me dishonest. We didn't know how the story was
going to end and so I have attempted to explain why we did what we
did, even when it turned out to be mistaken or counterproductive.
The reason why so many of the quoted conversations are in reported
speech is that they are taken from official records of the negotiations,
many of them written by me, and such notes are always written in
indirect speech. I have not attempted footnotes for the obvious reason
that no one has access to the sources. I should also mention that, in
referring to unionists, nationalists, loyalists and republicans, I have
aimed to follow the convention whereby capitalisation is used if the
term denotes a specific party or organisation and its members, and
lower case if it refers to the communities in general.

A number of the people who have helped me with the book have
asked not to be named, but I am nonetheless very grateful to them.
I would also like to thank Ronan Fanning and Paul Bew, who read the
historical section and offered suggestions. Quentin Thomas, David
Cooke and Tom Kelly all kindly read the manuscript and I am very
grateful to them, and to Bill Jeffrey, Jonathan Phillips and Robert
Hannigan, for being the best colleagues I could have had. Obviously
I am responsible for any mistakes that remain.

In the course of preparing this book, I read a number of books that
were helpful. Paul Bew's *The Politics of Enmity* and Richard English's
Irish Freedom were particularly useful when getting to grips with Irish
history, while Peter Taylor's *Brits* and *The Provos* give an excellent
account of the early years of the Troubles. More recent histories that

bring the story up-to-date are harder to come by. There are auto-biographies, like those of Gerry Adams, Mo Mowlam and George Mitchell, as well as biographies such as Don Macintyre's *Mandelson*, Frank Millar's excellent *David Trimble: The Price of Peace* (and his more general writing on the peace process) and Dean Godson's remarkable biography of David Trimble, *Himself Alone*. There are also some good academic books on the negotiations themselves, including Peter Neumann's *Britain's Long War* and Thomas Hennessy's *The Northern Ireland Peace Process*. Indispensable for anyone who wants an account of the whole period from 1921 to 2000 is David McKitterick and David McVea's *Making Sense of the Troubles*, complete with chronology. I also recommend David Trimble's website, which includes a transcript of his 'Antony Alcock Memorial Lecture', giving his account of the Good Friday negotiations. For a full bibliography of books on Northern Ireland, I suggest a visit to the online 'Cain Bibliography'.

This book would not have been written had it not been for the persuasiveness of Natasha Fairweather, my agent, and her continuous encouragement. I am also grateful to Rebecca Carter, my editor, for her quite remarkable work in producing a readable book from my musings by editing and re-editing right through Christmas, and to Dan Hind at Bodley Head who first came to me with the idea and brought it through to fruition, as well as to Drummond Moir who helped form the book into reality. Most of all, I am grateful to my wife Sarah and my children John, Charlie, Jessica and Rosamund for their tolerance. Northern Ireland has often taken me away from them; the negotiations did not respect weekends, holidays or even Christmas, and then there were the intense months I spent writing this book. I hope it will show them what it was all for.

Prologue

When Ian Paisley took the oath of office as First Minister of Northern Ireland on Tuesday 8 May 2007, in the old Parliament building at Stormont, people listened in absolute silence. I was sitting in the front row of the gallery, alongside Tony Blair and the Irish Taoiseach, Bertie Ahern, and I leaned over the balustrade, noting the way Paisley paused between words for maximum effect. As Martin McGuinness, the new Deputy First Minister, followed him to take the same oath, swearing loyalty to the Police Service of Northern Ireland, an oath over which we had fought so long and hard, I felt dizzy and slightly faint, as if I had just finished pushing a very large boulder uphill. If anyone had asked me when I first stepped into Downing Street as Tony Blair's Chief of Staff in May 1997 whether I ever expected to see Ian Paisley and Martin McGuinness sharing power in Stormont I would have thought they were mad. For ten years I had been involved in a series of grinding negotiations that, at many points along the way, had seemed as if they would never end. But now they *had* ended, and all the difficulties we had experienced seemed worthwhile. Unlike other governments before us, we had not just succeeded in managing the Northern Ireland problem, we had resolved it, we hoped, once and for all. It was a great moment for the people of Ireland and the people of Britain, but I also felt a real sense of personal triumph. Nothing in my thirty years in the public service had been harder to achieve or had given me so much satisfaction in its achievement.

I would have felt it to be an even more remarkable occasion had I realised the identity of the group of middle-aged men sitting in the next section along in the gallery. They looked harmless enough with their grey hair, but they were in fact the high command of the IRA, who between them had served over fifty years in jail and been responsible for more than a thousand deaths. It was only after the ceremony that we discovered who they were. Each of the key IRA figures were there, including the Quartermaster General, the military commander in Belfast, the head of intelligence and the chief ideologue – all sitting in the gallery just a few feet away from Bertie Ahern and Tony Blair. I had never met them and did not know what they looked like, but I felt I knew each one of them intimately. They had been the invisible presence at the negotiating table during all our talks. They were the people Sinn Féin leaders Gerry Adams and Martin McGuinness had needed to persuade to accept difficult compromises, usually going to meet them in an anonymous barn somewhere on the border with the Republic, in the middle of the night, with a running tractor engine in the background so their conversations couldn't be picked up. There was a powerful symbolism in the fact that these men, who had spent so much of their lives in hiding, had now come to witness openly the closing chapter of the long-drawn-out struggle.

Listening to Paisley's familiar booming voice, I reflected on the role fate had played in the bringing of peace, through two deaths narrowly avoided. In August 2004, Ian Paisley had come very near to death while in hospital. Of course, when he was discharged looking frail and gaunt, he couldn't resist upbraiding reporters for counting him out, but despite the usual irascibility he seemed a new person. His brush with mortality appeared to have changed his way of thinking. No longer content with being remembered as Dr No, he seemed determined to become Dr Yes, the man who had presided over the end of the Troubles and the beginning of a new period of peace, prosperity and devolved politics in Northern Ireland. If he had died instead of being metaphorically reborn, I doubt we would have witnessed those remarkable events on 8 May.

And there was another man who had been sick and came near to death, and whose survival helped secure the final settlement. He was someone I had never met, and who was not well known to the public, but was also sitting in the gallery along with the other members of the Republican leadership. Brian Keenan was at one stage the biggest single threat to the British state. He ran the IRA's mainland bombing campaigns (for which he served eighteen years in jail) and had persuaded Gaddafi to arm the IRA. But he was also instrumental in bringing the IRA round to the political strategy, and, as the secret intermediary with John de Chastelain, the Canadian General in charge of the International Commission on Decommissioning, was the man who had achieved the decommissioning of IRA weapons. If he had been against it, it would not have happened. If he had died, it might have been impossible to persuade the IRA to trade the Armalite for the ballot box. He too looked frail, but he had lived long enough to politicise the Volunteers of the IRA over time, and gradually to transform physical force republicanism into a political movement.

Although the events that day felt like the natural order of things, and commentators have tended to assume that peace in Northern Ireland was simply a matter of time, that it was destined to happen, that is far from the case. Right up to the last minute, it was dogged by unresolved issues that could well have thrown the whole thing off course. And the fact that it happened at all required extraordinary efforts by many people over many years.

But perhaps the main difference between this negotiation and all the previous efforts to resolve Northern Ireland was Tony Blair's determination that something could be done, and his refusal to accept that we had ever reached the end. In all the preceding attempts, British leaders had approached the problem half convinced that it was insoluble and that failure was inevitable. Winston Churchill's description of Northern Ireland after the First World War aptly caught the way British leaders saw it: 'As the deluge [of the war] subsides and the waters fall short, we see the dreary steeples of Fermanagh and Tyrone emerging once again. The integrity of their quarrel is one of the few institutions that has been unaltered in the cataclysm which has swept the world.' There was no political advantage to be gained in Britain in trying to resolve the dreary and incomprehensible dispute between two tribes somewhere on the periphery of the country. And the sense of impossibility meant that previous governments gave up when it all got too difficult. They shrugged, let the loyalists and republicans go back to killing each other, and tried to ignore the problem.

Tony has often been criticised for his messianic belief in other contexts. But for Northern Ireland that belief was essential. Tony had been an enthusiastic reader of Roy Jenkins's biography of Gladstone and saw some parallels with his own career, not least on the Irish question. He was constantly ordering me to make impossible things happen when the two sides completely disagreed, to make water flow uphill. And I lost count of the times I came back from exhausting all-night sessions with Gerry Adams or David Trimble to tell him it was all over, and Tony would refuse to let me give up, saying I had to get back in touch with them and start again. He was right. If republicans had ever become convinced we had lost interest in Ireland, as so many British prime ministers had before, the chance of success would have been lost. It was our interest and involvement they wanted above all else. Paying attention was nine-tenths of the battle.

But, in the end, one man is not enough. The question this book tries to address is why were we able to solve a problem that had dogged so many governments before ours, and why did we succeed at that particular moment in time? The Irish question bedevilled British politics in the second half of the nineteenth century, and even statesmen like Gladstone, despite their best efforts, were not able to resolve it. In the late twentieth century, Northern Ireland posed the biggest terrorist threat the country had ever faced, and was perhaps the major preoccupation of the British Army. Edward Heath, Harold Wilson, Margaret Thatcher and John Major all devoted considerable time to it without success. What's more, similar disputes elsewhere in the world have reached a stage of breakthrough like that brought by the Good Friday Agreement, but in each case – from the 1993 Oslo accords in the Middle East, the ceasefire between the government and the Tamil Tigers in Sri Lanka in 2002, and the ETA ceasefire in Spain in 2006 – the breakthrough agreement has got stuck in the eddies of politics and gradually unravelled, returning the dispute to violence. It is worth telling the story of the Northern Ireland talks in some detail for the light it can shed on other peace negotiations.

Obviously, this should be done with caution. Facile comparisons between Northern Ireland and conflicts elsewhere in the world are best avoided. Northern Ireland was *sui generis*. It was neither an ethnic nor a religious dispute, and although it was about nationalism it was only so in a very particular sense. It was very small scale, with no more than 1.7 million people in the whole of Northern Ireland, and the areas actually touched by the Troubles were tiny. Furthermore, it was taking place in a Western democracy, not a dictatorship or a developing country. Nevertheless, there are lessons to be learned, not least the crucial one that it was only by refusing to accept 'no' for an answer that we managed to build a lasting settlement, by never letting the talking stop and above all by using perseverance of a sort that had not been tried before.

Throughout the negotiations, Tony Blair and I often discussed whether our belief that the problem of Northern Ireland had a solution was, in fact, ill-founded. There were certainly many occasions on which that belief was challenged. At first we thought that, having achieved the breakthrough of the Good Friday Agreement, all we had to do was implement it. But, by the end of 1998, it became clear it was not going to be that simple, and we were facing an endurance test. I would tell Tony that, no matter what, we had to keep things moving forward, like a bicycle. If we ever let the bicycle fall over, we would create a vacuum and that vacuum would be filled by violence. It was a precept we stuck with, and I don't think that, deep down, either Tony or I ever really lost the belief that it could all be resolved eventually, if we were patient enough. By the end, we had realised peace was not an event but a process.

I

Taking Events at a Gallop: May 1997–March 1998

It is hard to explain now what the world felt like on the morning of 1 May 1997. I was light-headed, having flown down from Tony's constituency of Sedgefield in the early hours of the morning after two nights of very little sleep. I sleepwalked through the election victory celebration at the Royal Festival Hall, then drifted through the breaking dawn across Westminster Bridge to my flat near Victoria feeling numb and slightly panicked by the challenges ahead of us.

At the flat, I picked up the bundle of files I had been accumulating over the previous year on what we needed to do in the first hundred days, who would go to what job, how we should handle our European presidency, what announcements we would make in the first few days. Among them was a slim folder on Northern Ireland. Then I made my way to Tony's house in Richmond Crescent, Islington. The press were gathering outside and after an hour pinching ourselves to check that the enormity of what had happened was real, we jumped into the new official cars that had been sent for us and our motorcade swept off to Buckingham Palace, Tony and Cherie in the first car, Alastair Campbell and I in the second. After we passed King's Cross station, a remarkable thing started to happen. Along the route people began coming out of their houses and offices into the bright sunshine, and waving and cheering. They had been following our progress on TV as the news helicopters followed us from above and they wanted to be part of the celebration.

An hour later, as I made my way through the crowd lining Downing Street while Tony and Cherie shook hands with the throng, I could not suppress a grin. We had captured the citadel. When I walked through the door of No. 10, with the files crammed under my arm, and down the corridor filled with civil servants ready to clap Tony in, there seemed to be no limit to what we could achieve.

Northern Ireland was not the first item on our agenda. There were ministers to appoint, a Queen's Speech to finalise and domestic reforms – like the independence of the Bank of England – to set in motion. But it was in the first eleven, probably for the first time for a newly elected prime minister since Gladstone.

In opposition we had supported absolutely what John Major was doing on Northern Ireland and in government we planned to build on the structures he had created. But we had also observed the mistakes he made, in particular failing to get Sinn Féin into all-party talks quickly after the 1994 IRA ceasefire, and in raising decommissioning as a precondition for their entry into the talks. We had not criticised these missteps at the time but we were determined not to repeat them. We did not have a detailed, worked-out, point-by-point strategy, but we did have an idea. We would take events at a gallop and try to use the momentum of the electoral landslide to make progress in Northern Ireland before resistance had time to build up.

When Tony finally left the crowd of well-wishers and came into No. 10, he and I went into the Cabinet room at the back of the building where we were met by Robin Butler, the Cabinet Secretary. He handed over a pile of 'first day briefs' containing the Civil Service proposals on how to implement the policies in our manifesto. Included in the pile was a brief on Northern Ireland. It outlined the history of the conflict (starting with the civil war in 1921), and set out the next steps. It was clear what our priority was. The first IRA ceasefire of 1994 had collapsed in Major's last years in office and there was violence on the streets again. We had to get the IRA ceasefire restored and to bring Sinn Féin rapidly into the talks that were taking place in Belfast under the chairmanship of Senator George Mitchell. There was also a brief from the Northern Ireland Office (NIO). It told us it would be very difficult indeed to get Sinn Féin into the talks without losing the Unionists off the other side. But we were determined to try.

We were also greeted by John Holmes who had been Major's private secretary for foreign affairs since 1995. John, a professional diplomat, was quiet and self-effacing but formidably hard-working. Because Northern Ireland was seen primarily as a security issue, it had been dealt with at No. 10 for decades by the private secretary handling foreign and defence affairs. John, phlegmatic at all times, had wrestled with the problem through the collapse of the first ceasefire, keeping relations on an even keel with the Irish government and the Northern Ireland parties in the difficult period that followed, but he was in no position to drive the peace process forward by himself, and was probably faintly sceptical about our chances of success, having, unlike us, seen it all before.

Our first task was to reassure the unionists. Given the history of the Labour Party, they were naturally suspicious about our commitment to the Union. Of course, they had seen the changes Tony had made to Labour Party policy on Northern Ireland on becoming leader in 1994, including replacing the green shadow Northern Ireland Secretary Kevin McNamara with the iconoclastic Mo Mowlam in his first reshuffle. Mo had served as a junior spokesperson on Northern Ireland in 1989, but she had no history of association with either side to the dispute. However the unionists were still not convinced we were on their side in the way the Conservatives instinctively were. Tony's first comment on Northern Ireland after entering No. 10 was scribbled on top of a formal minute from John Holmes on 6 May. It said, 'I need to do a speech that sets out my view of the unlikely nature of unification.' He also proposed that he see David Trimble before he met the then Irish Prime Minister John Bruton, and we arranged a meeting for 7 May. They met in the House of Commons, in the Prime Minister's cavernous office behind the Speaker's chair, where Tony reassured Trimble that 'his aim was to sort out the Northern Ireland problem. He had no predilection whatsoever to a united Ireland.'

Tony had built up a good relationship with David Trimble in opposition. They had both been frontbench spokesmen on home affairs and Tony had seen Trimble a number of times after he became leader of the moderate Ulster Unionist Party (UUP). The UUP was the direct descendant of the original Ulster Unionist Party which had ruled Northern Ireland from its creation in 1922 onwards, representing the solid Protestant middle class, but in the decades since the Troubles began they had been increasingly outflanked by the Democratic Unionist Party (DUP) led by Ian Paisley and by other splinter unionist parties.

Tony was eager to deliver the reassuring speech to the unionists soon, and Alastair Campbell and I liked the symbolism of his first visit outside London being to Northern Ireland, so we chose the quintessentially unionist Royal Ulster Agricultural Show in Balmoral outside

Belfast as the setting. John Holmes proposed postponing the visit till after the Northern Ireland local elections in late May, but Tony was keen to get on with it.

It took me a while to get used to travelling by motorcade – the police motorcycle outriders screaming ahead as they took us down the wrong side of the road, people staring at us as if holding us personally responsible for their delay. On the morning of 16 May we drove to Northolt RAF station on the edge of London to get on to a small official jet. The airmen saluted as the doors of the cars were opened and we made our way through the gusting wind to the door at the back of the plane. I was clutching a series of files containing sensitive papers about the visit and just as I put my foot on the first step of the ladder to get into the plane the wind ripped the papers out of my hands and scattered them across the airfield. They were far too sensitive just to forget about, so, cringing with embarrassment, I had to ask the RAF to recover them. They sent two Land Rovers round the perimeter, collecting the pages from where the wind had pinned them against the barbed wire. Meanwhile, we all had to sit in the cabin of the plane waiting while Tony and Alastair teased me mercilessly for my clumsiness.

When we landed at Belfast international airport we were met by RAF helicopters to take us on to the site of the show. These were not the comfortable upholstered helicopters provided for French or American presidents, or even the small executive helicopters we had hired for election visits, but working military helicopters with canvas benches and ripped camouflage netting inside, and most of all unbearable noise for which they gave you little yellow plastic earplugs. The only way to communicate was by writing notes on scraps of paper and passing them around. The engines started and the overall-clad RAF man connected to the helicopter by the umbilical cord of his headphones jumped on, but kept both doors open as we took off, scuttling from side to side to look below to see we were in no danger.

The show itself was an incongruous sight. We entered through pens of the biggest bulls I had ever seen, with ruddy-faced farmers milling around looking at the animals. It didn't feel like the sort of place where a major political milestone would be passed, and the showgoers certainly didn't look as if they expected anything out of the ordinary.

John Holmes had produced a workmanlike draft of the speech that made all the key points, but Tony was congenitally incapable of delivering a speech written by anyone else. As a former barrister he could only speak with feeling if he had written out what he was going to say in longhand himself, on foolscap paper with a fountain pen. Over the years I repeatedly tried to recruit speechwriters to work with Tony to reduce the burden on him of writing all his speeches himself. I imagined something like the system in the White House where brilliant young writers labour through the night to produce beautifully crafted works of literature which somehow sound authentic in the mouth of the President when he reads them out the next day. Besides anything else, it would have saved so much time. It didn't work though, not because the young people we recruited were not brilliant, but because Tony could never get comfortable with words written for him except in very exceptional circumstances.

David Trimble later speculated that Tony had ad-libbed the key words in the Balmoral speech. But he had written them himself the day before and we had shown them to the Irish and the Americans, as well as talking to John Major about it. Paddy Teahon, the peppery Irish Deputy Cabinet Secretary, said when he saw the draft that he was not keen on the sentence 'None of us in the hall today, even the youngest, is likely to see Northern Ireland as anything but a part of the United Kingdom', but Tony insisted on maintaining it. The aim was to tell unionists that we were on their side, that their way of life was not under threat and that, as Tony had told Trimble when he first met him after the election, consent was the fundamental issue, rather than decommissioning.

It was a brilliantly judged speech in which Tony was explicit in his defence of the Union saying, 'My agenda is not a united Ireland. Northern Ireland is part of the United Kingdom alongside England, Scotland and Wales. The Union binds the four parts of the United Kingdom. I believe in the United Kingdom. I value the Union.' And he was explicit in reassuring the unionists that a Labour government would not slide back into its old policies, saying, 'Any settlement must be negotiated not imposed; it must be endorsed by the people of Northern Ireland in a referendum; and it must be endorsed by the British Parliament. So unionists have nothing to fear from a new Labour government. A political settlement is not a slippery slope to a united Ireland. The government will not be persuaders for unity.'

That the British government should be a 'persuader' for Irish unity was a key Republican demand, and had been the position of the Labour Party before Tony became leader. But Tony wanted to make it clear we would not be working for a united Ireland. Indeed, while we would of course accept the will of a majority in Northern Ireland for unification if that ever came about, until that moment arrived, we were in favour of a United Kingdom including Northern Ireland. This demand for a government to become a 'persuader' arises repeatedly in other peace processes too. For example, in Spain ETA have always wanted the Spanish government to become an advocate for uniting Navarre into the Basque homeland. But a democratic government cannot agree, under pressure from a terrorist organisation and under the threat of violence, to argue for a position it does not itself hold.

Tony went out of his way to make consent the centrepiece of the speech, saying, 'Northern Ireland is part of the United Kingdom because that is the wish of the majority who live here. It will remain part of the United Kingdom for as long as that remains the case. The principle of consent is and will be at the heart of my government's policies on Northern Ireland. It is the key principle. It means there can be absolutely no possibility of a change in the status of Northern Ireland as part of the United Kingdom without the clear and formal consent of a majority of people in Northern Ireland.'

One of Tony's remarkable attributes as a leader was his ability to go back to first principles rather than accepting what was given to him as conventional wisdom. Most of the moving parts in a Northern Ireland settlement had been on the table for years or even decades, from a power-sharing executive to the involvement of the Irish government in Northern Ireland affairs through North/South bodies. But Tony had zeroed in on the fundamental principle: what was the unit that had the right to self-determination? Was it Northern Ireland, the island of Ireland, or the islands together including Britain? He believed the key point to be that of the consent of the people being ruled, and that meant it had to be the people of Northern Ireland who should have the say. For the unionists this was of fundamental importance, unlike the issue of decommissioning which was purely transient because, after all, any group that gave up its weapons could easily acquire new ones. The principle of consent, which had been accepted by the Irish government in progressively stronger terms in the Sunningdale Agreement of 1973, the Anglo-Irish Agreement of 1985 and in the Downing Street Declaration of 1993, would be the most difficult concession for Republicans to make.

Although the pro-Union tone of the speech upset the Irish and unsettled the Republicans, it served its primary purpose of reassuring unionist voters and winning over David Trimble just because its message was such a stark and surprising statement of a pro-Union position by a Labour prime minister. So much of what we achieved in those early months of government was achieved in the same way; changing the weather by surprising people with the position we took, and jolting them out of their comfort zone so they looked at us and at the issue in a new way.

But reassuring the unionists was only part of the purpose of the speech. The other aim was to try to tempt the IRA back on to cease-fire, both by setting out the opportunities for them if they did so and by giving them an ultimatum that they must join now or we would go ahead without them. The first contact with Sinn Féin had already been made on 9 May by a phone call from Quentin Thomas, the NIO's political director, to Siobhan O'Hanlon, Gerry Adams's close aide, assuring Republicans there would be engagement before too long if there was no violence. After the Balmoral speech Tony authorised official meetings with Sinn Féin, and Quentin and his team met Martin McGuinness on 21 May. They reported a warmth and good humour that had not been present in the previous talks after the first cease-fire. Sinn Féin clearly saw the arrival of the new government as an opportunity to move things forward. Gerry Adams had told the Irish government separately that he could get a ceasefire within seven to ten days if we could convince them that they would be rapidly brought into all-party talks and if there were a deadline for the successful conclusion of those talks of six to nine months hence.

Dealing with Sinn Féin was not, however, a smooth and seamless process. An IRA group murdered two Royal Ulster Constabulary (RUC) officers in Lurgan on 16 June while we were at our first European summit in Amsterdam. Tony felt personally betrayed by this act of gratuitous violence, given what he had already communicated privately to Adams, and suspended official contacts temporarily, and we even contemplated withdrawing our offer to Republicans of early entry into talks. We had disapproved of John Major's willingness to resume contacts with Republicans after the Canary Wharf bomb of 1996. We were afraid that he had sent the hard men the message that such violent acts could help them to get their way in the negotiation, and we were determined to make it explicitly clear to the Republican leaders we met that if they ever returned to violence, we would cease to talk to them. But McGuinness contacted Quentin on the special telephone in his office reserved for them to say 'they had some problems'. It became clear that the attack had been unauthorised and was carried out by a rogue active service unit of the IRA, so we continued the official contact with Sinn Féin.

In these private talks, Quentin Thomas presented an aide-memoire setting out the basis on which we would go ahead if the IRA called a ceasefire. Six weeks after an end to violence we would assess whether the ceasefire was genuine and, if it was, include Sinn Féin in the all-party talks; those talks would be completed by May 1998; Sinn Féin would be expected to sign up to the principles of non-violence which former US Senator George Mitchell had set out in his report on decommissioning in January 1996; and they would need to agree that all parties were committed to working in good faith to implement all the Mitchell principles, including the principle on decommissioning. We made these conditions public so we could not be accused of negotiating a secret deal with Sinn Féin and Tony set out his pitch to Republicans in a statement to the House of Commons on 25 June, saying, 'The settlement train is leaving, with or without Sinn Féin. If it wants to join it is absolutely clear what it has to do.' He set deadlines for the all-party talks to start under the chairmanship of George Mitchell on 15 September, and for an agreement to be in place by May 1998. Actually, although we had set an ultimatum for Republicans, we had no way of going ahead without them as long as the nationalist Social Democratic and Labour Party (SDLP) was not prepared to do so, since it would mean we had no Catholic component to a cross-community consensus to carry us forward. That SDLP reluctance to move without Sinn Féin was a problem that was to bedevil us throughout the process.

Those first steps we took were a success. The IRA announced a new ceasefire on 20 July and three days later we said Sinn Féin could join the talks after a six-week period of quarantine. The public reaction in Northern Ireland was cautious, but at the end of August Mo Mowlam confirmed that the ceasefire had been genuine and talks would resume on 9 September, this time with the participation of Sinn Féin who had by then signed up to the Mitchell principles of non-violence.

Tony used to claim that every time he came across the Irish Sea it started to rain, but that this made you appreciate it even more when it stopped. When we crossed the channel on 13 October, Northern Ireland looked beautiful from the air in bright sunshine after the rain cleared. We had deliberately decided to hold the first meeting with Sinn Féin leaders in Belfast rather than London to get over the hurdle of seeing them by doing it in as low-key a way as possible. And we combined the meeting with other commitments, going first by heli-copter to Derry to open a factory and see SDLP leader John Hume, then crisscrossing the province to visit an army barracks in Portadown where we met representatives of the RUC. We then went by car to David Trimble's constituency office, and finally on to Stormont to meet the parties participating in the talks.

Our meeting with Sinn Féin took place in a little airless room with no windows in Castle Buildings. On their side there were Gerry Adams, Martin McGuinness, Pat Doherty and Siobhan O'Hanlon, taking short-hand. O'Hanlon was believed to have been a terrorist leader and was reputed to have been a member of the IRA Active Service Unit in Gibraltar made famous by the TV programme *Death on the Rock*. She had become a fiercely loyal member of Adams's inner team. Tony shook their hands one by one but Alastair, John Holmes and I had decided not to on principle. Both sides were nervous, with Gerry Adams's hand shaking slightly.

Adams started off the conversation with some rather wet jokes, including giving Tony a tiny harp made of Irish bog wood which he said he hoped was the only bit of Ireland he would keep. He then asked how it felt to be in power and Tony replied, rather shortly, that it was better than being in opposition: we wanted to make some changes. Martin McGuinness interjected they wanted changes too. Adams said he wanted to avoid history lessons and then proceeded to give us one, the burden of which was that the problem had been caused by the British presence in Ireland. He said that John Major had made a mess of the peace process and that we had to pick up the pieces. He also emphasised how determined they were to avoid the

Republican splits that littered Irish history, and to keep the movement together. He didn't want to create an Irish Hamas. McGuinness said Northern Ireland was a political problem not a security one and the dispute could only be resolved politically, whether now or in twenty-five years' time. Tony spoke rather well, with passion. He stressed the importance of consent and of their commitment to pursuing their ends through non-violent means, and warned them that the whole thing would be off if there was any return to violence.

I recorded in my diary that they were much more articulate and interesting than most of the other Northern Ireland politicians. John Holmes thought they were distressingly stuck in a rut but I found them more flexible than I had expected.

Tony did a brief press conference after the meeting and was asked if he had shaken Adams's hand. He had prepared his reply and said he had treated him as he would any other human being. The meeting had been long on symbolism – being the first meeting between Republican leaders and a British prime minister for eighty years – but light on substance. We hadn't really got a feel for their positions or even if they were serious about seeking peace, let alone why. It was a curiosity to meet people who had been demonised throughout my adult life. Television had not even been able legally to broadcast their voices and so for years the slightly threatening bearded face of Adams and the clear, chilling eyes of McGuinness had been overlaid by the voices of actors. Now we had heard their real voices. Their accents were thick and hard to follow, but over the years either I became more attuned to them or they became thinner as a result of international exposure.

After the meeting we rushed off to do a walkabout at the Connswater shopping centre, in the East Belfast constituency of the DUP deputy leader, Peter Robinson. Anji Hunter, Tony's close aide in charge of advancing the visit, paged me from the shopping centre saying we should go ahead and that there was 'a large (not hostile) crowd'. When we got there we discovered an organised demonstration by the DUP, who had been tipped off that we were coming, probably by a sympathiser in the police. The crowd was mostly made up of 'Hell's Grannies', whose contorted faces as they shouted 'traitor' and threw rubber gloves at Tony, saying he should wear them to shake hands with a murderer like Gerry Adams, were disconcerting if not really frightening. But their anger was real all right; they could not believe that their Prime Minister had been talking to terrorists. The RUC contingent protecting us overreacted, forming a flying wedge, literally raising Tony off the ground under his arms and hustling us off to the manager's office on the floor above the shopping centre. Tony was convinced the police had done it on purpose to suggest he was frightened. In my mind, they were just being overcautious. The result was some bad television pictures, but I thought at the time it was good to have some conflict, otherwise everything would look too easy. Given the way things worked out I needn't have worried.

Having got Sinn Féin into the talks, we had to do everything we could to persuade the UUP not to walk out. In every previous attempt at peace, as soon as the government got one community onside the other jumped overboard. Tony had explained his strategy to Trimble in June in the run-up to the ceasefire. The objective was to get Republicans into the talks so they could not go back to violence. Sinn Féin might well not be able to accept the outcome of the talks, but with the 'sufficient consensus' rule, which required only a majority from both communities to agree rather than unanimity, Republicans could not block any agreement as long as the SDLP went along with it. If they returned to violence because they did not like the outcome of a negotiation in which they had participated, they would lose all respectable support. He said the only alternative was to build out from the centre with an agreement between the UUP and the SDLP. But the SDLP and Irish government would only countenance that option if Sinn Féin had been given a chance and walked away from it.

Tony saw David Trimble and his deputy, John Taylor, along with other UUP leaders several times around the announcement of the IRA ceasefire, both in No. 10 and in the House of Commons. They were increasingly nervous, and criticised him for not insisting on decommissioning as a price for Sinn Féin entering the talks. Tony again explained the aim was to call Sinn Féin's bluff. The substantive negotiations would be difficult for Sinn Féin, particularly the issue of consent, and he did not want to break over the issue of decommissioning. The emphasis should be on consent, which was of far greater long-term significance for unionists than the issue of arms. We were determined not to get snagged on decommissioning in the way that

John Major had, but equally we could not ignore the issue and the Unionists were right that it should happen. As Tony told Bertie Ahern, the new Irish Prime Minister, at their first meeting after Bertie's election that summer, we would have to rely on a certain degree of ambiguity for the time being.

Immediately after the IRA ceasefire, Ian Paisley's Democratic Unionist Party refused to participate in the talks process, together with the even less moderate United Kingdom Unionist Party (UKUP) led by Bob McCartney, saying that the admission of Sinn Féin would result in 'a sell-out of the Union'. David Trimble sidestepped having to make a snap decision by announcing he was consulting the unionist community on whether or not the party should stay in the talks. At the time it looked as though the DUP walkout would make life more difficult for the UUP, but in retrospect, as George Mitchell observed, 'If their objective was, as they repeatedly insisted, to end the process, then their walkout was a fateful error. Reaching agreement without their presence was extremely difficult; it would have been impossible with them in the room . . . Their absence freed the UUP from daily attacks at the negotiating table, and gave the party room to negotiate that it might not otherwise have had.'

Tony saw Trimble and UUP leaders again in Downing Street at the end of August and tried to coax out of them their bottom line in the talks. Having failed, he set out what *he* thought it should be, including a sensible halfway house on decommissioning, and asked whether it was worth his while pursuing these ideas with the Irish government or whether the UUP would refuse to join the talks regardless. Trimble told him to go ahead on that basis and see what he could negotiate. They were holding open the door to remaining in the talks despite the flak they were taking at home. Tony met the same group again in the garden of Downing Street on 10 September, having had a session of negotiations with Bertie Ahern in between. He told them he thought he had persuaded the Irish to move on consent and agree that movement on decommissioning was necessary during the talks, as long as these steps would provide a sufficient basis for the UUP to stay in the talks. Trimble accepted what Tony said he could secure, including on decommissioning. We appeared to have a basis on which they would stay in the talks.

It was clear that a new relationship was developing between No.

10 and the Unionist leader. Trimble has said he found No. 10 much more accessible under Tony Blair than he had done under John Major and he had a friend at court in me. I had got to know the UUP leaders well during their visits to Washington in the early 1990s when I had been at the British Embassy and they were tentatively dipping their toes in the water of American opinion. They thought, rightly, that I was sympathetic. I saw them as misunderstood. They seemed such outlandish figures to the Americans and they had no natural constituency in the US. But after all it was not they who were killing people and their fundamental point, that it should be the people of Northern Ireland who decided their own future, seemed to me an entirely reasonable one. Visits to Washington were not always successful, even in 1997. Trimble met an Irish-American congressman during a visit in the autumn who earnestly praised Gerry Adams's simple search for peace and justice. Trimble replied that he hoped Adams would get his wish. 'Justice would put him behind bars.' As the Foreign Office memo of the meeting drily recorded, 'there was no real meeting of minds'.

As well as the key leaders of the party I also came to know and like several members of David Trimble's eclectic inner circle, including Paul Bew, the former Marxist intellectual, his friend the Irish Catholic polemicist Ruth Dudley Edwards and, most unlikely of all, Sean O'Callaghan, a chain-smoking, whippet-thin former IRA man from the South, who had repented after a term in jail and turned on the IRA leadership (I had met him when we were in opposition). O'Callaghan used to advise David Trimble on IRA thinking which Trimble took, together with snippets of intelligence leaked to him by the RUC, to build up a picture of Republican intentions, often completely wrong, but sometimes better informed than us, or at least more up to date since the police information seemed to get to him first. On the basis of this information, Trimble was convinced that Sinn Féin would not be able to meet the tests that were being imposed on them in 1997, and that therefore he would not face the difficult dilemma of whether or not to go into government with them. He did, however, have slightly odd notions of the IRA's capabilities. In one phone conversation with Tony in September he suddenly said they had to find another way to communicate because he was convinced the IRA were bugging his phone.

The most important aspect of the new relationship with No. 10 by a long way, however, was the personal relationship between the leaders. Tony used the Downing Street meetings with the Unionists to set out a political strategy for Trimble and the UUP, while getting them to believe it was their own. For his part, Trimble would use the meetings to educate his party colleagues on the risks and opportunities in the process. Tony persuaded them that this time they could be the reasonable party, rather than the party that always had to say no, if they agreed to go into talks and set conditions for the IRA. If the IRA met the conditions then Republicans would be on the road to reform, and if they did not, the SDLP would have no excuse not to go ahead without Sinn Féin on the political track to devolution that Trimble wanted to follow. Tony repeatedly reassured Trimble he would not let him down, and indeed did stand by him long after the Irish government, Sinn Féin, the NIO and even the Northern Ireland electorate had given up on him.

The fact that devolution was taking place in Scotland and Wales under the new Labour government, even if in very different forms, made it easier for Trimble. No longer was devolution a mark of the exceptional status of Northern Ireland, but rather a process going on across the whole of the United Kingdom. Politics in Northern Ireland had been stultified by the long period of direct rule. No one of any quality wanted to go into politics because they were not going to have any real power, confined to the role of protest organisation, criticising everything the government did but having no positive policies of their own. To Trimble's credit, he saw this as a political cancer and wanted to correct it by getting power restored to local politicians. Trimble was an odd mixture as a leader. He often saw his aims clearly and pursued them boldly. But at other times he could be infuriating in missing the strategic point, and his red-faced temper tantrums were already legendary.

The new relationship paid off and we were able to persuade Trimble to stay in the talks process even when the IRA threw a spanner in the works by announcing on 11 September that they, unlike Sinn Féin, would not abide by the Mitchell principles of non-violence. Trimble told us he had persuaded his party executive to give the leadership a free hand on deciding whether to go into talks, and it looked to me at the time as if he were looking for an excuse to participate rather than an excuse to stay out. As I recorded in my diary, he was clearly enjoying tweaking everyone's tail by keeping them guessing what he would do. He rang us again to tell us that he would not attend on Monday 15 September, the first day of the postponed talks, but he would announce that the party would be participating. On Tuesday a huge bomb placed by dissident republicans went off in the small town of Markethill and it was clear that he could not attend that day either, but he promised us he would go the next day. And on Wednesday 17 September, the UUP along with the two small Loyalist parties, the Progressive Unionist Party (PUP) and the Ulster Democratic Party (UDP), marched into the talks together. It was important for Trimble to have the two other parties with him because it enabled him to demonstrate he represented a majority of unionism even without the DUP and Bob McCartney's UKUP.

Once in the building, however, there had to be a major wrangle over wording to get the Unionists into a plenary meeting with Sinn Féin and, even once in the same room, it would be some months before Unionists would talk face to face with Republicans. All comments in the plenary meeting were addressed to George Mitchell in the chair rather than directly to Adams or McGuinness. Adams tried to engage Trimble in direct conversation at the urinals, but the advances were dismissed curtly by Trimble telling Adams to grow up.

I remember feeling a sense that the plot was falling into place that September. Despite the hiccups, we had pulled off the remarkable trick of getting Sinn Féin and the majority Unionist party in the same room in order to negotiate with the Irish government and other parties on the future of Northern Ireland.

The talks were divided into three strands. The first strand covered negotiations on a devolved Assembly for Northern Ireland and an Executive in which Catholics and Protestants could share power. (The Irish government did not participate in this, purely internal, aspect of negotiations.) The second covered relations between Ireland, North and South, and how cooperation could be managed through a ministerial council representing both sides, and North/South bodies that could implement the practical cooperation. The third strand covered East/West relations between London, Dublin, Belfast and the other components of the United Kingdom – Scotland, Wales and the various self-governing islands. This aspect of the talks was particularly important to the Unionists, because it helped them to present any agreement as being not about the Republic gaining a say in the affairs of Northern Ireland but of a recalibration of relations between all the parts of the British Isles. None of the issues making up the three strands was new. All had been wrestled with over many years and there was little reason to assume that we could overcome the strongly held opposing views this time, any more than previous British governments had been able to do. But our plan of taking things at a gallop was still working and there was a new sense of optimism in the air.

There was still, however, another symbolic hurdle to overcome and that was a meeting with Sinn Féin in Downing Street. We put it off as long as we could but eventually we had to agree to see them on 11 December. There was a huge sense of occasion and everyone in No. 10, from the principal private secretary, the most senior civil servant, to the messengers who delivered the tea, had been talking about it for days beforehand. Some had said they would not talk to Adams and McGuinness and others that they would not shake their hands as a matter of principle. Alastair had even sent me a memo proposing we put off the erection of the traditional Christmas tree outside the front door of No. 10 which was due to happen that day. He did not think we wanted a picture of Adams and McGuinness in front of festive decorations.

When the day came, the banks of cameras outside Downing Street were even larger than on the day after the election. Mo came into No. 10 through the internal door from the Cabinet Office to avoid them. Sinn Féin arrived ten minutes early with a big delegation and on Mo's advice we made them wait. It was with some trepidation that Tony and I together with Alastair, John Holmes and Mo hovered in the Cabinet Room in Downing Street waiting for Adams and McGuinness to be shown in with their delegation including Martin Ferris, a leading Republican from the South and a convicted gunrunner, Michelle Gildernew, Lucilita Bhreatnach, and Adams's two assistants Siobhan O'Hanlon and Richard McAuley. We waited on the Prime Minister's side of the Cabinet table where the only chair with arms sits in his place in the middle, with the portrait of the first Prime Minister, Sir Robert Walpole, on the wall behind it. Tony met them as they came through the door and shook their hands. Martin McGuinness came round to our side of the table to shake my hand, but I guided the others round to the opposite side. Martin Ferris was the most ominous.

A strong sense of the past hovered over the meeting. Before sitting down, McGuinness paused and observed, 'So this is where all the damage was done.' We all froze, taken aback by this opening gambit, and I said, 'Yes, the mortars landed in the garden behind you. The Gulf War Cabinet on this side of the table, including my brother Charles, the Prime Minister's foreign affairs adviser, dived under the table, before retreating to the Garden Rooms below. The windows came in but no one was injured.' McGuinness looked hurt. 'No, I meant this was where Michael Collins signed the Treaty in 1921.' We, with our shorter-term perspective, had been thinking of the IRA attack on Downing Street in 1991, while they, with their longer sense of historical grievance, had been thinking about the Treaty of Irish Independence signed with Lloyd George that had given rise to the Irish civil war.

Adams opened the meeting by referring to the pictures of past prime ministers in the hall, all of whose policies in Ireland had failed. He said he was grateful to Tony for taking the risk of holding the meeting and asked if the Labour Party policy of unity by consent had disappeared altogether. What was the government's strategic view? He did not want to appear to be lecturing the Prime Minister but his big fear was he would take his eye off the ball with all his other imme-diate preoccupations. Northern Ireland would be the most challenging test of his time in office. Tony said he would not be a persuader for a united Ireland but he did want to create a situation in Northern Ireland that was fair. He asked if Adams could go back and tell his people there was no possibility of a united Ireland. Adams said the question was rather how he could bring his people along. He had to show them there was an alternative way forward. McGuinness said the strength of the 'securocrats' in the British system worked against the peace process; the Prime Minister had to change it. Tony said he needed to look into Adams's eyes and hear him say that Sinn Féin were locked into the political process and would stick to their commit-ment to the Mitchell principles. Adams said they were. At the end of the meeting we asked them what they would say to the waiting press when they went out on to the street. Adams said jokingly they would go out and say the Prime Minister had promised British withdrawal and that all the prisoners would be released.

As I wrote in my diary at the time, Adams seemed intelligent, subtle and impressive. He had stuck to the big issues and asked Tony to look beyond the current preoccupations in the talks and draw up a strategy for the future. Once the meeting was over, Adams came round the end of the table to where two large pillars separate off part of the room so the other members of his delegation couldn't hear him, and said to Tony that he could of course split the movement any time we wanted him to, but that his aim was to carry them all along, and that he was at them persuading every day. Tony said he wanted longer and more informal discussions with Adams and McGuinness. After the meeting Tony said to John and me he was pleased that Adams seemed to accept he would have to live with something less than a united Ireland as the outcome of the process.

As they were leaving, Vera Doyle, a No. 10 messenger from a border area of the Republic herself, came up to Adams and McGuinness and told them what she thought of the IRA. Despite that, they became firm friends, and they made a point of looking her up every time they came back to No. 10.

Throughout the process that followed we had to deal with the duality of the Republican movement. The IRA was a proscribed organisation and we could not talk to its leaders as such. Of course we knew the people we were talking to as Sinn Féin leaders were also leaders of the IRA. And yet it wasn't as simple as the Unionist claim that the two organisations were one and the same. In the early days I, like the Unionists, would talk about the IRA/Sinn Féin in one breath. But the two organisations were different. There wasn't a complete overlap in their membership and their political imperatives were not the same. Some in the physical force Republican movement were not politically subtle and some in Sinn Féin were not engaged in physical violence. On a number of occasions during the negotiation Tony would offer to meet the high command of the IRA to try to reason with them himself. He was convinced that his remarkable powers of persuasion would succeed, but Adams would always say the time was not quite right, and maybe we should do it later. As he explained to me after the negotiations were finished and devolution in place, it was only he and McGuinness who could persuade the leadership of the IRA. A direct meeting with Tony Blair would have undermined trust rather than built it. The theoretical division was also convenient for the Republican leadership. As Mo observed in her autobiography, it gave them time to think, by saying they had to take their proposals away to consult the IRA on them rather than having to come to a decision there and then.

Adams and McGuinness were determined to carry the whole movement with them rather than repeating the history of Republicans, where any move forward had been accompanied by a split. The difference was this time we were in the same position. We did not want to have to make peace lots of times with republican splinter groups. We wanted to do it once. And so, uniquely, the British government had an interest in a united Republican movement as well, rather than trying to pursue a policy of divide and rule as it had in the past.

In the new year, our deadline of May 1998 for the conclusion of talks loomed into view. We had succeeded in getting the parties in the same room, but that was about it. The talks seemed to be going round in circles without getting anywhere. In an attempt to get the parties to focus on reaching a conclusion, we decided in January to put down some lapidary 'Propositions on Heads of Agreement', essentially the outline of a final agreement on just over one page. Since the parties were not prepared to make trade-offs between the different issues, the governments had to try to do so themselves. The Unionists were suspicious this would be a repeat of the Anglo-Irish negotiations that had produced the hated 'Frameworks' document published by John Major and John Bruton in 1995. This had been anathema to them, proposing what they regarded as joint Anglo-Irish authority over Northern Ireland. We tried to reassure them, producing a draft that covered what we considered to be the crucial six points: 1) changes to the Irish constitution to drop the claim to the territory of Northern Ireland; 2) acceptance of the principle of consent; 3) a devolved Northern Ireland Assembly and Executive; 4) a new British-Irish agreement to replace the Anglo-Irish Agreement; 5) a North/South council to bring together ministers from the Republic and from Northern Ireland; 6) a council which would cover the East/West dimension. There were also provisions on prisoners, policing, security, decommissioning and human rights. We showed the document to John Taylor and David Trimble on 5 January. They indicated they were content. The Irish, however, were not and produced their own, different version.

The ensuing negotiations were extremely complex. Tony had to leave for an official visit to Japan so he charged me with sorting the matter out. This involved managing an elaborate three-way discussion between the Irish, Trimble and Tony in Tokyo while taking account of the various time zones. Once Trimble had seen the Irish draft he rejected it out of hand and we had to abandon it and start again with the original British draft with a few Irish amendments that Tony and John Holmes drew up in Tokyo. On Saturday 10 January I recorded in my diary that I had made over a hundred phone calls during the course of the day, the last one at half past midnight with the news that Trimble had briefed the *Sunday Telegraph* with his account of the negotiations. All the other parties, not surprisingly, got into a state at being excluded. I got Tony to call Mo from Japan first thing in the morning on Sunday, even though he had been kept up till after three by the negotiations. At first she hadn't seen the story and was relaxed, but once she did she got into a terrible rage, putting the phone down on Tony once and then accusing us in No. 10 of undermining the whole peace process by leaving out the smaller parties.

Mo was a remarkable character and a very unusual politician. She was instrumental in making a Northern Ireland agreement possible by convincing republicans and nationalists that this was a different sort of British government. And she could not have been more different from her patrician, male predecessors with their military and colonial bearing. But her very success with the nationalists turned unionists against her. Trimble had already started to complain about Mo's nationalist bias as early as 28 May 1997 and the attacks on her and the NIO for duplicity became increasingly intemperate. At the end of August 1997 Trimble insisted that Mo was trying to drive him out of the talks and in January he said that 'most officials in the NIO were traitorous and he had no confidence in the Secretary of State'. Tony rebuffed these attacks, but Mo for her part complained about being left out of the meetings with David Trimble which she said encouraged Trimble to treat her and the NIO with contempt. Unionist criticism of Mo had been becoming increasingly public and she told us in December she couldn't stand much more of it.

As Mo said in her autobiography, she attached great importance to inclusiveness, wanting all the Northern Ireland parties, even the tiniest ones like the Women's Coalition, to participate fully in every step of every negotiation as well as the big parties. While an admirable goal, it was not practical politics. It is not possible to make progress in a sensitive negotiation if you require parties to make compromises and reveal their true positions in public. Neither side will move. So I went back to my telephone diplomacy, and after a Sunday on the phone from seven thirty in the morning to midnight I finally had an agreed text, having persuaded the Irish to retreat on the issue of North/South executive agencies. This was a crucial point for Unionists. They could not accept bodies that looked like a joint Anglo-Irish government of Northern Ireland with executive powers and depending on London and Dublin rather than a democratically elected assembly in Northern Ireland itself.

I went to bed pleased with having managed to agree a text but anxious that I might wake up in the morning to find there were problems. The Irish were not happy at the criticism they were getting from the SDLP and Sinn Féin for having conceded to Trimble on North/South bodies, and I wondered to myself if I had pushed them too far. But I was wrong. It was not the nationalists who pulled the plug. First thing on Monday morning David Trimble called me in a terrible state. He asked me to fax the document to a particular phone number in Northern Ireland. At nine he called me again virtually in tears. John Taylor had come in and read the document and hated it. Ken Maginnis, a party leader with responsibility for security and an ex-member of the Ulster Defence Regiment (UDR), was also opposed. Trimble told me he was going to attack the document since none of his colleagues would support it, even though he had agreed it himself the night before.

This was a perennial problem throughout the talks. I had been involved in many interstate negotiations as a diplomat – returning Hong Kong to the Chinese in the early 1980s and German reunification in the late 1980s – but never anything like this. I had to get used to a much more anarchic and loose process. Trimble would negotiate a document by himself, agree it, and only then show it to his colleagues. Each of them had a different view on what the sticking point should be, and you found yourself negotiating with a focus group, where you had to make individual concessions to each member of the group. On this occasion I got the Irish to throw in a few more concessions to meet the UUP's objections and Trimble won his party colleagues round. In the end it was all a great success. We published the 'Heads of Agreement' on Monday 12 January, and they became the foundations for the Good Friday Agreement. All the parties welcomed them. SDLP leader John Hume flew in to Northern Ireland and said it was a good thing. Taylor disappeared leaving Trimble to welcome it. And the process survived.

Sinn Féin, however, were not happy. Gerry Adams called Tony to complain that they had been left out of the negotiations. He said the Unionists were playing their usual game of putting on pressure to minimise change. This was understandable. The Unionists could only lose once, while Nationalists could afford to lose often, as long as they won once. But in the end Sinn Féin too welcomed the 'Heads of Agreement' and accepted them as the basis for progress, although they said they wanted to negotiate up from them. This was the first time Sinn Féin had accepted publicly that the negotiations would not result in a united Ireland.

These negotiations had been overlaid on a crisis with the Loyalists. In December 1997 unionists had started to criticise us for making too many concessions to republicans and this sense of unfairness was compounded when the Irish government released six IRA prisoners on 17 December without telling us. The Ulster Democratic Party, representing the Loyalist paramilitaries, the Ulster Defence Association (UDA), and the Ulster Freedom Fighters (UFF) announced they were reassessing their attitude to the peace process. Things were tense and then Billy Wright, the leader of the extreme Loyalist Volunteer Force (LVF), was shot inside the Maze prison by two prisoners from the fringe Irish National Liberation Army (INLA) and all hell broke loose. On 4 January the UDA prisoners in the Maze took a vote and two-thirds said they no longer supported the peace process. David Trimble went to see the prisoners, but this was not enough. Gary McMichael, leader of the UDP, a small and nervous man and the son of a prominent Loyalist who had been killed by the IRA, flew over to London to see Mo and appealed to her to go to the Maze herself to reason with the prisoners. Mo popped her head outside her office door and consulted her new permanent secretary, Joe Pilling, who had been head of the British prison service. When he agreed, she told Gary she would go. She didn't think of consulting us and went straight ahead and announced she was going to the Maze to meet the UDA prisoners. We didn't approve, and if she had asked us we would certainly have said no. But in the event she was right and we were wrong. Her visit had the effect of reassuring the Loyalists that she took them seriously, by both her presence there and her offer to look at their grievances. She managed to prevent them pulling the plug on the Process at a crucial moment. Her instinctive reaction turned out to be the right one.

The talks were constantly under threat of a breakdown as a result of the recurrence of violence on both the republican and loyalist sides. By 23 January it had become clear that the UDA/UFF had been responsible for a spate of loyalist killings in the previous weeks. The Chief Constable of the Royal Ulster Constabulary, Ronnie Flanagan, announced their involvement formally and we were gearing ourselves up to throw the UDP out of the talks when the UDA announced they had indeed been responsible for the killings but were going back on ceasefire. On the one hand we didn't want to set a precedent for the IRA reverting to killing while Sinn Féin stayed in the talks, so we felt we had to throw them out. On the other none of the other parties wanted to expel them. If they went there was a danger of the UUP walking out too because without the UDP a majority of the unionist population would not be represented in the talks. In the end we had to expel them on the first day of the session of the talks held in Lancaster House in London on 26 January, while making it clear that they would be allowed back in after a period of genuine ceasefire.

The next session of talks in Dublin was dominated by a similar expulsion crisis. Ronnie Flanagan told us on 11 February that he was going to say that two killings in the last forty-eight hours had been carried out by the IRA, the first of an alleged drug dealer, the other of a loyalist. He said the murders had been authorised at the highest levels within the IRA. The terrorists who carried out the attack were disguised as post office workers and the police had caught them red-handed changing back out of their uniforms. Presumably the IRA thought that murdering drug dealers and loyalists was normal business and no one would think it contravened the ceasefire.

Irish officials gave us the run-around all afternoon on 12 February, trying to block the expulsion of Sinn Féin from the talks, but finally

Tony got through to Bertie Ahern, who went up in my estimation by saying if it was clear the IRA had carried out the murders they should be thrown out. Sinn Féin struggled hard to stay in. Martin McGuinness said the killings had nothing to do with the IRA. This ability to say black is white without batting an eyelid had been a crucial part of running a disciplined terrorist organisation. But even allowing for the usual standards of mendacity in politics, it was difficult to get used to this amount of brass neck in a diplomatic negotiation. Over time we learned to compartmentalise the way we saw such statements. Duplicity about IRA operational matters was required but that didn't mean to say Republicans were duplicitous about everything.

William Hague demanded a meeting with Tony on Northern Ireland the next day and said he was worried the present situation would drive the government and opposition apart. Tony said we had held fast to bipartisanship in opposition despite the ups and downs of government policy. It would be a tragedy if the Tories backed out of it now. I believed Hague was acting under the influence of Andrew Mackay, the perma-tanned shadow Northern Ireland Secretary at the time. John Major offered to help bring the Tory Party back into line and succeeded in doing so.

We finally agreed to expel Sinn Féin on 20 February but then had a tense negotiation with the Irish about when we should let them back in. Everyone was conscious of the approaching deadline and how little time remained to find a settlement. The Irish insisted on letting Sinn Féin back in on 2 March and we were eventually pushed into agreeing 9 March, but I felt at the time it was ridiculously early and we were roundly criticised for pricing two lives at only two weeks' expulsion. David Trimble indicated to us that he would make a huge public fuss but not walk out of the talks. Adams and McGuinness acted in public as if they, rather than the men who were murdered, were the victims. Sinn Féin even went to court to try to prevent their expulsion, unsuccessfully. This became a pattern in the talks. Despite being opposed to the system, Republicans would repeatedly resort to the law to try to get their way.

When it came to being allowed back in, Adams and McGuinness made a song and dance. We announced on 5 March that they would be coming back, and they immediately started to quibble and said they wouldn't come back until they had had a meeting with Tony, so a meeting was arranged for 12 March. Adams was sweetness and light in private. He made it clear to Tony that Sinn Féin wanted to come back into the talks and then went into a long ramble about changes to the British constitution to balance changes to the Irish constitution, making it clear that either he didn't understand how the constitution worked or he wanted us to repeal the Act of Union.

Having had so much time wasted on diversions like this the talks had still made little progress and the deadline was looming. Officials in the NIO had been opposed to the deadline since the beginning. Mo thought we in No. 10 were fixated with it. Stability and peace on the streets was the overriding institutional objective of the NIO and they wanted a soft landing rather than a breakdown. We were in more of a hurry and believed we could only focus the parties on reaching an agreement with a hard deadline rather than carrying on negotiating indefinitely.

It was to become a recurring feature of the talks that Tony would set a deadline, and then as we approached it the NIO would worry about what would happen if we crashed the process, urging us not to stick to it too firmly. There were necessarily stresses and strains institutionally between No. 10 and the NIO, and these divisions long pre-dated the Blair government. The NIO understandably felt we were intervening on their turf on the basis of too little knowledge and rashly entering into undertakings that would fail, as well as allowing the parties to appeal over their heads to higher authority. They thought we should do more to empower them to make progress in the nego- tiations rather than trying to do it all ourselves. We, to some extent rightly, thought they were stuck in the mud and too imprisoned by the history of it all. We wanted a dynamic approach to rush the parties into an agreement without allowing them to stop and think too much. It was inevitable that the parties would appeal directly to No. 10, and Tony felt particularly strongly that we had to give the UUP support and encouragement, since they felt they faced a pan-nationalist front of the Irish government, the SDLP, Sinn Féin and the Americans, while coming under attack from less moderate unionist parties at the same time.

Tony's threat in January that if the parties did not agree then the governments would put their proposals to a referendum in Ireland North and South in May had been a useful way of galvanising the parties and it was a threat we kept coming back to even as late as the end of 2006, as a way of forcing progress. It was our perennial Plan B. But now, as the date approached, even John Holmes in No. 10 was becoming sceptical about the deadline. On 13 March he suggested we start looking for an exit strategy if it was clear that we couldn't meet the deadline, but Tony didn't want to consider the possibility of failure, though he came back to the issue on 26 March having begun to doubt the wisdom of the deadline himself. I, again, made the case that we had to push it through now. John, again, argued that we could always put it off. My fear was that if we did not resolve the question now we could continue to go through the motions later, as had happened in all previous attempts at making peace, but having once blinked we were unlikely to succeed. I argued we had to surprise the parties into an agreement.

Tony decided to stick to the deadline and we tried to drag the parties into an endgame. The problem lay on the UUP side. Tony had a series of difficult meetings with Trimble and his team in March. On 9 March Trimble started backing off even the 'Heads of Agreement' as he realised the moment of choice was looming and three days later he sounded positively ominous on the phone. We tried to engage him in a negotiation about the Assembly and the North/South bodies, but his answers showed how little he had thought about how they would actually work in practice. On 26 March Tony saw Trimble and John Taylor but they gave no signs of agreeing to anything. Taylor warned Tony not to get too personally involved in the search for an agreement. He thought the chances of success were not high, only 5 per cent in his view.

On Sunday 29 March Tony invited David Trimble and Jeffrey Donaldson to come down to see him at Chequers. We had to provide a No. 10 car and driver to get them there otherwise, they said, they would have to come by public transport since they had no official transport in Britain. In the two-and-a-half-hour meeting Tony tried to coax them into telling him what the UUP bottom line really was by showing them two papers outlining the possible agreement. He said some North/South bodies would have to be set up from the beginning but the language on them could be stripped down to a bare minimum. He suggested that we go for 'mutually assured destruction', a term borrowed from nuclear weapons theology, whereby the North/South bodies could only exist if the Assembly existed and vice versa. Trimble said that Sinn Féin could not be part of the govern-ment of Northern Ireland if they were hanging on to a private army. Tony agreed there had to be decommissioning and said it was hard to imagine a government continuing without steps towards it. But privately he was suspicious about why this issue had suddenly popped up again at this late stage when he had been urging the Unionists for months to focus on the more important issue of consent. John Holmes recorded at the end of the meeting that 'David Trimble and Jeffrey Donaldson seemed to accept the basic thrust of both the papers they were given, while reserving their position formally, and made few comments on the drafting'. He said there was nothing to suggest Jeffrey Donaldson was anti-agreement.

But Donaldson and Trimble appear to have gone away with the belief that Tony had agreed with them on decommissioning and that it would have to be an explicit part of any overall agreement, or at least they claimed so later. In any event the optimism with which the meeting ended was misplaced. It turned out we were all labouring under a misapprehension about how close the parties were to agree-ment. All the old problems that had dogged negotiations on Northern Ireland for decades were still there, from disagreement about an 'Irish dimension' in Northern Ireland to disagreement about the decom-missioning of weapons as a precondition for going into government. Any impartial observer with a sense of Irish history would have told us we were heading for a train wreck. Luckily Tony and I were sufficiently ignorant of Irish history to remain optimistic.

2

The Burden of History

I first met Tony Blair on 3 January 1993 when he visited Washington in the wake of Bill Clinton's victory in the 1992 US presidential elections. He came with Gordon Brown, whom I already knew from shepherding him around the Democratic Convention in New York in the summer of 1992. I met the two of them at Dulles airport and took them to dinner with the ambassador at the grand British residence on Massachusetts Avenue, which neither of them had visited before. They asked good questions, although I was surprised at their ignorance about the rest of the world. Tony impressed me particularly with his charisma and openness. I noted in my diary that he seemed genuinely radical in his commitment to reforming the Labour Party.

They wanted to meet Clinton's team, which I knew well having chosen Bill Clinton as the presidential candidate to follow around in 1991 – in part because he had been at my college at Oxford. During the next few days I took them to see the New Democrats of the Democratic Leadership Council who had succeeded in moving the party back to the election-winning political centre. Gordon left their headquarters staggering under an armful of policy papers. And I took them to see Clinton's election team, including Paul Begala, Elaine Kamarck and Stan Greenberg, who was Clinton's pollster and later became ours. A BBC TV crew traipsed around with us filming the two new hopes of the Labour Party at every meeting and in the car trips in between. They even enjoyed a mini-political crisis when John Prescott used the visit to attack the 'beautiful people', as he always, and misleadingly, described Tony and Gordon, for fraternising with the Democrats.

I kept in touch with Tony, and in September 1994 he asked me to come over and see him about the possibility of becoming his Chief of Staff. He was based in a spartan, bare room in the House of Commons, with a gaggle of offices around it and the Shadow Cabinet room next door. While I was waiting I met Pat McFadden and Alastair Campbell who had already started working for him and took to them straight away. Tony arrived and settled down on the dusty green sofa. It wasn't really an interview, more of a chat, but I was impressed. I had already placed him as the sort of pleasant TV-friendly personality necessary to succeed in modern politics, but he was tougher and more ruthless than I had at first thought, and that marked him out as potentially a truly remarkable leader. He knew what he wanted to do with the party and he asked me whether I was New Labour enough. I said I thought so.

Tony then sent me to see Derry Irvine, the shadow Lord Chancellor and his former pupil-master when he was a barrister, for a second opinion. Derry met me at the Peers' entrance to the House of Lords and took me up to the royal gallery – huge, intimidating and Victorian at its campest. He gave me a grilling asking why I had applied for the job. I explained I had not. He said I talked too fast and asked how the comrades were supposed to understand me when they didn't think as fast as I spoke. On my way back to Washington, I spotted Gordon Brown and Ed Balls at Terminal 4. They were coming over for a visit and I was to take them round Washington the next day, but I had to hide from them at the airport since my visit to see Tony was supposed to remain secret. I started work for Tony as his Chief of Staff a few weeks later.

Tony and I both have Irish antecedents, although of very different sorts. His grandmother was a Protestant from Donegal and his grandfather had been an Orangeman. As a child he had gone over every summer until the visits suddenly stopped with the advent of the Troubles. But he was in no sense a Protestant bigot, having married a Catholic and brought up his children as Catholics. I was descended on my mother's side from the Anglo-Irish ascendancy. A great-great-grandfather, a FitzGerald, had been Lord Chief Justice of Ireland in the nineteenth century and a great-grandfather, a Moylan, had had to leave Ireland under suspicion of being a Fenian. But neither of us knew much about our Irish antecedents and neither of us had any historical baggage on Northern Ireland, one of the advantages of relative ignorance about its history. We were of a younger generation and the war against Irish terrorism was not our war.

But it was impossible to stay ignorant about its history for long when meeting the party leaders in Northern Ireland. In those first stages of negotiation, it seemed that every meeting with either side began with a history lesson, or more accurately a catalogue of historical grievances. I would joke that if you broke off any of the meetings after just half an hour you would only have got up to the year 1690. To someone coming from outside, it was surprising how many of these grievances were ancient rather than present day, and how differently the two sides interpreted the same history. The real or objective history didn't matter so much, what was important was their view of it.

The nationalist and republican version of Irish history begins in the 1160s. In the words of the Fenian historian John O'Leary, writing in 1896, 'It is obvious to the meanest intelligence how far back I could look for the origin of Fenianism [a forerunner of Irish republicanism]. If the English had not come to Ireland, and if they had not stayed there and done all the evil so many of them now allow they have been doing all along, then there would have been no Fenianism. And here [. . .] I could easily go back to Strongbow [one of the Norman knights to come to Ireland in the 1160s].' Very much the same sentiment is still on the Sinn Féin website, 'Throughout history,' it says, 'the island of Ireland has been regarded as a single national unit. Prior to the Norman invasion from England in 1169, the Irish had their own system of law, culture and language and their own political and social structures. Following the invasion, the island continued to be governed as a single political unit, as a colony of Britain, until 1921.'

There is no particular reason why an entire island should be considered a unit for self-determination. After all, if that were the case, then the Scots and Welsh would have no right to be nations. And so it is crucial for Irish nationalists and republicans to maintain the myth of an original single, homogenised, Gaelic Ireland to explain why Ireland, and only the whole of Ireland, is entitled to self-determination, rather than Northern Ireland or the British isles. To them, the history of Ireland from the invasion of the Norman Welsh knights onwards is a story of repression by the British and the brave rebellion of a series of martyrs from Wolfe Tone to Bobby Sands. The difference between the nationalist and the republican threads of this history are, putting violence to one side, about the attitude to the unionists. Republicans thought that all you had to do was drive out the Brits and the unionists would give up. The nationalists thought the aim was not to drive out the Brits but to convince the unionists. They agreed, however, that the aim was to create a sovereign independent Ireland.

Bernadette Devlin talks of being radicalised at her father's knee by the tales of 'the English oppression and the risings'. In fact, medieval Ireland consisted of a small and reducing province around Dublin under the control of the Crown, and a large majority 'beyond the Pale' ruled by warring Irish and Norman princes who gradually chipped away at English control. The Tudor monarchs tried to establish their rule over the whole island and to impose the Protestant religion on its people but succeeded instead in forcing together the remaining Norman settlers, or old English, and the Gaelic Irish, who were united by a common Catholicism. When they rose up under Hugh O'Neill, the Earl of Tyrone, in the 1590s, Elizabeth suppressed the rebellion and the Stuart response was to import large numbers of Scottish and English settlers to 'civilise' the place and provide a strong Protestant garrison, as in the North American colonies. The most important of these 'plantations' imposed on the confiscated Catholic lands was in the north-east of Ireland.

In 1641 the Irish rebelled against this imposition, demanding full rights for Catholics, autonomy for the Irish Parliament and an end to the confiscation of Catholic land. The rebellion was again put down bloodily, this time by Cromwell, who massacred three thousand Catholics including one thousand civilians in the town of Drogheda, even though the town had surrendered. His brutality lives on in Irish memory.

In 1689 the Irish rose up again in support of the Catholic King James II who had been deposed in England, but were once again defeated and put to the sword, by William of Orange and his Protestant troops. This time the English were taking no chances and they turned Ireland into a colony of Britain, with a firm Protestant ascendancy and the use of penal laws to restrict the rights of Catholics.

In the eighteenth century there were occasional attempts to assert Irish rights, whether in Jonathan Swift's pamphlets or Henry Gratton's campaign for more authority for the Irish Parliament in the 1780s and 90s, but for republicans in particular, modern history begins with the Society of United Irishmen inspired at the end of the century by the example of the French Revolution. Every year republicans celebrate the death of its leader, Wolfe Tone, with a major speech at his grave at Bodenstown. Paradoxically for republicans, Tone was a Protestant, but he was also a revolutionary and dedicated to securing an independent republic in Ireland and to ending religious discrimination. His insurrection, despite support from the French, was rapidly and bloodily put down by British troops and Protestant militia in 1798 and 30,000 were killed including Wolfe Tone himself. The British responded by putting pressure on the Irish Parliament to abolish itself and imposing an Act of Union in 1801. But that did not entirely put an end to the United Irishmen and in 1803 Robert Emmet led a further attempt at rebellion. Again, the British had little difficulty in quelling the rising, but Emmet earned undying fame for his speech in court as he was convicted and condemned, largely because the romantic story of his tragic sacrifice was popularised in *Moore's Melodies*, the widely bought book of songs of the period. Both Emmet and Tone helped establish a tradition of heroic martyrs.

After the Napoleonic Wars another great wave of resistance was led by Daniel O'Connell, 'the Liberator', campaigning for Catholic emancipation and the repeal of the Union with the support of the Catholic Church. He drew huge crowds to his rallies and was dedicated to non-violence, but the threat of violence was never far away, and in parallel the 'Young Ireland' movement grew up dedicated to revolution. In 1848, inspired by the uprisings in Hungary and Paris that year, they mounted another doomed revolt. The defeated leaders fled to America or were deported to Australia.

A recurring theme in the narrative of nationalist history is the cruelty of the British, seen at its worst in the 'Great Famine' of 1845–9 where a potato blight caused the deaths of around a million and drove another million to emigrate. The charge is that the British stood by and let the Irish starve – if they did not, as the conspiracy theorists would have it, actually conspire to import the blight in order to thin out the Irish population. One of the first things we did, one month after entering government in 1997, was apologise for the British government's role in the potato famine, to try and remove at least that from the historical charge sheet against Britain.

In the second half of the nineteenth century the nearer ancestors of the IRA appeared in the form the Irish Republican Brotherhood

(IRB), a secret society more popularly known as the 'Fenians'. They were closely related to the transatlantic Clan na nGael founded by Irish emigrants to the US, who in 1866 put together a band of civil war veterans to undertake the quixotic mission of invading Canada in order to demand British withdrawal from Ireland. The Fenians rejected the constitutional approach and were explicitly committed to a violent struggle for independence, launching a rebellion in 1867, which collapsed as they vainly waited for Irish-American reinforcements. They had been heavily penetrated by informers and the rebellion was put down easily with only a handful of deaths. They also prefigured the IRA's spectacular jailbreaks of the 1970s and 80s, when they tried to release two of their members from Clerkenwell prison with explosives. They succeeded in blowing up the wall and killing twelve people but failed to release their comrades. They did, however, add to the roll call of iconic martyrs for independence when three of their members were hung for killing a policeman in Manchester as part of another, successful, jailbreak.

The focus of nationalism in the 1870s moved on to the Gaelic revival with the teaching of the Irish language and the resurgence of traditional sports like hurling, as well as to the redistribution of land from the Anglo-Irish landowners to small Irish farmers. The unlikely President of the Land League was a socially conservative, Protestant, country gentleman called Charles Stuart Parnell. He focused his land war on the evil of evictions, writing, 'It was a sad spectacle to see the old blind man, carrying a weak little child, beseeching the bailiff to accept bail for the amount of the decree unpaid.' Parnell, like Daniel O'Connell, was committed to non-violence, but he may have secretly joined the Irish Republican Brotherhood when released from prison in 1887, and his lieutenant William O'Brien was of the view that 'violence is the only way of ensuring a hearing for moderation'. This was a precursor to the belief of modern-day republicans that the only way to get the attention of the Brits was to ensure that the threat of violence remained present, otherwise they would sink back into their traditional comfort zone of ignoring Ireland. Parnell parlayed his Land League into the Home Rule movement, and the cause was taken up by Gladstone. Gladstone was just about the only British Prime Minister to enjoy a degree of popularity in Ireland until Tony Blair. In 1887 he was presented with a hurley stick and a match ball by the IRB-dominated

Gaelic Athletic Association (GAA) of Cork. Driven by his Christianity, he developed a crusading enthusiasm for Home Rule, in the end unsuccessful, and nearly broke his party on the subject. Parnell himself was brought down by the revelation of his affair with Kitty O'Shea, a distant relation of mine, whom my mother remembered seeing in her youth, and his movement split into factions. The split was to become a dominating feature of nationalist and republican politics, often exploited by the British to divide them against each other and weaken them.

There were two Home Rule bills in the 1880s and 90s both blocked by the Unionists and Conservatives. The third bill passed but was postponed in 1914 on the outbreak of the First World War. Meanwhile, revolutionary movements had been springing up in Ireland, including the Irish Republican Socialist Party of James Connolly, and the paramilitary Irish Citizen Army set up by the Irish Transport and General Workers Union to protect the workers in the General Strike of 1913. Arthur Griffith had set up Sinn Féin, eccentrically supporting a return to a dual monarchy on the Austro-Hungarian model. And in response to the establishment of the paramilitary Ulster Volunteer Force by Protestants in the north, nationalists formed the Volunteers, the direct antecedents of the IRA.

Twelve hundred representatives of the diverse republican movements mounted the Easter Rising on Easter Monday 1916 by taking over the General Post Office and other sites in Dublin, establishing a provisional government and declaring a republic. This was another quixotic rising that was relatively easily put down by the British security forces. But that was not the point. In the words of Patrick Pearse, one of the key leaders, 'It would take the blood of Irishmen to redeem Ireland.' The British proceeded to turn his vision into reality by executing sixteen of the rebellion's leaders and arresting three thousand, many of whom had not been involved in the uprising at all. The brutality of the British reaction built a huge wave of support for republicanism, and the decision by the government to attribute responsibility for the uprising to Sinn Féin, which had been hardly involved, gave the party a new popularity. It was promptly taken over by republicans. Despite the fact that large numbers of Irish Catholics had volunteered to fight in the British Army in the earlier part of the First World War the British government attempted to extend conscription to Ireland in the face of the German offensive in the spring of 1918, but met with a wall of opposition and managed in the process to solidify Irish nationalist sentiment.

In the post-war parliamentary election of 1918, Sinn Féin won seventy-three seats out of the 105 Irish seats, campaigning for independence. Instead of going to Westminster, their MPs set up their own independent parliament, Dáil Éireann, in Dublin in January 1919 and proclaimed an Irish Republic. The British government proscribed the Dáil and the situation tipped into a war of independence. The Volunteers became Oglaigh na hEireann, the IRA, and fought a mixed force of British soldiers, the Royal Irish Constabulary and the 'Black and Tans', an auxiliary force of demobbed British soldiers. The struggle followed the familiar pattern of guerrilla war with atrocity followed by reprisal followed by counter-reprisal. On Sunday 21 November 1920 the IRA killed twelve men in the morning, mainly government agents, and in the afternoon British forces went to Croke Park and killed twelve civilians at a Gaelic football match. By 1921 the two sides had fought themselves to stalemate and neither could win. In the North, Protestants conducted a pogrom and in the ensuing violence 555 lives were lost, mostly Catholics.

Michael Collins, the charismatic leader of the IRA, negotiated the Anglo-Irish Treaty with Prime Minister Lloyd George in Downing Street in 1921 which secured dominion status for the Irish Free State like that of Canada or New Zealand, but had to concede the maintenance of an oath to the King and other restrictions on full Irish independence. Collins did not try to argue it was perfect but he did claim it was the best deal available and gave Ireland 'the freedom to achieve freedom'. But the treaty was rejected by the Sinn Féin diehards led by Eamon de Valera, Collins's rival, and the two sides fell into a vicious civil war in 1922–3, which the Free State won. In 1926 de Valera abandoned abstentionism – the refusal to participate in the Dáil – left Sinn Féin and founded Fianna Fáil as a party for constitutional anti-treatyites. A rump Sinn Féin refused to accept their defeat.

The key to understanding the present-day IRA's claims to legitimacy lies in the 1919 Dáil. Republicans claim that the only time the Irish people were allowed to vote as a whole was in the 1918 election and they voted for independence. No one had a right to alienate that democratic decision and in 1922 the IRA Executive claimed the authority of that original Dáil on the basis that the Free State had violated its oath to defend the Irish Republic. Henceforth the Army Council would speak for the true government of Ireland until a thirty-two-county, united Ireland was re-established.

Partition occurred when the Ulster Volunteer Force, which had been formed by Protestants in the north-east of Ireland under the leadership of Edward Carson to resist the attempts of John Edward Redmond, Parnell's successor, to introduce Home Rule, posed enough of a threat for the British government to strike a deal with unionists and separate the north-east from the rest of Ireland. The Irish people were not consulted and regarded the six-county statelet created by the Government of Ireland Act as illegitimate, not least since it broke up the province of Ulster by omitting the three counties with the largest Catholic majorities in order to ensure a Protestant majority. The British government had given in to blackmail from the unionists. The Orange card (a phrase first coined by Randolph Churchill) had been played, as it would be many times again.

Northern Ireland was designed from its inception to keep Catholics in their place. James Craig, its first Prime Minister, made his aim clear when he said, 'I have always said I am an Orangeman first and a politician and a member of this Parliament afterwards. All I boast is that we are a Protestant Parliament and a Protestant state.' Catholics trapped in the statelet boycotted Stormont till 1926, assuming that its existence was temporary and that they would soon be rescued by their co-religionists in the South. Craig, determined to ensure one-party rule indefinitely, abolished proportional representation, introduced to protect the minority, and gerrymandered the constituencies so that even Catholic Derry could be ruled by a Protestant minority. All judges were unionists, appointed by the Northern Ireland government; the heavily armed auxiliary police force, the B Specials, were all Protestant; and the police force itself, the RUC, was 90 per cent Protestant. The jobs in the shipyards and the engineering works and the civil service were overwhelmingly kept for Protestants, while Catholics were twice as likely to be unemployed. In 1933 Basil Brooke, later Prime Minister, let the cat out of the bag when he said to a unionist gathering, 'Many in the audience employ Catholics, but I have not one about my place' (although it was revealed later that his cook at Brookebrough was a Catholic).

The unionists got away with this religious and political one-party state for forty years but in the 1960s a civil rights movement sprang up modelled on the equivalent movement in the American South. In 1967 the new movement, Northern Ireland Civil Rights Alliance, campaigned for one man one vote, changes to electoral boundaries, anti-discrimination in the provision of social housing, the repeal of the special powers and the disbandment of the B Specials. In 1968 the Nationalist MP Austin Currie symbolically occupied a council house in Tyrone near Dungannon that had been awarded by the Unionist local council to a Protestant girl of eighteen in preference to two Catholic families. He was evicted by the police but he had won publicity around the world for the abuses practised in Northern Ireland.

Unionists reacted violently to the growth of the civil rights movement. In January 1969 loyalists ambushed a civil rights march from Belfast to Derry in the open countryside at Burntollet Bridge and beat the marchers severely while the police looked on. The violence took off in August of that year after the Apprentice Boys March in Derry degenerated into the Battle of the Bogside, when the police would breach the barricades to allow loyalist mobs to run through wreaking havoc on Catholic neighbourhoods. The violence spread to Belfast with running battles as the two communities fought each other and Catholics were driven from their homes in mixed areas. The RUC comprehensively alienated the Catholic community, not least by killing an eight-year-old boy in his home in Belfast when a bullet from a heavy machine gun passed through the walls of the house. The Troubles had started.

Meanwhile the IRA had not gone away. It had continued sporadic attacks across the border in the 1920s and 30s, and in 1939 it launched the 'S-plan', a programme of sabotage in Britain, bombing power stations and other infrastructure targets. It also cooperated with the Nazis on a plan to invade the United Kingdom, with its Army Council sending a letter to Halifax, the Foreign Secretary, containing a war ultimatum. During the Second World War, the IRA mounted a campaign in the North which, while largely ineffective, was a sufficient threat that my father, an airman, was ambushed on his way home from Aldergrove to his isolated cottage and was issued with a revolver. De Valera was determined that the failure of the Irish state to move decisively against the IRA should not offer the British government an excuse for infringing Irish neutrality and, during the war, interned over five hundred IRA activists, including the IRA Chief of Staff, under Offences Against the State and Emergency Powers Acts. In the 1950s the IRA mounted a 'border campaign' and would send flying columns into the North to attack police stations and other targets before returning to the Republic. They stuck to rural areas because they feared that attacks in towns would invite retaliation against Catholics of the sort meted out in the pogrom of the 1920s. The police in Northern Ireland were easily able to contain the attacks and the campaign was wound up in 1962, leaving eight IRA Volunteers, four republican supporters and six RUC men dead.

In the 1960s the Dublin-based leadership of the IRA turned to Marxism, adopting the objective of persuading both Catholic and Protestant working classes to rise up together. But the sectarian violence of the late 1960s caught it unprepared, and it failed in its traditional duty to protect the Catholic neighbourhoods from attack. IRA came to stand for I Ran Away, and, in 1969, there was a split between a Marxist Official IRA, which went off to become a political party in the South (eventually merging with the Irish Labour Party in Dublin), and a new movement led by Sean Mac Stiofain and Ruari O'Bradaigh which returned to traditional physical force republicanism, styling themselves the Provisional IRA after the Provisional Government established during the Easter Rising of 1916. The ensuing violence between the two factions coloured the later views of two young Volunteers. Gerry Adams and Martin McGuinness had hesitated about which side to join, but in the end went with the Provisionals. Their experience made them determined to avoid any future splits and, at all costs, to stop republicans shooting at each other again.

The Troubles continued, but the IRA had a different opponent. Following the Battle of the Bogside in August 1969, the exhausted RUC was no longer able to cope, and so the Stormont government reluctantly called in the British Army. At first British soldiers were welcomed by Catholics as they took up positions between the two warring communities, but it was not long before they alienated Catholics as effectively as the RUC had, by appearing to direct their attentions exclusively at Catholic areas. In 1970 they imposed a curfew on West Belfast, cutting off a large part of the Catholic community for days and indiscriminately ransacking houses. Fourteen people died at the hands of the army in the process. In 1971 the rules of

engagement were further relaxed and the army shot dead two innocent Catholics in Derry. The SDLP walked out of Stormont when the
government refused to carry out an inquiry into the deaths. Then
came Bloody Sunday.

On 30 January 1972 the British Army killed thirteen people in
Derry and another died from his wounds. Members of the Parachute
Regiment appeared to have run amok, live on TV, and the pictures of
a Catholic priest running, half crouched, through the Bogside waving
a white handkerchief to try and help a fatally wounded victim will
haunt the British establishment for ever. Its effect was devastating.
Gerry Adams later commented that on the back of Bloody Sunday
'money, guns and recruits flooded into the IRA'.

So great was the place of Bloody Sunday in the memories of republicans and nationalists alike that one of their key demands as soon as
we came into government was that there should be a full and independent inquiry into it. The subject came up in early 1998, when Mo
wrote Tony a handwritten letter about the need for an inquiry. Both
Tony and I were opposed, feeling an apology would be sufficient. But
the Irish had told us that an apology would not be enough and that we
must hold an independent inquiry. Following Mo's request I read the
Widgery report into the incident, commissioned by Heath immediately
after the event, which doesn't take long since it is an extraordinarily
brief document. It was perfectly clear that what people had felt about
it at the time was correct: it was a complete and utter whitewash. I
did not see why we should not expose what really happened that day.
I discussed it with Tony and we agreed to change our position and
accept an inquiry. I had to contact Ted Heath and others to let them
know it was coming and no one complained. Tony made a statement
in the House of Commons a week later announcing the decision which
was welcomed by nearly all the parties, although the UUP grumbled.
But, by the weekend, I was already doubting the wisdom of what we
had done. I wrote in my diary that we had not thought the issue
through thoroughly enough. Sinn Féin were already pushing for the
soldiers to be punished even before the inquiry had started.

In fact, the inquiry cost the taxpayer around two hundred million
pounds that could have been spent on other things. It has still not
reported as of the time of writing. And it has failed to give satisfaction to either side. The nadir for me was when Martin McGuinness

said to me in a private conversation some years later he didn't know why we had done it: he thought an apology would have been quite sufficient. The aim had been to demonstrate to nationalists and republicans that we were even-handed and that the British government no longer had anything to hide. It had that impact in the short term. But we repented at leisure.

When Adams and McGuinness had come to Downing Street for the first time, Adams had spoken about how Bloody Sunday had turned his community definitively against the army. And he believed internment had helped create the modern IRA. The British government's decision to resort to internment in 1971 turned out to be a catastrophic error. The plan was well flagged up so all serious Republicans could flee, and Special Branch files were so out of date that the army found themselves seizing the wrong people and missing the right ones. The brutality with which they treated the people they did arrest, and the use of experimental techniques in interrogation such as white noise, sensory deprivation and spreadeagling suspects for hours, alienated a generation of Catholics. Those seized were imprisoned on a ship in Belfast Lough or in a military camp with Nissan huts and barbed wire at Long Kesh, which resembled nothing so much as a Second World War prisoner-of-war camp. No loyalists were arrested initially.

The British government was all at sea. In 1972 Willie Whitelaw, the Northern Ireland Secretary in Ted Heath's Conservative government, decided to try talking to the leaders of the Provisional IRA. He invited them to visit him in London and they brought with them two young up-and-coming commanders, Gerry Adams and Martin McGuinness. McGuinness, who was just twenty-two at the time, later described the bizarre visit: 'We assembled in Derry, six of us, and we were taken in a blacked-out van to a field in which a helicopter landed. We were put in the helicopter and brought to the military end of Aldergrove airport near Belfast. We were brought then by RAF plane to a military airfield in England where we were met by a fleet of limousines. They were the fanciest cars I had ever seen in my life. It was a most unreal experience. We were escorted by the Special Branch through London to Cheyne Walk and there we met Willie Whitelaw. We were offered drinks at the meeting and we all refused.[. . .] The only purpose of the meeting with Whitelaw was to demand a British declaration of intent to withdraw. All of us left the meeting quite clear in our minds that the British government were not yet at a position whereby we could do serious business.' It had been a terrible misunderstanding. Whitelaw thought they were going to be discussing extending the IRA's temporary ceasefire, and the IRA leadership thought the Brits were going to discuss terms of disengaging from Northern Ireland. The Provisionals returned to Northern Ireland determined to escalate the struggle.

The IRA proclaimed 1972 'the year of victory' and their new weapon, the car bomb, caused extraordinary damage. On Bloody Friday, twenty bombs went off in Belfast in one hour, killing nine, injuring 130 and causing complete panic. And in Claudy, a peaceful rural village, car bombs killed nine. But the fighting soon degenerated into tit-for-tat killings by loyalist and republican terrorists, largely of innocent civilians. On 11 July a drunken loyalist gang broke into a Catholic home and killed a mentally retarded child and raped his mother. In court they claimed their acts constituted 'political offences'. It didn't seem that things could get much lower. The leadership of the Republican movement came to appreciate it would be harder to get rid of the Brits than they had originally thought. In a speech in 1973, Gerry Adams asked, 'Does anybody think this war is going to be over in twenty years?' They realised they were in for a long campaign, a war of attrition that would make the cost so high that the Brits would not be able to stay in Northern Ireland indefinitely. The IRA switched from car bombs to carefully planned sniping attacks and bombings in England: in Birmingham, in Guildford and in Woolwich.

In 1973, the British government tried to introduce an Executive in which Catholics and Protestants shared power in what became known as the Sunningdale Agreement, but there was unionist outrage, and the government buckled in the face of the Orange card once again, when a loyalist general strike and the threat of violence forced them to abandon the agreement.

After the failure of Sunningdale, the new Labour government, under Prime Minister Harold Wilson, made secret overtures to the IRA, and the IRA leadership agreed to a ceasefire in 1974–5. This is seen now by IRA members as an unmitigated disaster in which Volunteers' morale plummeted and the movement was penetrated. The southern leadership of the movement had been duped by false promises. A coup was mounted against them and the organisation was restructured into a Northern and Southern Command, with the introduction of a modern cell structure to resist British informers and interrogation techniques. The list of targets was widened to include businessmen and prison officers.

The attacks became increasingly sophisticated. In 1979 the break-away Irish National Liberation Army killed Airey Neave, one of Mrs Thatcher's closest colleagues in the Conservative Party, in the Palace of Westminster and the IRA killed Lord Mountbatten by blowing up his boat off the west coast of Ireland. And on the same day, at Warren-point on the Irish border, the IRA killed eighteen soldiers, sixteen of them from the Parachute Regiment. A 800lb bomb hidden in a trailer beside the road blew up an army convoy travelling along the edge of Carlingford Lough, killing six. When new troops arrived to secure the scene they were shot at across the Lough from Irish territory. They returned fire, killing an English tourist. The remaining soldiers set up a defensive position behind nearby gates and a wall, exactly as the IRA had guessed they would, and a second bomb they had hidden at the spot went off, killing a further twelve soldiers. It was the biggest death toll for the Parachute Regiment since the Battle of Arnhem and the highest number of casualties from any IRA bomb.

During the 1970s the British security authorities had tried to ratchet up the measures to deal with the threat. Jury trials were replaced with Diplock courts. There was an increased use of plastic bullets to try and maintain control during rioting. Though such measures had been successful in reducing violence, they also provided new grievances. Plastic bullets had killed innocent bystanders, sometimes children. And there were a number of abuses by the locally raised and almost exclusively Protestant Ulster Defence Regiment. All this served to increase support for Republicans. Further ammunition was provided by the government's use of the SAS to undertake covert action against the IRA; the ambushes, including the attack on an IRA active service unit in Gibraltar, looked like a shoot-to-kill policy. Interrogation at Castlereagh was clearly pretty rough at times and Amnesty International investigated charges of torture. Most of all there were the allegations of collusion between the security forces and Loyalist paramilitaries.

The biggest gift of all, however, was the hunger strike. In 1972, when he was trying to engage with the IRA, Willie Whitelaw gave 'special category status' to paramilitary prisoners. Prisoners were allowed to wear their own clothes, reported to their own 'officers commanding' rather than to prison guards, and controlled their own compounds. They were more like prisoners of war than 'ordinary decent criminals' as the police termed them. But in 1976, Merlyn Rees, the Labour Secretary of State, withdrew these privileges and moved the prisoners out of the Nissan hut compounds into new purpose-built accommodation, called H blocks. At the same time he removed their special status and his successor, Roy Mason, reinforced the policy as he tried to 'criminalise' terrorist prisoners. IRA members refused to cooperate. They would not put on the uniforms and instead wrapped themselves in blankets. In response, the prison authorities removed all furniture, cancelled remission and banned prison visits. When the 'on the blanket' protest didn't work, the prisoners stopped washing and started spreading excrement on the walls of their cells, the so-called 'dirty protest'. That didn't garner much outside support either, so in 1980 they fell back on the hunger strike which had a revered place in the movement's history. They called it off in December when one prisoner was taken to hospital losing his sight, but began again in March 1981 with hunger strikers on staggered starts so that one would die after another. This time the protest broke through into the consciousness of the outside world. Republicans had the inspired idea of running Bobby Sands, the first hunger striker, as the Nationalist candidate in the by-election taking place in Fermanagh–South Tyrone, and he won. As ten prisoners died one by one, there was an enor-mous reaction of revulsion around the world. I was at the British Embassy in Lisbon at the time and there were huge demonstrations against the British government marching to our door.

In October 1981, the prisoners called off the hunger strike under pressure from their families. At first Republicans thought they had lost, but in fact they had made the key breakthrough into politics. They had shown they could win public support for their cause by the political path rather than being confined to the use of violence alone. Three weeks later, at Sinn Féin's annual conference, Danny Morrison, a Republican spokesman close to Adams, asked, 'Who here really believes we can win the war through the ballot box? But will anyone object if, with a ballot paper in one hand and the Armalite in the other, we take power in Ireland?' Although it came as a surprise to many of the delegates, Republicans had shifted from the purely physical-force strategy to a dual-track strategy.

When I listened to the unionists talk about the events of the late 1970s and early 80s, the hunger strikes might as well not have happened. Their focus was on the terrorist violence and the aftermath of the 1973 Sunningdale Agreement, particularly what they believed to be Brian Faulkner's betrayal in leading them into power-sharing. It was a situation that they were determined not to repeat.

The story of history the unionists told themselves was one of siege, resistance, sacrifice, loyalty and betrayal. You could tell this from their graffiti. While, on the green side, the walls were daubed with 'Our Time Will Come', on the Orange side it was: 'What we Have We Hold', 'No Surrender', 'Not An Inch' and most tellingly 'Still Under Siege'.

It was really the unionists who were 'ourselves alone' rather than Sinn Féin. For them, it all began with the plantations in the 1600s. The flight of the Catholic earls of Tyrone and Tyrconnel after their rebellion and the forfeit of their estates provided land for settlement in the north-east of Ireland alongside counties Down and Antrim which were already being settled from Scotland. In 1607 'undertakers', or subcontractors, brought over settlers and parcelled out the land between them. Derry was given to the corporation of London and renamed Londonderry in 1613, in return for the rebuilding of the city and its walls. The incomers, largely tough, obstinate, Lowland Scottish dissenters, cultivated the land assiduously, and regarded themselves in much the same way as early Israeli settlers saw themselves, perhaps not surprising since both based themselves on the Book of Joshua. Wesley, the great eighteenth-century Methodist preacher, a frequent visitor to Ireland, saw Ulster as distinctive: 'No sooner did we enter Ulster than we observed the difference. The ground was cultivated just as in England and the cottages not only neat, but with doors, chimneys and windows.'

In 1641 the Protestant settlers were attacked by the 'Confederate' Catholics and subjected to a sectarian massacre in which four thousand Protestants were killed. The events were recorded in official 'Depositions' that grossly exaggerated the scale and violence of the attacks, contributing to the insecurity, dread of massacre and fear of betrayal that characterised the Protestant people of Ulster; the sense that they were under siege. In 1649 Oliver Cromwell, the 'Liberator of Ireland', came to their rescue and drove the Catholics back.

History repeated itself in 1688 when forces loyal to the deposed King James II attempted to impose Catholic rule again. One of unionism's most potent legends is built around the decision of thirteen apprentices to ignore the instructions of Lt Col. Robert Lundy, governor of Londonderry, who wanted to surrender the city to the Earl of Antrim. Lundy's name entered the Protestant lexicon as a word for traitor, and his effigy is burned every year as we burn Guy Fawkes. (Later moderate leaders of unionism like Brian Faulkner and David Trimble were both called 'Lundies' for seeking compromises with Catholics.) The apprentice boys shut the gates of Londonderry against the advancing forces, and the city endured 105 days of siege, with the population reduced to eating rats until it was relieved by ships breaking the boom on the River Foyle on 1 August 1689. Those who had borne the suffering of the siege for loyalty to religion and to the United Kingdom became heroes. And once again the Protestant people were saved by the arrival of a Protestant British ruler who drove the Catholics back, this time William of Orange. King Billy and his victory at the Battle of the Boyne in July 1690 became powerful symbols for the Protestants of Northern Ireland who had precious few victories to celebrate in their history.

It was Protestant militias that helped suppress the Catholic peasant secret societies known as 'Ribonmen' at the Battle of the Diamond in Loughall in County Armagh in 1795, and it was there that they founded the Orange Order, named after King William of Orange, uniting all of the Protestant faith with an oath to 'resist the ascendancy of the Church of Rome by all lawful means'.

Presbyterians in Ireland were victims of the religious laws alongside the Catholics, but in the nineteenth century they were thrown into alliance with other Protestants (including members of the established Church of Ireland) by the common Catholic threat.

As the century went on, the Protestants of north-east Ireland increasingly thought of themselves not as Irish but as British. Belfast was dynamic and economically successful, more akin to Glasgow or Manchester than to the largely rural Ireland in which it sat. When moves towards Home Rule began in the 1870s, Protestant Ulstermen objected strongly. In George Birmingham's 1912 novel *The Red Hand of Ulster*, Protestants are described as fearing that 'Belfast will be the milch cow of the Dublin Parliament. Money will be wanted to feed paupers and pay priests in the south and west. We are the only people who have any money.' Determined to avoid isolation in an economically backward, tyrannical Gaelic and Catholic state, they banded together under the slogan 'Home Rule is Rome Rule'. And they suspected British politicians of wanting to sell them out. C. S. Lewis's father, a staunch unionist, wrote in 1882, 'I believe the cause of Irish agitation to be on the one hand the R.C. religion and the other the weakness and vacillation and the party selfishness of English ministers.'

The Protestants managed to see off the first two attempts at Home Rule in the late nineteenth century by forming an alliance with the Conservatives, who used their support to split apart the Liberals and unseat them. But they faced a real threat when the passage of the Parliament Act in 1911 made it clear that the bulwark of the House of Lords was no longer available to protect them from a further Home Rule bill. They turned to threats of violence, expressed in the earlier emotive words of one of their Conservative supporters, Randolph Churchill: 'Ulster will fight, and Ulster will be right.'

On 28 September 1912, Ulster day, 237,368 men, three-quarters of all Protestant males over the age of sixteen, led by Edward Carson, signed a solemn league and covenant pledging themselves to use 'all means which may be found necessary to defeat the present conspiracy to set up a Home Rule Parliament in Ireland'. They established an Ulster Unionist Council to be a provisional government, bringing together all the Protestant interests, and the Ulster Volunteer Force (UVF), a paramilitary body of 90,000 men which engaged in repeated shows of strength. Twenty-five thousand rifles and three million rounds of ammunition were imported from Imperial Germany in a ship named *Mountjoy II* after the ship that had relieved the siege of Londonderry. The unionists were not without support in Britain from such luminaries as Rudyard Kipling and Edward Elgar (a Catholic), and even had sympathisers in the British military; in the mutiny at the Curragh, sixty British officers resigned their commissions rather than be required to coerce the unionists into accepting Home Rule. In the event Home Rule was put on hold at the outbreak of the First World War. The

UVF went on to join the British expeditionary force, another manifestation of their loyalty to the British state, and vast numbers of them
were massacred at the Battle of the Somme, a source of pride and
sorrow still today in Ulster.

The partition of Ireland was not the unionists' desired outcome.
They would have preferred Ireland to remain in the United Kingdom.
But if there was going to be a separate Ireland they wanted no part
of it. In the words of David Trimble, 'Partition was inevitable. It was
a response to the social reality of two Irish nations.' Separation was
not easy, however. Of the nine counties of Ulster, three – Donegal,
Monaghan and Cavan – had substantial Catholic majorities. To ensure
there was a Protestant majority in Northern Ireland they had to be
excluded, leading to charges of betrayal from the Protestants left
behind in those counties. The unionists got their six-county province
in the Government of Ireland Act in 1920 and the new parliament was
opened by the King in 1921.

Some in unionist ranks argued for inclusiveness in the new Northern
Ireland. Edward Carson advised them in 1921: 'We used to say that we
could not trust an Irish parliament in Dublin to do justice to the Protestant minority. Let us take care that that reproach can no longer be
made against your people, and from the outset let them see that the
Catholic minority have nothing to fear from a Protestant majority.'
But this advice was not heeded by James Craig, the first Prime Minister
of Northern Ireland, whose government was determined to make
their power permanent and undiluted. Some Catholic councils voted
to join the South and nationalist politicians boycotted the Northern
Ireland government, so the Unionists changed the voting system and
altered the electoral boundaries. When the Catholics refused to take
up the one-third of positions in the new Royal Ulster Constabulary
reserved for them, the Unionists filled their places with Protestants.

David Trimble captured the mood well in his acceptance speech
for the Nobel Peace Prize when he said, 'Ulster Unionists, fearful of
being isolated in the island, built a solid house, but it was a cold house
for Catholics. And northern nationalists, although they had a roof
over their heads, seemed to us as if they wanted to burn the house
down.' Unionist politicians were traditionally populist, with a tendency
to follow the grass roots rather than lead them. This often resulted
in a failure to stand up to extremists. When an Ulster-born police

officer, Gerald Smyth, was killed by the IRA in Cork on 18 July 1920, loyalists responded a couple of days later by driving Catholics out of the Belfast shipyards. And when the IRA killed in Belfast, loyalists took revenge by driving Catholics out of their areas. Meanwhile, Protestants left the Free State in their droves and the Irish launched a boycott of the North. In 1937 de Valera amended the Irish constitution to claim that the territory of the Irish state included the entire island of Ireland. Unionists felt they were facing a hostile nationalist state to their south, a hostile nationalist minority within, and a London government of dubious reliability. They were not at all sure Northern Ireland would last, and they had nowhere else to go. They lived in constant fear that the British would abandon them, and they were not wrong to do so. Churchill secretly explored the possibility of agreeing to Irish unity in return for Irish assistance in the Second World War.

It was not until 1963, with the new Unionist Prime Minister Terence O'Neill, that the forty years of unbending rule began to give a little. O'Neill, more English gentleman than unionist, wanted to modernise Northern Ireland, initiating reforms and taking tentative steps towards reconciliation. He invited Sean Lemass, the Irish Prime Minister, to visit Belfast without telling his Cabinet colleagues and visited Dublin himself. But, as demonstrated by the French monarchy before the French Revolution, a few steps towards reform can prove to be a dangerous indication of weakness. O'Neill moved a little, but in the words of the distinguished Northern Ireland civil servant Ken Bloomfield who worked for him, he kept trying 'to buy reform at last year's prices'. His attempts at appeasing nationalists were a failure and all he succeeded in doing was alienating his unionist supporters. A new force appeared in the form of the radical Free Presbyterian firebrand Ian Paisley, who made his name by organising a protest against the flying of Belfast City Hall's flag at half-mast to mark the death of the Pope. In the 1964 elections the Sinn Féin office in West Belfast displayed a small Irish flag in its window. Again Ian Paisley organised a protest and threatened to lead a huge Protestant march into the Catholic enclave to remove it. Rather than risk sectarian violence, the RUC removed the flag themselves, causing some of the worst rioting Belfast had seen in decades. Paisley had a good line in colourful language and after O'Neill had met Lemass, he said, 'A traitor and a bridge are very much alike, for they both go over to the other side.' On the back of this populism, Paisley was elected to Stormont and to Westminster.

Unionists believed the IRA was behind the civil rights movement. 'There is all this nonsense about civil rights,' said William Craig, the Home Affairs secretary, 'and behind it is our old traditional enemy exploiting the situation.' They responded to the threat with force as they had always done. The pressure on them from Harold Wilson they saw as typical of unreliable British governments and did their best to ignore it. But it was not so easy to ignore the escalating violence in Londonderry and Belfast, and the Unionist government reluctantly had to call in the British Army to restore order. Its arrival proved a Trojan Horse, for it enabled Jim Callaghan, the Labour Home Secretary, to demand a say on what went on in Northern Ireland. Moreover, the Irish started to interfere, with Cabinet ministers like Charles Haughey providing guns to the IRA. Unionists were outraged by a speech by Jack Lynch, the Irish Prime Minister, in which he said the Republic would 'not stand idly by' while Catholics were attacked in the North (a statement Lynch was apparently forced into by members of his Cabinet).

As the violence got worse and worse, unionists were convinced that the British government were not being sufficiently tough in security terms, and that the army had one hand tied behind its back by political restrictions on what it could do. The Unionist party passed a motion saying 'we will be masters in our own house' and four thousand shipyard workers marched in 1971 demanding internment for IRA terrorists. In 1972, after the terrible events of Bloody Sunday, the Heath government looked for new ways of dealing with the problem. They considered three options, including repartition to give majority Catholic parts of Northern Ireland to the Republic, unification of Ireland and a referendum on the constitutional position. Brian Faulkner, the new Unionist Prime Minister, refused Heath's suggestion of a forced coalition with Nationalists, saying it would be a 'bedlam cabinet' and then felt betrayed when in March 1972 Heath pulled the plug on devolved government, replacing it with direct rule from Westminster. The collapse of Stormont was greeted with a rally of 100,000 supporters and a two-day unionist strike that brought the Province to a standstill. Willie Whitelaw's meeting with the IRA in July caused outrage amongst unionists. His White Paper on 'the future of Northern Ireland' ' in March 1973 talked about an 'Irish Dimension' and proposed the replacement of majority rule by power-sharing, an idea that horrified most unionists. But unionism was becoming increasingly fractured. Splinter groups had formed, like Vanguard, a party led by William Craig and containing the young David Trimble, which advocated semi-independence and tougher security measures to 'liquidate the enemy'. When Faulkner went into the 1973 Northern Ireland elections promising not to share power with any party 'whose primary objective was to break the link with Great Britain', this was assumed to be a promise not to share power with the nationalist SDLP. But immediately after the election Faulkner agreed to go into government with them. The Unionist Party was bitterly divided, but Whitelaw was determined to force the pace of negotiations about a power-sharing executive, at one point ordering his helicopter to land on the lawn at Stormont Castle in a dramatic attempt to convince the parties he was about to leave and push them into a decision.

In late 1973, Heath summoned the three parties (the Unionists, SDLP and the middle-of-the-road and non-sectarian Alliance Party) to meet the British and Irish governments at the Civil Service training college at Sunningdale just outside London. The hothouse negotiating sessions, which lasted late into the night, left a lasting impression on the collective memory of unionists, who tried to avoid such traps in future and Faulkner was driven too far in the compromises he was forced to make. He accepted a Council of Ireland and North/South cooperation exercising 'executive and harmonising functions' as a gesture towards the nationalist aspiration for an all-Ireland dimension. Later he tried to explain this away as 'nonsense' which would 'mean nothing in practice', but it looked to unionists like an embryo government of Ireland. And he was not helped by the Irish government which said publicly it had no intention of removing the claim to Northern Ireland in Articles 2 and 3 of the Irish constitution. They failed, also, to offer him anything concrete on cross-border security cooperation. The battleground for Faulkner was the Ulster Unionist Council (UUC) which brought together not just members of his party but also Orangemen and other affiliated organisations. The campaign against him was led by John Taylor, a Unionist minister and later Trimble's deputy as leader of the party. Faulkner lost the vote on the agreement at the UUC by 427 votes to 374 and resigned as party leader.

Faulkner's fate was a miserable one. He was spat on by fellow Union-ists in the Assembly and his Assembly members were physically attacked in the chamber. Police had to be called in to quell the fighting. Loyalist killings in the North trebled. And then Heath called a premature general election in which rejectionist Unionists won eleven of the twelve Northern Ireland seats. In May a general strike was declared by the Ulster Workers Council (UWC) and with the support of loyalist para-militaries they closed the roads, hijacked cars and cut off the electricity. After two weeks the British government gave in. Harold Wilson had tried to take them on with a televised address but in an ill-judged passage he called the loyalists 'people who spend their lives sponging off West-minster and British democracy and then systematically assault demo-cratic institutions'. The next day thousands of unionists sported bits of sponge in their lapels in proud defiance of the British government.

In the eyes of the unionists, the British government continued to betray them. The new Labour Secretary of State Merlyn Rees started contacts with the IRA again and legalised Sinn Féin in an attempt to secure a temporary ceasefire. Unionist politicians feared the worst and started consorting with loyalist paramilitaries and there was talk of a third force to protect Ulster again. The replacement of Rees with Roy Mason, a blunt miner from Barnsley, who opted for tougher meas-ures against the IRA, helped to reassure them, and security did get better. Unionists under their new leader James Molyneaux, elected in 1979, were content to live with the status quo rather than seek a deal with moderate Nationalists. Under the influence of Enoch Powell, who had become a Unionist MP, Molyneaux accepted the idea of integration as a full part of the UK rather than seeking the return of Stormont. He described himself as 'a general with an army that isn't making anything much in terms of territorial gains but has the satisfaction of repulsing all attacks on the citadel'. Any movement would mean paying a price in concessions to the Catholics, and contin-uing conflict was almost preferable to admitting that their view of history had been wrong. By the early 1980s, though stuck in defen-sive positions, the Unionists were relatively happy with the stalemate, and saw no reason to change.

These were the two different traditions, two different identities and two different histories Tony and I needed to comprehend as the negotiations progressed. Neither account of history was entirely right, but nor were they all wrong. They were internally consistent and mutually exclusive, and both were accepted completely by each side as a matter of faith. I also came to realise that the two sides spoke different languages. Republican speak was ornate, literary and didn't always mean what it said. Unionist language was blunt, direct, unyielding and always suspicious. There was one thing that both sides agreed on, however, and that was that the British government were to blame for it all. Our task was to convince them that we could now be a neutral intermediary, but we also had to take on board the legacy of previous governments who had attempted the role of go-between.

3

The Talking Starts:
1980–1998

By the early 1980s, people on all sides in Northern Ireland were becoming weary of the cycle of blood, and the pointlessness of violence was clear. The IRA realised they could not win militarily, and the British Army knew that, while it could keep a lid on violence 'at an acceptable level', it could not win either. Everyone started to look for the exits.

The Thatcher government which had come to power in 1979 had not given up on the consistent aim of British governments from Ted Heath onwards to devolve power back to Northern Ireland politicians and a new generation of senior officials at the centre of government wanted to have another go at finding a solution. In Dublin, the opening the British had shown to an 'Irish Dimension' in the Sunningdale Agreement of 1973 was a tempting hint that joint authority for the North might be possible, and they sought to begin talks with the British.

The first tentative contacts between the British and the Irish took place in 1982. David Goodall, a senior British diplomat attached to the Cabinet Office, from a Catholic family with connections to Ireland, began talking to Michael Lillis, a senior Irish diplomat, ferociously clever and with staunch republican antecedents. The NIO disapproved of the whole exercise and, as a result, was largely kept out of the loop. The negotiations were conducted in great secrecy, with Goodall joined by the Cabinet Secretary Robert Armstrong on the British side and Lillis by another senior Irish diplomat, Sean Donlon, along with Dermot Nally, the Irish Cabinet Secretary.

Margaret Thatcher was, of all modern prime ministers, the most sympathetic to the unionists, and it was therefore paradoxical that she should have been responsible for negotiations that led to the

Irish having more of a say in Northern Ireland. That she might be open to new thinking on Northern Ireland did not at first seem obvious, particularly after her intemperate reaction to the report from the nationalist 'New Ireland Forum' in November 1983 (she said the three options proposed – a united Ireland, a federal Ireland or joint Anglo-Irish authority – were 'out, out, out'). But Garrett FitzGerald, the new Fine Gael Prime Minister, was concerned that the mafia-style politics of the IRA and Sinn Féin risked infecting the whole Irish political system, and was determined to find a way of removing the alienation of Catholics in the North. He kept on doggedly pushing away at negotiations with Thatcher, and wouldn't be deflected until he secured an agreement.

Thatcher, for her part, had time for FitzGerald, unlike his predecessor Charlie Haughey, although she doubted he had the political strength to deliver on his undertakings. She was reluctant throughout about the negotiations, as I had seen her be about the talks with the Chinese on the return of Hong Kong a few years before. One of the reasons was Enoch Powell. It was important to Thatcher that she had been able to effect a reconciliation with Powell after her success in the Falklands War, and now that he had become an Ulster Unionist MP she did not want him turning on her again in the chamber of the House of Commons because of a deal with the Irish. Every time there was a new IRA atrocity she became more nervous about the whole enterprise. And then, in October 1984, the IRA attempted to kill her by blowing up the Grand Hotel in Brighton during the Tory Party conference. Five people died. The IRA statement issued after the bombing chillingly summed up their view of the equation of terror: 'Today we were unlucky, but remember, we have only to be lucky once. You will have to be lucky always.' Yet the principal impact of the bomb on Thatcher's thinking was to make her determined not to alter her course of action because of it, an unusually positive result of her trademark obstinacy.

The negotiations at a prime-ministerial level were undertaken either at the annual Anglo-Irish summits or in the margins of European summits in order to deflect any unwanted attention. On one memorable occasion, at a meeting with FitzGerald after a particularly long and tiresome EC meeting, Thatcher fell fast asleep soon after sitting down with him. FitzGerald looked at my brother Charles Powell, Thatcher's foreign policy aide, to ask what they should do. Charles suggested that

FitzGerald carry on making all the points he had intended to make and Charles would dutifully note them down. They could then wake her up to agree the joint press statement. To their credit neither FitzGerald nor the Irish Cabinet Secretary Dermot Nally who was with him seemed to mind, and as they finished the meeting Thatcher woke up and asked to be briefed on what they had agreed.

Thatcher saw the aim of the negotiations as being to improve relations with the Irish and to gain better security cooperation. At first she was bidding for the right of British security forces to go up to ten miles into Irish territory in hot pursuit of terrorists, but had to fall back to a zone of three miles. In the end FitzGerald wasn't able to deliver even that. Nevertheless, Thatcher, although emotionally uncomfortable with the Anglo-Irish Agreement, was intellectually persuaded of the case for it, and unveiled it together with Garrett FitzGerald at Hillsborough on 15 November 1985, despite a last-minute attempt by Tom King, the new Northern Ireland Secretary, to derail it.

The Agreement gave the Irish government a consultative role in Northern Ireland through a ministerial Inter Governmental Conference (IGC) and a small permanent joint secretariat based at Maryfield on the outskirts of East Belfast. The IGC had no executive powers but the two governments undertook to 'make determined efforts' to resolve their differences, allowing the Irish to have influence on what happened in the Province. On the other side, the Agreement made it clear that any change in the status of Northern Ireland could only happen with the backing of its people.

In the longer term, the important advance for the British was that it marked a switch in policy by the Irish government: instead of being a critic of British policy in the North, it now recognised that the two sides had to work together to resolve the problem. Without that new cooperation, no eventual settlement would have been possible. For the Irish, the long-term gain was, they hoped, the removal of the unionist veto, since for the first time Unionists had not been able to stop an agreement between the two governments. Henceforth, republicans would no longer be able to argue that the only way to get the Brits to move was through violence. And the threat of Anglo-Irish joint authority acted as an incentive to move the Unionists, over time, into power-sharing with Catholics. Although it took another twenty years before it happened, it was on exactly these grounds that Ian Paisley explained to his supporters his decision to go into a power-sharing Executive: in order to avoid joint authority over the North for the Irish government.

No attempt had been made to prepare the Unionists for the shock of the Anglo-Irish Agreement, and there was an outcry. They realised immediately that it meant the end of their veto, and reacted with fury. A group of unionists, including the moderate Ken Maginnis, gathered outside the gates at Hillsborough in the cold winter sunshine, enraged that they couldn't get in to stop their Prime Minister signing a deal with her Irish counterpart. There was a real sense of menace and lots of pushing and shoving between the unionists and the police. It was to be the first of many such confrontations.

The NIO delighted in saying 'I told you so', arguing that the problems arose from the fact that the Agreement had been negotiated by London-based civil servants and diplomats who did not properly understand the problem. One of the negotiators defended himself later, anonymously, by saying, 'We were aware of the history but we were not cowed by it.' The shock of betrayal was all the worse for the Unionists because it was so unexpected. UUP leader James Molyneaux had made the mistake of opting out of any negotiations, convinced that the veto was sufficient protection to ensure the government would not agree to anything of which he would disapprove. Now he was confronted by an agreement he didn't like but couldn't stop. Ian Paisley said the Agreement was to be 'resisted to the very death' and accused Margaret Thatcher of being prepared 'to wade knee-deep in the blood of loyalists for this document of treachery and deceit'. When the government refused to hold a referendum, the fifteen Unionist MPs resigned to cause by-elections, against the government 'diktat'. Unfortunately their message was blunted when one of them lost his seat to the SDLP. There was a huge rally against the Agreement at Belfast City Hall which, from then on, was draped with banners saying 'Ulster says No'. No British minister visited the City Hall again until 1991. In March, unionists mounted a day of action which brought the Province to a halt, but they were unable to repeat the success of the loyalist general strike in 1974. When a Portadown loyalist was killed by a RUC plastic bullet, loyalists started attacking the homes of policemen, and 150 police families had to move house. Separately, in one of the more comic moments, Peter Robinson, one of the DUP leadership at the time, 'invaded' the small market town of Clontibret across the border in the Republic but was arrested and had to pay a fine.

Thatcher herself was taken aback by the unionist response, and particularly saddened by the resignation of Ian Gow, her former parliamentary private secretary and closest political soulmate in the Conservative party. But while she complained at being bamboozled into the Agreement by officials, she never had any intention of giving in to Unionist pressure. That was not in her nature. So while the Unionists huffed and puffed, this time they were not able to blow the house down. What they did succeed in doing, however, was scuppering any hope the British government might have of devolving authority to a power-sharing government on the back of the Agreement.

The Ango-Irish Agreement, whatever its intentions, led to years of political sterility. For two years, Unionist leaders would not even talk to ministers, although in 1987 Tom King did manage to tempt them into 'talks about talks' which broached different methods of power-sharing. In parallel, the SDLP started talks with Sinn Féin at the instigation of Father Alec Reid, a Redemptorist priest close to Gerry Adams. The meetings, which took place at the Clonard monastery in West Belfast, got nowhere and collapsed in September 1988 but contacts between SDLP leader John Hume and Adams continued. However, aside from these unofficial contacts, all other negotiations stagnated. Then, in 1989, the Irish and British governments agreed to suspend the Inter Governmental Conference for long enough to allow exploratory talks to take place with the democratic parties, first under Brian Mawhinney, a junior minister in the NIO, and then, from the beginning of 1991, under the Secretary of State for Northern Ireland Peter Brooke. Crucially Brooke articulated, for the first time, the role of the British government as a neutral broker rather than as a party to the talks, happy to go along with anything the parties themselves could agree. This neutrality was never accepted by the parties, and the government could never be completely disinterested given its responsibility for security, but it was a key building block in the process that eventually found a settlement.

In March 1991 Brooke set out a three-stranded approach to the talks: the first strand dealing with internal matters for Northern Ireland such as the Assembly and the Executive, from which the Irish government were excluded; a second strand dealing with relations between the North and the Irish government; and the third strand dealing with relations between Ireland, North and South, and the rest of the British isles. This set the framework for all future talks through to the Good Friday Agreement and beyond. And in the process of the talks, the Unionists quietly dropped their earlier insistence on majoritarian rule. Another innovation was the fact that the talks were chaired for the first time by an independent, international figure, Sir Ninian Stephen, a former governor general of Australia. So, although by the end of 1991 little substantive progress had been made in the various abortive sessions of talks, many of the key structural elements for the eventual peace process were by then in place, and the habit of talking had begun which developed into that process.

In parallel to the talks, there was a stately minuet of speeches and public statements going on between Peter Brooke and Republicans. In November 1989, soon after being appointed Secretary of State for Northern Ireland, Brooke referred in an interview to the example of Cyprus and said the government would need to be imaginative and flexible in its response if there were an IRA ceasefire. His words created a frisson of interest on the Republican side. Martin McGuinness responded by saying that Brooke was the first Northern Ireland Secretary 'with some understanding of Irish history', urging him to spell out what he meant by 'imaginative steps'. In November 1990, in an important speech, Brooke said that the British government had 'no selfish strategic or economic interest in Northern Ireland', a crucial step in the view of SDLP leader John Hume in making it possible for the IRA to lay down its weapons. Gerry Adams responded, saying the remarks were interesting and the position Brooke was proposing deserved to be explored, while insisting the onus was still on those who believed there was an alternative to armed struggle to prove it.

In November 1990 John Major replaced Margaret Thatcher as Prime Minister. Among his first experiences of the Northern Ireland question was the mortar attack on 10 Downing Street on 7 February 1991. Major was in the Cabinet Room chairing a meeting of the Gulf War Cabinet. My brother Charles, his foreign policy adviser, was sitting to his immediate left. There was an almighty bang, quickly followed by several more. Their first thought was that it was an Iraqi car bomb on Horseguards Parade, and my brother shoved Major out of his seat and under the Cabinet table, afraid that the glass windows that looked over the garden to Horseguards Parade would come in under the force of the explosion. Certainly, when I visited No. 10 a few days later, you could still see jagged shrapnel in the ceiling of the White Room, which is immediately above the Cabinet Room. There the windows had been shattered and parts of the mortar had entered diagonally, slicing into the plaster. Luckily the windows in the Cabinet Room had recently been replaced by shatterproof reinforced glass.

While the members of the War Cabinet crouched under the table, four slightly portly police officers rushed into the room waving their revolvers. My brother took Major by the sleeve and led him down the stairs to the big walk-in safe on the ground floor, and they remained there until the all-clear was given and they could leave No. 10 for the underground Cabinet Office Briefing Room (COBR) under the Cabinet Office to continue their meeting. It was only then that they discovered that there had been an IRA mortar attack, with two of the missiles landing in Foreign Office Green just beyond No. 10 and one in the garden of No. 10 itself. It had been a close-run thing.

Despite this introduction, John Major was the first prime minister since Lloyd George to take a real and sustained interest in Northern Ireland. There was no political advantage to him in doing so, and he would get no thanks from the British people. But he was of a different generation and had a very different approach to Margaret Thatcher, who had come to the conclusion that the problem of Northern Ireland was insoluble. He was determined to prove it could be solved, and was convinced that he was a master negotiator who could bring it about. He received a letter from Gerry Adams two days after becoming Prime Minister (the first time Republicans had written to a prime minister), and he was dealing with the problem to his last day in office, for much of that time with the assistance of his remarkable private secretary, Rod Lyne, who worked all hours on the subject, despite for a large part of that time being under a personal death threat from the IRA which required round-the-clock police protection.

It was in 1991 that I too got my first introduction to Northern Ireland. I, like most British diplomats, had only the vaguest notion where Northern Ireland was, other than stuck somewhere in the 1950s. In preparation for my posting to the embassy in Washington, where it would be my job to defend the policy of the government against the attacks of the Irish-American lobby, I was sent to Belfast in June. I was fascinated by the anomaly of an ordinary, provincial Victorian city on which were superimposed fortified police stations, soldiers on the street and police Land Rovers with protection built down to the ground to stop bombs being rolled under them. I saw the problems of West Belfast from two very different angles. I was taken round first by a young, activist Catholic priest, who introduced me to republican and nationalist community centres. I then toured the area with an army patrol of young, nervous British soldiers initially in the back of an armoured Land Rover, watching all the time for coffee-jar bombs being hurled at them. I saw how they endured days and days of boredom punctuated by a sudden flash of fire that could maim you for life or even kill you. I was struck too by the young people on both sides. They were convinced that, if they strayed on to the territory of the other side, they would immediately be identified and dealt with because of the way they looked or the way they dressed. They all looked the same to me but a few well-directed questions about where they went to school or where their parents worked would betray their affiliation very quickly. Despite the violence and sectarian hatred, I wrote in my diary that I did not believe this was an insoluble problem.

It is very hard for democratic governments to admit to talking to terrorist groups while those groups are still killing innocent people. But on the basis of my experience I think it is always right to talk to your enemy however badly they are behaving. And luckily for this process, the British government's backchannel to the Provisional IRA had been in existence whenever required from 1973 onwards. When the Troubles had started, Northern Ireland was foreign territory for Whitehall, which had previously paid no attention to the subject, and they had sent British diplomat Oliver Wright over to Belfast to keep an eye on the Stormont government. As things got worse and Stormont collapsed, to be replaced by direct rule, it was a case of all hands to the pump, and a diverse collection of home civil servants, diplomats and spooks was sent out to try and make sense of the place. One of these was a remarkable Secret Intelligence Service (SIS) officer, Frank Steele, a former colonial officer and travelling companion to the explorer Wilfred Thesiger. Steele made it his job to get out into Catholic ghettos like the Falls Road in Belfast and the Bogside in Derry, which the Protestant government had hardly tried to administer at all, and to make contacts at all levels. Eventually he was able to get in touch with the Provisional IRA leaders and suggest they come to London to see Willie Whitelaw in 1972.

When Steele sat down with Daithi O'Conaill and Gerry Adams in a country house near the border with Donegal to negotiate the terms of the visit, he was the first British official to meet the IRA. While in Kenya, he had had to engage in dialogue with Jomo Kenyatta, considered a terrorist, and did not see much difference in talking to the Republicans. As well as arranging the Whitelaw meeting, Steele was able to use his contacts to prevent a bloodbath occurring when, in Operation Motorman, the British Army retook the no-go areas in Derry immediately after the meeting with Whitelaw. The IRA were advised of the situation and withdrew their weapons and ammunition, making no attempt to wage a pitched battle with the army.

When Steele left Northern Ireland in May 1973, his contacts were inherited by his successor, another SIS officer, Michael Oatley, a subtle and independent-minded intelligence operative who within a few months of his arrival managed to develop connections with and around the IRA leadership to see whether it might be encouraged in the direction of political activity. But maintaining those connections was now more difficult. IRA active service units were omnipresent in the areas into which Oatley made lonely forays to meet community leaders who might help him. He was also acutely conscious of the official injunction that there should be no further links after the embarrassment caused to the government by the meeting with Whitelaw in Cheyne Walk.

He was lucky. Cautious probing had produced three different potential lines of contact to the IRA. The most promising, and the one he pursued, involved a Derry businessman called Brendan Duddy whom Steele had met briefly and who had helped to engineer the peaceful passage of Operation Motorman. Duddy was very much an Irish republican, but he was a pacifist and a firm believer in dialogue, which he worked single-mindedly to create. In previous accounts of the period he has been referred to only as 'the Contact', his name a secret and his role as a brave and ingenious intermediary unpublicised for over three decades, yet he has a claim to have been among the most persistent and effective of the unsung heroes of the peace process. He partnered Oatley in building the connection through which the 1975 ceasefire was negotiated and took a leading part in managing those negotiations. When the ceasefire broke down he kept alive with Oatley's help a channel of communication to the British government which might one day be reactivated, and at intervals over the next sixteen years he used the position this gave him with elements of the Provisional leadership to canvass the attractions of a political programme. Duddy worked selflessly and at great risk to himself over many years to bring about a peaceful settlement in Northern Ireland and credit for his achievements is long overdue. In 1991 it was on his initiative that a meeting between Martin McGuinness and Michael Oatley took place which reactivated the 'Link' and helped lead eventually to the peace process. It was through him that the opening contacts leading up to the first IRA ceasefire in 1994 took place.

Oatley's initial contacts with the IRA through Duddy were cloaked in secrecy. Not even Merlyn Rees, the Northern Ireland Secretary, knew about them. Oatley informed Frank Cooper, the senior British official in Northern Ireland, of the existence of 'the Contact' and he in turn consulted John Hunt, the Cabinet Secretary, and Harold Wilson, who had had direct contact with the IRA himself when leader of the Opposition. After Wilson gave his approval, Oatley used the channel for some months to pass back and forth small pieces of non-sensitive information as a confidence-building measure, such as the date of release from prison of senior Republicans. His interlocutor at the other end was Ruari O'Bradaigh, president of Provisional Sinn Féin, backed by Daithi O'Conaill, the Chief of Staff. The intermediary, driving hundreds of miles up and down the country and doing everything he could to keep the IRA in play, was Duddy who, in the intervals of his journeying, joined Oatley in long meetings at a safe house in the mountains near Derry during which, over many hours, each educated the other in the political sensitivities affecting the opportunity for direct and positive engagement which they were trying to create. These meetings also fuelled Oatley's ideas for the next message or response, for which he then sought authority from Cooper reporting to Harold Wilson.

Neither the British government nor the IRA leaders felt able to take the next step and it was Duddy who pushed them into it. Recognising that the process must move on if it was not to break down, he engineered a meeting between Oatley and Billy McKee, a senior IRA figure who had recently emerged from prison and, although not yet identi-fied by the British in that capacity, had rejoined the Army Council. McKee reported to his colleagues that Oatley's overtures were worth pursuing and negotiations then began in earnest with O'Bradaigh, who was already committed to a political path, as the lead negotiator.

From a British government point of view there were no negotia-tions. Throughout the series of meetings which now occurred at ever more frequent intervals at a safehouse in Derry to which the Repub-lican participants were on each occasion smuggled from across the border under the eyes of the British Army, Oatley, later joined by his Foreign Office colleague James Allan, the political adviser on Merlyn Rees's staff, maintained the position that the purpose of the dialogue was not to negotiate, but to advise the IRA of what action the British government and security forces might take if there were a cessation of violence on the part of the IRA. It is unlikely that this distinction survived in what O'Bradaigh and his team reported to their colleagues. They had become convinced of the need to stop fighting and they had to be able to present concessions to the Army Council, and they were helped to do so.

The talks continued for weeks, with the hawks on the Army Council sending ever tougher demands. One was that their leaders be allowed to carry handguns when they returned to their areas after being 'on the run' in the South. The elaborate British response was to point out that, with the ending of violence, the army would withdraw from republican areas, senior IRA men might helpfully be designated as official points of contact for crisis resolution, and these contacts might then be given special passes which would make it very unlikely they would be searched if they stayed in their own areas. In the South this was interpreted as 'Agreed'.

They reached consensus on an indefinite ceasefire but needed a cover story for why violence was stopping. It was provided by the parallel talks going on in Feakle in County Clare with a group of clergymen in December 1974, and for nearly twenty years both sides kept secret what had actually taken place in Derry. The ceasefire itself stuttered on for some months and then collapsed in response to renewed loyalist violence. Oatley had, by then, left Northern Ireland for a more orthodox SIS posting but he deliberately continued his relationship with Duddy and they would meet or speak on the phone from time

to time despite the injunction from Roy Mason, the new Northern
Ireland Secretary, forbidding all further dealings, direct or indirect,
with the IRA as part of his tough new security approach. Oatley felt
that the reliable and secret channel of communication which had been
created was too valuable to waste, and without any authority to do
so he agreed with Duddy that the new IRA leadership, with Martin
McGuinness as a central figure, should be told that while there was
nothing now to talk about the channel remained available against the
day when there might be. It was, metaphorically, contained in a locked
box, the key to which was in the possession of Brendan Duddy and
behind which, wherever he happened to be in the world, was Oatley,
known to the IRA as 'Mountainclimber'. This arrangement gave Duddy
continuing access. He worked diligently to maintain the relationship,
meeting members of the leadership and providing political discussion
and strategy papers in his bid to promote peace.

The Link was resuscitated at the time of the hunger strikes in 1981.
Duddy phoned Oatley in London late at night and, talking in coded
language, indicated there might be a way of resolving the issue before
Sean McKenna, the first hunger striker died. Oatley went to see Ken
Stowe, the new permanent secretary of the NIO, to tell him about
the approach. Stowe called No. 10 to make sure Thatcher was content,
while Oatley spoke to Duddy on the phone from Stowe's office, and
then Oatley was bundled off to Belfast. There he met Duddy and
Father Meagher, the IRA prisoners' go-between, in a deserted arrivals
terminal at Aldergrove airport, and handed Meagher a document
setting out the concessions the government was prepared to make on
prison conditions. The first hunger strike was called off, but when the
government appeared to renege on its offer, the second, deadly hunger
strike began.

For the next ten years Oatley remained in contact with Duddy and
Duddy continued his relationship with the IRA leadership and his
advocacy of exclusively peaceful strategies. At last, early in 1991 he
told Oatley that the IRA might now be ready to discuss a political way
forward. He arranged for Oatley to meet Martin McGuinness in Derry
just ten days before Oatley's retirement from the SIS. Oatley told
McGuinness that while the British Army might never stop the IRA
altogether, it would always be able to contain it. Unless a political
track were found, the current leadership would be replaced by a new

one and the cycle of senseless violence would repeat itself all over again, but if the leadership were prepared to move in the direction of politics the British government might be willing to reopen the Link and to offer what help it could. McGuinness indicated they were ready for such a dialogue and asked what the channel would be. Oatley explained he was retiring but said he would talk to the government about who might replace him.

On returning to London, Oatley went to see John Chilcott, the new permanent secretary of the NIO, and told him he had opened a channel to Martin McGuinness who was ready to discuss a political way forward. Chilcott said he would consider how to proceed. Stella Rimington, then the Director General of the Security Service (MI5), was vehemently opposed to the idea of the SIS, which was normally confined to operations overseas, treading on their turf in this way, but the Security Service's Director and Coordinator of Intelligence in Northern Ireland, who had worked closely with Oatley on Arab terrorism, supported the initiative. Still, MI5 insisted that the oper- ation had to be mounted by one of their staff and found for the role a retired senior SIS officer who had recently been re-employed by the Security Service. This officer introduced himself to Duddy (who named him 'Fred') and took over running the Link.

At first the NIO used the Link in its latest phase with caution to provide information and receive messages. For example, they sent to the IRA an advance copy of an important speech Patrick Mayhew, the new Secretary of State, was to give in Coleraine in late 1992. In the speech Mayhew said that 'provided it is advocated constitutionally, there can be no proper reason for excluding any political objective from discussion. Certainly not the objective of a united Ireland [. . .] In the event of a genuine and established cessation of violence, the whole range of responses that we have had to make to that violence could, and would, be looked at afresh.'

The Link served a useful purpose, not least in focusing the British government's mind on what they wanted, but it really took off when, in February 1993, 'Fred' brought back a message purporting to come from Martin McGuinness. The message contained the following: 'The conflict is over but we need your advice on how to bring it to an end. We wish to have an unannounced ceasefire in order to hold a dialogue leading to peace. We cannot announce such a move as it will lead to confusion for the Volunteers because the press will interpret it as surrender. We cannot meet the Secretary of State's public renuncia- tion of violence [set out in the Coleraine speech], but it would be given privately as long as we were sure that we were not being tricked.'

Ever since it became public, there has been much controversy over the provenance of this message. Martin McGuinness denied he ever sent it, and claimed it had been invented by the British government to get him killed by other republicans. But it is fairly clear that 'Fred' believed it to be a genuine message. It is hard to be sure how it came to be concocted. Brendan Duddy had always been dedicated to bringing the two sides closer together in the search for peace and was not above painting the best possible picture in the messages they sent each other, but he would never have made something up. However, Denis Bradley, a former Catholic priest from Derry who had refused to have anything to do with the Link in its early days but played a minor part in it in the early 1990s, has suggested that he himself drafted the message, reflecting what he believed the true IRA position to be.

Whoever wrote the message, it inevitably created a stir within the British government. John Major convened a special Cabinet committee to discuss how to respond to it and, on 19 March, the government sent a substantive reply saying that, if the IRA proceeded to a cease- fire, the government would be 'bold and imaginative' in response. The Warrington bombs the next day, which killed two small children, nearly derailed the whole process, but the government held their nerve and there was a carefully orchestrated exchange of messages with the IRA. There was never a long enough gap in IRA violence to allow a sensible face-to-face discussion to happen, but unbeknown to officials at the government end of the Link, Duddy insisted on setting up a meeting in April for 'Fred' and the head of MI5 in Northern Ireland to talk to Martin McGuinness and Gerry Kelly, a leading Republican who had been imprisoned for the Old Bailey bomb of 1973. 'Fred' was pres- sured into turning up for the meeting but the Northern Ireland head of MI5 did not appear. On 2 November, there was a final message purporting to be from Martin McGuinness offering a 'total end to violence'. The IRA has subsequently denied ever sending such a message but the government responded enthusiastically, assuming it to be genuine, offering the guarantee of exploratory dialogue two and a half months after a permanent ceasefire was called.

The Link was shortly to go down, however. As 1993 drew to an end, its existence was leaked, probably by republican sources to Eamon Mallie, a Belfast journalist. After an initial effort to deny it, a shame-faced Mayhew had to publish the correspondence with the IRA in full. Unfortunately, in its haste, the government published a version of the correspondence that was full of errors, mainly typos, and when Republicans published their own, different, account, Mayhew had to come to the House of Commons again with a corrected version. Given that the Republican version of the dialogue, in a process I became familiar with later, would have been scribbled on lots of different scraps of paper in Adams's and McGuinness's crablike handwriting and then fitted together to read out as a message in a complicated version of Chinese whispers, it was amazing anyone had anything approximating to an accurate account of the correspondence at all.

Following its exposure, the Link went out of business for good. And what had been designed to bring the two sides closer, and had done so most successfully, at this last point created distrust. The Republicans insisted that Martin McGuinness had had a meeting with a British government representative. The government insisted that no such meeting had taken place. In fact, there had been the April 1993 meeting between 'Fred' and McGuinness, as well as the meeting between Oatley and McGuinness in 1991.

The real significance of the Link in the last chapter of its twenty-year history lay in the impact which McGuinness's supposed desire for an unofficial ceasefire had on Major and the Cabinet, who, with the exception of the sceptical Ken Clarke, were convinced there was at last the possibility of making progress towards peace.

In the meantime, the government's public focus had been on the talks begun in 1989 with the democratic political parties (the UUP, the SDLP, the DUP and the Alliance), where in April 1993 Paddy Mayhew carried on where Peter Brooke had left off. Although SDLP leader John Hume was uninterested in a process that excluded Sinn Féin, and Unionist leader James Molyneaux was not very interested in arriving anywhere in particular, making progress limited, Mayhew did manage to get closer to one important target: the idea that the Irish government would renounce the territorial claim on the North in the Irish constitution in return for new North/South institutions that would allow the Irish a say in Northern Ireland and replace those established by the Anglo-Irish Agreement, so hated by unionists. This became another key building block of an eventual agreement.

More useful dialogue was, however, taking place between John Hume and Gerry Adams. Adams and Hume had never broken off their contacts, but they had to come clean about them when Adams was spotted coming out of Hume's home in Derry in April 1993. Having been rumbled, they put out a joint statement on 26 April confirming the meetings, and carried on working together until they put out a further joint statement on 25 September, which said: 'We are convinced from our discussions that a process can be designed to lead to agreement among the divided people of this island which will provide a solid basis for peace.' Having dropped this bombshell, Hume disappeared to America on a visit to his political friends and allies and did not reappear until 7 October, when he went to see the Irish government in Dublin. He appeared to suggest at the time that he had handed over a piece of paper setting out the potential agreement that was to resolve the issue of Northern Ireland, but it seems clear now that he did not in fact give the Irish a document. Certainly the Irish government denied afterwards that any such document existed. But what Hume had done, in discussion with Adams, was to come up with the concept of a joint declaration by the two governments that could provide the trigger for the IRA to declare a ceasefire. He was roundly excoriated at the time for supping with the devil, but he persevered despite the criticism because he so desperately wanted peace. And he deserves an enormous amount of credit for his bravery in doing so.

The main event, however, was the negotiation between the British and Irish governments on a joint declaration. The British government's attitude was guided by what it knew of the Republican position from the Link and from the Hume–Adams contacts and of the other parties' positions in the talks process. It had an overview of all the different threads to the negotiations which gave it an advantage over the other protagonists.

The idea of a joint declaration had first come up officially in a meeting between Major and Charles Haughey in December 1991, but after Haughey resigned the following January his successor, Albert Reynolds, took up the initiative with huge enthusiasm. During this time, the Irish government were getting messages about it through

John Hume, as well as talking directly to Republicans. Martin Mansergh, the erudite Anglo-Irish adviser on Northern Ireland affairs to successive Fianna Fáil prime ministers, had a series of meetings with Gerry Adams at the Clonard monastery in West Belfast and in another Redemptorist monastery in Dundalk, again through the good offices of Father Alec Reid.

In 1993 Reynolds contacted Major and proposed that he come over secretly to Dublin because he had a paper of great importance to give him. Major explained patiently why a secret prime ministerial visit would be impossible, and instead sent his Cabinet Secretary, Robin Butler, to receive the document in his place. Butler flew to Baldonnel airforce base outside Dublin and Reynolds drove out from his office to meet him there. The document was a draft of the joint declara-tion that had been discussed between Adams and Hume and Adams and Mansergh. A week later, Hume handed over another slightly different version of the same document to John Chilcott. It only took one look at the document for Chilcott to be clear it was unacceptable to the British government (it demanded, for example, a date for British withdrawal from Northern Ireland), and on 14 June Butler relayed the British response to Irish Cabinet Secretary Dermot Nally: they could not negotiate on the basis of the document but would only provide comments. In November Butler flew back to Dublin again, this time to hand over a British draft of the joint declaration that was completely different to the Irish draft, and to tell Reynolds about the Link which was about to be splashed in the *Observer*. Reynolds reacted with fury on both points.

Major went over to Dublin himself on 3 December for a very diffi-cult session with Reynolds. The Irish were adamant that they would only negotiate on the basis of their text and Major eventually had to concede the point. He did, however, manage to remove all the objec-tionable republican elements and insert in particular the concept of the consent of the people of Northern Ireland to any change in its status. The Irish had already decided to relax their position on this issue. Their adviser, Martin Mansergh, had travelled to Cambridge University, where his father had been Professor of History, to conduct research on the examples of East Germany and North Korea, and had come back convinced that any change in the status of Northern Ireland could only be legitimate with the consent of the people of Northern Ireland.

Eventually, after further difficult and intensive negotiations between officials, Major and Reynolds published the Downing Street Declaration on 15 December 1993. The aim was to set out their stall for the circumstances in which Sinn Féin could be admitted to the talks process and to remove the excuses for violence once and for all. In contrast to the Anglo-Irish Agreement of 1985, Unionists had no difficulty this time. Major had been determined not to make Thatcher's mistake of blindsiding the Unionists with an unexpected agreement, not least since he depended on UUP votes on controversial legislation in the House of Commons. He had told James Molyneaux about the Joint Declaration and its contents in the summer of 1993, and although Molyneaux had initially made it clear he could not live with the approach, not least since he was under pressure from a new MP David Trimble to be more hard line, he came round when the British government produced its own version of the agreement.

From the Republican point of view, however, the document was not at all what they had been expecting after the discussions with the Irish government and with John Hume. Gone was the deadline for British withdrawal, gone the demand that the British government be a 'persuader' for a united Ireland, and gone the idea of an act of self-determination for all the Irish people. Adams and the leadership of the movement were thrown into crisis. They were being offered an entry into the political process but at a very different price to the one they had bargained for. They went into a holding pattern, with Adams trying to manage the divisions in Republican ranks by neither rejecting nor accepting the Downing Street Declaration but asking instead for 'clarification'.

John Major was desperate to avoid any suggestion that he was negotiating with Republicans while they were still committed to violence and responded by ruling out any further clarification. But this position had to be unwound in the following weeks because of pressure from the Irish, and when Paddy Mayhew was in Washington in April, two Congressmen came out of a meeting with him saying Mayhew had switched his position on clarification. He was now indicating that if Republicans asked questions of clarification on particular points then the government would be prepared to answer those questions. Sinn Féin took the hint and Adams wrote to Major putting twenty questions to the government about the Downing Street Declaration and the next month the government published answers to them all.

Adams announced a period of consultation over the summer, and finally on 31 August 1994 the IRA announced 'a complete cessation of military operations'. There was jubilation on the Catholic side with car horns blaring and flags being waved in West Belfast as if they had just won a football match. The Protestants, however, were much more uncertain. Ian Paisley said they faced 'the worst crisis in Ulster's history since the setting up of the state', and Molyneaux said the ceasefire 'started destabilising the whole population in Northern Ireland. It was not an occasion for celebration, quite the opposite.' Unionists were once again afraid they had been sold out by a British government as part of some secret deal. In fact they had not been, and there had been no more secret contacts with the IRA since November 1993. But nor had the problem been solved. The debate now moved on to the failure of the IRA to say that the ceasefire was 'permanent'.

Out in Washington I was caught up in the post-Declaration manoeuvrings when the embassy was instructed in December 1993 to try and stop the Clinton administration from granting Gerry Adams a visa to visit the US. Given that the IRA was not yet on ceasefire, the government believed it would send them the wrong message, indicating that talks could take place in parallel with violence.

It had been during the course of the New York Democratic Primary campaign of 1992 that Bill Clinton had assured Irish-American activists he would reverse American policy and give Gerry Adams a visa to visit the US. He made the promise after a long day campaigning, answering questions on a subject that was unfamiliar to him at a very tense time, and his foreign policy advisers, Tony Lake and Nancy Soderberg, were horrified. Once in power, Clinton in fact refused Adams a visa, and Irish-American activists assumed it was just another politician's promise. But in December 1993, after the Downing Street Declaration and under heavy lobbying from Albert Reynolds, Clinton returned to the issue. On 30 December the British Ambassador in Washington, Robin Renwick, went to the White House to lobby Lake, the National Security Adviser, not to grant the visa, and the month of January was given over to a vicious battle in Washington on the subject.

On 6 January I recorded in my diary that I thought we were losing. The Irish government were beating us in the lobbying stakes and it looked to me as though the Americans would give Adams a visa in the belief that it would help facilitate a ceasefire. By Thursday 27 January, however, we had won over Warren Christopher, the Secretary of State, along with the Attorney General Janet Reno, the head of the FBI and most of the Washington establishment. We still had to convince Tony Lake, and his number three at the National Security Council (NSC), Nancy Soderberg, my tennis partner and the White House's expert on matters Northern Irish, having worked for Ted Kennedy, but I thought we would win. By the weekend the problem seemed to be solved: the White House had agreed to set conditions on the visa and, as expected, when the Americans put the conditions to Adams he refused them. We thought that would be it, but the problem didn't stay solved. Adams gave an interview to NBC talking about peace and Tony Lake reopened the whole question. At the last minute there was a strange diversion, with an organisation describing itself as the Provisional IRA of Southern California calling a local radio station in San Diego saying there were three bombs in British shops in the city and linking the attack to a visa for Adams. I was highly suspicious of this obvious hoax, but Clinton took the matter seriously and demanded that Adams issue a denunciation. When he did, Clinton gave him the visa. The White House didn't tell us what their decision had been until it was already on the wires.

John Major was furious and No. 10 sent a very strongly worded message to the White House. They instructed us at the embassy to cease cooperation with the NSC on Northern Ireland matters. Major's relations with Clinton had never been good. Clinton was deeply suspicious of Tory attempts to damage him in the 1992 presidential election campaign by dredging through the records of his time at Oxford. I had set up the first phone call between the two men when Major was paying a farewell visit to George Bush in Washington in December 1992. I found a room in the Sheraton Carlton Hotel where Major could make the call privately and got Nancy Soderberg on the line down in Little Rock first then put Major on. I listened in. It was a very cold phone call, barely within the bounds of diplomatic courtesy. Clinton felt he owed Major little or nothing.

After the visa decision, however, Clinton was keen to make up with Major. The Adams visit had not produced the immediate ceasefire the White House had hoped for, and it had put the special relationship between Britain and America in the deep freeze, with, as the press put it, the worst crisis since Suez. Clinton invited Major over in February for a make-up visit with a sleepover in the White House and a flight in Air Force One from Pittsburgh.

The visa issue repeated itself in the summer of 1994. Having secured the first visa for Adams, Albert Reynolds discovered this wasn't enough for Republicans. They came back with a series of new demands before a ceasefire, including a visa for IRA veteran Joe Cahill, who had been sentenced to be hanged in the 1940s in Belfast for the murder of a policeman. Again we at the embassy tried to mount a campaign against the visa. I rang Nancy and asked if they had thought about what would happen if there was an attack while Cahill was in the US. Again the State Department were opposed. Nancy called me back on 30 August to say the President had finally decided at one in the morning to issue a visa. The IRA declared a ceasefire the next day.

Clinton had been motivated on the visa decision partly by Ted Kennedy's views in favour and partly by the desire to get Irish Americans on side for his re-election campaign. But he also genuinely believed that the symbolism of granting a visa would make it easier for the IRA to call a ceasefire. If Republicans could see there was a political way forward and see the respectability that came with giving up violence it might encourage them to move in the right direction. I wrote in my diary 'maybe we should have let both visas go ahead and used them to stop the killing, maybe the Americans really did have an influence' on bringing about the ceasefire and 'I hope Major doesn't back us into a corner on the lack of the word "permanent" in the ceasefire statement as he did on "clarification". We need room for manoeuvre.' At the time I opposed the visa vigorously as I was paid to do, but in retrospect Clinton was clearly right in the decision he made.

In the same month that the IRA announced their ceasefire, Tony Blair became leader of the Labour Party and moved to change Labour Party policy on Northern Ireland, giving a radio interview in which he abandoned the 'unity by consent' policy which had been the party's position through the 1980s and early 90s. This policy had been an uncomfortable compromise cobbled together in the early 1980s to split the difference between two irreconcilable wings of the party: a small

but highly motivated band of pro-unionists and the 'Troops Out' movement. The result was a green-tinged ambition to achieve a united
Ireland by persuading the unionists to participate in it, even though
it was perfectly obvious the unionists were not going to be persuaded.
Tony replaced this mishmash with a policy of neutrality, where the
job of the British government would be to help reconcile the two
communities in Northern Ireland and find a solution that both could
accept. This move was a reflection of what had happened in the Tory
party, which had switched from a strongly pro-unionist position to
one of neutrality. It put the party four-square behind John Major's
efforts to achieve peace.

The other big change Tony made was the replacement of Kevin
McNamara with Mo Mowlam as Shadow Secretary of State for
Northern Ireland. As a leading light in Tony's leadership campaign
and as a New Labourite before her time, Mo fitted in happily with
the change in policy. I got to know Mo a little when I first went to
work for Tony. She was a rare sort of politician, taking irreverence to
the next level. There was no limit to the outrageous things she was
prepared to say and do, and she was a naturally gregarious and friendly
person who immediately broke through to the people she met. Her
personality and her politics made her very attractive to nationalists
and republicans and convinced them that perhaps this time the Brits
would be different. There is no way it would have been possible for
us to reach agreement on Good Friday 1998 if Mo had not breached
the barrier with her ebullient personality. Mo was a necessary though
not sufficient condition for peace. But it was still some time before
we could get our hands on the negotiations.

John Major had reacted with caution to the IRA ceasefire. His caution
was not surprising given that intelligence was showing they were still
targeting members of the security forces, building stocks of weapons
and selling the move to cessation to their Volunteers as the 'tactical
use of armed struggle' rather than as a final break with the past.

The major blockage was caused by the disagreement over the decommissioning of IRA weapons. The nationalist critique is that the British
government never mentioned decommissioning during the negotiations
leading to the ceasefire, and only raised it afterwards as a serious issue.
John Hume said in 1997, 'He had never heard of decommissioning

until Sir Patrick Mayhew had mentioned it. He asked if there was anywhere a process which had begun with surrender'. And Albert Reynolds denied in August 1995, after he had left office, that decommissioning had ever been a major British demand during the talks on the Downing Street Declaration.

In the battle of the memoirs, the British tried to prove that they had raised decommissioning during the talks. Apparently Major had raised the surrender of IRA arms with Hume in September 1993 and raised decommissioning with Reynolds in October 1994 and he had not objected. In his autobiography John Major points to the reference in the Downing Street Declaration to 'the practical consequences of the ending of violence', which he said everyone understood as meaning decommissioning. Of course it did, but it also meant prisoner release and reducing the British military presence. If the British government had seriously intended to press ahead with decommissioning, civil servants would have been tasked to draw up detailed plans on how to go about it straight away, but they didn't really look into the issue until late in 1995.

In fact this battle of recollections misses the point. Major's original focus was, rightly, on getting the IRA to be clear that its cessation was permanent. The government and the Unionists were reluctant to enter negotiations with Republicans with a gun, literally, pointed at their head, so they wanted the IRA to be clear they had abandoned the threat of violence as well as violence itself. In the month after the ceasefire, Major demanded that the IRA say it had abandoned violence for good, but McGuinness responded by saying that the word 'permanent was not in the republican vocabulary'. Major tried again in October, saying it was the government's 'working assumption' that the IRA intended the ceasefire to be permanent. Having beaten his head against a brick wall on this approach, Major switched to decommissioning as a practical manifestation of the permanent end to violence. Unless there was decommissioning he said, there was 'unlikely to be confidence among the other political parties that Sinn Féin is committed permanently to peace'.

Yet even this – turning decommissioning into a surrogate for permanence – was not the problem. The problem was making decommissioning a precondition for talks, and it was this decision that snagged the process for more than a decade.

In December 1994 Major said 'huge progress' would have to be made towards the destruction of IRA weapons before exploratory talks with Sinn Féin could become formal. By March 1995 Mayhew had whittled this down to three conditions set out in a speech in Washington, which became known as the 'Washington Three'. The IRA had to: 1) disarm progressively; 2) agree what decommissioning would entail; and 3) undertake 'actual decommissioning of some arms' before talks could begin. So the British government had reduced the amount of decommissioning they required to a symbolic gesture but they were still making it a precondition. McGuinness responded by describing these conditions as 'ludicrous'; in private he said that there would never have been a ceasefire if decommissioning had been made an issue in advance. Sinn Féin made it clear that the IRA would not surrender weapons before a political settlement, demanding that the issue be dealt with in talks. Quentin Thomas, the NIO political director, later summed up the problem: 'The bad thing about decommissioning was that it kept inviting the Sinn Féin leadership to confront those within their movement who they did not want to confront for perfectly normal political reasons.' Adams put it another way to the Irish. Why on earth were the British government not content to let the sleeping dog lie? Why did they want him to kick it?

Interestingly the Unionists were not the ones, at this stage, pressing decommissioning as a precondition. Their new leader, David Trimble, made it clear this was a British government demand not a Unionist one. But, having created the hole, the British government would not stop digging, and since it was a public challenge to them, Republicans naturally dug in too. Eventually it was the Unionists who suggested a way out. In January 1995, UUP security spokesman Ken Maginnis floated the idea of an international body to oversee decommissioning, with American, Commonwealth and Scandinavian participation. The proposal was worked up over the summer by John Chilcott from the NIO and Tim Dalton, the permanent secretary of the Irish Department of Justice, a charming roly-poly, quietly spoken security expert who was to play a crucial role in the negotiations. George Mitchell, the former Democratic Senator and Clinton's peace envoy, was asked to take on the job of chairing the international body making recommendations on decommissioning with John de Chastelain, a Canadian general and former ambassador to Washington, and Hari Halkiri, a former Finnish prime minister.

However, Mitchell reached very different conclusions to Major. Late in 1995 he came to see the Prime Minister to alert him to his intention to recommend that the requirement for prior decommissioning be dropped in favour of parallel decommissioning and political talks. He said that when he had asked Hugh Annesley, the RUC Chief Constable, whether Adams could deliver prior decommissioning, Annesley had said that Adams wouldn't be able to deliver it even if he wanted to. He didn't have that much control. Major was furious. He thought Mitchell had exceeded his mandate and threatened to denounce the report, but Mitchell went ahead with the recommendation anyway.

Making decommissioning a precondition was not the only mistake the Major government made. The other was the appearance they gave of dragging their feet in bringing Sinn Féin into the talks process. Again this was because Major was sceptical about Republican motives and wanted a lengthy period of 'decontamination' before they could enter politics, to reassure unionists. He had a difficult meeting with Ian Paisley in No. 10 immediately after the ceasefire. They saw each other in the Cabinet Room, which Major used as his office, and Paisley was at his hectoring worst, accusing Major of lying about a secret agreement with the IRA. When he wouldn't withdraw the accusation, Major stormed out of the meeting, but was left in the awkward position of Paisley still occupying his office and refusing to leave. The moral of the story is: never storm out of a meeting in your own office. So, instead of the few weeks Republicans had expected before exploratory dialogue commenced, the gap dragged on till December 1994. The first contact for 'XD', as the exploratory dialogue was known, was a call on a dedicated phone line between Tony Beeton, a young NIO official, and Siobhan O'Hanlon, Gerry Adams's assistant.

The first meeting between Sinn Féin and government officials was highly symbolic, with McGuinness and his team chugging up the hill to Stormont on 9 December 1994 in an armoured black taxi. Quentin Thomas, political director at the NIO, tried to make the encounter as relaxed as possible, and McGuinness couldn't resist cheekily asking after 'Fred'. Sinn Féin denied they had any links with the Provisional IRA and insisted they should be admitted to all-party talks on the basis of their democratic mandate. Quentin tried to get them to think about how they might demonstrate that they would not return to violence even if they didn't get what they wanted. Then Sinn Féin ran through a long list of demands on the Irish language, economic development, prisoners, policing and justice, and warned against making decommissioning a precondition.

Meetings with officials continued at a stately pace but Sinn Féin were getting increasingly exasperated. Major saw the exploratory talks as the point, while they saw them as something to get through so they could move on to the holy grail of all-party talks. Meanwhile, Quentin Thomas saw the process as devoted to 'the progressive adjustment of expectations'. At the fifth meeting on 9 February 1995, Sinn Féin added some light relief by walking out of the talks, claiming their meeting room had been bugged. But when the RUC went to check, they could find no listening devices and came to the conclusion that the Republicans' anti-bugging device was picking up emanations from the photocopying machine.

Sinn Féin demanded meetings with ministers but John Major was holding out until the IRA started moving on decommissioning. Eventually the government gave in and agreed to a private meeting with Michael Ancram in May, at which Ancram handed over a paper on decommissioning. That led to a public meeting between Paddy Mayhew and Adams in Washington on 24 May that got over the handshake hurdle. There were then private meetings with McGuinness in Derry in July, where McGuinness complained the IRA was being boxed in on decommissioning and Mayhew floated the idea of a twin-track approach in which decommissioning and political talks moved in parallel. Although there were further ministerial meetings in the autumn, Mayhew detected a new hard-line approach from Sinn Féin. The government had left it too late and Republicans had concluded that the Brits were messing about and had no intention of letting them in to all-party talks except at an impossible price. On 3 November 1995, they withdrew from the exploratory dialogue with the government.

To be fair to Major, he was conducting a very difficult balancing act. He did not want to go all out for an agreement on the republican side just to end up with an even bigger problem with the unionists. And the Irish and American governments were rushing ahead with concessions to Republicans. One week after the ceasefire Reynolds had met Hume and Adams for a public handshake without giving the British government any warning, and started talking about an amnesty for prisoners. Clinton had invited Adams to the St Patrick's Day celebrations at the White House in 1995 and given him a visa for fund-raising in the US. Major was livid and declined to return Clinton's apologetic phone calls for three days thereafter. Added to this, the IRA were still up to no good. In November 1995 they killed a post office worker in Newry in a bungled robbery. And while they turned off punishment beatings and killings during Clinton's visit to Northern Ireland at the end of November, they turned them on again at a higher rate after he had gone.

The problem was exacerbated by the fact that Major was depending increasingly on Unionist votes as his government unwound. To his credit, he never did a deal with Unionist leaders, sacrificing the peace process to the survival of his government. But he could not afford to alienate them by taking bold steps towards Sinn Féin and he had to trim his policy accordingly. Despite this he did make gestures towards republicans by moving terrorist prisoners to Northern Ireland, increasing remission, reducing security levels and reopening border roads. But Republicans were not convinced. On 9 February 1996, a huge bomb went off in Canary Wharf, killing two people and causing millions of pounds' worth of damage. Republicans had been patient for eighteen months since the ceasefire but had convinced themselves they needed to give the British government a short sharp shock. The bomb came as a surprise to the government. They had not anticipated the attack. McGuinness said privately that the Brits had wanted a victory not a ceasefire, and the IRA publicly demanded an 'inclusive negotiated settlement'.

When the message sent by the Canary Wharf bomb failed to get the response they wanted, the IRA returned to a stop–start terrorist campaign with occasional spectaculars like the bomb in the centre of Manchester and the bomb inside army headquarters in Lisburn in Northern Ireland, and culminating in the shooting of a young soldier, Bombardier Stephen Restorick, in South Armagh in February 1997. The government response should have been that they would never deal with the IRA again until they had put violence aside for good, but instead officials were in touch with Sinn Féin two weeks later.

The Major government fatally undermined their credibility with Republicans by insisting they would not, as a matter of principle, talk to them while a terrorist campaign was going on, but then in practice doing exactly that, as it had through the Link. It made Republicans believe the British government had no position of principle on the subject and helped convince them to continue with their dual strategy of violence and politics together.

The focus in these years was not, however, exclusively on Sinn Féin. The British and Irish governments had been working since the spring of 1993 on a 'Frameworks for the Future' document to serve as a basis for talks once Sinn Féin were admitted. The document was worked up by Quentin Thomas and Sean O'Uiginn, the complex and searingly intellectual head of the Anglo-Irish Division in the Irish Department of Foreign Affairs. Both were to become high in the pantheon of hate figures for Unionists, David Trimble describing Quentin many years later, when John Reid was appointed as Northern Ireland Secretary, as 'one of the undead'. The 'Frameworks' were published by Major and John Bruton, the new Fine Gael Prime Minister, in February 1995 and were immediately condemned by the Unionists for, in their view, like the Anglo-Irish Agreement, appearing to create joint authority with the Irish over Northern Ireland. Major had tried to show the draft agreement to Molyneaux early on, but when he pushed it across the Cabinet Room table Molyneaux declined to read it, not wishing to be compromised. The Unionist reaction forced Mayhew to set out the 'Triple Lock' as a way of reassuring them they were well protected from any outcome they did not like. He said any agreement would have to be accepted by the parties in Northern Ireland, accepted by the people of Northern Ireland in a referendum and approved by Westminster.

It was, however, a Unionist suggestion that helped John Major out of the complete impasse he was stuck in on decommissioning. When UUP leader David Trimble proposed calling elections to a negotiating body in Northern Ireland as a way forward, Major seized on the idea. He persuaded George Mitchell to include an oblique reference to such elections in his report, and when it was published in January 1996 chose that as the next step, rather than Mitchell's more difficult recommendation of sidestepping decommissioning through parallelism.

John Hume and the Irish opposed elections to a negotiating body as just another means of delay, but Major pressed ahead and they were held on 30 May 1996. Sinn Féin were the greatest beneficiaries, increasing their vote to an unprecedented 15 per cent. But others also gained an advantage. The criteria for the elections had been constructed to ensure that the two small parties representing the Loyalists made it past the threshold, but the unintended side effect was to let in the maverick Unionist Bob McCartney and his supporters. McCartney was a very bright barrister who devoted his political life to trying to frustrate agreement, and the inclusion of his party, the UKUP, made it much harder for the DUP to be even as constructive as they had been in the talks in 1991–2, because they would not allow themselves to be outflanked by another unionist party.

All-party talks began on 10 June 1996 under the chairmanship of George Mitchell. Sinn Féin were excluded because the IRA had gone back to violence and enjoyed the propaganda coup of marching up to Stormont and being confronted by a locked gate. Although the talks got nowhere and were wound up in March 1997 when general-election blight set in, they did establish a process with George Mitchell in the chair which we would inherit after the election as the vehicle for achieving the Good Friday Agreement.

The Mitchell report also set out the six Mitchell Principles on Non-Violence which were crucial in eventually bringing Sinn Féin into the process. They demanded commitments from the parties to: 1) democratic and exclusively peaceful means; 2) total disarmament of all paramilitary organisations; 3) disarmament taking place in a manner verifiable by an independent commission; 4) renunciation of the use of force and the threat of force; 5) acceptance of the agreement reached without attempts to alter it by force or the threat of force; and 6) an end to punishment beatings and killing. As a device they are applicable in other similar disputes where there is no confidence in the permanence of the ceasefire called by a terrorist movement.

Throughout Tony's time as leader of the Opposition, we always maintained a policy of bipartisanship, supporting John Major's government in whatever they did on Northern Ireland, even if it was sometimes politically uncomfortable, for example when he pressed ahead with elections to the negotiating body in 1996 in the face of

strong opposition from John Hume and the greener elements of the
Labour Party. And sometimes we strongly disagreed with what he
was doing, most particularly when he was prepared to re-engage
after Canary Wharf, which we thought sent the wrong message to
the IRA. But Tony took the view that since we did not know the
inside story of what was going on in the negotiations, we should
not try to second-guess Major on the basis of ignorance. The only
sensible thing to do was support him and hope he got it right. Once
we were in government, the Tory Party maintained the facade of
bipartisanship but often tried to make our lives as difficult as possible
by constantly harrying us at difficult moments. They also put the
Unionists in an impossible position by trying to outflank them as
more extreme defenders of the Union. But without at least the facade
of bipartisanship we would have found it much more difficult to
make progress, as the Socialist government in Spain has found, where
any contacts with ETA have been subject to a full-frontal attack by
the opposition Partido Popular.

We also managed to resist the temptation of trying to use Unionist
votes in the House of Commons to bring down the Major government. Tony's good relationship with David Trimble might have allowed
us to do this. But Tony took the view that it was more important not
to compromise our position on the peace process after the election
than it was to put the government out of their agony early by a squalid
compromise with the Unionists.

We used the time in opposition to prepare ourselves for what we
would do in Northern Ireland once we were in government. We visited
Dublin to meet the Irish Prime Minister John Bruton and the new
leader of Fianna Fáil, Bertie Ahern, with whom Tony hit it off immediately. And, at the beginning of 1997, we held an important dinner
in the Travellers Club on Pall Mall with John Chilcott and his team
at the NIO to discuss exactly what we would do when we took over,
so we could be ready to move quickly. We decided in particular to
make it clear that we would bring Sinn Féin rapidly into talks if there
were a ceasefire, and Mo let the cat out of the bag during the course
of the general-election campaign by saying we would require only six
weeks between a ceasefire and talks.

John Major deserves enormous credit for his efforts on Northern
Ireland even if he didn't succeed in clearing the final hurdle. Although

the Unionists tried to kill off the 'Frameworks' document, it served as the quarry for our negotiations in 1998. But there was one part of it that would bedevil the process. The Unionists hated the notion that the Irish and British governments might appoint North/South bodies with executive powers, and their refusal to countenance them got the negotiations on the Good Friday Agreement off to an appalling start.

4

Good Friday: April 1998

By Friday 3 April 1998 Senator George Mitchell had all of the draft agreement in place ready to give to the parties except for the Strand 2 section dealing with North/South relations. That he had left to the two governments, and Tony met Bertie Ahern in the margins of the EU summit with Asian countries in London that day and had a desultory discussion of the text. It was basically agreed, apart from a few passages in square brackets for further discussion, but Tony and Bertie decided to leave it unfinished for the moment. They feared that if they gave it to George Mitchell for circulation too early, the parties would pull it to pieces over the weekend. From Tony's office in No. 10 they made a joint phone call to Mitchell in Belfast to tell him there would be a delay. He was not happy because he had promised to distribute the document to the parties. The Irish said publicly as they left No. 10 that we had been unable to agree and there were still important differences. I wrote in my diary that evening that my gut told me we could do a deal by the following weekend but my brain told me it was unlikely.

John Holmes and Irish Cabinet Secretary Paddy Teahon resolved the outstanding points by phone over the weekend and gave the text to George Mitchell for circulation on the evening of Monday 6 April. We sent an advance copy of the North/South section to David Trimble and Tony called him that evening to judge his reaction. He did not jump up and down too much although he did say there would have to be changes. But on Tuesday morning Trimble called in a terrible state. He had been going through the draft with colleagues and it was 'ghastly and hopeless'. He was desperately worried in case the long list of proposed North/South bodies discussed in the Strand 2 section and in two associated annexes to the agreement became public. He said that if it did he would be dead in the water. In case we hadn't got the message, his deputy, John Taylor, went on breakfast television to say he wouldn't touch the agreement with a forty-foot barge pole.

Tony and I had to spend Tuesday morning in a summit of European Socialist leaders that Tony had convened as President of the European Union. The meeting was taking place in the Locarno Room of the Foreign Office, the vast Victorian treaty room that had once been divided into little cubicles (in one of which Douglas Hurd had worked when he first joined the FO as a third secretary), but was now a brightly gilded cavern. We had all nine of the European Socialist prime ministers there, as well as the leaders of all of the Socialist parties in Europe, but both Tony and I had to keep rushing out to make calls to Bertie Ahern, to David Trimble and to George Mitchell. Tony endeavoured to chair the meeting but his mind was not on it. He asked everyone he spoke to on the phone whether he should go to Belfast himself with Bertie to intervene in the talks process. Bertie said he worried that once they got to Belfast they would be trapped there and unable to leave. Other of Tony's advisers thought it would be a huge risk for him to go. There was very little advantage to be gained in British politics by succeeding in Northern Ireland, while being associated with a major failure at this stage of his premiership would have been very damaging indeed.

By lunchtime Tony had decided to ignore the advice and go. He called George Mitchell and Mitchell agreed Tony needed to come over to Belfast to see if he could salvage the process. We checked with Bertie. He wasn't sure when he would be able to make it as his mother had just died but he raised no objection to Tony going. As soon as the Socialist summit was over, we hopped into the motorcade out to the airport.

We helicoptered into Hillsborough pretty much without a plan. Tony was looking for someone to blame and he said that John Holmes had let him down. I gave him quite a sharp lecture. The week before he had been singing John's praises and now he said he had lost all confidence in him. He had in any case agreed the text of the draft agreement himself. And John had tried to persuade Mitchell not to table the two offending annexes giving details of North/South bodies, but the Irish had insisted. Besides it didn't matter how we had got to this point; it mattered to find a way out of it.

In the early evening, we swept past the media into Hillsborough Castle, the stately home which served as the bed and breakfast for the Secretary of State for Northern Ireland, in my view nicer than any British Ambassador's residence elsewhere in the world. Tony needed to make a statement to the waiting TV cameras in the entrance portico, and Alastair and I propelled him straight back out without giving him time to prepare carefully what he would say. Normally Tony would take a good few minutes rehearsing in his head the words he would use. But we were anxious to get on with the negotiations and didn't give him a chance. It was for that reason that he tripped into one of his most awkward, but equally one of his most memorable, sound bites: 'A day like today is not a day for sound bites, we can leave those at home, but I feel the hand of history upon our shoulder with respect to this, I really do.' Alastair and I were in fits of giggles. Tony couldn't explain afterwards how he had come up with the formulation, saying it had just popped into his head.

Trimble was waiting for us and Tony took him for a stroll in the beautiful grounds. As they walked towards the lake down the yew avenue paved in moss, he assured Trimble that we would stick with him through the negotiations whatever happened. We then spent two hours going through the draft agreement with Trimble in the Lady Gray room, working out what amendments might make the document acceptable to the Unionists. In essence Trimble's problem was not so much the North/South bodies themselves, as the amount of space given to them in the agreement. Seven out of eleven pages were devoted to the all-Ireland elements as well as the two long annexes. It was proposed that there should be eight North/South bodies created by legislation passed in the House of Commons so that they would not be accountable to the Assembly, and between them the two annexes set out forty-one areas of cooperation. What's more, he wanted all North/South bodies to be accountable to the Northern Ireland Assembly rather than imposed by Westminster. By the time Trimble left we had a raft of detailed amendments.

Tony phoned John Hume to get the nationalist perspective. Hume was aware that Trimble had a problem, but urged us not to let the Unionists veto the agreement. John Alderdice, the leader of the cross-community Alliance Party, and a good bellwether of unionist opinion, then came to see us in the big drawing room overlooking the garden.

He confirmed to us that the agreement was not deliverable as it stood in the unionist community. The annexes were far too long. After him we saw David Ervine, the charismatic leader of the small loyalist Progressive Unionist Party, who agreed that the document, as it stood, was unsaleable to the unionist electorate. And finally we talked to George Mitchell who, having spent so long negotiating with the parties, took the same line. We had to get the Irish to back down on their ambition for so heavy an emphasis on North/South cooperation or there was no prospect of success. Bertie Ahern was flying in the next morning for a brief meeting between his mother's wake and her funeral. Mitchell agreed to speak to Bertie before we did, to persuade him of the need to accept amendments.

We got our last full night's sleep. For the next fifty-eight hours we were to go pretty much without. First thing on Wednesday morning, we gathered in the grand Queen's bedroom where Tony was staying and he phoned Trimble to reassure him we would get the amendments he needed from the Irish. We were terrified he would just walk out of the talks without further ado. He had said to us the previous day that perhaps the best thing to do was just wait till after Easter and see what could be rescued.

We then had breakfast with Bertie Ahern who had helicoptered up to Hillsborough from Dublin, having kept watch over his mother's body the night before. He had made a big personal sacrifice to come. Visiting Hillsborough was still a problem for the Irish. It reeked of viceroy status with its green lawns, its throne room and regal portraits. And Tony had to give Bertie a very hard message. We needed to rewrite completely the North/South part of the agreement that was so dear to the Irish. Bertie explained how difficult this would be. He was already going to propose to the Irish people that they amend their constitution to remove the territorial claim to the North. If he did so and got nothing in return he would look like an idiot. And he had no confidence that the Unionists would actually agree to the creation of the North/South bodies at all unless they accepted them in advance and they were enshrined in Westminster legislation rather than left to the goodwill of the Assembly. After all, he pointed out, such bodies had been agreed in 1921 and in Sunningdale in 1973, but had never actually been delivered. What was more, if he conceded on this point, the Unionists would be back asking for further concessions. But despite all this, Bertie did not rule out making amendments because he realised they were essential to get the UUP back on board. He therefore agreed to leave Paddy Teahon and Dermot Gallagher, from the Irish Foreign Ministry, to negotiate changes while he returned to Dublin for his mother's funeral.

Bertie Ahern was above all a practical man, who had made his political career as a negotiator with Irish trade unions in different government positions. There would have been no agreement in Northern Ireland if it had not been for his unadorned common sense. When Tony had first met him, he had told Bertie that 'he came to the issues with no ideological or historical baggage. He regarded the present situation as irrational and stupid and he simply wanted to stop people killing each other.' Ahern had said that 'he too came to Northern Ireland with no historical baggage'. And it was because these two men were of a new generation that was not weighed down with the prejudices of the past that they were able to work together so closely for so long, not just resolving the problem of Northern Ireland but putting wider relations between Britain and Ireland on a new footing. Bertie came from a family with firm republican credentials and led de Valera's Fianna Fáil party, but he had no complex about the Brits, and never tried to see a conspiracy where there wasn't one. He was quiet and understated, lacking Tony's soaring rhetoric, but he was always looking for a way through, and was far better at working the bars and corridors at a negotiation, while Tony tended to stay in his room. Above all, Bertie took the broad view. It was often difficult in the Irish political system and with his background to decide not to take the traditional Irish position but to take a risk for peace. Bertie Ahern showed real political courage in doing so.

We left John Holmes negotiating with the Irish officials at Hillsborough and helicoptered to the Stormont estate, for the talks. In Gerry Adams's words, Stormont 'reeks of a Boer mentality'. It is very grand, looking down both literally and metaphorically on everyone who approaches. But in the 1960s some misguided architect had built a squat five-storey office block – Castle Buildings – down in the dip by the main road, and it was here that the talks were taking place.

Castle Buildings felt like a sick building. Its Formica panelling was chipped and crumbling; its maze of anonymous corridors made sure you were disorientated as soon as you opened a door. And after months of negotiations, it stank of sweat and stale food. The malaise of the building affected the mood of the people inside it. If ever there was an unpropitious place in which to reach an agreement, this was it. It left an undying impression on us. In later years, when we were in some sweltering barracks in Afghanistan or Iraq, Tony and I would say to each other, 'At least we aren't in Castle Buildings.'

Mo showed us to our assigned suite of offices which normally belonged to Tony Worthington, one of the junior ministers in the NIO. It was on the fifth floor, just down the corridor from George Mitchell and consisted of two nondescript offices opening on to each other with Civil Service green and grey steel and Formica furniture and windows looking out on to a blind courtyard. Some of Tony Worthington's ornaments and photographs were still there.

As soon as we arrived, Tony saw Trimble and a UUP delegation. He told them he had made it clear to the Irish that they had to amend the text on North/South matters radically and that there could be no progress elsewhere until this was unblocked. But to do this he needed a clear commitment from the UUP that if he unblocked this issue they would be prepared to move on other matters, particularly Strand 1 dealing with a power-sharing executive. Reg Empey, one of Trimble's deputies, kept insisting that amending the text was not enough; it had to be taken off the table altogether so they could start again. Eventually Trimble, who had got the point that Tony was making, shut him up. Then Ken Maginnis, the UUP security spokesman, started complaining that the security parts of the agreement, including the sections on policing and decommissioning, were unacceptable. Tony instructed me to go off with him and sort out the details.

Maginnis and I sat with officials in a small office next to Mitchell's as I went through all his concerns. I drew up some tough amendments in a limited number of areas, particularly on the proposed review of the RUC. As soon as we finished George Mitchell collared me. He was feeling frustrated at sitting twiddling his thumbs, and asked if he could bring me together with the Irish officials to talk through these amendments with them. I readily agreed, but the Irish refused, not wanting to address any more UUP amendments until the North/South issue had been agreed. So Mitchell passed on the amendments himself. When the Irish saw them, they had a collective fit.

Paddy Teahon and Martin Mansergh stormed into our office, their faces a very unattractive shade of puce, and in front of Tony raged about perfidious Albion trying to go behind their backs. Word soon spread around the building that I had nearly brought the negotiations to their knees, but the row did my standing with the UUP no end of good. They were convinced that all NIO officials were traitors, in the pocket of the Irish, so it was useful to have someone in the building they thought was on their side.

Tony sat in his room and saw all the parties in turn, but little progress could be made until Bertie returned from Dublin and approved the amended text on North/South bodies in Strand 2. We soon began suffering from claustrophobia. The only way we could get out into the fresh air without being live on television, since the building was besieged by the media, was to persuade the security men to open up the walled courtyard of the building, and walk round and round on the gravel. It was an appropriate reminder of life in prison. Tony was jittery, uncertain that we would succeed, and his mood was volatile. Alastair was convinced we would never get an agreement. I, on the other hand, was convinced we would. Looking back I'm not entirely sure what I based my optimism on, but it was my job to be optimistic and keep everyone's spirits up, so I kept telling them it would be all right.

Tony decided the best use for me was down with the UUP on the ground floor since they liked and trusted me. I sat in their suite and worked with Reg Empey on how they might be brought to accept the North/South bodies. They would tell me their ideas as great secrets, and I would pass them on to the Irish in a suitably modified form to try and build an agreement.

When Bertie returned late in the afternoon, and once I had apologised for my sins on the security front, we convened a tripartite meeting with the Irish and the UUP in Tony's office. Bertie indicated to the meeting that the Irish could now agree to radical changes to Strand 2 and John Taylor said theatrically that, if this was indeed the case, then business could be done. It was agreed that the Irish and UUP should go away and agree a text between them. Yet when they did meet late on Wednesday evening, they failed to focus on a new text but spent their time on a generalised discussion of the difficult issues. An exhausted Bertie soon gave up and went to bed.

Meanwhile, Gerry Adams had wandered into Tony's office and asked to see him on his own. He said Sinn Féin definitely wanted to sign up for a deal, but we had to give him a deal he could sign up to, and not just on the key issue of prisoner release. He suggested to Tony that we might not make it: an agreement was perhaps too difficult. Tony was convinced he was sending us a covert message and for the next thirty-six hours was constantly nervous that Sinn Féin would not be able to accept the agreement. I recorded in my diary that I thought Adams was just play-acting to attract some attention away from the Unionists. We flew back to Hillsborough from Castle Buildings at one o'clock in the morning. I was terrified by my first helicopter flight in the dark, and even the young pilots looked a little concerned as they tried to manoeuvre the big military helicopter down between the trees on the Hillsborough estate.

When Tony discovered that the Irish and UUP had failed to stay up negotiating a text, he was furious. We should probably have kept the negotiations going through the night. By taking our foot off the pedal at this crucial moment, we let everybody slip back, away from an agreement. But we craved a few precious hours in bed. First thing Thursday morning, Tony called David Trimble to say that Bertie's pragmatism meant a deal was possible on Strand 2, but Trimble should not push his luck on other issues. Trimble said he understood. Over breakfast Bertie was still suspicious of the Unionists, but Tony proposed that the Irish sit down with them again to see what they could agree. Once we returned to Castle Buildings, however, it became clear the two sides were congenitally incapable of solving the problem between themselves because of their mutual distrust and hostility.

At midday everything seemed as if it might be back on track. David Trimble brought us a UUP draft accepting six North/South bodies and giving a list of sample areas of cooperation between Northern Ireland and the Republic to be laid out in an annexe. It wasn't that different an approach to that in Mitchell's original draft, but it was acceptable to the Unionists because it was their idea. Tony put the UUP proposal to Bertie and persuaded him he had to work from it. The Irish came back with a few amendments. David Trimble indicated he was willing to accept the majority of them and we thought we had an agreed text.

However, things soon began to unravel. Both Sinn Féin and the SDLP raised difficulties with the document, and Tony had to see both of them to explain why the changes were essential. Having finished with them, we could not find Bertie for several hours. His disappearance should have sounded alarm bells: when he came back a few hours later, he handed over a completely new text on North/South matters having come under pressure from his own delegation to renegotiate the issue. Tony completely flipped. He shouted at all of us and was mildly impolite to the Irish. He told Bertie that there was absolutely no chance of selling the new Irish draft to the UUP: the Irish had to negotiate on the basis of the UUP text. Fortunately Bertie could see the point of this. Tony suggested seeing if the UUP would move on one or two elements of the agreement, and once Bertie and his officials had acquiesced, managed to persuade Trimble and John Taylor to accept a handful of minor amendments. By now the North/South text had been dramatically slimmed down and the Unionists had secured the 'mutually assured destruction' they wanted. If the Assembly collapsed so would the North/South bodies, and there would be no return to the bad old days of the Irish having a say in the affairs of Northern Ireland when the people of Northern Ireland did not.

Success on Strand 2 unlocked negotiations on Strand 1: what should happen in Northern Ireland itself. Under the chairmanship of Paul Murphy, Mo's soft-spoken and popular Welsh deputy, the Unionists rapidly ditched their long-standing proposal of a committee-based system and agreed instead to SDLP proposals on an Executive with ten ministers selected by the d'Hondt method (a particularly complicated system of proportional representation devised by a nineteenth-century Belgian mathematician), a unionist First Minister and a nationalist Deputy First Minister. They also agreed to the idea of a 108-member Assembly, and cross-community voting on key issues. These were all ideas that the Unionists had been rejecting for years. John Hume couldn't believe how easy it had been and, according to Gerry Adams's autobiography, came into the Sinn Féin offices laughing and doing a jig. But actually it was entirely logical for the Unionists to want an executive if power was to be devolved to Northern Ireland, not least since they would be occupying the position of First Minister. In parallel we agreed new words on decommissioning and on policing, and the UUP accepted the proposed amendments to Articles 2 and 3 of the Irish constitution removing the claim to the territory of Northern Ireland. By the end of Thursday things were beginning to fall into place, and it looked as though the Unionists were going to be on board.

Ian Paisley and a few hundred demonstrators provided a welcome distraction at this point by taking the gates into the Stormont grounds off their hinges and marching up the 'Stormont mile'. After some negotiation with officials it was agreed Paisley could hold a press conference if they would go away afterwards. He did so and denounced Trimble as a traitor, but he was constantly interrupted by heckling from members of the small Loyalist parties who had come out of Castle Buildings to see the press conference. The event was a farce.

The problem now was on the other side. Sinn Féin resented being taken for granted and, in order to let us know this, sent out one of their spokesmen on Thursday evening to say to the press that there would be no agreement. Their action engendered a collective panic. We did everything we could to keep them on board. Bertie spent hours sitting with Adams and McGuinness trying to persuade them to stick it out. And late into the night Tony and Bertie had two long meetings with Adams and McGuinness alone. I slipped in and sat quietly at the back with Alastair to see what happened. Adams and McGuinness were mounting quite an effective 'good cop, bad cop' routine, presumably on the basis of decades of practice. Adams was careful never to say he would reject the agreement but McGuinness said he couldn't recommend it, perhaps in the hope of putting the fear of God into us with unstated threats of a return to violence.

Adams and McGuinness had been together longer than most married couples. Ever since they first joined the Provisional IRA as young men, they had been the yin and yang of the Provisional movement, alternating with each other in leadership positions. Adams represented Belfast, the centre of gravity and ideological heart of the movement, while McGuinness represented Derry, its emotional stronghold on the other side of the Province. Adams was more cerebral, while McGuinness was more popular with the military Volunteers. McGuinness tended to defer to Adams. If he came to meetings alone he would take notes and say he would refer back. Adams, however, would give on-the-spot answers. He would often say, as a negotiating device, that he had not yet had a chance to consult McGuinness on such-and-such a proposal, but he was prepared to put it forward anyway – an indication that he wanted us to think he was being particularly daring. Adams's eyes were hard to read, while McGuinness was more human, although we suspected he had more first-hand operational experience. He was emotional and could go off on long tirades against the securocrats, laced with references to what people were saying on the street, which Adams would gently mock. For me, Adams's approach was summed up by a comment he made in 1999 when we were caught up in heated negotiations in the Sinn Féin centre on the Falls Road. He leaned over the table towards me and said, 'The thing I like about you, Jonathan, is that you always blush when you lie.' Bill Jeffrey, the Northern Ireland Office political director at the time, who was sitting next to me at the table, responded immediately, 'Unlike you, Gerry.' We all laughed, but there was more than a grain of truth in the quip. He was a ruthless and focused negotiator who believed absolutely in his cause. And I respected him for that because it was he, rather than us, who carried the burden of persuading the hardliners in his movement, knowing that if he made a mistake he could end up paying with his life.

In the second of those two late-night meetings on Thursday 9 April, Adams and McGuinness came back with forty pages of detailed changes that their backroom team had worked up. They covered policing, the Irish language and prisoners. Bertie and Mo sat down with them and went through the detail, and Mo offered them a letter of comfort on some of their concerns although there were very few we could actually accept. As the night wore on, the security people told us that among those coming into the building were an increasing number of hard-core IRA members, presumably to be consulted, since Adams and McGuinness could not leave to talk to them.

We got ourselves in a frightful muddle about prisoners. We had always been clear that the best we could do was release terrorist prisoners after two years if there was no return to violence. Sinn Féin were pressing for them to be released after one year. They even tried to enlist the loyalist parties in support, but to their credit the Loyalists refused to make common cause on such a sensitive issue. Mo seems to have suggested to Adams and McGuinness that we could, after all, release them after one year. Tony got very cold feet when she came to tell us. Alastair and I were worried about the response of the British public who were not at all prepared for the extraordinary act of releasing murderers. Tony asked to see the senior NIO official on the subject, John Steele, who was appalled at the idea. He was precisely the kind of moderate unionist on whose support the Agreement would depend and, after speaking to him, it was clear we could not go down to one year. But when we tried to pull the concession back Adams got very difficult. He explained that 'released prisoners are the best ambassadors for the peace process'. And it is true that prisoner release is a crucial part of any peace process of this kind, with prisoners usually being the members of a terrorist movement most in favour of a lasting peace. In the end Tony agreed to give Adams a private oral assurance that if Sinn Féin signed up for the deal and if the circumstances allowed, we would bring forward release from two years to one. This promise has never been made public. Adams would remind us of it from time to time, but he never called it in and never revealed it. The prisoners were released after two years.

The final thing that seemed to get Adams over the hump was Tony assuring him that he would meet him again after Easter to discuss all the issues further. One of the principal Republican concerns was that Tony would turn his back on Northern Ireland as soon as the agreement was signed, as so many British prime ministers had done before. It was the promise to remain engaged, and in their words 'work for change', that was crucial to them. For good measure Tony phoned President Clinton and asked him to call Adams. At the time we thought Clinton had called Adams once, but it turns out from Adams's memoirs that he in fact called him three times – at 1 a.m., 2.30 and 4.45. The President stayed up all night following what was going on in the negotiations and talking to George Mitchell, and, if Adams's account is to be believed, called Adams to shoot the breeze, rather than to put pressure on him.

So, at 2 a.m. we were sitting in our office, exhausted, thinking we had an agreement. John Holmes was so tired he had gone to sleep on a table in his suit. Tony was fretting about not being at Spanish Prime Minister Aznar's official holiday residence in the south of Spain, where he was due to spend Easter. His family were already there and he was concerned about what his mother-in-law, Gail, might be saying to Aznar. To keep his spirits up, he joshed with Alastair about my newly acquired paunch, the result of sixteen-hour days at my desk in Downing

Street sustained by a diet of Mars bars. They had decided to rename me 'Five Bellies Powell' in honour of Jimmy Gardner, much in the papers at the time as Gazza's drinking companion of choice (they were forever going on about football). Every so often one would say to the other in a mock-Geordie accent, 'Go and get us some pork scratchings and a pint of mild, Five Bellies,' and both would collapse in hysterical laughter. Mo would pop in from time to time and ask how things were going. She was like a hyperactive hostess, going round the conference keeping everyone's spirits up by serving them food and drink.

The more tired we got, the more the gallows humour came to the surface. Alastair was briefing the press aggressively about who was to blame at any given moment. After Adams and McGuinness came to complain about a bias against Sinn Féin, I said to Alastair that they knew where he lived. It became a running gag between us for the next few years. The line reflected our ambivalence about the 'Shinners', as Sinn Féin were known colloquially in Northern Ireland, stranded some-where in between terrorists and politicians, a physical threat to our personal safety as well as our negotiating partners. Yet I came to like and respect Sinn Féin members, including Gerry Adams's assistant Siobhan O'Hanlon, now sadly dead, who ferried me around Belfast on a number of occasions. She was tough but straight and entirely reliable. I particularly regretted a joke I made when, late on Thursday afternoon, she drifted into our office, asking if Gerry could have a meeting with Tony. I said Bertie was in with Tony but we could get rid of him. She said, 'Oh no, no need,' and I threw in that I did not mean 'get rid of him' in her usual sense. She left with dignity and I felt bad.

It turned out we had been wrong to think we had an agreement. In the early hours of Good Friday morning, things started to come apart again. It became apparent the Irish had tried a side route to get what they wanted on the North/South bodies. Paddy Teahon and Dermot Gallagher, who were unhappy with where the negotiation had ended up, had told us in the course of the night that they had persuaded the UUP to agree to two additional North/South bodies: one to deal with the Irish language, the other on international trade promotion. We were surprised by this, since the UUP had been particularly opposed to Irish involvement in these two areas, and David Trimble had even given us a lecture on the importance of the recognition of Ullans, the Scots-Irish dialect, if we were to recognise Irish, which had left us in hysterics once he left the room. But we took Paddy's word for it and added the two bodies to the agreement. When the UUP discovered them first thing Friday morning, they blew a fuse. According to Teahon and Gallagher, they had cornered Ken Maginnis and a young UUP staffer in a bar and agreed the new bodies there, but that wouldn't wash with the Unionists. There was nothing for it but for Tony to bring together Bertie and Trimble and their delegations once again to discuss the matter. The Irish dug their heels in, and Trimble came across as appallingly rude to Bertie, who came within an ace of hitting him, as he told us after the Unionists had left the room. In the end I had to appeal to Trimble on bended knee to add a meaningless body ensuring cooperation between the health services in the two territories that the Irish wanted and he agreed.

But this was only a taster of what was to come. The real trouble started later on Good Friday morning as we were tidying up all the different parts of the agreement. Trimble's delegation had stayed at Castle Buildings while he got a few hours' sleep at the nearby Stormont Hotel. They were in a state of nervous exhaustion and, as soon as he returned, started raising new issues. The first of these was that Maryfield, the headquarters of the Anglo-Irish secretariat, be closed by the end of the year. The Unionists saw the whole point of the new agreement as being to replace the hated Anglo-Irish Agreement, and the physical manifestation of it at Maryfield. We couldn't find Bertie so we decided to send a letter to Trimble unilaterally assuring him this would happen.

Then Ken Maginnis came to see me to say he had heard rumours that we had made all sorts of concessions to the IRA. He made a big fuss about how he hadn't agreed to any of the changes the Irish claimed on the North/South bodies. His main concern was prisoner release, an issue the Unionists had picked up on only late in the negotiations. He wanted clarification about exactly what was involved. I provided him with a handwritten letter explaining how the scheme would work and referring back to the Stormont government decision to grant a general amnesty to all terrorist prisoners at the end of the last IRA campaign in 1962. He seemed content and the UUP later published the letter.

By this time Alastair had been out to tell the press that a deal was done. But when all the parties got the new text of the agreement at midday, all hell broke loose. Most of the parties hadn't seen any text since Monday and big sections of it must have come as a surprise. The UUP delegation had been swollen by this time as supporters piled in, apparently without check. David Trimble broke them up into groups to read through different sections of the agreement. Fairly rapidly he realised he had a problem. Trimble called me and asked me to talk to Jeffrey Donaldson, the most prominent of the objectors, suggesting I had a good relationship with him. I went down to the ground floor and dragged him out of their conference room, but he wouldn't speak to me. The younger UUP members, attracted to the party by David Trimble's leadership, were working themselves into a lather. In the corridor, one of the young staffers grabbed me by the shirt collar and started jabbing me in the chest saying, 'It's unacceptable, no way, no way.'

Trimble told me the party were in general revolt. I suppose that, confronted with a document that put Sinn Féin in government with no guarantee of decommissioning, with prisoners being released, doubts about the future of the RUC, a new relationship with Dublin, with nationalists holding a veto in the Assembly over major issues, and without preparation from their leaders on any of these points, it was not so surprising they had difficulties. It was clear that Trimble had failed to pave the way for an inclusive agreement, believing that Sinn Féin would not be able to swallow the principle of consent and would therefore not sign.

Tony called David Montgomery, a Northern Ireland unionist and proprietor of the *Mirror* who was close to David Trimble, asking him to persuade Trimble to sign up the agreement. But Montgomery's call failed to sway him. Tony then tried Clinton, despite the fact the President had been up all night talking to Adams and Hume and other participants. Clinton agreed readily, and I rushed down to the UUP offices to tell Trimble. Opening the door, I found Trimble, already on his feet to receive the call. He clearly thought it appropriate to rise for the President of the USA, even on the phone.

But not even the call from Clinton did the trick. In the early afternoon, Trimble brought a delegation to see Tony in his office. They said the situation was hopeless. They could not be expected to sign up to an agreement that failed to make it clear Sinn Féin would be thrown out of the government and Assembly if the IRA did not start decommissioning. Tony was despairing. He begged them to look at the big picture. Look what they had gained. They had just secured the Union, and even Republicans were accepting it. They had changed the Irish constitution, got themselves an Assembly, won North/South bodies they could live with and have a veto over. But they were totally focused on the issue of decommissioning. What guarantee did they have that, if there was no decommissioning, Sinn Féin would be excluded? Tony explained that, with everyone waiting to sign, he could not reopen the agreement on such a fundamental point at this stage. The other parties and the Irish would just not tolerate it. Adams had already made it clear he was not in a position to accept the agreement there and then without consulting his party, let alone one that moved backwards on this sensitive issue. He sent them away to reflect.

Once they had gone, we made an effort to snap out of our depression. Tony was determined that, having come this far, we were not going to fail. He decided we should send Trimble a side letter offering the guarantee on exclusion he wanted. Tony stood at my shoulder dictating the letter while I typed it at top speed on to my laptop and John Steele of the NIO offered comments. The key paragraph read that we would 'support changes to provisions for excluding parties from the Executive in Northern Ireland if during the course of the first six months of the shadow Assembly itself the provisions have been shown to be ineffective'. I snatched it off the printer and raced down to give it to Trimble. There was no time to lose because we feared he was about to walk out. But down on the Unionist floor, I was confronted by a locked door. They were debating whether or not to accept the agreement inside, and I couldn't get in to give Trimble the letter. Finally I attracted the attention of one of the young Unionists near the door and he let me in. Trimble read the letter, with John Taylor looking over his shoulder, and Taylor said almost instantly, 'That's fine, we can run with that.' I raced back up to tell Tony.

Nevertheless, there was a tense hour before we got an official acceptance. Trimble carried on his meeting with the UUP delegation, letting them all express their views before he did, despite our attempts to hurry them up. 'This is just what they did to Faulkner at Sunningdale, put us under pressure,' said Taylor. 'We'll not be panicked.' But Trimble knew he was safe with the support of Taylor as well as Empey and Maginnis, and he concluded the meeting by saying, 'Right, I am going for the agreement.' He asked Jeffrey Donaldson if he was coming to the plenary session for the signing. He replied he had to leave for a family holiday. Trimble thought Donaldson was skipping the drama, but in fact he was walking out of the negotiations. It wasn't until the press conference, when Trimble was asked about Donaldson's walkout, that he realised what had happened. It marked the beginning of the civil war in the UUP that, in the end, cost Trimble his job as leader, and broke up the party. He made the brave and right decision on Good Friday, but he paid a terrible price for it.

Tony's letter on exclusion was clearly precious to Trimble because he read it out at the press conference. He said later that his biggest worry was that the ink would run in the rain. Little did he know that, if it had, we would not have been able to give him another copy. In the rush I had omitted to save the letter on the computer or keep a copy and it wasn't until the NIO eventually plucked up the courage to ask the UUP for a duplicate a few years later that we had a record of what we'd written.

The plenary was a low-key affair at which all the party leaders assented to the agreement except for Adams who said he was very positive but had to consult his party conference. There was no applause, just stunned silence. Tony and Bertie left before the votes of thanks and mutual congratulations so that they could be the first out to explain the agreement to the media before the other party leaders tried to put their spin on it. They stood together on the steps of Castle Buildings as the rain began to fall. 'Finally,' Tony said, 'the burden of history can at long last start to be lifted from our shoulders.' So the hand of history had come and gone in three long days and nights.

We raced up to Stormont Castle and into the helicopters. As we were taking off I got a call from Buckingham Palace saying the Queen wanted to speak to the Prime Minister. I explained it couldn't be done now but he would call her as soon as we landed. In the helicopter Tony, John, Alastair and I collapsed in exhaustion-induced hysterical laughter having, we thought, concluded a peace agreement that would resolve the problem of Northern Ireland once and for all. In front of us, an RAF gunner sat on the floor, with his legs dangling out into open space, pointing an oversize machine gun at Castle Buildings below us.

Of course, it turned out not to be the end at all but the beginning.

5

The First Test:
April–July 1998

In essence the Good Friday Agreement was an agreement to disagree. The two sides couldn't even agree on its title: the unionists called it the Belfast Agreement and the nationalists called it the Good Friday Agreement. The republicans and nationalists still wanted a united Ireland; the unionists still wanted Northern Ireland to remain part of the United Kingdom. Neither had given up their aspirations. But they had agreed that both would pursue those aspirations by peaceful means rather than by violence. There was a trade-off for each side. The republicans had to accept the principle of consent; the unionists the republican aspiration for a united Ireland, reflected in the All-Ireland elements including the North/South bodies. The trade-off we were unable to secure then, however, was that unionists should agree to share power with Catholics, and that republicans would demonstrate (in a manner acceptable to unionists) that they really had ended the terrorist campaign once and for all.

The problem that was to dog us in the years that followed was the constructive ambiguity we had to deploy to get the Good Friday Agreement. If we had insisted on making decommissioning of terrorist weapons a precondition for entry into government, the Republicans would not have signed up for the Agreement. Traditionally in peace agreements, the giving up of weapons is something that happens at the end of the process, not at the beginning. And there was no way Republicans would have agreed to surrender their weapons at this stage of the process however much we insisted (even though, as events showed, they did not intend to use them again). So we needed ambiguity to get us through: Sinn Féin saying it would use its best efforts to secure decommissioning, and Unionists saying they wanted decommissioning in parallel to going into government. Afterwards, however, this ambiguity led to an impasse.

In the view of the IRA, decommissioning could only start once 'the causes of conflict' were truly resolved and there was real equality, with unionists demonstrating they were really prepared to share power with Catholics. But for unionists, the failure of the IRA to decommission was proof that they had not yet permanently ended their terrorist campaign. How could they be expected to go into government with a political party that had a fully equipped army at its back?

In retrospect, it was probably necessary for a lengthy period of time to elapse after the conclusion of the Good Friday Agreement, to allow the history of distrust to work itself out of the system on both sides, the ambiguity to be squeezed out of the process and true power-sharing to happen. But, at the time, it felt as if we were failing. We had managed to get the Agreement because of the unstoppable momentum we had built. It was a case of an irresistible force meeting an immovable object, and moving it. Both sides were surprised to end up with an agreement the other side could sign up for. But neither side had wanted to get the blame for collapsing the process. Now, though, it was becoming clear that the race was a marathon not a sprint.

The paradox was that it was so much harder to sell the Agreement to the unionists than to nationalists and republicans. In many ways, republicans had had to concede more. After all, if they accepted the principle of consent, that it was for the people of Northern Ireland to decide their future, what had the armed campaign and the suffering been for? But given the zero-sum nature of Northern Ireland politics, the fact that nationalists and republicans came out smiling meant the unionists took more convincing that they had won. They thought there must be something wrong in the Agreement, and they had plenty of doubters on their side to play to those fears.

On Easter Saturday, David Trimble succeeded in winning support for the Good Friday Agreement from the Ulster Unionist Party's Executive by fifty-five votes to twenty-three. But over half his Westminster MPs were opposed to the agreement and he faced a very difficult ride. On Wednesday 15 April, I got a call from one of his confidants, David Montgomery, saying Trimble was in difficulty on the subject of prisoner release. This was followed shortly afterwards by a call from Trimble himself saying things were going terribly. He had problems on prisoners, on police and on decommissioning. He needed our help. I got Tony to speak to him and then, at Trimble's request, Tony called Jim Molyneaux, whom Trimble feared would become the focus of opposition within the party. To help reassure unionist opinion, Tony announced that the RUC would remain a unitary force, a key demand of the unionists, and made it clear that only those prisoners of organisations on ceasefire would be eligible for the new early-release scheme.

But Trimble was rightly fixated with the fate that had befallen his predecessors as leaders of unionism when they tried to say yes rather than no. He was even concerned that the letter about decommissioning he had squeezed out of us on the morning of Good Friday might end up damaging him. His colleagues remembered Brian Faulkner brandishing a telegram from Ted Heath after Sunningdale, which was shown not to be worth the paper it was written on. The ghost of Faulkner and his humiliating defeat after Sunningdale was inevitably to haunt Trimble from April 1998 onwards. It was Trimble's deputy, John Taylor, who had administered the *coup de grâce* to Faulkner at the Ulster Unionist Council in 1974. Taylor was therefore deliberately chosen to introduce the debate at the UUC on Saturday 18 April, Trimble's big test in the party. The yes vote won by 540 to 210.

The battle for unionism was not over however. The key thing Trimble wanted us to do was to persuade Jeffrey Donaldson and his mentor Jim Molyneaux to support him when the Agreement was put to the referendum scheduled for 22 May. In particular, Trimble wanted us to neutralise the possibility of a leadership challenge from Donaldson, a plausible alternative. Tony started the cultivation early, calling Donaldson on Easter Monday and seeing him after Prime Minister's Questions on the first Wednesday after the Agreement. Donaldson told Tony he did not plan to lead the campaign against Trimble by urging a no vote in the referendum. He would keep his head down and not take any position for the moment. Molyneaux said the same.

At Donaldson's request Tony met a group of his young Unionist supporters on 6 May, during his first visit to Northern Ireland for the referendum campaign. Then, on 12 May, Tony spoke to Donaldson again and offered to use in public some of the wording Donaldson had proposed which talked about Sinn Féin being inextricably linked with the IRA, and hinted at the need for legislation to stop Sinn Féin serving on the Executive if there were no decommissioning. Donaldson said that, if the Prime Minister did use such language, he would switch from a reluctant no vote to a yes vote. Tony tried the words out tentatively, first in response to a question from David Trimble at Prime Minister's Questions in the House of Commons the next day, and then in a TV interview. On Thursday 14 May, Tony went ahead with his undertaking to Donaldson and used the language in a major speech. I was terrified that, in doing so, he would push the Republicans off the other side, and indeed the Irish were upset, with Gerry Adams rather notably unable to take a call from Tony telling him what was in the speech. Not that it did us much good. The next day, while Tony was chairing the G8 summit in Birmingham, he asked me to call Donaldson and find out when he was switching his position. Donaldson didn't return my call but later in the afternoon he issued a press statement supporting the No campaign. It appeared that he had enjoyed the flattery of the Prime Minister's attentions but couldn't in the end deliver Molyneaux and his young Unionist supporters. We felt badly let down and the result was highly damaging for the Yes campaign.

For the next three years Trimble would constantly have to defend himself against a guerrilla campaign from Donaldson and his wing of the party. Donaldson never managed to challenge him successfully for the leadership or defeat him in the party, but Trimble was never secure, always worrying about whether he would survive the next party meeting. In one respect this was a result of Trimble's poor people skills and the bad management of his party, something we tried to help him with from time to time, but there were also deeper forces at work as unionism reconfigured itself in the face of the Agreement. The division in the party compounded the sense in the unionist community that there was something wrong in the Good Friday Agreement, that somehow they had lost.

On the surface at least, things were easier on the republican side. Gerry Adams sailed through his party executive, or Ard Chomhairle, on the Tuesday after Easter. His next hurdle would be the special party conference (Ard Fheis) called for 10 May to debate the Agreement. When Tony spoke to him on 17 April, Adams said if it were only Sinn Féin he had to convince there would be few problems, but the 'others' would be more difficult.

Adams's major task was to win over the party from its traditional position of 'abstentionism'. Abstentionism went back to the origins of Sinn Féin as a party. They did not recognise the UK Parliament or any Northern Ireland Assembly because they did not accept British rule in Northern Ireland: if they won a seat in Parliament or the Assembly they would not take it. To plead the cause, Adams and McGuinness spread out across Ireland, North and South, seeing party members in small groups, arguing they had to be in the Assembly if they were to influence the North/South bodies that depended on it. Adams needed a two-thirds majority at the Ard Fheis to make the changes in Sinn Féin's constitution that this required and as a result he became very cautious.

When Tony called him on 27 April, Adams said McGuinness had been given the job of persuading the 'others'. He asked if, to help him win people over, we could begin taking down military installations in Northern Ireland. Tony declined and asked him in turn if he could persuade the IRA to begin decommissioning or take any other steps to help Trimble in the campaign. Adams said it was very difficult to do anything like that at such a sensitive stage in winning republicans over. But he said he wanted an open relationship with Tony of the sort he had with Bertie Ahern and had had with Albert Reynolds. He said he would not 'do the dog on him' which, according to the po-faced civil service memo of the conversation, 'appeared to mean go back to violence without warning'.

Adams called again on 6 May to remind Tony of his difficult promise during the Good Friday negotiations to release prisoners after one rather than two years. Tony said it wasn't possible then because things were too fragile on the unionist side. Adams accepted the judgement but when Tony pressed him for concessions of his own he said he was having a difficult enough time winning over people on his side, and 'he had run out of imagination for this week'.

Adams needn't have worried. He won the vote in the Ard Fheis by 331 to 19.

But if he was in control of events in Sinn Féin, things were more problematic in the murkier world of the IRA. Even before the Good Friday Agreement, Mickey McKevitt, the long-time Quartermaster General of the IRA responsible for all their weapons and materiel, had formed the dissident 32 Counties Sovereignty Committee with his wife Bernadette Sands McKevitt, the sister of the famous hunger striker Bobby Sands. McKevitt was the biggest challenge to Adams and McGuinness's determination not to repeat previous republican splits. He was a credible figure and, after all, they were settling for much less in the Agreement than had been originally demanded by Republicans in 1993.

On 7 May, the dissidents announced the formation of the 'Real IRA' and on 8 May declared the ceasefire over and said they were at war with the British Cabinet. We had difficulty establishing how serious a threat they were. Bertie told Tony on 2 May that those joining the dissidents were relatively few and not the brightest. But, as May went on, Irish officials became increasingly worried, telling us of high-level defections. They saw the RIRA as a serious and growing threat with between 160 and 200 terrorists.

It is hard to speak with certainty of anything that went on inside the IRA at any stage in the peace process, but it is clear that fear of a major split prevented Adams and McGuinness from being as bold in their opening steps after the Good Friday Agreement as they might have been. It is probable that it took considerable skill and persever-ance to hold the movement together during this period, and to convince republicans that they had provided a real democratic alternative to physical force. They had to show they were being taken seriously by the British government without having to blow people up to get their attention. But the price they paid was, probably, accepting in return that the IRA would not begin decommissioning, as it made clear in its statement put out on 30 April. This concession may have been necessary to avoid a major split but it was, combined with the weakness of Trimble's position, to become the root of our inability to move the process on at the speed we wanted.

We were ourselves a little complacent at the start of the referendum campaign. An opinion poll on 16 April showed 73 per cent of the population of Northern Ireland in favour of the Agreement. But our overconfidence didn't last long. A published poll on 19 May showed one-third of unionists in favour, one-third against and one-third undecided. Our internal polls showed unionist opinion hardening against the Agreement in late April and early May. I wrote in my diary that 'it looks as though we will win the referendum but lose the unionists'.

The No campaign of Paisley, McCartney and dissident UUP MPs got off to a good start, especially since immediately after launching the Yes campaign, Trimble went to the US for a speaking engagement at the University of Chicago and Maginnis went off on holiday to Northern Cyprus. We began to panic. Unionist opinion was drifting away from us and the moderate Unionist leaders had left the country. We set up our own steering group on 28 April with a grid of activities and initiatives, and we arranged for Tony to go to Northern Ireland three times in the course of the month-long campaign. When Trimble came back from the US, I couldn't help noticing that he'd had a complete makeover and was playing the role of world statesman, but I wasn't sure a new haircut and new glasses were going to do the trick.

There were some left-field ideas thrown up by our efforts to put life into the campaign. Alastair Campbell sent me a memo on 12 April proposing we arrange a football match between Rangers and Celtic, Glasgow teams with traditional Protestant and Catholic followings, playing each other in Northern Ireland but wearing each other's strips as a sign of reconciliation. Rather more successfully U2 held a concert in support of a yes vote and Bono persuaded a sheepish Trimble and Hume to come onstage and punch the air in front of a young audience.

We endeavoured to make the campaign as bipartisan as possible. William Hague agreed to help and suggested that he, Tony and Paddy Ashdown visit the Province together. Later, though, Hague became tricky, urging that prisoner release be linked to decommissioning, and Tony had to ask him to be careful in his use of language. John Major, by contrast, was extremely supportive and went to Northern Ireland with Tony on his 6 May trip to demonstrate cross-party endorsement of the Agreement. We even persuaded Robert Cranborne, who had been one of a handful of Tory MPs to vote against the Anglo-Irish Agreement, to campaign for a yes vote, as well as unionist-friendly Labour MPs like Kate Hoey, who played a crucial role in supporting Trimble throughout the campaign. We also talked to President Clinton about the possibility of a visit, but Trimble made it clear that such a visit would be counterproductive. Instead, we got Clinton to issue a joint statement of support with Tony at the G8 summit in Birmingham on 17 May.

Within the Province itself, Tony did everything Trimble requested to try and bring round the doubting unionists. First he saw the Orange Order, led by Robert Saulters, a man who had been quoted as saying that Tony had 'sold his birthright by marrying a Romanist and would sell his soul to the devil himself'. Tony was never surprised by sectarian bigotry. He liked to tell the story of his unionist grandmother who, on her deathbed, wanted him to promise that he would never marry a Catholic. He succeeded in preventing the Order from condemning the Agreement outright, despite their misgivings. Tony also saw the RUC on his 6 May visit, and we found £5 million for Victims Groups. Finally Gordon Brown visited Belfast to announce an economic package for the Province. We were appalled to discover that it was the first visit to Northern Ireland by a Chancellor for twenty years.

Meanwhile, concern was growing about the impact any announcement from the new Parades Commission might have on opinion. Almost as soon as Labour came into power, Mo Mowlan had set up the new Commission under Alistair Graham, a Leeds-based employment lawyer, to arbitrate on controversial marches. It was expected to announce its decision on rerouting virtually all the Orange marches on 22 April. Everyone knew the decision would go against the Orange Order, and Trimble worried, rightly, that it would play into the hands of Paisley and the No campaign. Mo was reluctant to interfere with the commission's independence, so Tony called Alistair Graham, whom he had known slightly as a lawyer, to try to persuade him to postpone the publication of his decision. Graham was difficult and, to cover his back, insisted that Tony put the request in a public letter. We did so and the decision was put off until after the referendum campaign was over.

Yet, despite all our efforts to help the Yes campaign, one fatal event served to undermine unionist support for the Agreement even further. After Good Friday, Mo Mowlam had agreed to the transfer from England to Ireland of four members of the notorious Balcombe Street Gang, an IRA group responsible for a series of mainland bombings and assassinations in the 1980s. Without telling us, the Irish government decided that they should be released on parole to attend the Sinn Féin Ard Fheis in Dublin on 10 May. Presumably Adams had confided his worry to the Irish that he would be unable to win a two-thirds majority at the conference and argued this would help. The Republican leadership thought it would be a good idea to parade all four of the released prisoners on the stage at the conference, live on TV, to a heroes' welcome. Adams records in his autobiography that there were ten minutes of cheering and shouting after they appeared. The triumphalism went down extraordinarily badly in the unionist community and increased their sense that they had lost something. There was no constructive ambiguity in those graphic pictures.

The problem was compounded by Mo's decision to release Padraig Wilson, the commander of the IRA prisoners in the Maze, and to allow Michael Stone, the crazed loyalist killer famous for his shooting spree in a West Belfast cemetery, to leave prison to attend a UDA/UDP rally at Ulster Hall. Moderate unionists thought that if this is what the agreement meant, they were not for it.

So, by the middle of May, things were worse rather than better. We tried to claw our way back. Tony returned to Northern Ireland on the anniversary of his Balmoral speech and gave another unionist-friendly speech setting four conditions for prisoners to be released. We also sent Philip Gould, our pollster, over to Belfast to conduct focus groups to see what would make a difference. He divined that for unionists the position of Prime Minister still carried great weight and if Tony made promises in that capacity rather than just as a charismatic politician, his guarantees would have more impact. Alastair Campbell and John Holmes drew up five pledges, imitating the New Labour pledge card of the 1997 general-election campaign, and Tony wrote them out in his own hand on a huge card during his last visit to Northern Ireland before the vote. The pledges were: 1) no change in the status of Northern Ireland without the consent of the people of Northern Ireland; 2) power to take decisions returned to a Northern Ireland Assembly, with accountable North/South cooperation; 3) fairness and equality guaranteed for all; 4) those who use or threaten violence excluded from the government of Northern Ireland; 5) prisoners kept in unless violence given up for good. The pledges had been carefully drafted, and they probably had an impact on the vote, but they caused dreadful problems later as anti-Agreement unionists used their interpretations of what the promises meant to claim that we had reneged on them.

Finally, in the last days of the campaign, the unionist vote began to swing back. It is hard to say whether this was because they had to focus properly on the issues as the time came to make a decision, or because they were swayed by last-minute events, such as David

Trimble's good performance in the TV debate against Ian Paisley, or Tony's simultaneous article in the unionist *Newsletter* and nationalist *Irish News* on the day of the vote. But shift they did.

Predictably in the South, 94 per cent voted in favour of the Agreement. In the North the turnout was 81 per cent, nearly as high as the turnout for the 1922 referendum on separation. Seventy-one per cent voted in favour, made up of 96 per cent of the Catholic population and about 55 per cent of the Protestants. This was scarcely a resounding triumph on the unionist side but at least we could claim that a majority of Protestants had voted yes.

The referendum was swiftly followed by a campaign for elections to the Northern Ireland Assembly on 25 June. Tony went to Dublin on 1 June where he agreed with Bertie Ahern that our aim was to get through the elections with our achievements intact. He went on to Belfast to meet the parties, and was disappointed to be told that he could not campaign in the election for Trimble as the moderate unionist leader.

Trimble would have been wise to be magnanimous to Jeffrey Donaldson after the referendum. I was lobbied by a group of young Unionists asking us to appeal to Trimble to do just that, and Tony spoke to him on 21 May urging him to reach out to Donaldson. I also tried to persuade Trimble myself immediately after the referendum, arguing that it made sense to get Donaldson back on board. But he wouldn't do it, mainly because of pressure from Ken Maginnis and Reg Empey not to reward a rebel. Instead, he refused Donaldson the exemption he needed to run for the Assembly while being an MP, leaving him firmly on the outside.

With his party split, David Trimble fought a defensive campaign in the run-up to the Assembly elections. The referendum had turned out what he called the 'flymo' vote, the middle-class unionists who certainly wanted the Union to remain but looked down their noses at those engaged in politics in the Province and had been little bothered by the Troubles in their comfortable suburbs with manicured lawns. But these people did not turn out in the Assembly elections (60,000 fewer Protestants voted in the elections than in the referendum) and the UUP suffered accordingly, receiving their lowest ever share of the vote. For the first time in the history of such elections, a Catholic party, the SDLP, came top of the poll. Sinn Féin did well too, and the anti-Agreement unionists fell only two seats short of being able to block the work of the Assembly. Surprisingly, this was not because the DUP triumphed, but because of the unexpectedly good showing of Bob McCartney's splinter party, the UKUP, and a gaggle of independent anti-Agreement unionists.

Tony phoned all the party leaders after the results were announced and said he wished he had been able to come over to campaign. He was convinced he could have got more votes for Trimble. From Trimble to Adams, they all disabused him of that illusion, but he still believed it. Trimble told Tony 'he had only just made it by the skin of his teeth'. He had a mere twenty-eight loyal Assembly members and he was fatally weakened before the Assembly even started. He would not have the space to be courageous. Paisley said he didn't usually take political calls on a Sunday but deigned to take Tony's call anyway. I listened in, and Paisley was almost hysterical, attacking Tony for hypocrisy and betrayal during the campaign. I spoke to Tony afterwards, worried that he would be in shock, but he said he could not really take the call seriously as he was with the children watching *The Simpsons* on TV at the time.

On 1 July the new Assembly met in temporary offices in Castle Buildings. They elected the shadow First and Deputy First Ministers but not the Executive. In the event that step was only to happen many, many months later. David Trimble became the First Minister designate, and Seamus Mallon, deputy leader of the SDLP, became Deputy First Minister. David Trimble was pleased to have Mallon rather than John Hume. He suspected Hume of being too well disposed to Sinn Féin and thought Mallon might be more sceptical about republican intentions and more unionist-friendly. He was both. But Trimble and Mallon were both proud and prickly and could never get on at a personal level. On their first trip to the United States together Mo rang me to say she was thinking of sending them back because they were behaving so badly. When they met President Clinton they spent the entire half-hour arguing with each other in front of him. The White House staff were bemused, given how hard it was even for heads of state of major countries to get half an hour with the President.

Tony and I saw the new First and Deputy First Ministers and the other political leaders in Northern Ireland on 2 July. But there was not much rejoicing. Both sides had come out of the two campaigns further constrained and, by then, their and our minds had already moved on to a new political crisis, the marching season, and in particular the threat of sectarian violence surrounding the Drumcree march in Trimble's constituency of Portadown.

Trimble said he had been wounded by the election. Drumcree might finish him off.

6

Off the Hill:
The Summer of 1998

Orange marches are one of the things that an English person finds most incomprehensible about Northern Ireland. The sectarian marking of territory with flags on the lamp posts, or kerbstones painted red, white and blue may come as a shock to a first-time visitor. But the marches in which the Orangemen dress in their best suits, with bowler hats, rolled umbrellas, white gloves and their 'collarettes' – symbolic halters around their necks – look like a throwback. Why do they want to do it? And there are not one or two marches every year, but hundreds of them, with the main season concentrated in July. Throughout the 1980s and 90s, they would impede political progress, which had to be suspended, or rushed to a conclusion at the end of June, and were sure to result in rioting. In Northern Ireland middle-class people used to go on holiday in July to avoid the marches.

Yet if you despise the motivation for marching rather than understand it, you will not get to grips with the real problems of Northern Ireland. The annual marches of the Orange Order, and its slightly upmarket cousin, the Black Preceptory, are not just an old tradition. They express the centuries-old obstinacy of a Protestant people determined not to be driven from their land by the majority community in Ireland. Walking, as they call it, is a refusal to allow their freedom of expression to be restricted. The result is a classic clash of rights: on the one hand, the right of Orangemen to march down the Queen's highway and express their cultural identity, and on the other, the right of Catholic residents not to be terrorised in their own homes.

During the summer of 1998, all eyes were on the Drumcree march which had been the source of major tension in the previous three years. In the words of Jack Hermon, the former Chief Constable of the RUC, Drumcree outside Portadown, County Armagh, is the

'Vatican of Orangeism'. It is not for nothing the local Orange organisation is known as Loyal Order Lodge Number One. Every year since
1807, on the Sunday before 12 July, when unionists celebrate the Battle
of the Boyne, the Orangemen of Portadown have marched out to a
service in Drumcree church, and then marched back to the Carleton
Street Orange Lodge in the centre of town. And judging by the
pamphlets both sides gave me when I started trying to mediate, for
two centuries the march had been surrounded by sectarian violence
on both sides.

But it wasn't the ancient history that was the problem in 1998. It
was the recent history. Portadown is a town divided by sectarianism.
The two traditions live in their own areas and don't mix. Often they
come to blows. Soon after we came to office, a young Catholic boy,
Robert Hamill, was killed in the centre of Portadown by a loyalist
mob. In the 1980s the return route of the march back from the church
had been moved, to avoid going through a Catholic area on the way
back into Portadown, on to a main thoroughfare called the Garvaghy
Road. But over time, the area along this road had become a Catholic
suburb. The Catholic residents objected to the march. But the
Orangemen had expected the change of route to be permanent, and
they weren't going to be moved again.

On the day of the march in 1995 tensions reached their peak when
the RUC tried to reroute the return leg away from the Garvaghy Road
because the Catholic residents were holding a sit-down protest there
and the police wanted to avoid clashes between the marchers and the
demonstrators. The Orange Order didn't take kindly to this denial of
their rights. They, too, refused to move and, for several days, their
local MP David Trimble slept in his car outside Drumcree church to
be with them. A loyalist crowd of 30,000 gathered and Ian Paisley
turned up. There were loyalist protests and violence across the
Province. Eventually the police backed down, unable to resist the
weight of numbers, and allowed the marchers down the Garvaghy
Road. Ian Paisley and David Trimble were pictured arm in arm
welcoming the Orangemen back. And it was in part his role in 'the siege
of Drumcree' that propelled David Trimble to leadership of the UUP
in September 1995.

In 1996 it was even worse. The police were again overwhelmed by
numbers after some abortive negotiations between the two sides at a

local carpet factory. There was serious violence on both sides. The police were seen to have been unable to maintain the rule of law under pressure from the loyalists. In the eyes of nationalists, the British had once again ceded to the 'Orange Card', and the SDLP walked out of the negotiating forum.

In response Paddy Mayhew announced a Parades Commission to arbitrate on these controversial marches, but he couldn't give it teeth because of opposition within the Tory Party, and because the Major government depended on Unionist support in crucial votes in the Commons. After the election, Mo Mowlam introduced legislation for a new, more powerful Parades Commission, but it had not come into force by the time of the 1997 marching season. During our first year in government, the decision on whether or not a particular march could go ahead still rested in the hands of the RUC Chief Constable, Ronnie Flanagan, who took the decision on public order grounds.

On 1 July 1997, John Holmes minuted Tony about the imminent Drumcree march. Tony was reluctantly of the view the march should go ahead, but with strict limits on the number and behaviour of marchers (for example that they should march without their bands, and that if any of the conditions were breached, they should not march the next year), but he also recognised that we had to accept Ronnie Flanagan's judgement on public order, whatever it might be. This was an operational matter in which the police had independence.

Saturday 5 July was decision day. The army rolled razor wire across the entrance to the Garvaghy Road in a way that made it look as if they were going to block the route of the march. In fact, they were just holding the situation while the Chief Constable made his decision. At ten in the evening, he decided the march should be allowed to go ahead without restrictions. He said it was the lesser of two evils, worried the police would be overwhelmed both at Drumcree and across the Province if he tried to block it. So, at midnight, the army rolled back the razor wire and, catching the residents unawares, occupied the Garvaghy Road to allow the march to take place. Tony called Bertie Ahern at eight o'clock the next morning to let him know the decision. Nationalist Ireland, North and South, were disappointed in the new Labour government, which they had hoped would stand up to the Orange Order, and once again the Province exploded into violence.

In 1997 we in No. 10 had not been closely involved in the decision-making process on Drumcree. But in 1998 we could not avoid it. There was too much at stake just to leave events to take their course. We had persuaded Alistair Graham of the Parades Commission to delay his decision on the rerouting of marches during the campaign for the Good Friday Agreement referendum, but on 29 June he published his conclusions. The Garvaghy Road leg of the Drumcree march was to be banned. Two of the three Protestant members of the Commission wanted to resign, probably because they were unhappy with his decision on Drumcree.

The first I had heard about the issue was from Trimble's friends, journalist Ruth Dudley Edwards and ex-IRA man Sean O'Callaghan. They both came to see me in late May, saying they had a plan to resolve Drumcree. Their idea was to allow a small parade with restrictions, such as those Tony had contemplated privately the year before, and they wanted us to press John Hume, Gerry Adams and President Clinton to back this policy and help save David Trimble. I mentioned the approach to Tony, and when he saw Gerry Adams on 2 June he asked if Adams would help Trimble on Drumcree. Adams said he would be happy to sit down with Trimble to discuss the matter. But of course Trimble declined. He was saving his first face-to-face meeting with Adams for a bigger prize, as he told us: to secure a commitment from Republicans to the war being finally over.

Later in June, the Reverend William Bingham came to see me. He was the Deputy Grand Chaplain of the Orange Order, but unlike anything I had expected from someone with such an archaic title. He was intellectual, mild, young and sensible. And he brought with him Trevor Ringland, a former captain of the Ireland rugby team. They seemed remarkably sane people to be raising such a recondite subject, but they felt very strongly about it. They argued that the only way to bolster moderate unionism was to find a compromise that allowed the march to go ahead. I asked why the Orange Order couldn't negotiate directly with the Catholic residents. They explained that it was because the residents were led by Breandan MacCionnaith who, in the eyes of the Orangemen, was a terrorist, convicted of kidnap in the context of the blowing up of the Royal Legion Hall in Portadown in 1981. I said I would see what I could do. I wrote in my diary: 'Whether they can stop the conflagration that is about to hit us I do not know.'

In the end, they couldn't. On 29 June, just before Alistair Graham's Parades Commission was about to announce its decision, William Bingham called me at home to ask if I could stop the Parades Commission announcing their decision that day. He said he and a local Orange businessman, Dennis Watson, had potential contacts with the residents, and might be able to find a solution. I called the NIO but they said it was too late and, anyway, the Chief Constable didn't think their contacts amounted to much. But we wanted to help. Tony spoke to John Hume and to Bertie Ahern, whom he saw at an event launching the European Central Bank in Frankfurt, asking them for support. He argued that what was needed was a magnanimous gesture by nationalists towards unionists on the back of the referendum and election campaign. Bertie agreed and sent Eamon O'Cuiv, a junior minister in his government with impeccable republican credentials (he was de Valera's grandson), to see the residents.

Meanwhile, Tony told me he wanted to go over to Northern Ireland to sort the problem out. When I told Mo, she said it was part of his 'Jesus complex': a belief that his personal presence could resolve problems. I suspected she had a point but, nevertheless, after Cabinet on 2 July, we flew over to Northern Ireland.

We started by visiting a burnt-out Catholic church near Aldergrove airport, destroyed in the sectarian violence leading up to the march. I was shocked. It was upsetting to see the charred altar. We then helicoptered to Stormont for a photo opportunity with Trimble and Mallon to congratulate them on their success in the Assembly election. They were pretty depressed. I wrote in my diary that if only they could get through this together they would be much strengthened. However, our meetings with Adams and Hume offered little comfort. Adams protested he was not in control of the residents' leader MacCionnaith. His suggestion was that Trimble send someone close to him to see the residents. We also saw Chief Constable Ronnie Flanagan who was very worried about loyalist violence in the wake of the Parades Commission's decision. He would have preferred the march to go ahead, but he said he would hold the line. We met the church leaders, but they said they couldn't do anything to mediate between the two sides. John Holmes, thank goodness, managed to persuade Tony that he should not insist on staying there till the problem was solved. We would have been there a very long time indeed.

Late that evening, while we were at Stormont with the political leaders, the DUP mounted a demonstration at the top of the hill behind Parliament Buildings. They were beating on big Lambeg drums, the huge eighteenth-century drums that Protestant marchers play to terrorise and mark their ascendancy. Hearing them in the night like that, I could physically feel how they threatened the Catholics with their tribal hate. The whole thing looked hopeless and we flew back through the dark to London.

The next morning, when I got in to No. 10, Tony summoned me to his den next to the Cabinet Room and said he was disappointed with progress and demanded that I go back to see what could be done. Mo was furious when she found out. She thought it was a vote of no confidence in her ability to resolve the situation herself. Nevertheless, Tony was adamant I should go, and I took a flight that day. I was met off the plane by a NIO official who planned to take me to the Garvaghy Road to meet the residents. I decided on a change of plan. Trimble had sent David Thomson, the chair of his constituency association, to see the Garvaghy Road Residents' group and I thought it best for me to go to Castle Buildings for a debriefing with Trimble and the Orangemen. Thomson reported back that he saw no sign of movement and indeed MacCionnaith had told him he would not be safe if he came to the residents' meeting that evening. I tried to bring Seamus Mallon into the negotiations but he was slow to react and said MacCionnaith couldn't be cut out. I then phoned MacCionnaith and talked to him for half an hour. He invited me to address his meeting, but I turned him down. He appeared to be convinced we would over-turn the Parades Commission's decision and allow the march down the road.

I spent the evening holding meetings at Hillsborough. The Irish minister Bertie had sent to see the residents, Eamon O'Cuiv, told me that he, too, had failed to persuade them to compromise in any way. David Trimble, William Bingham and Dennis Watson made it clear the Orangemen were adamant they would not talk face to face with MacCionnaith.

*   *   *

The next morning Mo, who I had not seen the previous day, came into my grand bedroom at Hillsborough, woke me up and told me she wanted me to go. While we were in the 'family room' on the first floor, having an 'Ulster fry' breakfast (a guaranteed heart attack of black pudding, fried bread and everything else unhealthy you can imagine), she picked up the phone and booked me a ticket back to London on the lunchtime flight. She said she was highly offended that Tony had sent me over. Her irritation was entirely understandable. As a secretary of state it must be very undermining to have the Prime Minister try to second guess your decisions and show such apparent lack of confidence in your abilities. But Tony was right to think that the only way to convince Trimble and the Orangemen we were serious was to have direct No. 10 involvement.

After breakfast, Mo insisted on taking me to her security meeting in the war room with Ronnie Flanagan and the General Officer Commanding (GOC), the top military officer in Northern Ireland, to demonstrate she was in charge. Ronnie was fairly cheerful since this year he hadn't had to take the decision on whether the march should go ahead. He anticipated violence across the Province but not necessarily at Drumcree itself. Some of the loyalists had manufactured shotguns that looked like short sticks or batons. Others planned to block the road to the airport.

I went on to Castle Buildings to join Trimble and Mallon in an effort to get them to work together. They issued a joint statement and did a press conference calling for calm. Despite Mo's pressure to leave, I stayed with them till mid-afternoon when they went home and I spent the rest of the day on the phone. Gerry Adams called me and I urged him to be more responsible in what he said publicly, particularly if he wanted to avoid provoking Trimble into a public outburst. He invited me out for a pint which I declined.

Tony spoke again to Alistair Graham, and urged him to allow the Orangemen to march down the Lower Ormeau Road in Belfast, another controversial march that had been banned the year before following the violence at Drumcree. Graham wanted Tony to speak to Seamus Mallon and persuade him to say that moderate Catholics were in favour of allowing the march, but when Tony called Mallon, he absolutely refused for reasons of principle. I flew home that night but spent the whole of Sunday on the phone.

That day the violence started in earnest. There were ninety petrol bomb attacks and twenty-seven hijackings, but the police managed to keep the roads open by clearing the burning barricades. Despite an announcement by an extreme Orange group that they planned to attack the homes of police families, the police and army made it clear they were serious about blocking the march. They dumped huge containers of concrete on the road leading from Drumcree church to the Garvaghy Road, deployed miles of razor wire, built a small fort at the top of the rise on the road from which they could look down on the marchers, and drafted in an extra thousand troops from Britain. In the evening I set up a conference call between William Bingham, Dennis Watson, Seamus Mallon and Brid Rogers, the local SDLP representative for Portadown, to see if we could find some common ground. In the event there was not a lot, but we at least made progress in establishing a dialogue. David Montgomery called to tell me David Trimble was ready to resign.

On Monday there were 10,000 loyalists at Drumcree behind the razor wire. There were 130 sectarian attacks, as well as 215 petrol and blast bombs, the latter being particularly unpleasant small home-made weapons designed for close combat to kill or maim policemen. Sixty-six vehicles were hijacked, 237 roads were blocked by loyalists, and the police came under fire five times. Even their homes were under attack. Ian Paisley announced ominously that the following Sunday would be 'the settling day'. I arranged two conference calls, including David Trimble in both this time. We agreed that Brid Rogers would go and talk to the residents' group. She came back to report that they were willing to be flexible about the march next year but were adamant it couldn't take place this year. The Orangemen appeared to believe that we would eventually give in and allow them to march down the road. My worry was that the good weather would increase the violence: what Bertie Ahern called the early-summer 'white nights' in Northern Ireland tended to encourage outdoor violence.

On Tuesday the security forces reported the violence was building. Brid Rogers dropped out of our conference calls, I imagined that she had been frightened off by threats from the residents. The remaining group of us agreed that Seamus Mallon and David Trimble would go and talk to their respective communities and then report back. William Bingham again told me the Orangemen believed we would give in and let them down the road.

Mallon took a long time to get moving and on Wednesday, when he finally went to the Garvaghy Road, he was nearly mobbed. He got nowhere, but at least he bought us a little more time. Trimble was getting increasingly agitated. Bingham called me, worried about what the reaction of the Orange Order would be when they came to see Tony the next day in Downing Street and got nothing out of us on any of their demands. He had chosen a delegation from among the more reasonable Orangemen, but, when they came on Thursday, they showed little sign of leadership. Tony kept saying they needed an exit strategy. They sheltered behind the hard men saying their only exit strategy was to march down the road. We floated the idea of a march in September instead, on Ulster Day, and a peace camp until then, but they rejected it. Nor were they prepared to accept a limited march, and warned us about violence at the weekend. We suggested proximity talks, which Mallon had told us the residents would accept, but even that appeared to be difficult for the Orange Order. Mallon said the talks would need to be held away from Portadown itself, given the disastrous episode of the talks in the carpet factory in Portadown in 1996.

On Friday morning, I faxed letters to Dennis Watson of the Orange Order and to Breandan MacCionnaith of the Garvaghy Road Residents proposing proximity talks starting the next day. The rules were that the talks would take place in separate rooms and I would shuttle between the two parties. There would be no preconditions, drafting would be carried out by me and nothing would be agreed until every-thing was agreed. The NIO officials suggested the Reverend Roy Magee, a Presbyterian minister who had negotiated the Loyalist cease-fire in 1994, as a facilitator on the Orange side and started looking for one on the residents' side. I got on a plane and arrived in Belfast late on Friday evening.

Belfast International was deserted as I came through arrivals, and the tension in the air was palpable. There was something resembling a medieval siege going on at Drumcree, complete with battering rams and the modern equivalent of boiling oil (water cannons). The confronta-tion between the police and the loyalists was visceral. The loyalists thought the police were supposed to be on their side, and seeing them enforcing the laws against them rather than against nationalists had enraged them. Tony had spoken to Ronnie Flanagan on the phone, and he'd assured him the morale of the RUC was good, despite what they were facing. He said that, earlier in the day, the TV news had broadcast shocking video footage of Orangeman in full regalia encouraging attacks on the police across the front line at Drumcree. Both the police and the loyalists were crossing the Rubicon: their relationship would never be the same, but it came at a high price for individual policemen who lived in loyalist areas and suffered along with their families.

My NIO driver was nervous this late at night and he took the back roads to Hillsborough. Even so we ran into a barricade of burning tyres blocking the road in a lonely spot. Luckily it was deserted and we managed to make our way round. Once I was settled in the Queen's Room at Hillsborough, I started on late-night phone calls. Breandan MacCionnaith wouldn't agree to talk anywhere except in his enclave. He even suggested the train station. I gave him the letter of guarantee he had requested, stating that the march would not be forced down the road while I was talking to him. And eventually, by perseverance, and because someone had probably leaned on him, he agreed to talks in Armagh.

Sorting out a venue for the talks at such short notice wasn't straightforward. Our first choice – the Armagh campus of Queen's University – was rejected because the police judged it too dangerous for the Catholic residents. Luckily we were able to use the District Council buildings. They were set in parkland, which we hoped would keep the press at bay. We put the Orangemen in the reception room, which had big paintings of William and Mary, and the residents in the large council chamber. The facilitators and I, along with our superb NIO team, were left with the slightly more modest room in between. The residents turned up at two thirty, accompanied by a group of eight thick-necked men wearing earrings and tracksuits who served as their drivers and bodyguards. The Orangemen were in a sulk because they had been there since before lunch and had been made to wait. The two sides refused even to share the same toilets.

I had been involved in many negotiations in my life, with the Chinese over the return of Hong Kong, in the 'Two-plus-Four' negotiations over German unification in the late 1980s and with the former Soviet Union on human rights abuses and arms control. But I had never before encountered such unreasonableness from both sides. The

Orange Order's idea of a negotiation was to turn up with an opening position and stick to it. When you asked them if they could compromise, they would be adamant they couldn't. The Garvaghy Road Residents were the opposite: they came from the school of tricky negotiators, who would start by negotiating about parking places before they got into the building and work up from there. I felt under huge pressure. I had never entered such an unpropitious negotiation nor one which would impact so immediately on whether people would live or die depending on what we did.

I started with the Orange Order. They set out their prejudices at tedious length. There were two middle-class businessmen representing the Order and two stalwarts of the local lodge. 'Do you realise they are shooting plastic bullets at Orangemen?' one of them said to me in horror, as if such things should be reserved for Catholics.

We had eventually found a facilitator for the residents' side in the form of Peter Quinn, a businessman from Enniskillen, and a former head of the Gaelic Athletic Association. He was recommended to me by Gerry Adams, and he turned out to be remarkably able. He needed to be. The residents were like an old Labour constituency general committee. They immediately raised ten points of order and wanted two sets of notes taken at each meeting. I tried to address all their points straight away. One of them concerned the presence of Eamon McKee, a young Irish diplomat close to the residents. John Holmes had agreed with the Irish Cabinet Secretary Paddy Teahon that McKee could stay in a nearby hotel, but he had turned up at the negotiations themselves. I said that whether or not the residents had an Irish diplomat with them was between them and the Irish government. I liked Eamon, whom I had known in Washington, but he was not universally popular in the Irish system because of his extravagant reporting and was known in the Irish Justice Ministry as 'Jesus McKee', because every time they read something he had written, they all said 'Jesus!'

When Trimble found out McKee was there, he had a fit. In fact Trimble was in resigning mood most of the day and I had to spend a good deal of the time calming him down. He had his man there too, in the form of David Campbell, a farmer and political adviser, known as 'the Undertaker' because of his lugubrious looks. Actually he was a very wise head who later went on to play a key role in the peace process.

The two sides stated their opening positions. The Orange Order offered to limit their march to the 1,400 members of the local lodge, with no music and only two standards, walking four abreast so they would pass down the road more rapidly. They wanted agreement not just on a march this year, but for all future years too. In return, they were prepared to discuss economic and social issues in a new civic forum. The residents said there could be no march this year, but they were prepared to 'explore the possibility of an Orange presence on the Garvaghy Road in the future' and discuss that possibility in a civic forum. We rapidly got nowhere. I suggested to the residents that the Orange leaders had marched their men to the top of the hill and wanted to find a way down. Perhaps the residents could help, since there was no advantage in humiliating them. My words fell on deaf ears.

I went back to the Order. Would they consider moderating their position so I could broker a compromise between the two sides? No, they said. They had already set out their position. They saw the notion of compromise as somehow immoral. The sacrifice of principle to a pragmatic end was anathema to them.

Time was ticking away. It was already six o'clock on Saturday and the Orangemen wouldn't be available again until the following Wednesday since Sunday was the Sabbath, Monday the 12 July celebration and Tuesday the Black Preceptory marching day across the Province. They had said they were prepared to negotiate until midnight, but this wasn't much help since the residents, who were willing to come the next day, said they had to go home at seven. Later the residents agreed to stay on, but asked for safe passage home through back roads with an armed escort. They did not want to be travelling by themselves at night with rioting going on. I offered them a RUC escort but they wanted the army, so we got them two army vehicles if they agreed to stay till midnight.

At the last minute the residents hinted they might agree to a parade later in the year if we established a civic forum and put £5 million a year into the area. But it was too late by then. The Orangemen believed the negotiation wasn't going anywhere. I got Tony, who was at No. 10, to call Dennis Watson to press him to agree the process was not dead. Meanwhile, William Bingham told me a deal might be possible but not that night. We put out an emollient press release, saying progress had been made and bilateral contacts would continue with the aim of resuming the talks process later. I went to bed thinking that at least the talks were serving as a pressure release for the violence, but awoke on Sunday morning to the horrifying news that sectarian murderers had killed three young Catholic children, the Quinns, aged ten, nine and eight, by burning them alive in their beds, in their home in Ballymoney in County Antrim.

In retrospect this ghastly event expedited something that was already happening in Orange ranks. Many Orangemen were already disgusted by the violence at Drumcree. This was the last straw. I spoke very early to William Bingham, who said he was sick at heart. He said he was thinking of preaching about it in his sermon later that morning, and I encouraged him to do so. When I spoke to him again at eleven-thirty as he was going into church, he said he would make his views plain. I had got a TV news crew down to his village and the impact of his words, 'A road is not worth a life', was incredibly powerful. In taking this stand he was very brave. He and his family were later subject to attacks and harassment for his perceived disloyalty to the Orange cause. But he did what he believed to be right without thinking about his safety. It was one of those moments when the bravery of one man can turn events.

David Trimble went on television as well and made it clear the protest must end. He showed no hesitation. He did not consult his colleagues. And he took a big political risk. But it paid off. A corner was turned and the steam was taken out of Drumcree. We had a moment of anxiety later on Sunday afternoon, though. I had spent the day with Trimble and Mallon at Castle Buildings where we had seen the Orange leaders. I put Tony on the phone to them and bit by bit we'd won them over to calling on their men to come off the hill at Drumcree. But when we virtually had it settled, things were nearly blown apart by a false report that the murder had in fact been a domestic dispute, carried out by the former husband of the children's mother, and nothing to do with Drumcree. We had to get hold of the investigating officer so that he could make it clear to the Orangemen that it was indeed a sectarian attack. That steadied their nerves and we sent them off. Ronnie Flanagan later mentioned to me that it was a senior DUP politician who had spread the story. Northern Ireland, as a small province, is a place where rumours, however outlandish, can gestate quickly and then spread like wildfire. Killing them off is never easy.

Having seen the Orange leaders, Trimble and Mallon held a very effective joint press conference calling for the men to come off the hill. I wrote in my diary that Mallon had the 'patience of Job sticking with Trimble' who came across not just as angry and rude but as making no effort to keep Mallon informed of what he was up to. But between them, miraculously, they got it right. Monday passed with only a minor hiccup. Gerry Adams called me several times from the Lower Ormeau Road in South Belfast where the march was due to take place. He said he had persuaded the residents not to block the march and to hold a silent black-flag protest instead, but his attempts were being undermined by the police arresting residents. I called Mo and she spoke to Ronnie Flanagan, who in turn managed to defuse the situation.

So, in the end, the height of the marching season had passed and the turmoil we'd expected – massive protest and a partial rerun of the Loyalist Workers strike that finished off the Sunningdale Agreement – did not happen. Mallon and Trimble had survived their first test and I wrote in my diary: 'I think there has been a sea change in Northern Ireland. When we look back on it, this will have been an important step. I think there is a chance we can make it work.'

We did not, however, give up on trying to solve the problem of Drumcree then. It is never good to leave one side feeling defeated and humiliated, and we wanted to help David Trimble, in whose constituency the festering sore remained. Although we had persuaded most of the protestors to leave the hill, a hard core stood firm, led by Harold Gracey, who would stay on the site in a caravan for years to come. Sporadic violence continued, and Trimble became convinced that elements in the Orange Order were trying to use the dispute to ensure that he was replaced by a DUP MP at the next election.

The residents agreed to go back into talks as early as Monday 14 July, but Gerry Adams thought he should visit them before talks began. He continued to push for a face-to-face meeting with David Trimble to discuss the subject, but Trimble refused. Nor were the Orangemen eager to come back to the negotiating table. Eventually they agreed to talks the next weekend. They said that, unlike the residents, they were working men and could not leave their jobs for talks in the middle of the week.

I spent some of the next week in Germany meeting Gerhard Schroeder's inner team in Hanover before their election victory, but I flew back to Northern Ireland on Friday. This time when I arrived the burning barricades had gone, but there was still plenty of tension. I was dispirited to find that, back in the Armagh District Council offices, the issues hadn't changed. The Orange Order wanted to talk about a march in 1998, but the residents said they were only ready to consider a march once the civic forum was up and running. MacCionnaith said, 'The Orange Order should be reassured to know that when the Garvaghy Road Residents' Coalition says "no", it does not mean "never".' Unfortunately, the Orange Order weren't reassured. They wanted the residents to accept their offer of a civic forum, plus another forum where they could all meet in the same room to discuss the march, and address each other through a chairman, *if* the residents allowed them down the road later in the year. I suggested to the residents that it was in their interest to offer the Orange Order an honourable way out, and I called Martin McGuinness to ask if he could reason with MacCionnaith. But all this led to was MacCionnaith calling me to his room to complain in demotic terms about putting pressure on the residents through Sinn Féin. He also accused me of trying to take away the money we had offered the residents of the Garvaghy Road, an area he compared in perhaps slightly overstated terms to the Warsaw ghetto. We tabled a composite document in the evening setting out a possible agreement, but it was rejected by both sides and we had to call it a day.

Even that wasn't the end of our efforts to resolve the stand-off at Drumcree, however. For the next two years we stayed engaged, trying to find a solution. The security services were worried about a renewed outbreak of violence around Drumcree at Christmas 1998, so I wrote to the two sides proposing new talks. Once I had resolved MacCionnaith's usual procedural points, we managed to gather both sides at the appropriately named 'Nutts Corner' training centre near Aldergrove airport on 16 December. Both sides were intransigent as ever, and for the Orange Order the bottom line was a march back down the Garvaghy Road. To my surprise MacCionnaith indicated some flexibility to Peter Quinn, the facilitator, and we prepared a paper that tried to build on it, but the Orange Order were too flat-footed to take advantage of the opportunity and we failed again to find an agreement. I just managed to catch the last plane back to London, listening on the radio to statements by Tony and by President Clinton on the bombing of Iraq.

In 1999, Mo appointed Frank Blair of the Scottish industrial mediation service, ACAS, to act as mediator. Our aim was to keep travelling in the talks even if we couldn't immediately arrive at a solution. But on 15 March, Rosemary Nelson, a Catholic solicitor who had helped the residents as their legal adviser, was blown up by a bomb placed under her car which exploded just outside her eight-year-old daughter's school. This ghastly murder made any hope of agreement even more remote.

Frank Blair gave up his quest in June and Tony and I met both sides in Castle Buildings when we were in Belfast for talks on 15 June. The residents were cheerful but the Orange Order were angry. We met them around a long table in Mo's office. They brought with them Richard Monteith, a Protestant solicitor, and as tempers flared he accused Tony of lying. I am usually a mild-mannered and restrained public servant, but Monteith made my blood boil and I jumped to my feet and tried to grab him across the table, saying he could not speak to the Prime Minister like that. I don't know what came over me, but I could easily have hit him. Some splinter of Northern Ireland must have entered my soul. Tony had to tell me sharply to sit down and restrain myself, and later said to me he never lost his temper in public situations unless he did so deliberately for reasons of calculation.

It was at this time that Tony almost lost heart. On 21 June he recorded a TV programme with children from Northern Ireland who were almost more bigoted than their parents and grandparents. Afterwards he was so depressed he said he would never go back to the Province, although this didn't stop him sending me back almost immediately for another session of shuttling between the Orange Order and the residents. My first stop was to visit the Garvaghy Road, with two hours of meetings in the residents' community centre and then a drive round the route of the march with MacCionnaith. The Orange Order spotted me in his car and became convinced I had gone over to the other side.

The next day was awful. I noted in my diary that it was 'the sort of day that would drive you mad. It is hard to work out which side is more unreasonable, the Orange or the residents.' My NIO team and I set up shop in the Craigavon council offices. The residents had given us a completely outrageous proposal in the morning and David Trimble came to tell us at lunchtime that the Orange Order rejected it out of hand. Then Gerry Kelly, the Sinn Féin security spokesman, came to see us to tell us that a march that year would be very difficult. I sent David Campbell off to see the Orangemen and Peter Quinn to see the residents but neither came back with anything workable. Tony called me from London to tell me to get on with it, and I suggested that he do something useful instead of harassing me, like calling Alistair Graham to have another go at persuading him to put off his decision.

Overnight I finally had a good idea and decided that, instead of allowing myself to be subject to mental torture by the two sides for another day, I would summon the residents to direct face-to-face talks at Stormont House with four Orangemen – David Trimble, David Campbell, David McNarry and Graham Montgomery (the latter two UUP officials). Admittedly they were not the leaders of the Portadown Orangemen, but they were senior in the Order and the residents had been demanding face-to-face talks. When we put the proposal to the residents, they began to argue among themselves in front of us and I had a frisson of triumph at finally having wrong-footed MacCionnaith. They had no option but to attend. Once we got the talks going at Stormont House, and after a few hours of rather sterile point-scoring, the residents suddenly suggested the idea of an act of reconciliation with marches by both sides. This bought us a bit of time and we went to see the Parades Commission in central Belfast late at night to get them to put off their decision. Tony saw the Orange Order and the residents when he came over the next day for political talks with the parties but was unable to get to an agreement on the march. He hinted that there might be a march in 1999, which gave the Orange Order enough of a glimmer of hope that we were able to avoid any serious violence for another year.

The process meandered on with a review of the Parades Commission that had been demanded by the Orange Order, and a new, more sensible choice for the chair in the form of Tony Holland, a distinguished solicitor. The new commission set out ways in which the Orange Order could satisfy their conditions and secure their march later in 1999, but in their usual pig-headed way the Order managed to ignore this concession. Brian Currin, a South African mediator, then tried his hand at finding a solution in 2000. By the time Harold Gracey, who refused to leave his caravan at Drumcree, died on 29 March 2004, the problem of Drumcree had still not been solved. But, by then, the peace process had moved on, and it had become a dead letter.

Byzantine though the process of negotiation had been, it had served two purposes. The first was to prevent serious rioting around the issue of the march, since violence was less likely while the two sides were talking. The second was the quashing once and for all of the 'Orange card' that had bedevilled British rule in Ireland for over a century. In the first part of the twentieth century it was Carson and the threat of Loyalist paramilitary violence in part that had pushed the British government into partition. In 1974 it was the Loyalist Workers strike that had finished off Brian Faulkner and the Sunningdale Agreement. Loyalists had faced down Harold Wilson after his disparaging comments about 'spongers' in the 1970s. And they had boycotted the Thatcher government's plans after the Anglo-Irish Agreement. They tried to do the same after the Good Friday Agreement, and their battlefield was Drumcree. Yet we stood firm, and as a result of fate, the terrible death of the three Quinn children, and endless patience in negotiation, the Orange card failed to work and the Agreement had passed its first test. But my optimistic diary entry on Sunday 12 July 1998, stating that I could see a 'sea change' in Northern Ireland was premature.

In fact, it was going to take another nine years before we could implement the Good Friday Agreement and the Province was about to face the worst terrorist atrocity in its history.

7

Getting Through Decommissioning: August 1998–October 1999

On Saturday 15 August 1998, at ten past three in the afternoon, a bomb of between two hundred and three hundred pounds went off in the sleepy market town of Omagh, killing twenty-nine people and injuring hundreds, many of them horrifically. When the smoke cleared, the main street was a scene of carnage with destroyed buildings and water spraying from burst water mains. It was strewn with the twisted wreckage of cars, and limbs torn from bodies by the force of the blast. Among the dead were a woman pregnant with twins, whose mother and daughter also died, and four children on a Spanish exchange programme trip, as well as one of their escorts, who had come over the border from Buncrana in Donegal for a day out. The Real IRA had given a warning to Ulster Television using a recognised code word and saying the bomb was a hundred yards from the courthouse. The police had started evacuating people away from the courthouse and right into the force of the blast which was in fact four hundred yards from the building.

The peace in the peace process had been shattered, but no one saw it as a reason to give up. Rather it was seen as a reason to redouble our efforts to ensure such senseless violence never happened again. In an internal note to the key people in No. 10, Tony said that the bombing shouldn't be seen as a return to the past and that the political process could, and still would, move forward. All the party leaders in Northern Ireland said something similar. If Drumcree had been a test of the government's will to defend the Agreement, then Omagh was a test of the people's resolve. The peace process was in the balance immediately after Omagh and if the people of Northern Ireland had lost their nerve the process could have ended then.

The day after the bomb, Tony came back from holiday in France to visit Omagh. He was appalled at what he saw, and particularly upset by a little girl who had lost her sight in the explosion. I did not visit Omagh until we went there with President Clinton on 3 September when we met seven hundred representatives of the victims and their families and saw the site of the bomb. I found the visit harrowing. I met a man who had lost his pregnant wife and two-year-old daughter, and was left with three children under five to bring up by himself. There were so many individual tragedies like his.

One of the few good things to come out of the horror was that the RIRA was fatally discredited and never recovered. On 18 August they announced they were suspending operations and on 7 September they announced a complete cessation of violence. Shortly thereafter they started making overtures to the Irish government through a Catholic priest, in the hope of securing the release of their prisoners. At the time of writing, they remain in existence, but badly split and, thank God, unable so far to mount an effective operation. Their failure was not predestined. As a republican commented at the time, if the RIRA had managed to kill policemen and soldiers instead of mounting a ham-fisted and indiscriminate massacre of civilians, it might have become a convincing rival and successor to the Provisional IRA.

Tony saw the Omagh bomb as an opportunity for Sinn Féin to say the war was over. After it happened, Adams and McGuinness were quick to condemn the attack, describing it as 'indefensible' and saying they were 'appalled' and 'disgusted'. But Tony wanted them to go further. Adams explained why it was impossible, under republican theology, to announce the end of the war when the causes of conflict were still unresolved. However, he said privately to Tony that 'as time passed the chances of the mainstream IRA going back to violence were reduced. People were becoming rusty and getting on with their lives.'

Tony also moved rapidly on the security front. He wanted measures to reassure the public that the terrorists would be dealt with. In his note after the attack he proposed that the RIRA be proscribed and that membership become an offence which could be proved merely by the evidence of a senior police officer. He ruled out, however, a return to internment. When I saw the legislation, I was worried it was a bit of a mouse, but it was certainly preferable to a return to the policy that had been so disastrous in the 1970s. The Irish government was, as ever, more robust than us. Having passed legislation outlawing membership of the RIRA, they successfully prosecuted several RIRA leaders, while we fenced our legislation about with so many restrictions that, in the UK, it was more or less impossible to convict anyone of membership just on the word of a senior police officer.

Tony tried to persuade Adams and McGuinness to support these security measures, but again they explained it was not yet possible for them to endorse action by the RUC, and in the end Tony gave up pressing them. Parliament was recalled on 2 September so that Tony could make a statement on the bombing and the emergency legislation could be passed. He was unused to attending debates in the House, and sitting there in the Chamber this time he got worried when the Liberal Democrats started making a fuss about the 'guillotine' motion that allowed the bill to pass quickly, not realising the noise they were making was just part of the usual silliness that went on. Tony thought we were actually going to lose the vote. He even summoned the chief whip. She was able to reassure him, and Paddy Ashdown called up later to apologise.

President Clinton visited Northern Ireland on 3 September at the height of the Monica Lewinsky row. I left London with Tony at five thirty in the morning to arrive in Belfast in time to welcome him. Air Force One pulled into Aldergrove airport with great pomp and we whistled off to Stormont in the biggest motorcade Northern Ireland had ever seen. We were anxious to avoid photographs of the Prime Minister with leading Republicans and went to great lengths to do so, but there was nothing we could do when New York Congressman Peter King, a long-term IRA supporter, took out his camera and snapped Tony with Gerry Adams, Tony with Martin McGuinness and even Tony with Gerry Kelly. Fortunately, none of these pictures made it into the press but the possibility of a similar photo opportunity arising worried us all day. At the opening of the Springvale campus, which was in Gerry Adams's constituency, Adams made a huge fuss, demanding that he be on the stage with Clinton and Tony. In the end we allowed him up there, but kept him to one side, at a distance from them. Before the event, Tony took Adams aside in order to bend his ear on decommissioning. Clinton pressed him too, but then fell fast asleep on the Green Room sofa. I came in to the comic picture of Clinton snoring away and Tony jabbing at Adams.

At the Waterfront Hall, David Trimble made an ill-judged speech, harsh and divisive rather than warm and inclusive as the situation demanded. David Trimble was not a natural politician and could be an intensely irritating man. He was irascible and over the years managed to alienate the members of his party one by one. He had an irritating habit of picking up a book and starting to read it while you were talking to him or answering his mobile phone to talk to a journalist in the middle of a meeting, and flying into a towering, red-faced rage at what seemed to be only the slightest provocation. For all that, David Trimble was a vulnerable figure and I found it hard not to like him even when he was being impossible. He had the one cardinal political virtue of being brave. On the really important decisions he always did the right thing, even though it cost him his political career and the future of his party.

Later that afternoon, we helicoptered down to Armagh city for a big rally. It was inspirational. Clinton lit up in contact with the crowd. He ditched his prepared speech and ad-libbed, 'When I go to Israel and Palestine, I say, look at Northern Ireland; when I go to India and Pakistan and they are trying to sort out Kashmir, I say look at Northern Ireland; when I go to Sri Lanka and all the other trouble spots of the world, I say look at Northern Ireland. Peace is within reach.' Tony followed suit and threw away his prepared speech. I would have come away feeling optimistic if I hadn't put my foot in it. I was standing at the back of the crowd with the American delegation and spotted a woman who looked remarkably like Nancy Soderberg, my ex-tennis partner and former adviser to Clinton on matters Irish. I walked up behind her and said, 'Nancy,' leaning forward and puckering my lips for a kiss. She said, 'Yes,' and turned round, but then pulled away. 'Aren't you going to kiss me?' I asked. 'No,' she said, and stalked off. A couple of Americans were sniggering behind me, so I asked them what the problem was. It turned out the woman I had tried to kiss was not Nancy Soderberg at all but one of Hillary Clinton's secret service agents. I was very lucky not to be shot.

The only good news we had that autumn was the award of the Nobel Peace Prize. We had been terrified they would award it to Adams and Hume, and were mightily relieved when they chose Hume and Trimble.

We invited Trimble to address the Labour Party conference in October, a first for both the Unionists and the Labour Party, and rather risky given there was no love lost between the two. Clare Short, who was chair of the conference at that point suddenly tried to move the time of the lunch break so that Trimble would be addressing an empty hall. We managed to pull it back just in time, and he was politely received.

Meanwhile, we continued to push for the establishment of the Executive at Stormont. The central conundrum we faced was still, inevitably, decommissioning. The two positions were pithily expressed by the graffiti on the walls of the two communities. On the unionist side, it read 'No guns, no government' and on the republican side, 'Not an ounce, not a bullet'. The UUP would not agree to the establishment of the Executive until the IRA had begun to decommission its weapons, but Adams said the IRA would not decommission until the causes of conflict had been resolved, in part through the establishment of the Executive. The 'constructive' ambiguity we had built into the Good Friday Agreement was now destructive. It required decommissioning by May 2000 but didn't say how we got there other than through the 'best efforts' of the parties. Adams said we should leave decommissioning to de Chastelain and the International Independent Commission on Decommissioning (IICD) but Trimble said it was politically necessary before the Executive could be established.

We did not have a crisis, or the collapse of the process, but we had an impasse and no one seemed to have any clear idea how to get round it. In early September, some in the NIO, and even John Holmes in No. 10, began to suggest we should give up on our seemingly hopeless quest for decommissioning. Tony refused. He said privately decommissioning was something we had to get through, not round, and the process must not be allowed to stagnate.

Interestingly, it had been the aftermath of Omagh that provided Tony with the germ of an idea for the next stage in the process. On 26 August, eleven days after the bomb, he had travelled down from Northern Ireland to Ashford Castle in the Republic to meet Bertie Ahern. He had been flown in an Irish Air Force helicopter and called me afterwards to complain about the bumpy flight, and that the seats were too small and the roof too low. He liked to travel in comfort. Then he said he'd come up with a six-point plan which he thought he had agreed with David Trimble: Adams was to say something to the effect that the war was over and Trimble would convene a meeting of all the parties; McGuinness would become the interlocutor with General de Chastelain and the IICD, and Trimble would agree to meet Adams; finally the IRA would decommission some weapons and Trimble would agree to form the Executive. I told Tony I was sceptical either side could accept anything like it, but it was an idea.

It was becoming increasingly important to get Adams and Trimble to meet face to face. Following Tony's six-point plan, we worked away at a statement by Adams that would make a meeting possible, and he eventually came up with something halfway acceptable, which he delivered on 1 September. We massively hyped it up, so that Trimble had to welcome it, even if begrudgingly. But then he declined to convene the all-party meeting as he had promised, saying it would look too choreographed. Eventually we managed to manoeuvre Trimble into a meeting with Adams. Even though it was behind closed doors and there was no handshake, it felt like an historic occasion: it was the first meeting between Republican and Unionist leaders since the 1920s.

Both men complained to us about the meeting afterwards. Trimble felt that Adams was failing to deliver on decommissioning, thereby putting him in an invidious position with his party. And he asked us to stop Mo trying to bounce him into the Executive, warning the party would desert him if he agreed to that without decommissioning. He was also adamant that if we went ahead without decommissioning and ran d'Hondt to appoint the Executive he would have to resign and had no certainty of being re-elected as First Minister. Adams said the meeting had been fine at the personal level but Trimble had been 'unrealistic' in his demands.

The Assembly met on 14 September but still failed to nominate the Executive. And it was late December before we could get the parties to agree even on the number and nature of the ministries to be filled and the precise nature of the North/South bodies. Bertie Ahern got depressed about the tortuous negotiations on such trivial issues. I was surprised that no one else seemed to share my sense of déjà vu from the final stages of the Good Friday negotiations on exactly the same points.

I tried to get Adams to meet me so we could start frank discussions, but he came up with every sort of excuse: it was his wife's birthday; the meeting would become public. I think he was afraid of being put in a corner. We finally agreed to meet in the margins of the Labour Party conference. Tony called Trimble to tell him what I was doing, and got him on his mobile just as he was being bundled by the police out of the Orange hall in Portadown through a crowd of protestors, having addressed a hostile gathering of the local Orange Order.

My meeting with Adams didn't lead to any movement, however. He told me that 'historically the IRA has never decommissioned weapons and it is not going to start now'. If the political context changed then that might change. I disabused him of the notion that Trimble was posturing, and suggested that de Chastelain set the timetable for decommissioning. But Adams said I wasn't listening: the IRA wasn't thinking of decommissioning, so it wouldn't agree to a timetable. I said to him we had a stand-off. Everyone kept saying we must find a way through but there was no obvious route out.

In the course of the next month we went round in circles. The Irish suggested it would be sufficient for McGuinness to assure Trimble privately that decommissioning was going to happen and for de Chastelain to declare publicly that he believed it would happen. But this didn't work: it wasn't enough for Trimble; McGuinness wasn't prepared to give the assurance; and nor was de Chastelain prepared to make the assertion without some evidence it was true. The IICD tried to find a way out of the impasse by suggesting the idea of 'a bang in the woods', whereby the IRA destroyed some of its own explosives and weapons. But while John Taylor agreed to this on behalf of the Unionists, McGuinness said it was not possible at that moment.

Trimble became increasingly anxious about his party, confiding in me that they were plotting against him in the run-up to their conference in October. They hoped to use Molyneaux as the rallying point for opposition. The key question was whether they had enough strength to requisition an Ulster Unionist Council meeting. He had made sure Jeffrey Donaldson would be out of the country at the time of the conference, and in the end he got through unscathed.

On 10 November McGuinness called me wanting to talk. He asked me to come to Derry incognito without telling anyone, so the securocrats would not know I was there. I said jokingly I would come as long as they didn't kill me, but I thought quite deeply about whether the visit was sensible before I went. I wasn't particularly afraid of what would happen to me, but I was worried about cutting the NIO and the security forces out of what I was doing. I checked with Tony and he wanted me to go, so I called McGuinness and agreed. I took a scheduled flight on 18 November, and then a taxi all the way from Aldergrove airport to Derry. The driver was delighted to get such a long journey and talked all the way about his former career as a professional cyclist. When I got to Derry I stood apprehensively outside the Trinity Hotel waiting for someone to recognise me. Two seedy-looking men came up and said, 'Martin sent us,' then ushered me into a waiting car. The men were as taciturn as the taxi driver had been talkative. They drove me around and around the town in what appeared to be a series of circles on our way to the safe house where we were to meet. While we were in the car, my phone rang. It was the office. They told me Paddy Ashdown had called in a rage that we were apparently not going to reintroduce the European elections bill, and was threatening to call the whole Lib-Lab deal off. I explained I couldn't deal with it from where I was and said that Tony would have to speak to him.

Eventually we pulled into a close of small, neat, newly built houses and I got out and rang a doorbell. Martin McGuinness appeared at the door on crutches. He had broken his leg. He ushered me in without coming out from behind the front door himself so no one could see him and led me into the kitchen where he was making a cup of tea. The house was extraordinarily tidy and festooned with Celtic knick-knacks and embroidered prayers to the Madonna. The lady of the house had gone out, leaving a plate of biscuits and not asking what the house was to be used for.

There was a fire burning in the small sitting room, and we settled down in the easy chairs. McGuinness was polite and never threatening. I said that we were under pressure from the Tories, who felt we were being too lenient on prisoner release. We needed something to work with. I tried redefining decommissioning. Perhaps Semtex and detonators and a bang in the woods? Perhaps they could tell de Chastelain where the dumps were? Or they could agree a timetable for decommissioning ... He said it was all out of the question. The history meant it would look like surrender. Their troops were getting restive at the non-implementation of the Agreement. Only once the Executive was up and running would decommissioning cease to be a problem. Major and Mayhew had made decommissioning the issue at the behest of the securocrats and it had become a block on progress. We should not make that mistake again. The more we focused on it, the harder it would be to do.

According to McGuinness, all that was needed was a statement from de Chastelain saying that all the parties were cooperating fully. I suggested this was problematic, given that the only thing de Chastelain currently had to go on was a statement from the IRA saying there would be no decommissioning. We needed something new. Could the IRA make a different statement? McGuinness said he and Adams were stopping the IRA making a worse statement. I urged him to use his imagination and think of something new to say to de Chastelain, but he said he had run out of imagination, something we were to hear pretty often from him and Adams during the process. As I left, escorted by the same two men, I said we could bring the party leaders together again in December and try to get the Executive up and running, but it would only work if he could come up with some new idea on decommissioning. We both agreed we had to find an answer where de Chastelain took some of the weight, but it wasn't at all clear what the answer might be. I was glad the Republicans had enough confidence in me to invite me to their inner sanctum for such a conversation. I assumed they wanted to talk to me because I was close to the Unionists and could give them a sense of what would and wouldn't work with them.

We saw all the party leaders again on 25 November, but nothing came out of the meeting, apart from a wonderful but pointless argument between Trimble and Mallon in front of us. Tony tried to sell the idea of letting the weapons rust in the ground to Adams, then asked me to try it on de Chastelain, who made the obvious point that modern weapons do not, like pikes or muskets, 'rust in the ground', and Semtex has a life expectancy of twenty years.

In fact, the battle over decommissioning was entirely symbolic. We all knew perfectly well that any terrorist movement could acquire new

weapons whenever it wanted, so getting rid of them was no guarantee of peace. The issue was really trust. Could republicans convince
unionists that they had really put violence behind them for good and
opted for exclusively peaceful means? Tony would often compare our
negotiations with those going on in the Middle East. The unionists
were the Israelis and the republicans were the Palestinians, and we
were the Americans trying to bring the two sides together and get
them to trust each other, while also having cards in our hands (in the
form of subsidies and security guarantees in the case of the US in the
Middle East). He had a point, and sometimes the parallels between
the two processes were eerie, but I would point out the differences.
In this case the British government was not only a facilitator of the
talks, but a major player. We were actually ruling Northern Ireland
so we could determine what happened on the ground even if we did
not have any selfish interest in what the outcome was, other than that
it was peaceful and that it was acceptable to the two sides.

As we tipped into 1999, the Irish began to see signs of Republican
flexibility on decommissioning that were not apparent to the naked
eye. Bertie told Tony privately that the IRA had been on the verge of
approving an act of decommissioning to follow one month after the
establishment of the Executive. Rather more surprisingly, David
Trimble started having similar fits of optimism. On 16 February Sean
O'Callaghan called me to tell me that, on the basis of his reading of
their tactics, he had assured Trimble that the IRA would decommission. On 11 June Trimble told me he had heard of an indirect approach
from Francie Molloy, a leading Sinn Féin figure, saying that they were
arranging a major decommissioning event in the Republic and had
approached a distinguished figure in Northern Ireland, who Trimble
declined to name, to verify it. On another occasion, a visit by Gerry
Kelly to the Maze prison produced a rumour that he was consulting
the prisoners on an act of decommissioning.

On the other hand, Martin McGuinness was perfectly clear with
me when he came to see me on 9 February (smuggled in through a
side door to No. 10 so the press didn't see him). He said that 'we had
to understand, no bullshit, that there was no chance of an act of
decommissioning or of them making a promise on decommissioning'.
He went on to say that RIRA were waiting for decommissioning as

an opportunity to act. Young republicans were restless. 'There was a real threat that someone would give a gun to some impressionable seventeen-year-old and get them to shoot Adams or him.'

John Holmes, being cautious, commissioned work at the beginning of January (before he left No. 10 to become ambassador in Lisbon and was replaced by another senior diplomat, John Sawers) on what would happen if the IRA ceasefire broke down again. He did not want us to be caught unawares, as Major had been with Canary Wharf.

Having failed to get anywhere in 1998 we decided to resort to deadlines again in 1999. The date proposed for the setting up of the Executive was 10 March, but it came and went without any agreement. As did 25 March. Meanwhile, Bertie Ahern had suggested the idea of an 'act of reconciliation' in a phone call to Tony on 8 March. He said he had discussed it with Sinn Féin. The idea was that, on a chosen day, the IRA would destroy some of their weapons at the same time as the British security forces destroyed some of theirs. The weapons would then be built into some sort of monument, verified by the IICD, allowing the Executive to be set up.

Bilateral discussions between Sinn Féin and the UUP had been getting nowhere so Tony and Bertie Ahern went to Belfast on Monday 29 March to see if they could make progress towards an agreement. The war in Kosovo was under way at the time and Tony was distracted. I really wanted to go too but my second daughter was due imminently so I decided to stay at home. John Sawers went with him. I recorded in my diary that I had a sense they wouldn't find a way through that week, although I hoped I was wrong.

The symbolism of the discussions taking place on the anniversary of the Good Friday Agreement was obvious to all. Tony called me on Tuesday from Hillsborough to say that he saw a glimmer of hope and he thought he had the UUP and Sinn Féin on the hook. They were working through all the options for getting through decommissioning. He returned briefly to London for Prime Minister's Questions on Wednesday 31 March and called me again on his way back to Belfast. It seemed to me they were a long way from finding a resolution. They worked through Wednesday night, but then Sinn Féin turned up with a long shopping list of demands at two thirty in the morning so Tony sent the UUP off to bed. Trimble went home to sleep, but Tony gave up his own bed at Hillsborough to Ken Maginnis.

On the morning of Thursday 1 April, Tony and Bertie stood on the steps of Hillsborough Castle and announced the proposal for an 'act of reconciliation' in the 'Hillsborough Declaration'. Tony had wanted to stay on to get the parties to sign off on the proposal, but Bertie said it was madness to stay till Easter given all Tony had to do on Kosovo and other issues, and so they left the parties to consult and come back with their reactions. While the UUP was positive, the Republicans were harder to convince. Adams had spent much of the time at Hillsborough consulting his colleagues in the gardens because he didn't trust the walls, and had even disappeared altogether for a couple of hours. But he hadn't succeeded in convincing them, and on 2 April Sinn Féin rejected the proposal. Even if they had been able to agree to it, we would have had a serious problem with the security forces who hated the idea of equivalence between their weapons and those of terrorists.

After the failure, Adams called Tony to make up on 14 April. Tony said he understood why the IRA did not want to be told what to do. Adams said he 'could not just wish away the last thirty years': the IRA said to him that cessation of violence should be enough, but now the Unionists were demanding they give up their weapons, which was entirely unacceptable. Still Tony wanted to try again. On 19 April, he and Bertie Ahern summoned the three major parties to Downing Street. I'd spoken on the phone to Trimble, who was optimistic, and thought Sinn Féin were just negotiating. But in another phone conversation between Tony and Adams, Adams had said he did not see any way forward. Decommissioning would only happen if political circumstances changed. He went on: 'There was a huge risk that it [decommissioning] would be seen as a sell-out by some and there would be a split in the IRA. His contribution was his ability to deliver, otherwise he was just another nationalist politician.' It looked as though we were stuck again, but Tony was determined to avoid a vacuum. He did not want a delay or a review and was considering putting our proposals to an all-Ireland referendum if the other parties would sign up to them.

We began looking for a new way of resolving the problem posed by the refusal of either side to go first. We tried to break the process into little steps which would then be choreographed so that both sides had confidence they were moving together, rather than feeling as if they were having to trust the other side to reciprocate if they made the first move. Things looked a little more interesting when, on 5 May, we met the Irish and Sinn Féin in Jury's Inn, an Irish hotel in west London, and Adams told us that, in a big meeting he'd had with his team two weeks before, they'd agreed that he could say they were confident that decommissioning would be complete by May 2000. Tony put the proposition to Trimble the next day, in a meeting at Downing Street with Bertie Ahern, and, to my surprise, Trimble didn't turn red and storm out. He did, however, appear nervous, as he always did when confronted with a decision. I was sent off with the Irish Cabinet Secretary Paddy Teahon to negotiate possible texts with Sinn Féin. When we came back, Tony and Bertie had another meeting with Trimble. This time, John Taylor and Reg Empey were also present, and Tony put the proposition to them, admittedly in a rather oblique fashion, and they too didn't react badly, although I wasn't sure they had grasped the full import of it. The UUP then met bilaterally with Sinn Féin and even that went well. Things were looking so promising that Adams and Bertie Ahern became worried the Unionists had misunderstood the proposal.

By the end of the day, the UUP position appeared to be that they could accept the promise of decommissioning in statements from Adams and the IRA, as long as they had failsafe legislation that gave them a way out if the IRA did not actually decommission once the Executive was in place. However, Trimble didn't want to pursue this option until after the European parliamentary elections in June because he was afraid any initiative now might affect their prospects in the election, and Sinn Féin were saying it had to happen immediately. While we were meeting the parties downstairs at No. 10, Cherie Blair was showing fashion designer Ralph Lauren around the state rooms upstairs. They ran into Martin McGuinness in the White Room, and he in turn introduced Ralph Lauren to Gerry Kelly (notorious for his dapper turnout) and made a great show of asking for an assessment of Kelly's matching grey and beige outfit. Adams and McGuinness themselves always opted for a version of smart casual we called 'terrorist chic'.

We had several more meetings in Downing Street in the course of May, although we were mainly preoccupied with Kosovo. I began every day's entry in my diary under the heading 'War and Peace'. The proposal was that Sinn Féin would undertake to 'successfully persuade' the IRA to decommission within the timescale of the Agreement; the IRA would make a statement backing this up; the Executive would be set up and then the IRA would appoint a representative to the IICD in order to agree how decommissioning was to be carried out. Trimble agreed to work on this approach as long as he had a guarantee that decommissioning would take place in reality, but on Friday 14 May I noted that John Taylor left the negotiating session early and Reg Empey failed to turn up at all, which was a clear sign we would have problems on the Unionist side.

My fears were borne out over the weekend when the UUP rejected the deal and we had to create yet another deadline for agreement on setting up the Executive, this time for 30 June, after the European elections. As I noted: 'Adams thought he could sell "Hillsborough" but failed. Trimble thought he could sell "Downing Street" but failed. So it is 1-all.' Thinking back over the events of that week, during which Downing Street had been taken over by the Northern Ireland parties, each based in a different state room, the images that stayed in my mind were not so much of the negotiations themselves, but of Bertie Ahern, David Trimble, Gerry Adams, Martin McGuinness, John Hume and Seamus Mallon all joking away in Tony's office after he had gone to bed, exhausted after a day of endless meetings (the personification of the old saw that the Brits leave and don't say goodbye, while the Irish say goodbye and don't leave). And of the moment Adams and McGuinness managed to escape from the building and into the No. 10 garden – years of training, I suppose. I looked out of the window to see them playing with the Blair children and trying to ride Nicky Blair's skateboard down the path through the rose garden. I was terrified they would be photographed and rushed outside to shepherd them back in.

Having been fed up with Adams and McGuinness after the collapse of the Hillsborough Declaration, we were now fed up with Trimble in May and June for failing to get his party to agree to the Downing Street approach. The UUP were spending so long negotiating with themselves they were leaving no time to negotiate with the other side. Trimble complained to me that we were distancing ourselves from him.

Tony now wanted to put more weight on what de Chastelain could do on decommissioning – get him to report on the timetable and how it was to be done. I said we should be aiming to get both sides to jump together by agreeing devolution and a timetable for decommissioning simultaneously. This was what we tried to achieve through late May and June, but Taylor, Empey and Trimble were very negative when we invited them for an informal discussion over dinner in Downing Street on 10 June. They were adamant that absolutely no progress could be made without an act of decommissioning. Taylor tried pushing his idea of limited, Welsh-style devolution, but even his colleagues rejected it. Tony made it clear he was serious about the 30 June deadline, and set out our proposal: a Sinn Féin statement setting a date for decommissioning; an IRA statement; and de Chastelain then dealing with the modalities and timetable of decommissioning. There would also be an escape clause if decommissioning did not take place. The three of them didn't give us an outright 'no' this time, but they didn't engage.

Tony used a speech he gave at Stranmills College on 14 June to say publicly what he had been saying privately for a while: 'Decommissioning can be got through, but it can't be got round.' It was not, he said, a precondition for devolution but it was a requirement of the Good Friday Agreement. He appealed to the people of Northern Ireland to urge politicians on both sides to be more flexible.

Trimble expressed his displeasure to me immediately after the speech, complaining that we were continuing to distance ourselves from him, and saying that John Taylor had threatened to resign if they settled for anything less than an act of decommissioning. The following week, he mounted an attack on the government in the press, criticising Tony personally and calling for Mo's resignation. Tony responded by writing an article for *The Times* on 25 June setting out publicly what was on offer and urging all sides to accept it. I had some reservations about revealing our hand in this way but was persuaded that throwing a grenade into the process might be the only way to save it, given Trimble's position. The Irish came to London that day so that Bertie could attend Cardinal Hume's funeral with Tony. By lunchtime the Irish had got over their irritation at the article and the British and Irish teams flew off together to Belfast. We met the parties and to our surprise persuaded them to agree to the three principles we had set out in advance: an inclusive Executive; decommissioning by May 2000; and the manner of decommissioning to be determined by de Chastelain – even with Jeffrey Donaldson as again part of the UUP negotiating team.

We then went into six days of discussions in which Tony held a total of seventy-five meetings with the parties. This time we had decided to hold the negotiations in Castle Buildings, despite our hatred for the place, rather than Hillsborough, in the hope some of the luck that had produced the Good Friday Agreement would rub off on us. On Tuesday 29 June both Sinn Féin and the UUP were telling us we were in the ballpark, and the first day of talks became infused with optimism despite the fact that we hadn't actually pinned anything down. I was charged with keeping de Chastelain happy; what he said was crucial to making the plan work. Quite correctly, he jealously protected his independence and objected when Alastair Campbell announced publicly he would be putting a report out. But in the end, we needn't have worried: his report was excellent. The timetable stated that the process of decommissioning would start a couple of days after devolution and that the act of decommissioning would be complete a few weeks after that.

However, as dawn came up over Castle Buildings on the day of the 30 June deadline, we were still faced with a problem. Although Adams and McGuinness were forthcoming in private about the IRA's intentions, they could not express them publicly. The statement Sinn Féin had produced was hopelessly weak and the IRA had yet to produce theirs. Among those coming into the building in the course of the night were some increasingly senior paramilitary figures, who went in to see Adams, so that I thought Tony might end up meeting the entire IRA Army Council by morning.

At 5 a.m. we drove back to Hillsborough and had a brief rest before reappearing at Stormont at midday. In order to try to get the UUP on board, Tony bounced the Irish by making a statement to the waiting TV cameras as we were coming back into Castle Buildings about introducing legislation to exclude the IRA if there were no decommissioning. As a result Bertie spent a good part of the day refusing to speak to him. But once the Irish had come out of their sulk, they came to us with a proposition about how to break the deadlock. They wanted us to persuade the UUP to agree that we should set 15 August as the date for an act of decommissioning and run d'Hondt to set up the Executive at the same time. They added that they wanted us to go ahead with the election for the Executive even if the UUP did not agree. Tony persuaded Trimble to support 15 August as the trigger date. But when we went back to Paddy Teahon to tell him of our success, he said their proposal had been rejected by Sinn Féin and he wanted us to put another, different, proposition to the UUP. We should put off devolution to September and decommissioning to October. Tony went back to see Trimble again, and even addressed the UUP Assembly group, who accepted the proposal. But when we went back to the Irish they said that wouldn't run either. Now they wanted us to propose that de Chastelain set the timetable for decommissioning. This left us with a huge handling problem. We had persuaded the UUP to accept two different proposals at the instigation of the Irish, but now the Irish wanted us to go back to them again and sell a third idea. Tony tried, but not surprisingly they rejected it, while pointing out they could accept either of the two previous ideas. The problem was not so much one of substance as that they felt they were being messed around. Throughout all this process Tony kept going when most of us had given up. He eventually managed to persuade Trimble, Taylor and Maginnis to accept the third proposal but they were unable to sell it to the rest of their party.

On the afternoon of Friday 2 July, Tony and Bertie launched the 'Way Forward' document on the steps of Castle Buildings as they had the Good Friday Agreement a bit more than a year before. Tony said he detected a 'seismic shift' in the Republican position. This time, however, the deal had faded by the time we got to the airport. We listened to the radio news and it talked of sinking feelings. They could have been describing our mood in the motorcade. McGuinness called me to say he was disgusted by the failsafe clause giving the Unionists a way out if the IRA did not decommission and would not even try to sell the deal to Republicans. But the real problem was on the Unionist side. Tony spoke to Trimble a few days later and he sounded close to despair about the possibility of getting it past his colleagues. He had said he would try to be helpful, but I didn't see much sign of it. Although Trimble, Taylor and Empey still seemed ready to accept the deal when they came to see us on 7 July, two days later the UUP executive criticised the 'Way Forward' document, saying it was profoundly unfair on unionists. Meanwhile, Adams complained to us that *An Phoblacht*, the Republican newspaper, was asking why the Brits thought decommissioning would happen. They were raising suspicions about what Adams had said in private, making his job more difficult.

We tried to keep the deal alive in the following days. We produced the failsafe legislation the Unionists had wanted and forced it through, despite the Irish complaining like mad and going to the length of calling the Clinton administration in the hope of getting them to lean on us. Irritatingly, Trimble told us afterwards he was more interested in the IRA statement than the legislation. He seemed constantly to be moving the goalposts, and we were a way off getting a decent statement. In fact, far from providing an IRA statement, Adams produced an article in his own name denying he had ever made any commitments on decommissioning. That drove a coach and horses through our hope of a positive decision by the UUP. The next morning it became clear Trimble was not even trying to persuade his colleagues: he came out of his party executive after only fifteen minutes and announced he was saying 'no'.

The UUP's decision depressed me, but didn't make me want to give up. That day I noted in my diary the words of a taxi driver: 'Well done for trying but the problem of Northern Ireland is essentially insoluble.' I didn't agree with him: I knew the participants well enough still to think that, in the long term, we could make the Agreement work and that, at the very least, there wouldn't be a return to serious violence. We were, however, trapped on the escalator to running d'Hondt to establish the Executive, as we had promised to do if Sinn Féin agreed to the deal.

We set Thursday 15 July as the day when the Assembly would meet to choose the ministers in the Executive. At 10 a.m. Trimble called us to say the UUP would not be attending. The result was a farce. I watched on TV as they postured. Ian Paisley even thought about nominating DUP ministers to wrong-foot Trimble. But in the end only the Catholic parties put forward nominations, congratulating each other as if they were already real ministers. The appointment that caused the most ribaldry was that of Martin McGuinness as Minister of Agriculture: there were lots of wry comments about responsibility for fertiliser and sugar, the two key components of the IRA's home-made bombs. We tried desperately to get Seamus Mallon not to resign as Deputy First Minister, but in what appeared to us to be an extra-ordinary act of self-indulgence he ignored Tony's pleas and did so.

We found out at the last minute that the rules did not mean that Trimble was deemed to have resigned as well, so he remained as First Minister, which was just as well as it would have been difficult to get him re-elected. Paradoxically, though, these events had strengthened David Trimble within his own party. Unionists always like a leader who can say no. He told me he now believed he could get a deal done in the autumn. He needed to reform and modernise his party so he could get a better grip of it, but he wanted Tony to stay involved and wanted to assure him 'there had been no long-term damage to the relationship'.

We had tried two different ways to decommissioning but neither had worked, so this time we decided to try bringing in an outsider. On 20 July Bertie Ahern and Tony met George Mitchell in Downing Street and agreed Mitchell should conduct a review of the Good Friday Agreement to see if he could make progress where we had failed. The aborted nominations to the Executive led to a new mood among the parties. Tony was due to meet Adams and McGuinness on 21 July, but that morning, the IRA issued a hard-line statement that contained an element of threat, and was at first seen as an indication that they were ending the ceasefire. Tony called me suggesting he cancel his meeting with Adams and McGuinness, but I talked him out of it. Instead, he was very firm when he met them, saying that 'if the IRA carried out another Canary Wharf-type bombing, then it would be the last time he would see anyone related to the republican movement'. David Trimble, on the other hand, was full of beans the next day. The IRA statement had given the UUP the high ground and put them in a comfortable place. He came in through the side door to No. 10 to see me privately first and then went out again through the Cabinet Office, so that he could enter Downing Street openly and denounce the IRA to the assembled media outside the front door. When he saw Trimble, Tony advised him to reach out and make friends in other parties. Trimble retorted, 'Why should I make friends in other parties when I have none in my own?' He said the UUP would carry on discussions with Sinn Féin over the summer. Tony assured both Trimble and Adams that he would return to the issue in the autumn and sort it.

In the meantime a new problem had appeared in the form of the Patten report on the reform of the RUC which was to complicate negotiations further. Chris Patten had come to see us privately as early as 15 April to tell us that he aimed to achieve balance between the two sides by changing the name and symbols of the RUC while making sure that enough remained .of the old force to prevent republicans claiming it had been abolished. I'd had a further briefing on 21 July, when Bob Pierce, Patten's key adviser, came in to hand over the contents of the report. The recommendations seemed very sensible: they were for a smaller, more modern, more accountable police force, with some changes to the symbols, but with an emphasis on the fact that the RUC was not being disbanded. We had, however, failed to reckon with the curious nature of Northern Ireland politics where symbols can be more important than substance. After the report was published on 9 September, Trimble denounced it as 'the shoddiest piece of work he had seen for thirty years', and 'gratuitously offensive' to the RUC. Patten was shocked. He had been sure the attack would come from the republican side. For the next year we then had to deal with constant demands from Trimble to maintain the name of the RUC and its insignia. At times this issue seemed more important to him than decommissioning. From his point of view, the Good Friday Agreement had been intended to settle once and for all that Northern Ireland was part of the UK. It meant that it should be fine for the government to use the symbols of that Union, whether by flying the Union Jack over police stations or putting a crown on the police badge. For unionists, such symbols were an important mark of their identity. But of course they were anathema to republicans and nationalists who wanted the police to represent their aspirations as well.

A further question mark had also arisen over the IRA's ceasefire. A number of republicans had been arrested by the FBI in July for attempting to smuggle handguns from Florida, and an alleged IRA informer, Charles Bennett, had been murdered. When I saw Gerry Adams in Belfast on 4 August he was in a curious mood. He distanced himself from the gun-running and the murder. He was clearly worried we were going to exclude Sinn Féin and said he would resign as leader if we did. I said if anything more like this happened we would be in an intolerable position. He called Tony on the same subject after the summer break and said he was 'depressed, annoyed and politically frustrated by what had gone on. The silliness of what had been going on in the States was beyond him.' We felt there was insufficient evidence to declare the ceasefire breached, and Mo made the announcement to that effect in early September. But it was a worrying indication the IRA had not given up, and was persisting in pressing the boundaries of what was acceptable behaviour.

Trimble, too, was in a gloomy mood when I saw him on 2 September in Downing Street. (In order to avoid meeting him in my cycling shorts, I'd had to go into the building through the basement and change because he'd arrived before me.) He said the reaction of the unionist population to the concessions he had made was so negative, he wasn't sure he could even go on living in Northern Ireland. It was true: our focus groups showed unionist opinion drifting away. People were coming to believe the gap was too big for this generation to close.

Our main focus from July to September, however, was Mo herself. It is clear from Mo's autobiography that she thought the standing ovation she received at the Labour Party conference in 1998, when Tony had mentioned her name in his speech, had been a source of envy and dissatisfaction at No. 10. On the contrary, it was a big plus for the government and we were thrilled about it. Mo was one of the most popular figures in the Cabinet and her unconventional manner provided some interest and colour to politics that otherwise tended to be dull and monochrome. She naturally disliked Tony's attempts to run Northern Ireland policy himself and it irritated her to be cut out of some of the negotiations. But no one in No. 10 was gunning for her.

It was at the beginning of 1999 that she began to indicate to Tony that she would like to move on from the NIO into a bigger job. As usual there was lots of uninformed reshuffle speculation in the newspapers, some of it suggesting that Mo might be moved and she paid attention to it. I made a faux pas by making a joke on the subject. It was during the May talks between the Northern Ireland parties and we were all hanging around in my office waiting for the negotiations to conclude. Mo was feeling particularly fed up at being left out of the meetings, and I tried to lighten the mood with what I thought was a bit of friendly banter about a reshuffle being round the corner.

She stormed out of the room and I had to chase her down the corridor to the Cabinet Office to apologise profusely. I think she probably had me down as an enemy from that point.

A year had elapsed since Peter Mandelson had resigned from the government over Geoffrey Robinson's loan, and Tony was eager to bring him back into government. Clearly he couldn't put him back in a top-flight position, or anything the parliamentary Labour Party might consider enjoyable, such as Aid or Culture, since he was expected to do penance. Tony had therefore fixed on Northern Ireland, which would be seen as a suitable form of punishment. He also wanted to move Mo, not least because the Unionists had said they could no longer work with her. Unfortunately, Peter couldn't resist putting in the papers the suggestion that he was to take over. It sent Mo wild, and she immediately took an opportunity to say publicly that she wanted to stay on as Secretary of State for Northern Ireland. Tony saw her on Monday 19 July and suggested she move to Health or another big delivery department, but she wouldn't move for anything less than Foreign Secretary, Chancellor or Home Secretary. Tony explained these posts weren't on offer, but he really wanted her to move to one of the big jobs he was offering. She refused point-blank. As an afterthought, Mo offered to take Peter Mandelson as her deputy, and then went straight out and briefed the papers she wasn't for moving.

By the autumn, however, she'd changed her mind. Tony had been thinking of putting Peter in Defence, but Mo had had a pretty miserable summer in Northern Ireland, under public attack from the Unionists and with the process in stasis. She told Tony not to waste any more time on the problem of Northern Ireland, nothing could be done for three years or so and she indicated she was now ready to go. Even so, she was pretty bruised when, on Monday 11 October Tony appointed Peter as Northern Ireland Secretary and moved her to the Cabinet Office, and she continued to believe No. 10 had done her in. When there were stories in the papers suggesting that she should be the Labour candidate for Mayor of London she attributed them to me. It was true Tony thought she would be a good candidate but I had certainly never talked to the press about it. Later some really unpleasant articles appeared, particularly in the *New Statesman*, saying she was too ill to do her job properly and that she was not up to it intellectually.

Politics is a rough old business but these were well beyond the realm of normal bitchiness. I thought of writing to her to sympathise, but I feared she already suspected me of being behind any story about her and so decided not to. Shortly afterwards, stories appeared in the *Mail* newspapers accusing me of being the 'poisoner of Downing Street', implying I had been responsible for briefing the papers against Cabinet members, particularly Mo and Frank Dobson. I chose a suitable moment to assure Mo I was not briefing the media at all, and she insisted, rather theatrically, that we go and have a drink together and we went to the terrace at the House of Commons to make up publicly within sight of all the MPs and political correspondents.

Mo and I were never soulmates, as she made clear in her autobiography, but I had immense respect for her. She was the perfect foil for her predecessors like Peter Brooke and Paddy Mayhew. Instead of a patrician figure with a military bearing, we had a very human and spontaneous woman doing the job, and her presence was fundamental to convincing republicans and nationalists that the new British government was different. The trap she fell into was the trap waiting for all Northern Ireland Secretaries. If they lean over too far one way then they alienate the other side. She had concentrated so much on the Republicans that the Unionists became suspicious and then tried to undermine her by calling, both publicly and privately, for her to go. She argued in her autobiography that Tony should have stood up to them and insisted on keeping her. But that would have been miserable for her and disabled us from making progress on peace, which was just too important to put at risk.

The Northern Ireland political parties were past masters at trying to divide No. 10 from the NIO, and had repeatedly done so under Major. We probably should have been better at slapping them down when they tried to do so with Mo, and we did learn our lesson and get heavier about it when they tried it again with Peter Mandelson and, later, John Reid. But in the end, the political life expectancy of a Northern Ireland Secretary during the peace process was not very long. And it was best to move on before it was too late.

8

Peter Mandelson:
October 1999 – January 2001

Peter Mandelson was, and remains, a much misunderstood figure. Of the original New Labour three, Tony, Gordon and Peter, it was Peter who was the one who thought about the long term. His real contribution was his ability to turn the vision into a coherent narrative that made what we were doing comprehensible to people. It was this skill that was far more important than his abilities as a practitioner of the black arts with the press. But once you have a reputation as an effective spin doctor, it is hard to convince people you are not responsible for every piece of character assassination or negative briefing that appears in the press. The trouble with Peter came when he switched from a behind-the-scenes role as an adviser to a front-of-stage job: he had a tendency not to take his own advice and to irritate colleagues with his apparent haughtiness. Indeed, he would have been his own worst enemy, if he had not created so many even worse enemies along the way. But there is no doubt that Peter was one of the most talented people in the government, and we hoped his appointment as Secretary of State for Northern Ireland in October 1999 would be an opportunity for No. 10 to step back and leave more of the burden to the NIO. I personally was very glad to have him back. His resignation had been a traumatic event for all of us, and it was wonderful that he had a chance to rebuild his political career.

The arrival of new blood in Northern Ireland enabled us to refocus our efforts. George Mitchell had started his review on 22 September, with a strict rule that the talks were to be confined to the Northern Ireland politicians themselves with no ministers or officials admitted. I'd seen Martin McGuinness in the margins of the Labour Party conference on 29 September, and he had indicated they were ready to do a deal on the basis of the Castle Buildings negotiations, and asked if

Trimble was in a position to negotiate. I'd said he was, but that McGuinness would have to show that something had changed since July – like a decent IRA statement and a timetable for decommissioning. McGuinness had said that, if we wanted that, we'd have to drop the failsafe legislation that allowed the Unionists a way out if the IRA did not decommission.

But by the time Peter came to the NIO on 10 October, George Mitchell was finding the talks process very difficult and was indicating to us that he thought he might fail. At the end of October he took the party leaders out of Northern Ireland and transferred the meetings to Winfield House, the grand residence of the American Ambassador to the UK in Regent's Park, a strategy that had a positive effect since, in early November, it looked as though there might be the basis for a deal. The party leaders went off to consult their constituencies, but Mitchell wasn't convinced he had heard the end of their demands. When he came to see us on 3 November, he described Adams and McGuinness as 'natural-born chisellers' – they would always come back asking for one last concession. It was true that the Republicans were addicted to over-negotiating. They would keep going, hoping that they could squeeze out one final thing, when often they would have been better off settling earlier, because each time the talks broke down, the price they had to pay next time had gone up.

As predicted by Mitchell, Adams called the next day to make a series of further demands. We tried to accommodate them in a letter on 5 November making it clear we would change the legislation so that politicians could serve both in the Northern Ireland Assembly and in the Irish Dáil, and that we would deal with the outstanding issues of wanted IRA terrorists who had escaped abroad and now wished to come back to Northern Ireland (called 'On The Runs') and demilitarisation, or security normalisation, in Northern Ireland (the British government always called it the latter and Republicans always called it the former, but in either case it meant reducing the military presence and infrastructure in Northern Ireland). But McGuinness called me at home the next day, a Saturday, to say that they had had 'a night session with people' and it was going badly. There was active opposition from about one-third of the organisation. They wanted more from us on top of the letter, particularly on demilitarisation in South Armagh. (Garnering support in South Armagh, the base of IRA Chief of Staff Tom 'Slab' Murphy, was crucially important to them, and they needed to show that something had changed on the ground for them there.)

It was late and I phoned Tony at home in the flat above No. 11 and we agreed we should give them a further letter of comfort without waiting for Peter who was away in France. On the 7th, Gerry Adams called me at home, his voice like slow treacle, both wheedling and threatening, demanding yet more concessions, particularly the removal of the watch tower in South Armagh overlooking 'Slab' Murphy's farm. I spent most of the day avoiding further calls from him as I could not answer his questions. I finally phoned him late in the evening once Tony had agreed yet another letter, and spoke to him as he was driving towards the border to a meeting with the IRA Army Council. I read him the letter on his crackly mobile and he noted down what I had to say before the line went dead as his mobile went out of range. He was then unreachable for twenty-four hours, his phone switched off for security reasons while he met the IRA high command. When he contacted us again he said he had 'lift-off this end'.

When Peter got to hear that we had been making further concessions to the Republicans he threw a fit and tried to stop us. Tony thought he was just covering his back by dissociating himself from the concessions we had made: we had, after all, asked him to lean towards the Unionists in order to compensate for Mo's perceived favouritism of the Republican side. I thought it was more to do with resentment at being left out though. Peter had a point in saying that we may not have strictly needed to make further concessions to Adams and McGuinness to get them on board, and could have faced them down. But at each stage we had to make a best guess as to the real bottom line on each side. There was no science to the judgement; it was a matter of feel. In this case we thought Adams and McGuinness probably did have real problems with the IRA and that the last-minute concessions were necessary. The risk of losing the Agreement, or of the IRA statement being watered down, was too great to refuse concessions that were, in the big scheme of things, fairly trivial, just for the pleasure of feeling we had got the deal at the lowest possible price. The problem was, as I noted in my diary, that we were back in the usual circle: the Unionists would be next in demanding concessions from us.

★   ★   ★

Getting the Unionists on board was difficult. Adams had given the draft IRA statement to David Trimble who insisted on amending it. (I was amazed when Adams came back to us again on Tuesday with the statement further revised to meet those amendments, which he joked had been drafted by 'David O'Neill' rather than 'P. O'Neill', the traditional signatory of IRA statements since the time of the Easter Rising.) Adams said Trimble had 'intellectualised' his way into the Mitchell agreement, getting there rationally rather than emotionally and Trimble had made no attempt to sell it to his party. On Tuesday 9 November I felt he was chickening out of the deal he had himself negotiated even though Republicans had delivered everything he asked for. Peter was struggling manfully to keep him onside. John Taylor was the key, not just as Trimble's deputy but as an important weathervane of the mood within the party. Over the weekend we discussed what incentives we could offer Taylor, and Peter flippantly suggested making him ambassador in Turkey after the election, given his liking for holidaying in Northern Cyprus. Frankly he could have asked for whatever he wanted. We then discovered that he was off to Iran for four days so we needn't have worried. In the absence of Taylor, Trimble rallied and started fighting for the deal. Tony spoke to Conrad Black to try and get the *Daily Telegraph*, the only British paper read by unionists and virulently anti-Agreement, to be more moderate, which was only partly successful since what Black used to call 'the militant tendency' on the paper stuck obstinately to their attempts to undermine the Agreement.

On Tuesday 16 November, the day before the Queen's Speech, the IRA issued its statement saying it was ready to discuss decommissioning and would appoint a go-between to meet de Chastelain. As agreed with Mitchell, the UUP statement followed. The initial public responses were favourable, but there was still the Ulster Unionist Council to win over. David Campbell, Trimble's special adviser responsible for running the party for him, called me and said it was 60/40 their way in the party judging by the returns from the constituencies. Campbell was a perfect antidote for Trimble, always calm and collected however difficult the circumstances. John Taylor returned from Iran and Peter went to work on him. Peter still thought our efforts were going to fail and proposed that, if the deal did go down, we make David Trimble and Seamus Mallon junior ministers responsible for

Northern Ireland in the British government. We returned to this idea a number of times during subsequent crises but it was not really practical politics, and it was hard to see anyway how a nationalist could agree to be a minister in a British government.

As always this turned out not to be the last word. Trimble pulled out a surprise at the UUC by handing a post-dated resignation letter to the president of the party to come into effect if there were no decommissioning and said he would return to the UUC in February 2000. This established a new deadline. Campbell told me it was the only way they could get the deal past the dissidents in the party without them resigning. As the news was coming in, Gerry Adams called me from his sick bed with flu saying he was putting out a statement denouncing Trimble for misleading people about what had been agreed about decommissioning with Mitchell. I pointed out the danger of losing the UUC vote, which had still to take place. He said he was doing it anyway. I asked Tony to call him from the train on his way to his constituency, but he too failed to persuade him before they were cut off. When I got Adams back, he sounded resigned rather than ready to knock the whole thing over and he went back to bed without putting out a statement.

When the result of the vote came through with a narrow victory for Trimble I called David Campbell who said they had been let down at the last moment by the president of the party who, in the debate, had failed to call John Taylor, instead calling James Molyneaux, who had denounced the deal. He thought, without that complication, they would have got 60 per cent support rather than scraping through with a narrow victory.

On Monday 29 November the Assembly met, the elections for the Executive took place using d'Hondt, and the Northern Ireland Executive was finally established a year and a half after the Good Friday Agreement. The Unionists were unwise enough to let Sinn Féin select both the education and health minister slots, responsible for nearly three-quarters of the budget. The Irish government repealed Articles 2 and 3 of their constitution, thereby renouncing their claim on Northern Ireland, and on 2 December the Executive met for the first time.

Two weeks later, the first British-Irish Council (BIC) took place, a bizarre body that brought together the devolved administrations of the UK, the Irish government plus the Isle of Man, Jersey and Guernsey. It had been a key part of the Good Friday Agreement, created to give the Unionists the reassurance of what they called an East/West element to reduce the apparent uniqueness of Northern Ireland by making it clear it was in a similar position to Wales or Scotland and together they were all discussing common issues with the Irish. The public significance of this meeting was largely confined to the first public handshake between Tony and a Republican leader. The cameras outside Lancaster House were all waiting for the moment when Tony came out to shake Bairbre de Brún's hand as she arrived as Northern Ireland Minister of Health.

It was amusing to note the pleasure the representatives of the islands derived from being on an equal footing with the Prime Ministers of Ireland and the UK. We also had a comic moment when Gerry Adams called me on the morning of 8 December to say a bug had been discovered in his car and he was planning to hold a press conference to reveal it and attack the securocrats. He asked me to keep our response low-key. There was a division of opinion in our ranks on how to respond. Peter wanted us to welcome the announcement and say it was a good thing. But we decided to refuse to comment, and when Adams called Tony later, Tony said there was not a great deal he could say about an intelligence matter.

Most of the calls from Adams, however, were devoted to complaining that we had not delivered on the promises he had squeezed out of us in the run-up to the IRA statement. I explained what we were doing and why it was not possible to magic away overnight all the cases of terrorists 'on the run' he had raised with us. Then Adams came in to Downing Street to complain about our failure to pardon leading Republican Rita O'Hare (who had escaped to Dublin having been charged with the attempted murder of a soldier in the 1970s), and, unintentionally, I managed to achieve another historic first by bringing Adams out of the Cabinet Room and slap bang into Chief of Defence Staff Charles Guthrie and all the other military top brass, who were waiting for a meeting on Montenegro. They did not look too delighted.

We were all holding our breath about decommissioning. If it did not happen after Christmas, David Trimble's resignation letter would tip us straight back into crisis in the new year. I wrote in my diary on the day of the BIC meeting that 'everyone behaves as if decommissioning will happen. Perhaps it will. But Sinn Féin are showing no sign of it.'

The Irish weren't convinced it would happen either. On 2 December Bertie Ahern told us that Martin McGuinness was thinking of disbandment of the IRA rather than decommissioning. And on 9 December Ahern's senior adviser Martin Mansergh said, 'An army without arms made no sense,' and so he, too, thought they would just disband. Then, at the end of December, Adams shocked us by making it clear there would be no decommissioning in January. Father Alec Reid, the Catholic priest close to Adams who had been instrumental in bringing about the dialogue between Hume and Adams, explained the logic to our ambassador in Dublin. He said 'to be seen to be faced down by the Unionists and the British government would lead to the emergence of a new IRA which would do nothing to solve the historical problem'. Adams explained to us that the IRA had been brought reluctantly to accept the Good Friday Agreement even though they did not like it. But that stretched them as far as they could go.

This left us with the problem of what had actually been agreed at the Mitchell talks. Although Mitchell had briefed Bill Jeffrey, the agreement had not been written down and the government were not party to the talks so we did not know for sure. Adams insisted that, if we asked Mitchell, he would be clear that Republicans had never said that the IRA would actually decommission by any particular date. Trimble was equally clear that they had committed to decommissioning in January. When we arranged for George Mitchell to be asked for his version of events, we were told that 'Mitchell said in the final negotiations he had been very direct with Sinn Féin about the expectation of decommissioning before the end of January. Sinn Féin insisted that nothing they had said [during the negotiations] could legitimately give rise to such an expectation, although they were pledged to do their very best to secure decommissioning as quickly as possible.' So ambiguity had once again led us into an impasse.

Trimble, for his part, was more interested in discussing the name of the successor to the RUC and its badge than decommissioning. He said he thought Adams was just 'hardballing' it and would decommission when it came to it, but discussions with Adams were more depressing. Adams said decommissioning had become a totem for the IRA. It would be easier for them to disband than to decommission their weapons. Tony warned him that, in that case, the process would collapse. The only flexibility we had was on how decommissioning could be brought about in practical terms, and what links there might be between it and security normalisation. But when we asked President Clinton to press Adams, Adams told him that public pressure on decommissioning merely made it harder to do. There may have been some truth to this, but Sinn Féin used it as a catch-22. We would ease off and then nothing would happen. We came to believe that they simply used this line in order to reduce the public pressure rather than with any intention of actually solving the problem.

January was very tense but finally, at the end of the month, Adams started to show a bit of ankle, as I'd expected. In a meeting with Tony he said that, while they could not do any decommissioning now, he was prepared to seek an IRA statement committing them to decommissioning and to the search for a new way to discuss how and when it might happen. There was also the possibility that they might hold an Army Convention later in the year to disband the IRA altogether. 'It's always jam tomorrow,' I noted in my diary.

Miraculously, on 31 January Adams came up with a draft IRA statement, which the Irish termed the 'Angel Paper' because it was supposed to be totally deniable and to have come from the angels. But it was pathetically useless, with a hedged commitment to decommissioning and no timescale at all. It wasn't even close to being enough to get the Unionists on board, most of whom wanted an actual, concrete act of decommissioning. A series of late-night phone calls later that day involving Bertie Ahern, Bill Clinton, Tony and Adams failed to make progress. At 1 a.m. Adams sounded completely finished. It was clear we were not going to get enough to keep the Executive in place. Peter became obsessed with how much of the dirt was going to stick to him from the failure, saying that we weren't thinking enough about his position. A few days later, de Chastelain issued his report stating that he had no information from the IRA on when decommissioning would start, spelling an end to the Executive unless a miracle happened.

Tony started looking for a soft landing so that we did not lose the whole process. He had a difficult discussion with Adams, who was hectoring, saying that we couldn't suspend the institutions after five years of ceasefire. Tony said that the IRA were not free agents on decommissioning as they had been on the ceasefire. They could not handle it in their own way of choosing. Adams explained the difficult position he found himself in, saying 'the more involved one became in politics, the more liberated one was on such issues. The British government could order its securocrats. But Sinn Féin did not have the same luxury.' He was worried he wouldn't have the same space to move once the institutions were suspended. Tony insisted we had to suspend: we had a moral obligation. He could not leave Trimble to be cut to ribbons by his own dissidents. If we lost Trimble it would be ten years before a new unionist leadership was ready to do a deal.

At this point the Irish started sheering away from us. They said they had legal advice from their Attorney General that suspension was unconstitutional and they could not acquiesce in it unless there had been a default by one of the parties. Instead, they entered into a mad dash to see if they could persuade Adams and McGuinness to give something more that might keep the institutions in place before the deadline for Trimble's resignation of 11 February. Bertie saw them in Dublin on 2 February and called us to say that they might be able to agree to a timetable for decommissioning. Adams and McGuinness then went back north to consult their colleagues. Bertie said he wanted to come over to brief Tony on the outcome, but he had to wait for Adams to return with the answer. Tony was on a regional tour of the south west, so first the plan was to meet at Heathrow for breakfast; then it was lunch in Exeter; then tea in Plymouth; and finally dinner in St Austell. We had a plane on hold all day as we waited for the Irish. When we finally saw what the IRA were prepared to offer it was not worth the wait. All they had done was cobble together the same words in a different order but without making a significant commit- ment on decommissioning. Tony told Bertie that Adams would have to be able to say that there would be substantial decommissioning and indicate when the first steps would take place. He proposed that Adams meet Trimble and talk to him direct, but in their brief meeting Adams did nothing but ask Trimble a series of questions about what he required and they got nowhere.

While the Irish continued to scrabble away to find some way through, Tony spoke to Adams again and reiterated that the institutions were going to be suspended. We would have to put the Executive and the Assembly back together again afterwards. Adams reminded him of the tale of Humpty-Dumpty; putting things together again wouldn't be so easy. On Saturday 5 February Martin McGuinness called me to try and explain an IRA statement that had just been issued. He said we should ignore the guff at the beginning attacking Peter for his unhelpful role and try to respond positively to the bit at the end saying they would find a way to disarm. Unusually the communiqué was in comprehensible English, but the section on decommissioning wasn't strong enough. On Monday Paddy Teahon came to see us again, this time with a preposterous proposal from the IRA. The good news was they were prepared to disband. The bad news was they weren't prepared to do so until 2001, and in the meantime everyone else had to take their promise on good faith and do all the things they wanted. We made it clear it wouldn't fly and Teahon got rather overheated. The Irish would break with us, he said. They came to see us yet again the next day with still more unacceptable words. Teahon claimed he had almost come to blows with Adams and Gerry Kelly. Finally he called me on Thursday to say they had been summoned to a meeting in a safe house in west Belfast that night with some 'serious people'. The Irish were very sensitive to any suggestion that the meeting might be with the IRA rather than Sinn Féin, since they were banned from talking to the IRA. I observed in my diary that 'no doubt Republicans will try and pull something out of the hat tomorrow. But it will be too late.' Peter was due to sign the order suspending the Executive at midday the next day, Friday 11 February.

We didn't hear from the Irish on Thursday night, and I had to call them on Friday morning. Teahon said they did not have much but they did have something. It was a clever attempt to excite our interest. Then Bertie called Tony to say that a new secret IRA leadership position had been handed to the Irish at three in the morning, in which the IRA would commit to putting arms 'finally and completely' beyond use. But the position would be withdrawn if it became public because, as Adams told us later, the leadership was a hundred yards ahead of the Volunteers and the text could cause a violent backlash. We could not even show it to Trimble and de Chastelain could not refer to it. Bertie pleaded for more time and we agreed.

Given that we couldn't reveal the IRA plan to anyone, we didn't have much to work with. When we eventually saw the draft IRA state-ment it sort of suggested they were willing to disband and decom-mission without actually saying so. Peter spoke to Trimble in general terms about the new IRA position and he was interested, but Reg Empey was firmly against. We suggested that McGuinness meet Trimble, because only if he could convince him of the importance of the new IRA position and the need for delay in suspension, could we make progress. I spoke to McGuinness myself in advance, stressing the importance of the meeting and the need to make an impact on Trimble. He said he understood. But when he eventually saw Trimble after lunch, McGuinness was at his charmless worst, threatening and failing to tell him anything new. Trimble called to brief us on the meeting and said it didn't give him anything like enough to persuade others. He was getting increasingly nervous. His resignation letter was in the hands of the unpredictable Josias Cunningham, the UUP president and no friend of Trimble's, who kept threatening to deliver it. It was now 4.30 p.m. and, under pressure from Peter, we agreed he should sign the order. When, five minutes later, Tony called Adams to tell him our decision, Adams seemed anxious to end the conver-sation quickly. We later discovered why. Although Peter signed the order at 5 p.m., we did not issue it immediately so that Tony could work on the terms of the announcement. In the meantime, at 5.15, Adams rather sneakily made the IRA position public in a modified form, despite having told us we could not discuss it with anyone. He tried to present the statement as a great leap forward and urged us not to suspend. Bertie called Tony to repeat the plea, and persuaded President Clinton to do the same. We decided to deploy some Nelsonian blindness by applying the telescope to the wrong eye and said there was nothing we could do because the suspension order was already beyond recall. Then we rushed it out.

Even then the Irish did not give up. At 8.30 that evening Bertie, with Paddy Teahon standing over his shoulder, called Tony arguing we should agree to a hopelessly over-positive joint statement to welcome the de Chastelain report on the half-step forwards and on the basis of it commit to reversing the suspension as soon as possible. Tony explained this was impossible, but we wanted to publish de Chastelain's report before the nine o'clock news, which required the agreement of both governments. After twenty minutes of getting nowhere Bertie handed the phone to Teahon who tried to push us into reversing suspension by threatening to break with us. In the words of the Civil Service minute of the conversation, he was in danger of 'coming very close to the limits of what is unacceptable from officials of another government'. As the clock got closer and closer to 9 p.m., Tony got firmer and firmer on the need to publish the report. Eventually, at 9.01, Teahon agreed and we published. Trimble breathed a sigh of relief: he would survive his party conference. In order to avoid damaging their relationship with No. 10, Sinn Féin saved most of their venom over the suspension for Peter, both in public and in private.

While Mo had been Secretary of State I had to fill the gap as friend of the Unionists, but now my role changed. Peter had taken to heart our request that he cultivate the Unionists, but he rather overdid it and became their favourite Secretary of State since Roy Mason, the bluff former miner who, when he occupied the position under Jim Callaghan, decided to go for a purely security solution in Northern Ireland. As a result Peter fell into the Northern Ireland Secretary trap in the opposite way to Mo, and I ended up having to manage relations with slighted Republicans rather than Unionists. This occasionally caused friction between myself and Peter, who felt that I was leaving him out. But any disagreement there was between us bore no comparison to the stories in the press. On 20 February the *Sunday Telegraph* ran a piece about the supposed seething tensions there were between me and Peter, making up a series of quotes from me and claiming that Peter's dog Bobby always barked at me. I wrote to them pointing out that their report might be a little inaccurate since I had never actually met Peter's dog (an experience I was to enjoy later when he insisted on taking his *two* dogs on the small private plane he used to go back and forth to Belfast – it was cramped enough with the officials on board, but it became unbearable with the dogs leaping all over the place and trying to eat your sandwiches).

In this new phase I found myself conducting a number of clandestine meetings with Adams and McGuinness to try to find an imaginative way through the decommissioning impasse. Adams first indicated to me that quiet meetings might prove productive when he came into No. 10 on 21 March to talk about the IRA tradition of dumping weapons at the end of a campaign. His suggestion was that dumping could serve as a confidence-building measure. After the meeting he insisted I follow him into the ground-floor toilet (so we could speak away from his people, and possibly our bugs) to ask me to come up with some ideas on how this could be done and then come over to see him. As a result, I began consulting the Security Service and the army on ways the IRA could build confidence short of all-out decommissioning. I got a whole menu of technical suggestions out of these discussions, but it was my meeting with General Roger Wheeler, the head of the army and a former GOC in Northern Ireland, that produced the best idea. He said we should consider what had happened in Bosnia and in Kosovo as a precedent. There, weapons had been put in dumps that were sealed and regularly inspected by international observers to ensure they were still secure, until they were eventually destroyed.

I used a meeting scheduled with the Irish on 28 March as cover to go and talk privately to Adams about this. Having got up at five thirty to fly to Belfast, I held talks with the Irish now led by Dermot Gallagher, the head of the Anglo-Irish division in the Irish Department of Foreign Affairs, and soon to succeed Paddy Teahon who was retiring. The Irish argued that if we did more on demilitarisation in South Armagh we could get a more forward IRA statement. It was hard to give the discussion my full attention when I was thinking about my next meeting with Adams. I was picked up by his PA, Siobhan O'Hanlon, in her beat-up old blue car and driven through west Belfast. She told me about her new baby while taking me to a safe house on the outskirts of town, near a Gypsy encampment, where Adams and McGuinness were waiting.

I read out the different ideas we had come up with for ways of dumping the weapons. They noted them all down carefully and then told me why the IRA would not agree to any of them. I could sense that they were trying to draw me into a negotiation on the IRA statement, which they said could be tweaked and amended, but, other than saying that any statement would have to be utterly clear not hedged with conditionality, I resisted talking to them about it, conscious of what the Irish had said to me in the previous meeting about not selling ourselves short. Still, I was encouraged that they were looking for a way out. Siobhan drove me back to the airport by the back roads, and I will long remember the section of road through rolling countryside, known as the Nine Mile Straight for self-explanatory reasons. It is a narrow lane with barely room for two cars to pass and she decided to take it at full speed to make sure I made my plane in time.

Unfortunately, the Irish found out about my meeting with Adams and McGuinness which Adams had asked me to keep private. In an attempt to ensure they remained relevant, they handed over to Sinn Féin the documents we had been negotiating. These were a long way from being agreed, and it would put me in a difficult position when I next met Adams, since I would have to disown them, but he would now know our thinking. Despite this, I went ahead with another private meeting on 5 April. Aidan McAteer, a key member of Adams's brains trust, picked me up at Belfast City airport, explaining to me how dangerous it was for republicans like him to come into east Belfast. I didn't really give much attention to which areas were safe and which were not; perhaps I should have. He then drove me to a house in the strongly republican Ballymurphy estate. Adams and McGuiness didn't come out, but they opened the door and I slipped in. They were halfway through some huge doorstep sandwiches. Adams offered me half his tuna sandwich which I politely declined.

They talked very frankly about the way ahead. Adams said that some of the confidence-building measures on weapons dumps I had proposed might well happen next year. McGuinness said the organisation would wither away, and talked about the IRA becoming a veterans' organisation to bury old Volunteers under the tricolour. Adams said the draft IRA statement that was contained in the papers the Irish had given them had to be put in the IRA's own language, particularly on constitutional issues like the holding of an Army Convention, which we knew to be the fundamental decision-making body of the IRA bringing together representatives of all the Volunteers. I said that was fine, as long as their redraft was not obscure and ambiguous. Adams warned me that they could not go back to the IRA and ask for more halfway through a negotiation as they had had to do on the last two occasions. As leaders they had lost all credibility. This time they needed to go to the IRA with a complete deal, and they would need time to brief the 'middle management'. It was around this time that the Irish told us they had got wind of Brian Keenan's attitude to decommissioning. Keenan was not on the Army Council but was a key figure in the organisation as chief ideologue. In Keenan's view the war was clearly over, but the organisation couldn't say so because that would mean that the rationale for the IRA was at an end and some other organisation would take over the mantle. It was crucial that he continued his work on politicising the Volunteers and it cheered me up to hear that he was firmly committed to the peaceful path.

Two days later, I went to meet the Irish in Dublin with Bill Jeffrey, the political director in the NIO and a key player in the negotiation. Bill was as dry as one would expect of a lowland Scot and determined to make sure there was fair play. So when we were negotiating with the Republicans he ensured the Unionist point of view was heard in the negotiation and vice versa. He was crucial to keeping me honest in the negotiations, although his bluntness occasionally frustrated my plans to sell ideas to the Republicans, when he would interrupt and elucidate some point I was deliberately keeping opaque, having learned the skill of creative vagueness from my boss. It was the first time I had been in the Taoiseach's office in Dublin and I commented on the amazing opulence of the surroundings, which the Irish officials blamed on Charlie Haughey. We agreed that, from then on, we should have joint meetings with Sinn Féin rather than competing with each other. They pressed us hard to be more forward on demilitarisation, and this issue turned into a bone of contention between Peter and me. Peter was taking a deliberately hard line, saying we could not move further, while I favoured trying to accommodate some of their demands. I wrote in a note to Tony that, although the securocrats might leak what was going on and encourage the *Daily Telegraph* to accuse us of taking risks with security, if we weren't bold, we would rightly be criticised by later generations for not taking enough risks for peace. So I favoured being forward on demilitarisation.

On Monday 10 April, Tony and I met the security chiefs with Peter. As I expected, General Wheeler was the most outspoken. He said we could not remove the towers in South Armagh while the dissident threat remained. The Chief Constable of the RUC, Ronnie Flanagan, was much more reasonable, but his force did not run the towers. Tony didn't try to overrule the military, and Peter of course played to them as the hard man on security. It made me see the army in a new light. I did not like their attitude. They were playing a political game, fulfilling the caricature of securocrats favoured by McGuinness. In the end, in a democracy, the army have to do what the politicians decide. But I could also see why it was a high-risk game. They argued that we needed the towers to control the threat from the dissident republican terrorists. But I thought this meant we were giving the RIRA a veto over the whole process. And there was something to what McGuinness had said to me the week before about the best friend the dissidents had being 'the British government moving slowly to implement the agreement'. Changing the attitude of the people in South Armagh would do more to bring them on board than a thousand British soldiers. Adams said the IRA in South Armagh had always supported the leadership in the peace process, and the leadership was relying on their supporters in South Armagh to keep the RIRA in check in the pubs and clubs. We in turn had to show them that something had changed by reducing the army patrols in South Armagh and removing the towers. South Armagh had been a lawless area for generations and the topography made it impossible to police without army protection and helicopters. It was home to the most proficient IRA brigade as well as its Chief of Staff. For the British Army it was the principal battleground and they were not going to be defeated there. It became the main focus of our efforts to bring about security normalisation.

Tony cleverly moved slowly on this issue, allowing pressure to build up on the military as the negotiations went on, so he did not have to confront them. But it left me in a very difficult negotiating position, constantly having to turn up at meetings with the Irish and Sinn Féin over the next few months with nothing new to say on the subject. I flew over to Dublin on 12 April for a meeting in the Irish equivalent of the Royal Hospital Chelsea, half historical monument and half home for the elderly. It turned into a Feydeau farce, with the Irish holding a meeting with Sinn Féin before we arrived, hoping we wouldn't notice, but then being embarrassed when we turned up early. The Irish met us to say what Sinn Féin had said to them, and then we all met together so Sinn Féin could say it again. Sinn Féin had brought Rita O'Hare with them to make us feel guilty about not resolving her case so she could return to Northern Ireland and see her sick father.

I decided to take a soft-spoken, no-bullshit approach to the negotiations, cutting straight to the bottom line. The NIO used to criticise me for this style of negotiating, which they thought encouraged Sinn Féin chiselling because they couldn't believe there wasn't more to come. Adams and McGuinness liked negotiation to be a drama, with emotional speeches back and forth. But that day I couldn't be doing with the laboriousness of it all: we didn't have time to waste. Adams made it clear they would not agree to a timetable on decommissioning but he did float the idea of a confidence-building measure in which weapons were placed in a dump to be inspected by a third party. Tim Dalton, the permanent secretary in the Irish Department of Justice and the Irish official most trusted by Republicans, told me privately that they had taken up the idea I had put to them based on what had happened in Kosovo and Bosnia.

Peter came back onside after a dinner with Tony and me at No. 10 and he and Joe Pilling, the permanent secretary at the NIO, started the softening-up process with the military. Ronnie Flanagan was fine but he said we needed to woo the GOC. On 17 April, after Peter and I had seen David Trimble together, I went on to west Belfast where McGuinness gave me a list of military installations they wanted taken down, including the emplacement on the top of the Divis block of flats overlooking west Belfast, the towers in the walls of Derry and the towers in South Armagh. Paddy Teahon called me at home over the weekend saying we should press ahead regardless of what Trimble said, thinking, I imagined, about his forthcoming retirement and desire to go out on a successful note. It wasn't that easy, though. The NIO called me shortly afterwards to warn me that the GOC would resign if we insisted on taking down the towers in South Armagh.

Meanwhile, Trimble was still obsessed with the Patten report on the RUC. At the UUC on 25 March, David Burnside, who had been a close supporter of David Trimble but was now becoming more critical as he tried to win a parliamentary constituency, succeeded in passing a motion that required the leadership to secure the word 'Royal' in the title of the new police force before it could agree to go back into the Executive. Trimble's hands were tied. Instead of concentrating on decommissioning, he spent most of his time negotiating with Peter on the title and symbols of the new police force. Despite Peter's popularity with the Unionists, he and Trimble didn't have the easiest of relationships, perhaps unsurprisingly, given how difficult both of them could be. They had a number of spectacular bustups. I remember particularly clearly one incident in early February 2000. Peter and I were supposed to join Trimble behind the Speaker's chair in the House of Commons, after Peter had made a statement to the House about the possibility of suspending the Executive, in order to go to the Prime Minister's House of Commons office for a meeting. But Trimble came storming out of the Chamber shouting at both of us that Peter had failed to give a date for suspension, and, instead of heading for Tony's office, stomped off down the stairs. Peter and I went running after him, pleading with him to calm down as he strode, red-faced, across the Speaker's courtyard, but it wasn't until we got to the main court-yard facing on to Parliament Square that he had calmed down enough to have a rational conversation. We had our meeting standing outside in the cold night air.

When we did get Trimble to focus on the idea of inspection of weapons dumps, we faced a tough sell. According to UUP information, the IRA rank and file were not being briefed to expect decommissioning, and it was extremely difficult to convince them to accept the idea of inspections of weapons dumps without a firm commitment for subse-quent decommissioning. However, when I explained the Kosovo and Bosnian precedent to Trimble, he became more interested, and in a meeting with Tony on 20 April confirmed he could agree the package, provided there was a safety net in case Republicans did not deliver on decommissioning. We had dinner with Trimble, Taylor, Empey and Maginnis in Downing Street on 3 May and they accepted the proposal, and the next day we went to Hillsborough for talks on a new deal.

Finally we had a breakthrough. After two days of negotiations the IRA issued a statement committing themselves to decommissioning in the context of the removal of the causes of the conflict. They declared they would resume contacts with the IICD and we agreed the inspection of three dumps by Maarti Ahtisaari, the former Presi-dent of Finland, and Cyril Ramaphosa, the former General Secretary of the South African ANC, both of whom had been called by John Sawers and agreed to take on the task. On Friday evening we ended with a handshake between Gerry Adams and David Trimble. Devo-lution could be resumed and the Executive could be put back in place again.

There's an entry in my diary for 29 May 2000 that reads: 'You never get any time to enjoy success in this process because as soon as you have solved one problem you are pitched straight back into another

Gerry Adams and Martin McGuinness meet Tony Blair and Jonathan Powell
in the Prime Minister's Office in the House of Commons in 2007.

Kitty O'Shea, Charles
Stuart Parnell's mistress
and a distant ancestor
of the author's.

Wolfe Tone,
leader of the United
Irishmen celebrated
by Republicans.

The *Mountjoy* relieving
the siege of Londonderry
in July 1689.

Edward Carson,
Unionist leader.

Gerry Adams on the Falls Road in 1984.

Ian Paisley addressing a rally against the Anglo-Irish Agreement, flanked by Peter Robinson, in 1981.

Brendan Duddy, the man who ran the secret link from the British government to the IRA from 1974 to 1993.

Gerry Adams and Martin McGuinness outside 10 Downing Street in December 1997, with Martin Ferris behind McGuinness and Siobhan O'Hanlon to the right of Adams in the trouser suit.

(*Below*) David Trimble flanked by UUP delega-tion on the steps of Castle Buildings on 10 April 1998 announcing their acceptance of the Belfast Agreement.

Tony Blair, John Hume and David Trimble on the last day of the Referendum campaign in May 1998.

Tony Blair and Bertie Ahern in Dublin in 1998.

Trimble slips through police lines at Drumcree in 1995.

The Orange march approaches the army barricade at Drumcree in 1998.

Loyalist riots in support of the Orangemen in July 2000.

The aftermath of the Omagh bomb of 15 August 1998.

Bill Clinton meeting Omagh residents in September 1998.

Hillsborough Castle from the gardens; scene of many of
the negotiations, with the Lady Gray room on the right.

Mo Mowlam receiving a standing ovation during Tony Blair's speech
to the Labour Party Conference in September 1998.

David Trimble and Seamus Mallon after their election
as First and Deputy First Minister in July 1998.

Stormont: Parliament Buildings.

IRA arms discovered in County Meath in 1994.

George Mitchell, John de Chastelain and Harri Holkeri.

Tony Blair and George
Bush in the gardens of
Hillsborough, 7 April 2003.

Ian Paisley giving a press
conference after his release from
hospital in September 2004.

Tony Blair and the author in 2004.

Sinn Fein's Gerry Kelly during intercommunity violence in north Belfast in 2001.

Ian Paisley, Peter Robinson and Jeffrey Donaldson meeting Tony Blair in Downing Street in 2005.

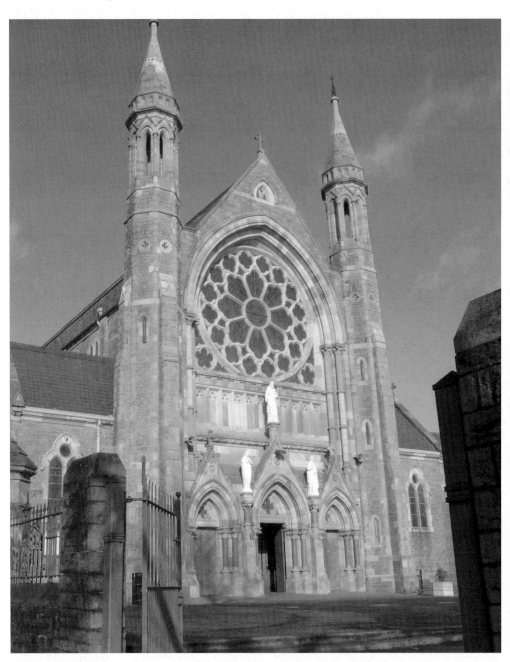

The Clonard monastery in west Belfast where many of the negotiations took place.

The fiancée and sisters of the murdered Robert McCartney on Short Strand in March 2005.

Gerry Adams and Martin McGuinness carrying Siobhan O'Hanlon's coffin in April 2006.

Gerry Adams and Ian Paisley at the apex of the diamond-shaped table in March 2007.

Martin McGuinness, Bertie Ahern, Tony Blair and Peter Hain laughing at Ian Paisley's joke in the First Minister's office in Stormont on 8 May 2007.

crisis.' The crisis this time was the promise Peter had made to the Unionists on policing in order to get them onside for the new agreement: he'd promised the word 'Royal' would be in the new police force's name. When I saw Adams and McGuinness on 24 May in Northern Ireland, they told me the inspection would be off the table if we continued to make concessions to the Unionists on the Patten reforms to the police, and indeed we needed to move towards the Republicans on this, not away from them. They didn't yet know of Peter's promise, and when Peter heard what they'd said, he went into a spin. In the end, we had to pull the announcement on the RUC he had promised the Unionists, and instead have Peter write a confidential letter to Taylor, giving him secret assurances on policing. Taylor was in Taiwan on a trip and I had to arrange for him to be bumped on to the British Midland flight back to Belfast otherwise he would have missed the UUC meeting where they would be voting on the new deal and his vote was crucial. Unfortunately, in a press conference after the UUC, Taylor couldn't resist showing off that he had government assurances in black and white on the name of the police force. The Republicans made a huge fuss. McGuinness called Peter and had a very tense conversation with him. Both sides retired hurt. Peter took his dogs for a walk and was uncontactable. McGuinness called me to complain. I kept making the point to him that they couldn't issue threats now they were a political party.

The situation didn't help Peter's mood. There had been an incident on 23 May when Peter had got shirty about my involvement in Northern Ireland and forbidden me to go back there. I'd said I'd be very happy not to, given that the RUC had recently told me I was on the RIRA's hit list, but Tony had intervened, accusing me of winding Peter up by being too 'prickly' in the way I handled him, and insisting on sending me back off to Belfast at the earliest opportunity. In the coming months, I continued to have trouble with Peter over security issues as I tried to find a way through the Republican demands on demilitarisation and terrorists 'on the run' (OTRs).

Demilitarisation came up when, on 2 June, I met Adams and Kelly in the VIP suite at Heathrow as they were on their way to see weapons dump inspectors Ahtisaari and Ramaphosa. We had a room on the edge of a runway which meant we could barely hear what was said. I observed it was like meeting round a tractor. They used the occasion to complain about our failure to deliver on OTRs. Tony had been unable to persuade Gareth Williams, the Attorney General, that there was a public-interest case for not proceeding against them. And the only other alternative was legislation. Adams and Kelly went on to meet the two inspectors and apparently spent most of their time discussing whether they should use plastic or paper seals on the dumps.

Before we could squeeze the inspection of the arms dumps out of them, Adams demanded one more meeting with me, Tony and Peter because, he joked, I always said yes, Peter always said no and Tony always said maybe. In the end, we managed to get Sinn Féin some demilitarisation. The army agreed to take down some towers in South Armagh and other prominent installations, and Peter sent Tony and me a message saying, 'You will be pleased and relieved to hear that demilitarisation, as you call it, is leading radio and television news in Northern Ireland. There is limited bunting in the streets.'

Without pausing for breath, Adams went straight on to demand that I sort out the situation on OTRs. I was supposed to go over and see him on 19 July, but I couldn't get out of Downing Street because of a RIRA bomb threat which had closed Whitehall. He did not seem to appreciate the irony, complaining about how I was disrupting his programme. Instead, I went to meet him in the VIP suite at Dublin airport on 27 July on his way to the US and he used the opportunity to give me a hard time on our failure to deliver on the promises we had made, threatening that the inspections would not take place and the IRA would not make contact again with de Chastelain. We had a difficult passage of arms about the dismantlement of one of the towers in South Armagh at a place called Cloghue. NIO political director Bill Jeffrey and I insisted that the tower there had been destroyed, but Adams insisted that it had not. As neither I nor Adams knew precisely where the place was, the argument was conducted in a certain fog of ignorance. After the meeting I got a picture of the site from the military and it turned out there were two structures at Cloghue. We had destroyed the observation tower, but not the aerial below it. The picture showed Conor Murphy, the local Sinn Féin representative, in front of the observation tower. But it seemed to me that Adams had more right in the argument than us: if we were only going to knock down one part of the structure there we should have made it clear at the beginning.

Meanwhile, the IRA had honoured their side of the bargain. On Monday 26 June Ahtisaari and Ramaphosa came to have breakfast with us in No. 10, and told us some wonderful stories of being driven round and round country lanes in blacked-out vans and of scrambling up hillsides in the dark to inspect bunkers. Ahtisaari, who was very large and had bad knees, had had a terrible time climbing down into the bunkers themselves. But their IRA minders had been very thoughtful. They provided overalls, although Ahtisaari's were too small, and provided toothbrushes and toothpaste in the houses where they were put up. They said it had been a professional operation.

Yet, despite these steps forward, I think it was plain to all of us that we were heading for another autumn crisis. I wrote in my diary that perhaps Northern Ireland was insoluble after all, given the fact that every time we made a breakthrough we faced a new crisis immediately, and maybe the only thing we could do was manage the problem, keep talking so that people didn't go back to killing each other.

Since I saw it as my job to be the optimistic one, things must have seemed particularly black. I met Adams in Belfast after the summer break and he was pushing for more and faster demilitarisation. Once the meeting was finished he sent the others out of the room and told me I had to understand how terrible things were with the middle management of the IRA. The leadership were facing ridicule everywhere, even in places like the Felons Club in west Belfast, where you could only become a member if you had served time for a terrorist offence and where loyalty to the movement came with the membership card. The community was losing its 'blitz spirit' that had kept it cohesive during the Troubles. We had to give him something to sell. But try as we might, all autumn we could not persuade Attorney General Gareth Williams to move on the OTRs. So we were stuck. On 23 October I called Adams to tell him that Gareth had refused to accept a national security case on Rita O'Hare, and that I was going into hospital with an infected foot. He quipped he hoped it wasn't a knee-capping. As a result of our failure to move, the IRA announced that, while it was going ahead with another inspection of the dumps, it was not going to re-engage with de Chastelain.

Trimble was equally apocalyptic. He thought unionist opinion had moved so far it would be hard ever to get it back. He said they saw the Agreement as a slippery slope where everything moved against them. Our focus groups also suggested unionists were demoralised, and while Catholics were enjoying the experience of republicans and nationalists in power, unionists focused mainly on the negative side of the police reforms. Trimble thought that Sinn Féin were deliberately trying to split the UUP by holding back on decommissioning. So, when Jeffrey Donaldson put down a motion for the UUC in late October 2000 calling on the party to pull out of the Executive if decommissioning had not taken place by Christmas, Trimble, instead of trying to beat him, decided to join him in supporting the motion. He added his own motion promising, as First Minister, to prevent Sinn Féin ministers attending North/South bodies until the IRA had re-engaged with de Chastelain. Northern Ireland was back in crisis.

On 31 October Tony called me very late at night to talk about Northern Ireland. I was very frank with him about the way I saw it on demilitarisation, and hoped he didn't shop me to Peter. He suggested a visit by Clinton in his last few weeks in office. I said a presidential visit might well help focus the negotiations but we would need to plan it carefully. On 10 November Tony called Clinton, who was on a golf course, to explain the situation and urge him to come over in the hope that he could serve as a catalyst to an agreement. He followed this up with a written message to Clinton setting out the seven elements of a possible deal: 1) the IRA re-engaging with de Chastelain; 2) weapons put beyond use; 3) the IRA stopping killing, punishment beatings and buying weapons; 4) agreement on the Patten policing reforms; 5) legislation to resolve the OTRs; 6) security normalisation; and 7) the UUP dropping the ban on Sinn Féin ministers attending North/South ministerial meetings.

On 16 November I met Jim Steinberg, Clinton's Deputy National Security Adviser, at the Ritz. He had come over to meet all the parties to the peace process and he said to me the White House was pretty sceptical about the President taking a big role in Northern Ireland at this point, or even visiting. He wanted to check that the Irish, Trimble and Adams would also welcome presidential involvement, and even though, later, they were eventually persuaded, Clinton's team continued to be nervous right up to the visit. Sandy Berger, the National Security Adviser, called me on 27 November worried we were putting the President in the middle of negotiations that might possibly fail.

The problem was that, yet again, Peter was very reluctant to get back into the issue of security normalisation. He had taken me aside on 9 November to complain that Tony was undermining him by constantly making concessions to Republicans. For his part, Tony was getting increasingly fed up with Peter, saying he was trying to appeal to the Prince Charles/*Daily Telegraph* element in what he was doing in Northern Ireland. Tony and I met Ronnie Flanagan on 13 November and he agreed to more steps forward but warned that the army would be difficult to move. He suggested we wait until the new GOC was in place because he might be more flexible. The Irish got increasingly irritated with our failure to engage on the issue. At a meeting with them on 16 November, Martin Mansergh and Tim Dalton suddenly suggested we offer to close the huge security base in Crossmaglen in the heart of South Armagh, in return for real decommissioning. I was willing to explore it, but it was too radical for the security forces and wasn't in any case high on Sinn Féin's wish list.

Sandy Berger called me again on 2 December to bully me about Clinton's visit. He said he couldn't let the President walk into a major failure in his last few weeks in office. He threatened to cancel the visit unless we could make an offer to the Republicans on demilitarisation. I didn't find the threat particularly convincing and told him not to lose his nerve. It was always going to be difficult. I explained the bind we found ourselves in with the security forces. These negotiations were high stakes for high gain. Nevertheless, the American pressure continued. Steinberg called me two days later from Singapore. He said we should hold some of our concessions back so the Americans could be seen to squeeze them out of us at the last moment. He said Clinton would be prepped for a negotiation rather than for a visit and pressed me again on demilitarisation in South Armagh. I said, 'We could not find ourselves in a situation where, following the removal of certain installations, a bomb went off in Northern Ireland or elsewhere in the UK and the resulting deaths were blamed on the Prime Minister. I described the analogy in the US: what would the President do if his security advisers told him that unless he took certain steps terrorists would blow up the World Trade Center?' He said it was all very well but we should not allow a political issue like this to be resolved by the security forces. I urged him to come over and talk to the parties again. He said there was no

point in coming till we were ready to enter serious negotiations with
Sinn Féin.

We met the Irish again in the margins of the Nice European summit.
We made some advances on other issues but still we could make no
progress on demilitarisation. Tony was driving me crazy. He had clearly
not decided his position on the issue and was making my life a misery
by his prevarication. I went back to Belfast two days later to meet
Sinn Féin, Jim Steinberg and the Irish. Adams walked out of the
meeting because I couldn't reveal what we would do on demilitarisation. It was clear that there would be no chance of a deal when Clinton
came to Northern Ireland on 12 December, but I still hoped to use
his visit to crystallise things.

Clinton got a wonderfully warm reception in Ireland, North and
South. Tens of thousands of people turned out to see him in Dundalk,
and thousands more lined the roads in South Armagh. We arrived in
Belfast on the eve of his visit by a bumpy flight from Bradford where
Tony had recorded a difficult audience-participation programme with
David Dimbleby (part of the so-called 'Masochism Strategy'). We had
breakfast with Ronnie Flanagan and the new GOC who were both
sensible about security normalisation. Peter did a bit of posturing
during the discussion that irritated Tony. He commented afterwards
on how pompous Peter had become.

Tony saw Clinton on his arrival and suggested a game plan to him
for his meetings with the parties. But Tony had been focused on other
things and Clinton was too tired and we were unable to make the
progress we wanted. We held a big rally at the Odyssey Centre in
Belfast and Trimble surprised all of us by standing up halfway through
Clinton's speech and walking out. Everyone assumed he must have
taken offence at something Clinton had said. But when I came to
check later, it turned out he had left to catch a flight from Belfast
airport because he was afraid he would miss his connection at
Heathrow to attend a UN sponsored conference on organised crime
in Sicily and receive the Freedom of the City of Palermo. Given that
the British government was represented at this insignificant conference
by a first secretary at the embassy in Rome, to me this demonstrated
a strange sense of priorities.

★   ★   ★

After Clinton's departure, we spent the last month of 2000 trying to get a deal. At first Gerry Adams refused to come and see us, but eventually we persuaded him to meet us at Chequers on 15 December on his own. Tony set out the entire security normalisation proposal for him, including the removal of towers in South Armagh, which we had agreed with the GOC and the Chief Constable at breakfast at Hillsborough two days before. He was completely flummoxed. He had not been expecting a concrete and specific offer and spent some time talking about other issues while he regained his composure. When he did, he said it was completely unacceptable, but he asked me to come over the next week with a written offer. Tony also put a scheme to him to resolve OTRs which required them to return and submit to the courts and then be released. Adams said if Tony 'had read Biggles and Colditz stories he would have a better understanding of escapees, and why they would refuse to return under the scheme we proposed'.

That weekend I went to a bizarre dinner with Tony and Peter in the Blairs' flat above No. 11 to talk about Northern Ireland and the forthcoming election. Tony said it looked like a try out for the film *Three Men and a Baby*. Cherie had gone out leaving Tony in charge of Leo, and I spent the evening trying to get him off to sleep by jiggling him around while Tony burned the garlic bread and served up a rather inedible lasagne. We didn't make much progress on Northern Ireland and spent most of the time discussing the election campaign.

On 19 December I flew over with Bill Jeffrey to meet Adams and Kelly in a living room in west Belfast. Normally I knew where I stood after these meetings, but not this time. I put the proposals to them. They didn't ask for more. They just said a deal was impossible before Christmas and moved on to a discussion of policing issues from the Patten report. They gave Bill and me a bottle of Irish whiskey each for Christmas and Siobhan O'Hanlon drove us through Andersonstown with Bill sitting on the back seat next to her baby. I went to see Peter to talk things through, but he was in a festive mood and instead of engaging showed me his Christmas card with a picture of himself and his dogs.

I went back to Northern Ireland again two days later. This time Bill and I took the early flight and met Adams and McGuinness and the Irish in the west Belfast community centre on the Falls Road, where the rooms were full of anti-drugs posters and whiteboards covered in notes from recent gender awareness courses. Sinn Féin indicated they could concrete over the dumps inspected by Ahtisaari and Ramaphosa and have them verified by de Chastelain. They even proposed to get an agreement on how decommissioning would be carried out by 1 March and to complete decommissioning itself by 1 May. We and the Irish then retired to Stormont to revise the texts. When we returned to the community centre, the mood had suddenly changed. Sinn Féin were no longer amenable and were clearly looking for an excuse to break the talks. In the end they chose to do so over the sequencing, arguing that the army towers be taken down first before the dumps were concreted over. They insisted we had to go first, and I insisted the IRA needed to go first. Adams stormed out and Bill and I left to catch our flight home late in the evening, wondering why things had gone so badly wrong so quickly. Sinn Féin put out a press release while we were on our way to the airport saying the talks had broken down because of the line taken by the securocrats.

When I got back, Tony was cross with me and said I should have carried on talking. Having had to get up at five in the morning two days before Christmas Eve, I wasn't contrite. He was of course right that we should always go on talking, but it had seemed to me that there was something artificial about the way in which Adams had broken things off.

My suspicions turned out to be correct. When Adams called the next day, it was clear that the break had been a deliberate tactic. I think they were surprised by our putting forward a concrete position on demilitarisation and had got themselves out on a limb where they could not deliver decommissioning in response. There was a certain pattern to negotiating with Adams and McGuinness. First they would titillate and suggest things were possible, to get you interested. You would then have to go through a lengthy and tough negotiation on all the detail of what they wanted, before, at the eleventh hour, they poured a large bucket of cold water over you to reduce your expectations.

After Christmas Sinn Féin said decommissioning was now off the table. The Irish made a half-hearted attempt to persuade us to accept a mini deal on the republican side, with just an IRA statement committing them to re-engage with de Chastelain, in return for the big deal on our side on demilitarisation. Sinn Féin were making it clear they could not move on policing now. I was afraid they had just decided it was all too difficult before the general election in the spring and had gone into a holding pattern again.

But before we could make any more progress we were catapulted into another Peter crisis.

I saw the *Observer* story about Peter and the passports for the Hindujas on Sunday 21 January and thought it was bad. I was conscious of doing nothing about it and was rather pleased no one called and asked me to. On Monday I told Tony I thought it was really serious. He hadn't focused on it, being preoccupied elsewhere. Alastair came in to see him in the afternoon and said it made him worry too. Tony demanded to know if Peter had done anything wrong. On the face of it making a representation about a passport was not a crime. There was no scandal at the centre of the story.

On Tuesday Alastair decided he would correct Peter's story on the passports at the press lobby in the morning having spoken to Jack Straw about it. He asked Tony if this was OK, but Tony wouldn't focus on the issue. Alastair asked me and I did not object. His comments set off a firestorm by implying that Peter had been misleading. Tony finally got involved in the evening, but by then it was too late. He called Jack Straw and Peter to try to get the story straight – the problem in all these sorts of crises is pinning down the facts in the short space of time available. Jack explained that he and his junior minister in the Home Office, Mike O'Brien, had discussed the issue with Peter the week before in the context of agreeing an answer to a parliamentary question and Peter had admitted then that he had indeed spoken to Mike at the time. At midnight Tony confronted Peter with this point and asked for reassurance he had not taken favours from the Hindujas, which he had not. Peter was tearful. In my view there was no need for him to go; I hoped it could be resolved by an outside inquiry. Ironically we had spent all day in No. 10 seeing the Northern Ireland parties, but making little progress.

By the time I got in on Wednesday morning Tony had already spoken to Derry Irvine on the phone and decided that Peter had to go. Derry had put his finger on the problem. He argued that the passport issue was not by itself a dismissible offence, if unwise, but that appearing to mislead the media, Alastair and Tony was. It could not be sustained. Alastair, Anji Hunter, Sally Morgan and I gathered in Tony's flat above No. 11. Derry and Richard Wilson, the Cabinet Secretary, joined us. I made the case for the defence. We should have an inquiry and see what the facts were before we took any action. But Jack Straw called me during the meeting to say his private secretary had checked her recollection: she was clear on the fact that Peter's private secretary had called her on 11 January to say that Peter regarded the conversation with Mike O'Brien as private and did not want it revealed.

Alastair was pushing for a decision by the eleven o'clock press lobby. He said if he postponed the lobby the journalists would scent blood. I summoned Peter over to No. 10 and he chatted to me about Northern Ireland, apparently unsuspecting, while waiting outside Tony's office. When Tony saw him Peter tried to argue for his survival, but after a bit more than an hour he gave in. Having been tearful the night before, he put a brave face on it, even though I felt like crying. We'd had our differences over Northern Ireland, but he was a real talent and a friend. Like King Charles, 'nothing suited him like the leaving of it'. He went out on to the street and gave a composed and restrained statement about leaving government. He did Northern Ireland parliamentary questions in the House and he sat through Prime Minister's Questions before walking into the sunset.

Peter later came to resent both his departure and the manner of its happening, and it is probably true we should not have been rushed into making a decision so quickly by the deadline of the press lobby. He was a big loss to the government both in his own right and as a balancing factor. Even his Irish opposite number, Brian Cowen, the Foreign Minister with whom Peter had had a falling-out, paid tribute to him. Cowen was a tough and extremely clever politician, known universally in Ireland as BIFFO – big ignorant fella from Offaly. Peter and he were never going to be a marriage made in heaven, but their relationship foundered when a record of a dinner between the two of them was leaked, making it clear what Peter thought of him. Relations were distinctly frosty for a while after that, but they had made up enough by the end for Cowen to say in January 2001, 'We couldn't have done it [kept the peace process going] without Peter having steadied the Unionists.'

During Peter's tenure as Northern Ireland Secretary we had managed to set up the Executive for the first time, albeit only temporarily. We had made progress on IRA weapons. And Northern Ireland had enjoyed another year and a bit of peace and prosperity. But a general election was looming and we had still not found a solution to the blockage posed by decommissioning.

9

John Reid:
January 2001 – October 2002

There was a strange dynamic in the peace process: some things never seemed to change, like the problem over decommissioning; while other things were constantly in flux, like the people dealing with the process. I appeared to be becoming an old hand, although nothing like as much of a fixture as Gerry Adams and Ian Paisley. At the beginning of 2001, we had a new American president, and a new Secretary of State for Northern Ireland. We had also bid goodbye to the Irish Cabinet Secretary Paddy Teahon at a farewell dinner in Downing Street. Although he was often a thorn in our side, we would miss him now. He was always aggressive and tough with us, but we comforted ourselves with the thought he was tougher and ruder to Sinn Féin.

Not surprisingly President Bush was not as engaged in the issue as President Clinton had been, but he made it apparent from the beginning he was willing to be helpful whenever we asked him to intervene. As for the new Northern Ireland Secretary John Reid, it was clear from the start he would be a good thing. He was the first Catholic to hold the job and had been angling for it for years. John was probably one of the few people in the Cabinet who could be called an intellectual. He had a fast and complex mind, although he did do a lot of his thinking through talking. Later, when he'd been in the job a few months, Charlie Falconer and I flew over to a brainstorming session in Hillsborough with him. We stayed for as much of the meeting as we could and when we left commented to each other that John had not once paused for breath for the three hours we had been in the building.

John was also aggressive and quite capable of starting a fight in an empty room. With David Trimble around, this was always going to be easy, and at least once during John's tenure I would almost literally have to pin him to his chair in Tony's office in Downing Street or he would have been out of it and pounding Trimble for accusing him of lying or some other unmentionable offence. He said from the start that he didn't want there to be division between No. 10 and the NIO, and he succeeded in keeping it that way. Instead of worrying about Downing Street having a role, John tried to use us as a resource, always addressing me as 'Slab Powell' in a reference to my opposite number, the Chief of Staff of the IRA. And he managed more or less to balance the two sides in Northern Ireland so that neither camp hated him more than the other.

He couldn't have joined us at a more unpropitious moment. Tony had seen Ian Paisley on 18 January and commented that 'he had never witnessed the DUP so cocksure they would smash Trimble at the forthcoming elections'. He regretted that he hadn't previously understood the depth of the problem in the unionist community.

We were still trying to salvage the deal we had missed during the Clinton visit in December, before the blight of the impending spring general election set in. On 19 January we had seen Sinn Féin, the Irish and the Americans, in the form of Jim Steinberg, at Chequers for a day of talks. We were pushing Sinn Féin to set a date for decommissioning before the elections, but they were more interested in talking about policing. They were considering signing up for the reformed police force but wanted changes to the Patten legislation to limit the power of the Chief Constable and make the police more accountable to local communities. Tony told them their proposals reminded him of old Labour's attempts in the 1980s to limit the police in unworkable ways. He said it was in their interest to have an effective police force. We kept the talks going until midnight and the Irish booked the Sinn Féin delegation into the Crown Hotel at Amersham, and paid for them, so they would stay late. Despite a call to Adams from President Clinton, just before his departure from the White House, we were unable to get them to agree a package, but they did say they would go away to consult on it.

After this meeting, Sinn Féin went through a prolonged period of constipation, unable to tell us whether they accepted the deal or not. Instead of sending us a proposal of their own on policing as we'd asked, they provided yet another long commentary on the Patten reforms. Bill Jeffrey and I flew over to Belfast again in early February to see if we could unblock the issue. We arrived at the west Belfast community centre before Sinn Féin and the Irish and had to hang around waiting for them, first outside on the Falls Road and then in one of the meeting rooms. Once they arrived and negotiations started, we went round in circles. Sinn Féin wanted us to make an unqualified commitment to revising the policing legislation after a review. We insisted it must be qualified because we didn't know what the review would recommend. We left without having made any headway but I decided to call Adams from the car to see if anything would shift him. He was walking down the Falls Road away from the community centre when I called. I asked him, against instructions, whether if we dropped the qualification he could accept the rest of the overall package. He said he could, but only if the review of the legislation was over in six months rather than the twelve months we needed.

I arrived back in London at midnight and spent the next morning helping Tony with his speech setting out his vision for a second term before flying back to Northern Ireland at lunchtime. When I got back to the community centre, I took Adams aside to remind him of our conversation. He avoided the subject by initiating a series of intricate negotiations on matters of simple wording that dragged on till one o'clock in the morning. I had to stay in the NIO dormitory at Stormont House and then got the six o'clock flight back to London that morning. I was intensely irritated by the end and let it show. It was becoming clear to me that Sinn Féin were just playing for time. Meanwhile, the Irish clearly thought that I had conceded too much to Sinn Féin on policing and were worried I would thereby undermine the SDLP position.

The issue of policing was difficult for Republicans. The leadership had to be cautious on how and when they moved on it. As long as Republicans refused to cooperate with the police their communities would demand that the IRA provide a form of vigilante justice to deal with joy riders and drug dealers. But the transition from violence wouldn't be complete until they ended punishment beatings. Equally, they didn't want to be outflanked by the nationalist SDLP in demanding a high price for joining the police. We never had a good fix on the real attitudes of the Republican leadership on the subject whatever intelligence we got. Indeed sometimes it felt as though they were feeding us what they wanted us to hear. So when they said things were too difficult we had to take their word for it.

On 11 February, Adams called Tony and said 'a final deal had to be sustainable on his side too. His people were a close, tightly knit community clustered in small parts of Belfast and Derry. There would be a huge debate within this community which he would have to win if the current leadership was not to be banjaxed. It would be a disaster if parts of the IRA or Sinn Féin were to break away.'

At the beginning of the following week, Dermot Gallagher, now in Bertie Ahern's office, came to Downing Street with a series of further demands from Republicans. They were all unacceptable, even though the Irish said they had beaten Sinn Féin down. I got Tony to come and talk to Dermot himself to say we were at our bottom line. He followed up with a phone call to Adams to say we were faxing him a revised text, which was as far as we could go. It proposed that the sequence of events should be: an IRA statement announcing their re-engagement with the IICD; the Decommissioning Commission announcing agreement on how arms would be put beyond use; a report that weapons had been put beyond use and a private understanding on the timetable for all these steps so that weapons were put beyond use by Easter 2001. He told Adams he had until tomorrow to tell us whether or not there was a deal.

Their answer was swift in coming. Adams and McGuinness flew over to see us on Thursday 15 February. They said there was no deal. They did not try to show a glimmer of hope. They just said no. We had wasted several months. Tony and I were furious. Nevertheless, when we had dinner with Bertie Ahern on 21 February just before our first visit to meet President Bush at Camp David, we agreed we would have one last push before the beginning of the general-election campaign. We arranged to go to Hillsborough on Thursday 8 March for another round with the parties.

I was curious to see what would happen at Hillsborough. Although I wasn't against a last attempt at an agreement pre-election, I was pretty sure that Sinn Féin had simply decided to string things out. I wanted to be proved wrong, but I wasn't.

It all started to go awry before the talks even began. On the morning of 8 March I got a call at Hillsborough from Dermot Gallagher to tell me the IRA were issuing a statement saying they would re-engage with de Chastelain but nothing more than that. The aim was to put themselves in a good tactical position before the day's negotiations began. It was an act of bad faith, but the result was not the one they intended. The UUP were delighted. All they had to do now was make their position conditional on the IRA taking the next step and actually undertaking some decommissioning. As a result they were under no pressure at all.

This was a boost for Trimble, who was not in a good frame of mind. David Campbell described him as 'worn down and resentful about the way in which the UUP had had to take the strain of implementation over the last two years with minimal reciprocation from the other side'. Trimble complained about the way in which he had been left out of the negotiations since the Clinton visit the previous December, and it was true that despite our best efforts we sometimes fell into the trap of negotiating an agreement with Sinn Féin before we even started talks with the Unionists. But he insisted he wanted to fight the election from within the Northern Ireland Executive if he possibly could.

As the day wore on, it became increasingly clear we weren't going to get anywhere. The SDLP were on the brink of signing up to the reformed police service regardless of Sinn Féin. That would have given us cross-community support for the police, but the Irish put huge pressure on them not to do so, wanting to hold out for an inclusive agreement on the nationalist side with Sinn Féin as well as the SDLP. During the day, relations between the Irish and the SDLP were at rock bottom, with the two sides snarling at each other. A few weeks later Seamus Mallon told us he wouldn't forgive the Irish government for their lack of support on policing. So, in the end, the only thing to come out of the day was an agreement between Adams, McGuinness, Trimble and Empey to create a small contact group between the two sides. We were effectively deciding to put the whole thing off till after the elections.

The election campaign took our attention away from Northern Ireland for the months of April and May. We had to wrestle with the Foot-and-Mouth outbreak, which put back the date of the election to June. It was a fraught period and we were exhausted by the time we returned to No. 10, in government again. We turned rapidly back to Northern Ireland. The election results were bad for Trimble, with the DUP replacing the UUP as the largest party. But it was not yet disastrous. When Tony called him on 9 June, two days after the election, Trimble said the UUP had missed meltdown by the narrowest of margins. Three seats could easily have gone the other way. He told John Reid he was 'mortally wounded' and might not be able to survive his annual conference at the end of the month. Trimble had already announced before the elections that he was giving a post-dated letter of resignation to the Speaker of the Assembly to shore up his position at his conference. He had called me on the morning he handed the letter over to tell me what he was doing, adding that he was ringing only fifteen minutes before the announcement was made public, to stop me talking him out of it.

Tony and Bertie Ahern went to Northern Ireland on 18 June for a post-election session with the parties. Trimble was at his most fatalistic, almost glorying in his decision to resign. He had brought Donaldson with him to the negotiations as his meal ticket to survival. The UUP said that they had taken the strain for too long. Conditions for Sinn Féin to carry out decommissioning were as favourable as they would ever be, given their success in the election. Adams and McGuinness, instead of making a concession to Unionists from a position of strength, couldn't resist being cocky, claiming that their increased vote in the election was a vote of confidence by their community in the strategy of putting off decommissioning. It seemed to me that, while Sinn Féin's current success meant it was unlikely the IRA would go back to killing, we risked jeopardising the peace process if we allowed things to drag on: I worried it might go the way of the Oslo peace accords in the Middle East, with people giving up on it before we could revive it.

Tony was completely fed up with the lack of progress. He drafted a note on 22 June proposing that he and Bertie issue a statement saying we would implement the Patten reforms of the police in full and requiring the IRA to provide a programme for decommissioning weapons. If this was not accepted, the overall package should be put to an all-Ireland referendum. I said I was not sure Bertie would be that keen on another referendum having just lost the referendum on the European Treaty agreed at Nice. Nor was it clear the UUP would support it. After yet another session of talks with the parties on 29 June – during which everyone was jolly, Sinn Féin because they had already decided what to do and Trimble because he had decided to resign – Tony thought we needed a forcing session of negotiation where we could drag the parties away from their constituencies and their home environment and make them think more imaginatively. I suggested the stately home of Weston Park in the West Midlands, which had served well when we'd held part of the G8 summit there in 1998.

Meanwhile, Tony continued to suggest mad ideas for the way forward, which I had to wean him away from. I was trying to find a way to put the process back on a stable footing, but it depended entirely on the IRA being prepared to decommission its weapons soon, and none of the evidence from all the sources available to us told us this was likely. However, I had a breakthrough in late June when Adams began to appear a little nervous about Sinn Féin's isolation and asked me to come over to Northern Ireland privately. He suggested we meet at the Clonard monastery in west Belfast, where his meetings with Hume had happened in the 1980s, and where Martin Mansergh had come to meet him as part of the early contacts between the Irish government and Sinn Féin in the early 1990s.

I got the early-morning flight to Belfast on Wednesday 4 July with Bill Jeffrey. Our unionist driver couldn't find the Clonard monastery at first and crawled nervously around the narrow roads of west Belfast, past street signs displaying resonant names like Bombay Street, where the Troubles had first started in the 1960s, and gable-end murals glorifying the IRA hunger strikers. He insisted on leaving as soon as he'd dropped us in the monastery car park, saying he was going back to the centre of town and we could call him when we wanted to be picked up. We walked past the Victorian church and in through a reception where old ladies were buying candles. A well-scrubbed monk in sandals met us and escorted us to a small room on the first floor with a sign on the door reading 'meeting in progress'. We sat and waited. An ethereal voice came through the internal speaker system saying 'Father Gerry, Father Gerry, will you come to main reception'. The place smelt of wood polish and a clock ticked in a distant room.

Eventually one of Adams's assistants came to fetch us, and took us to a room down the corridor where Adams and McGuinness were stuffing their faces with soda bread and butter. McGuinness said he had switched the meeting from the west Belfast community centre to Clonard because he was worried about a possible dissident attack on us there. Bill and I sat down on the two metal chairs remaining. There was no table and, with all of us sitting in a circle, it was like a prayer group. Appropriately enough, we started with an hour of philosophy. Rather than cutting to the chase, as I usually did, I decided to try a more lyrical approach myself, and make an impromptu plea about recognising the wider picture, to see if I could dislodge something on decommissioning.

My record of the meeting states that I talked about how 'we had managed to keep the peace process going for three years with bits of sticking plaster and avoiding the hump of decommissioning. Now we had to get over the hump if it were to survive. Sinn Féin had to abandon the dual strategy of the Armalite in one hand and the ballot box in the other and move on to an exclusively political strategy.' I said that I understood what Adams had said about the IRA being unwilling to accept the same old promises from us again. This time it needed to be more than another 'sordid' deal. It needed a sense of higher purpose not a cynical haggle. I finished up with something about how we had to transcend the situation, and that the British government would want to make a bigger statement committing itself to bringing about change.

Adams and McGuinness perked up at this point because they had been going on at Tony in our last few meetings about a united Ireland and thought I must be making a hint in that direction. Realising this, I said Tony had made it clear that we were not going to commit ourselves to a united Ireland. Afterwards Adams took me aside on the stairs at the back of the monastery overlooking Bombay Street, from which you could see the loyalist Shankhill Road in the distance, and asked me what I had in mind when I said a 'bigger statement'. I said I would send him some ideas. I also told him privately that leaving decommissioning till the autumn would be too late. There would be nothing left to save. He said he understood: we would be waiting for ever if we waited for 'P. O'Neill' to propose how weapons should be put beyond use. He asked us to put forward a scheme for decommissioning. I said they had to put weapons permanently beyond use in a manner acceptable to de Chastelain on a clear timescale and as part of a continuing process. Adams carefully noted down what I said and appeared to be back in a negotiating mindset.

I flew back to London for a dinner with Tony and Bertie to concert our positions prior to the Weston Park meeting, which was due to take place on 9 July. The Irish consistently took the position that they would sort out the Republicans and we should be responsible for sorting out the Unionists. We kept trying to explain to them that it did not work like that, and we were in no position to deliver the Unionists, but they never really believed us. Although the Irish were not keen to be bound too closely to us, we had prepared together a series of papers for the meeting. They said they agreed with us on decommissioning but did not agree with us on policing. I had breakfast the next morning with Trimble and told him about the timing of Weston Park. He pulled out his diary and said he would have to vote on the electoral fraud bill on Tuesday and then he and his wife would be attending the Buckingham Palace garden party on Wednesday so he wouldn't be able to be there the whole time. He said he had assumed we were going to suspend the institutions and resume talks in the autumn. He did not like the talk of calling elections in Northern Ireland if we failed to reach agreement. Elections looked like pressure on him, when what we needed was an alternative Plan B that disadvantaged Sinn Féin, to apply pressure on them.

We had booked Weston Park for a week, but it became clear that none of the parties would stay there the whole time, so we decided to make it a game of two halves, with preparatory negotiations, a chance for parties to go away and consult and then return to conclude a deal. Tony and I helicoptered over in the morning and went for a walk with John Reid and his team in the lovely gardens. The sun was shining and the whole setting was like something out of the film *Gosford Park*, only with a mixture of politicians, activists and recently released terrorists drifting in and out of sedate libraries stuffed with eighteenth-century tomes and wandering through huge ballrooms dominated by complicated chandeliers. I was glad I was not the person who had to worry about counting the silver spoons afterwards. Hughie Smyth, a particularly engaging member of the Loyalist PUP delegation, confessed to Tony that at a meeting before the election he had pressed him on the sex of the baby he and Cherie were expecting and possible names, and then had placed a bet at the bookies and cleaned up when it was a boy named Leo after Tony's father. Gerry Adams revealed a new side of himself too by wandering around the park hugging the stately trees. Martin McGuinness was mercilessly teasing him as a 'tree hugger'.

David Ervine, the leader of the PUP representing supporters of the Loyalist UVF (and one of the cleverest and most charismatic of the party leaders), used the opening round table to confront Gerry Adams with the pertinent question of what he regarded as 'the causes of the conflict'. His point was that, if the IRA was linking its decommissioning to the 'causes of conflict' being resolved, we needed to know what those causes were. Would they be resolved when the Good Friday Agreement was implemented, or only when there was a united Ireland? Adams defensively and in a patronising way refused to answer the question, and Ervine led his party in a walkout from the talks.

We tried to focus the negotiations on three issues: decommissioning, policing and the stability of the institutions (a guarantee required by Republicans that Trimble would not pull the institutions down again once they had been re-established). Monday and Tuesday were spent going back and forth on the key texts, and we then broke on Wednesday morning for the parties to go away and reflect. We didn't truly expect to get a final agreement by Friday, but the intention was to give the parties an agreement to take away on Friday to consult on and then publish it later.

In the negotiations, the SDLP had pressed hard for inquiries into murder cases where there was a suspicion of collusion by the security forces, including the case of Patrick Finucane, the Catholic solicitor who had been killed by loyalist murderers allegedly in collusion with some in the security forces. We were very reluctant to agree to this. After the continuing Bloody Sunday inquiry, the last thing Northern Ireland needed was to spend more of its time looking back rather than preparing for the future. But in the end, in order to get the SDLP to accept the police reforms, we had to support the idea of an international judge looking at whether there were grounds for public inquiries into a series of individual cases. For their part, the Unionists wanted the list of cases to be considered to include Billy Wright, the LVF leader murdered in the Maze prison, to balance the otherwise exclusively Catholic bias.

When it came to discussions on decommissioning at Weston Park, Adams held parallel talks with the Irish security expert Tim Dalton, trying to persuade him that they should take place without the IICD being present. We said that would not be acceptable and Dalton began to discuss methods by which the IRA might decommission without an Army Convention being required under the IRA constitution to approve it, since the leadership were always worried about the risk of losing at such a convention. But we insisted equally strongly, as did de Chastelain, that decommissioning had to be real and weapons had to be rendered genuinely unreachable and unusable. Sinn Féin finally decided on acceptable methods with de Chastelain on 25 July.

By the time we returned to Weston Park on the Friday we had agreed seven papers with the Irish: on security normalisation, on decommissioning, on policing, on inquiries, on OTRs, on an all-party statement about the stability of the institutions, and a statement by the two governments with an agreed sequence in which the steps would take place. As expected, we couldn't get the parties to sign up to any agreement at Weston Park, although none rejected the package out of hand. Since they needed still more time to consult we decided not to publish the documents at that stage and instead issued a statement that, in the view of the two governments, we had reached a fair and balanced package, and that further negotiation was not necessary. We decided with the Irish that, if the Republicans failed to decommission, or the UUP refused the package for other reasons, we would publish the texts and blame the offending party for blocking progress.

On Sunday 22 July I called Adams to tell him that Tony and Bertie would meet on the following Friday and issue a statement to the press saying they were sending out a draft agreement to all the parties and expected a positive response. He said he thought the IRA would decommission but he didn't know if it would be now, in six months or a year. I said that was no good. Now was the moment.

We arranged for Bertie to meet Tony up in his constituency of Sedgefield on Friday 27 July, and together they held a press conference at a country-house hotel not far from Tony's home in Trimdon Colliery. Then both Tony and I went off on holiday. I was in Cornwall when Adams called me on 5 August to say cryptically that something would happen the next day and he hoped our response would be generous.

I rang Tony at the hotel in Cancún where he was staying with Cherie and the children. He had just been speaking to George Bush on the phone with me listening in. Bush had tried Spanish on Tony asking, '*Donde esta?*' to which Tony had replied, '*Muy bien gracias.*' I pointed out to Tony the correct reply would have been 'Mexico', but Spanish was clearly not one of his best languages. I told him about Adams's call and we hoped that it might presage actual decommissioning. Later, once we realised it was not the real thing but only the IRA announcing publicly that it had agreed modalities for decommissioning with de Chastelain, we agreed to welcome the half-step but make clear it was not sufficient to unblock the situation.

We and the Irish spent some time in the autumn trying to work out why Republicans had pulled back from decommissioning. After all, we had been told that Volunteers had been briefed to expect a move then. Bertie and Tony thought Adams and McGuinness had believed they could deliver but were turned over by the hard men of the IRA. Bertie said that, when he had spoken to them, Adams and McGuinness claimed they had not known what the IRA was going to do. In that case, he had asked, who was in charge? I argued that they were far less strategic than they were given credit for. In fact, they had an eventual goal – Irish unity – but they had no medium-term strategy. That was why they kept coming to us looking for new ideas every time one bit of road ran out.

The summer in north Belfast had been violent, with regular rioting. It was clear the IRA were encouraging rather than trying to restrain the violence. I met Trimble at the end of August and urged him not to let Republicans out from behind the eight ball by doing something stupid himself. He said that, after what had happened, Unionists now wanted more than just decommissioning. Jeffrey Donaldson and David Burnside had the votes to call a UUC and he would have to do something to get through his executive. At about the same time he told Sylvia Hermon, one of his few loyal MPs, that he had lost the party.

I wrote Tony a note on his return from holiday arguing we really needed to call Sinn Féin's bluff. We could not tolerate indefinitely the continuing criminal and paramilitary activity we had turned a blind eye to so far. If we couldn't get the SDLP to share power without them, then we had to find some other way to force them on to an exclusively peaceful path. We'd always known it would be a long process – that the scales wouldn't suddenly fall from their eyes making them realise the error of their ways – and we couldn't give up on them because that would leave them permanently outside politics. So we needed a process that bore down on the criminal and paramilitary activity progressively. Tony responded by suggesting that we ask ex-President Clinton to conduct a review, but I said Trimble would object because unionists suspected Clinton of favouring nationalists.

When Tony saw Bertie Ahern on 3 September he got these points across. We could not let Sinn Féin exploit a dual approach of legitimate and illegitimate political methods indefinitely. They were building a political base in tandem with IRA intimidation, and other political parties would get fed up with being disadvantaged. We had to move on from the ceasefire to the end of the armed struggle. Bertie agreed. And of course his Fianna Fáil was one of the parties being disadvantaged in competition with a well-funded Sinn Féin, and his MPs were urging him to get tough with them.

Then 9/11 happened and everything changed.

At first it seemed as if all the change was going on in the rest of the world, and Northern Ireland, as in Churchill's famous quotation, had remained 'unaltered in the cataclysm'. In the immediate aftermath of the attacks on New York and Washington, our attention was distracted from the province as we helped to rally support for the United States and prepare the invasion of Afghanistan. But Bertie Ahern, when he called Tony on 12 September, pointed out that the tragedy in the US might have repercussions for Northern Ireland. He was of the opinion that it might bring pressure to bear on the IRA to turn away from terrorism for good. And he was right. A few days later, on 15 September, Adams called Tim Dalton to say that the IRA would definitely decommission but he needed more time to get it all agreed.

Adams has always argued that 9/11 had no impact on the IRA. But the fact was that their brand of terrorism had been rendered obsolete. They could not compete with terrorists prepared to use suicide bombers to kill people in their thousands rather than tens. In my view the IRA would have decommissioned even if there had been no 9/11: their time had passed. But events in New York speeded up the process.

Adams called in mid-September demanding a meeting with Tony

but Tony was playing hard to get. Adams asked if we had any ideas and I said it was his turn to have an idea. Sinn Féin had managed to drag out the final steps of the process for weeks but they had lost their bargaining power. Finally, on 22 October, Adams issued an appeal to the IRA to decommission: 'I do not underestimate the difficulties this creates for the army. Genuine republicans will have concerns about such a move. The nay-sayers, the armchair generals and the begrudgers, and the enemies of Irish republicanism and of the peace process will present a positive IRA move in disparaging terms. This is only to be expected.' The next day Adams called me at lunchtime to say the IRA would issue a statement at 5 p.m. and the IICD would do theirs at eight. The IRA said they had implemented the scheme of decom-missioning agreed with de Chastelain. The IICD said they had witnessed an event in which the IRA had put a quantity of weaponry completely beyond use. The materiel in question included arms, ammunition and explosives. Tony made a statement on TV welcoming the news which he said was not an act of weakness, but what we had been working for, for over three years, and was a sign that politics was working. You could see in the Middle East what 'no process' meant – continuing bloodshed.

We had been waiting for this moment for so long that when it eventually came it was a bit of an anticlimax. If it had happened a year or so before, it could have helped to build trust among union-ists. But now it was too late to convince them that things had changed. It is hard to be sure just how much difficulty Adams had with his own side in extracting this concession. He called me the day after and said people were coming up to him in west Belfast weeping and asking why they had done it. It was a blow to their core support. Adams told us later there had been a real risk of elements within the movement calling an Army Convention, where divisions would have fed into the wider republican community. He said that 'had the alignment of personalities been different, things could have been more problematic'.

On 30 November we went to Dublin for a meeting of the British-Irish Inter Governmental Conference (BIIGC) which brought together the British and Irish governments and the Northern Ireland Execu-tive. We had a bilateral meeting with Bertie Ahern and, for the first time ever, Northern Ireland was not mentioned. On 13 December David Trimble and Mark Durkan, who had replaced John Hume as

leader of the SDLP and taken over Seamus Mallon's role as Deputy
First Minister, came to see Tony as a team, and, again for the first
time, discussed budgets and development rather than the usual crises
and terrorism. The low-key and less moody Durkan got on far better
with Trimble than Seamus Mallon ever had, and the two actually
worked well together. Martin McGuinness used their meeting with
Tony to complain cheekily about the coalition bombing of Afghanistan.
He should know a thing or two about bombing campaigns, we thought.
Peter Mandelson made our life more difficult by giving an interview
saying that we were soft on the IRA, and that he expected there to
be a united Ireland in his lifetime presided over by President Gerry
Adams.

John Reid had worked away throughout this period in tandem with
us in No. 10. He had said to me when he was appointed he did not
want to be picked off by one side or the other like his predecessors,
and was equally aggressive to both. This didn't stop the Unionists
trying to have a go at him in the same way that they had tried to
disable Mo. In late November Trimble had got in a fury with John
over the appointment of George Quigley as chair of the review of
the Parades Commission and over a series of other minor issues, and
had started to attack him in the press, causing me to have to ring
Trimble's adviser, David Campbell, and give him a very heavy warning.
I said that if we saw any more signs of an attack on John Reid by the
UUP, we would regard it as an attack on Tony himself and deal with
it accordingly. It worked this time. David Trimble came in the next
day, much more constructive.

It always seemed to me in Northern Ireland that, paradoxically,
when things looked at their bleakest from the outside there were
reasons for hope in the private conversations going on inside, and
conversely when things seemed to be going swimmingly from the
outside they were just about to collapse. This is certainly what
happened in 2002.

The IRA suspension of punishment beatings and similar activities
for the duration of the Irish election campaign in the spring of 2002
flagged up the need to push them to suspend such activities permanently, while Bertie Ahern's insistence he would not share power in
the South with Sinn Féin until the IRA had disbanded raised the

question of why Unionists in the North shouldn't demand the same conditions.

On 10 May I wrote a note to Tony saying the only way to re-establish confidence in the unionist community was to make it clear to Republicans that no targeting, preparations for terrorism, acquisition of weapons or killing would be tolerated. Trimble suggested to me on 23 May that we should call for the disbandment of the IRA. I said what we needed was the suspension of all activity rather than disbandment. Tony commented on the note, 'this [the peace process] is heading for the rocks', and when he saw Adams and McGuinness at the beginning of June, told them that we were in a crisis that did not look like a crisis from the outside. We had reason to believe the IRA was continuing to procure weapons and carry out targeting. This was not, he said, 'the manifestation of a securocrat's imagination but what we know to be true'. It was fine to have some activity during a transition but it was not acceptable as the permanent state in a peace process. The IRA had to take a leap forward or the process would collapse. He said we were always going to face a clash between Sinn Féin as a political party and the IRA as a revolutionary movement. Ultimately, the IRA had to disband, although it was not helpful to say so for the moment, but it did have to stop these activities now and say it had done so. Adams said the IRA would fade away if politics continued. Some of its members would go into the party and others would remain in a veterans' organisation. He reiterated the point that we should not create an impasse like decommissioning, which we had inherited.

In the end it was the accumulation of events that brought the whole structure crashing down again. The root cause was the same – the lack of trust in the unionist community that republicans had finally put terrorism behind them. They were no longer focused on decommissioning but on the continued paramilitary and criminal activity of the organisation.

First, in August 2001, there was the arrest of three republicans in Colombia who were reported to be engaged in technology exchange with the FARC, one of the nastiest and most brutal terrorist organisations in the world, sustained by the cocaine trade. Adams's denial that they had anything to do with the IRA was soon undermined by the revelation that one of them was the Sinn Féin representative in

Cuba. Colombia was a long way away, and the evident embarrassment it caused Republicans made it of less impact by itself on the
unionists. Adams actually asked me at one stage to put in a word with
the Colombians to help get the arrested men out. Eventually they
skipped bail.

Then, in March 2002, there was a break-in at Castlereagh police
headquarters and the theft of sensitive papers. On instructions, I had
to give Adams a warning. I told him that evidence was mounting of
IRA involvement in the Castlereagh break-in and if it were proved we
would face huge pressure to declare the ceasefire over. In the aftermath we had to move a large number of police officers from their
homes because their addresses had been compromised and I had to
tell him if anyone was killed as a result of the break-in, the whole
process would be over. It is still entirely unclear to me why the IRA
might think this break-in was a good idea, other than to cock a snook
at the Brits, and because they could.

As these events progressed it was no good trying to hide what was
going on from Trimble. He was getting reports of IRA activity from
unionist contacts within the police more quickly than we were.
Inevitably, these reports were turning unionist opinion away from the
Agreement. Trimble didn't seem to think this was a huge problem for
him. He came to see me on 12 June and said he was pretty upbeat
about his position in the party. But in our experience, his judgement
about such things was awful, and he was in what Alastair Campbell
and I used to call his 'dum de dum de dum' mood where he would
hum to himself in confidence just as the chopper was about to come
down and cut off his head. I told him that the information we had
suggested he might be wrong, and Tony commented two days later
that 'David Trimble's position is dire, although he has only just realised
it'. Shortly afterwards, Donaldson wrote a public letter to Trimble
calling on him to resign because the IRA was no longer on ceasefire,
and the party was in open turmoil again.

We tried to persuade the Republicans to act to save the situation.
Adams indicated they were in the market for new ideas, and I went
over to meet him and McGuinness at the Clonard monastery on
17 June. I took with me a draft IRA statement saying the war was over,
the IRA would stand down and that they would not engage in paramilitary activities, training, targeting, and acquisition and development

of arms or weapons. Adams agreed to consider the text but asked if we were not creating a rod for our own backs. We would be hostage to one person doing something stupid. I said they could distance themselves from an unauthorised individual. He said he didn't think it would run with the IRA. I said we had to speed up the transition.

I went back to see him again at the beginning of July. I had booked an NIO driver but Siobhan O'Hanlon insisted on collecting me so we could meet in a safe house in west Belfast. She said the international airport where we had agreed to meet was not safe. Instead we met in a house on a small, quite smart estate. Siobhan told me the houses sold for £130,000, which seemed a lot in those days. Adams said he had seen David Trimble in the morning and asked him what he wanted and he had replied 'peace on the streets'. He said our language for a draft IRA statement wouldn't fly with the IRA and offered instead local initiatives to keep the peace on the streets of Belfast over the summer. I said that was fine but it did not address the fundamental problem.

On the way back to the airport, Siobhan's husband Pat drove. She told me rather disarmingly that he used to be a hunger striker. I felt a bit comic sitting there clutching my official briefcase with its royal crest.

During this period the Irish did not share our assessment that the IRA were still engaged in paramilitarism and violence. They believed that the IRA was giving up the violent path. When I went to see Irish officials in Dublin on 27 June, Bertie Ahern unexpectedly dropped in on the meeting and said IRA members were going political all across Ireland. When Tony met him a week later Bertie told us the Garda (the Irish police) said all the evidence we had provided on IRA activity was 'waffle'. They were not keen on specifying the paramilitary and criminal activities the IRA should give up. I said, if they didn't think the IRA were engaged in such activities now, there shouldn't be a problem with Republicans renouncing them.

Trimble was gearing up for another breakdown in the talks. He was sufficiently weakened that he had to agree a motion with Donaldson for the UUC on 21 September to pull out of the Executive within three months unless the IRA disbanded. He came to see me a few days afterwards in Tony's den in No. 10 to tell me there was wiggle room in his motion and he was not demanding the immediate disbandment of the IRA. He proposed the idea of an independent assessor of the ceasefire, either a US general or a committee of privy councillors, an idea he had been given by a Northern Irish friend in Washington. Later he suggested Baltasar Garzon, the legendary anti-terrorist judge in Spain. John Reid resisted the idea, since the power to determine whether or not the ceasefire was breached was vested in the Northern Ireland Secretary by law, but we came back to Trimble's idea in time.

We went on to have a heart-to-heart conversation which I recorded in a note for Tony. 'Trimble said to me rather melodramatically this morning that this was a turning point. We had to decide whose side we were on. No unionist believed we were on their side. And we risked making the mistake that Mrs T made in 1985 with the Anglo-Irish Agreement, so alienating unionist opinion that we had no one to engage with. That would condemn us to another ten years of pointless violence and political vacuum.' He asked how we could expect him to serve in an Executive with Sinn Féin when Bertie Ahern had made it clear in the Irish elections he would not allow Sinn Féin into the Irish government until the IRA had stood down.

I commented to Tony that we had managed to stay one step ahead of the sheriff for the last four years by constantly moving the process forward before the consequences caught up. But the sheriff was about to catch up with us. We needed to give back to the process some credibility. But before we could do anything, there was Stormontgate.

Tony and I were caught unawares by the police raid on the Sinn Féin offices at Stormont. We'd been given advance information that something was afoot by John Reid, who'd called us on 19 September to give us a cryptic warning, but we had not really grasped the full significance of what he was telling us. Only on 4 October, when I saw the raid on television did I realise that this was what John had been talking about. The queues of police, male and female, trooping in and out of Parliament Buildings in full body armour made for gripping viewing, a bit like the arrest of Guy Fawkes. The media focused on the political documents discovered, including records of one of Tony's conversations with Bertie Ahern and one of my conversations with David Trimble about decommissioning. But that was humorous rather than dangerous. The real problem was all the material relevant to targeting that was found on the computers, including the addresses of police officers in Northern Ireland and the details of the GOC's car. Adams disappeared as he always did at moments of difficulty.

John Reid immediately recommended suspending the institutions and putting the Agreement into review. We saw Trimble who was like the cat that has got the cream. He said that either we had to exclude Sinn Féin or suspend the institutions by 15 October. He complained bitterly about Republicans gathering political intelligence on his meetings which gave them an unfair advantage. An opinion poll that came out the next day showed that support for the Good Friday Agreement among unionists had sunk to only one-third. We saw the SDLP leader Mark Durkan and asked him if he would support an exclusion motion. He said he could not and would prefer suspension. We therefore opted for suspension on 15 October.

Trimble hadn't been keen to specify precisely what the IRA had to do to ensure the institutions were restored in future so, on 9 October, I minuted Tony that he should plan to go to Belfast and give a speech to win back credibility with the unionists and make it clear that the IRA now had to stop all paramilitary and criminal activity. The transition must be complete. It was high-risk but we had to force the choice. He agreed and started thinking about what he would say.

The Irish were not at first as convinced as we were that this was a serious setback, but we persuaded Bertie Ahern to put out a statement calling on the IRA to end its transition from violence to peaceful means as a quid pro quo for keeping the North/South bodies going after suspension. Tony said to him that the timelines for IRA transition and unionist tolerance of their behaviour were out of sync. Sinn Féin had to make a choice. Bertie said he would make a speech in parallel to Tony's. The Irish were attached to going ahead with the scheduled May elections to the Northern Ireland Assembly and some of the Irish officials made barbed comments about Paisley being easier to deal with than Trimble.

Trimble himself was convinced we were writing him off and looking to other Unionist leaders. He said we were briefing against him. I assured him we were not. In fact, John Reid and the NIO were of the opinion we would be better off with Paisley, but Tony remained obstinately committed to Trimble until the very end. He wrote to me, 'I have advised John [Reid] to be very careful on this and discount any natural personal desire to be shot of Trimble – he is still our best hope.'

Adams and McGuinness were apprehensive when we met on 10 October thinking we were going to be tough with them, but Tony was, as ever, scrupulously polite. He repeated what he had said to Bertie about the IRA and the Unionists being on different timelines, and said 'we needed a big bang so that it would be clear Republicans had abandoned the dual-track approach'. Simply another act of decommissioning wouldn't help. The one negotiating card the Unionists had was the continued existence of the IRA. Adams said he shared our objective of disbanding the IRA but it was a question of how to bring it about. He asked what timescale we were talking about. He also suggested the reason it had all collapsed was because we were distracted with Iraq and had lost any strategic view of the process, a criticism we didn't take terribly seriously.

It looked as though the institutions we had worked so hard to create in Northern Ireland were falling, irreparably, apart. Trimble was pushing for a continuing, undefined, role for himself and Durkan after suspension. The Irish, meanwhile, wanted us to inflict pain on the Unionists by presenting British/Irish cooperation as a move in the direction of joint sovereignty. We had struggled for four years to implement the Good Friday Agreement, by giving a few concessions to one side and then a few to the other in the hope that we could build trust between the sides over time. But time had worked against us: the peace process had become badly discredited and morally undermined. It no longer seemed to be based on principle. Now we had to restore its credibility and force the Republicans into a choice between the ballot box and the Armalite.

10

An End to Ambiguity:
October 2002 – November 2003

'There is no parallel track left. The fork in the road has finally come. We cannot carry on with the IRA half in, half out of this process. Not just because it isn't right any more. It won't work any more . . . So that's where we are. Not another impasse. But a fundamental choice of direction, a turning point.'

The speech Tony gave in Belfast on 18 October 2002 was an important one which marked the opening of a new phase of the negotiations. There were no meetings with party leaders or appearances with the police or army. We just flew in, Tony delivered the speech at the Belfast Harbour Commissioner's Office beside the docks in central Belfast, and we flew back again. There was a small Sinn Féin demonstration outside but they didn't have much heart in them.

Our press secretary, Tom Kelly, who as a unionist and a long-time political journalist in Northern Ireland was our best guide to the mood there, had had the first crack at writing the speech, but Tony had rewritten it in his own words on the flight from Moscow and we had discussed it back and forth. Tony was nervous about its impact right up to the last moment. Was it a good idea to be so clear about what we were demanding? What would the reaction be? Would we burn our boats with Republicans?

The speech's core idea was that we could no longer try to implement the Good Friday Agreement by small steps, but had to do it by one giant leap. The ambiguity that had made the Good Friday Agreement possible in the first place had ceased to be constructive and had become a hindrance. Unionists needed to know that the IRA's armed campaign was over for good and Republicans would resort only to political means. Nationalists needed to know that the unionists were not just messing about but were really prepared to share power and respect their rights. On both sides we needed 'acts of completion'.

The 'securocrats' had told us that they did not believe that the IRA would really cease until Irish unification was achieved. We believed we had to persuade Republicans that the answer to David Ervine's question at Weston Park was that 'the causes of conflict' would be resolved, not when unification took place, but once the Good Friday Agreement was implemented in full. The key message to Republicans in the speech was the one Tony had been giving them privately for some time. 'The continuing existence of the IRA as an active para-military organisation is now the best card those whom Republicans call "rejectionist" unionists have in their hand.' In other words the threat of the IRA returning to violence was no longer a negotiating lever to make the Brits do what they wanted but had become the key blockage to progress.

In the event, reaction to the speech was generally good. The Irish were a little sore at not being fully consulted, and put out a statement the press interpreted as a rejection. But the speech made the impact we had intended, helping to restore Tony's standing in Northern Ireland, particularly among unionists, by describing things as they actually were rather than as we wished them to be. The DUP liked it so much they later took up the conditions Tony set out in the speech and turned them into the 'Blair necessities' in their 2003 election manifesto, representing their demands before they would go into government with Sinn Féin.

I had warned Adams about the speech and sent him a copy in advance. We awaited his reaction with bated breath. He called me a few days afterwards to say he had seen 'some people' and the situation was slipping away from him. But he was interested in what Tony had said about taking away excuses from rejectionist unionists and about steps to stop the unionists wrecking the Executive and North/South bodies again. And then to my surprise he asked for my help in drafting his response. I was rather taken aback and asked if he wanted me to draft part of his speech, and he replied yes, he was giving a keynote speech on Saturday and could I send him a draft of what he should say in response to Tony's speech.

This was a crucial opening. If we could get Adams to respond constructively and hint in public at what he had said to us in private, we might have something we could build on to replace the discredited old negotiations. I tried my best to give an approximation of republican-speak, and sent him the following:

> Tony Blair's speech was portrayed by the media as no more than a call for the IRA to disband. It was in fact a serious and detailed speech, and deserves a considered response. He recognised Catholics in the North had been treated as second-class citizens. I agree. He said the overwhelming majority of people want the institutions to remain in place. I agree. He said that the time for transition had come to an end. There was a need for acts of completion. I agree. He said that the British government thought the Good Friday Agreement should be implemented in one fell swoop instead of a concession to one side here and a concession to the other there. I agree. The IRA is never going to disband in response to ultimatums from the British government or David Trimble. But I do believe the logic of the peace process puts us all in a different place. So if you ask me do I envisage a future without an IRA? The answer is obvious. The answer is yes.

I was absolutely amazed when he delivered the speech on 26 October with the draft passage contained within in it pretty much unchanged, saying the IRA would disappear. I had considered the ideas I had provided as probably too challenging. It was a thoughtful speech which we could build on. But now I was terrified someone other than Tony and Tom would find out I had been the author of part of it.

A few days later, the IRA came back with a response, in their usual convoluted language. 'In our view the full implementation by the two governments of their commitments could provide a political context with the potential to remove the causes of conflict.' So the answer to David Ervine's question at Weston Park was 'maybe'. This was followed, shortly afterwards, by a more concise public declaration by McGuinness who said, 'My war is over.'

We now had a new basis for final status negotiations. We all accepted that the aim was not further small steps towards peace but an agreement that would bring about the disappearance of the IRA and the beginning of genuine power-sharing. Of course, getting there wasn't going to be easy but there was a fresh sense of optimism. And we had a new Northern Ireland Secretary in Paul Murphy, the second

Catholic to hold the job. Paul had been a minister in the department with Mo, was well liked by all the parties, and had been instrumental in concluding the internal political part of the Good Friday Agreement dealing with the Assembly and the Executive.

Bertie Ahern had said to us that he believed the winter was the time to make progress in the negotiations, before the return of the 'white nights' in the summer. On 31 October I wrote a note for Tony setting out our objectives for this new 'big bang' approach. I said we were not seeking disbandment of the IRA but its standing down. We wanted, as we had said in the summer, an end to all training, targeting, acquisition or development of arms or any similar preparations for terrorist violence. But now we were also seeking an end to punishment attacks, exiling and organised rioting and street disturbances. Decommissioning or saying the war was over was helpful but not sufficient. Reality was more important than words this time. We agreed this 'big bang' approach with the Irish on 12 November and McGuinness told us they were 'up for it'. I said we were not being prescriptive. It was up to the IRA to implement these objectives within the context of their history and traditions.

We made little progress in November and December, with Sinn Féin just demanding more and more papers from us on different aspects of the deal. And David Trimble was uncertain. He called me in late November to say he understood we were cooking up a deal with Sinn Féin to accept an oral assurance from the IRA that they would stand down in return for a series of concessions the Unionists would be unable to accept, including handing over the police to ex-IRA members. I assured him it wasn't true. He did at least provide a little light relief on 19 December by walking out of multi-party talks in Northern Ireland when, according to the press, an Irish official inadvertently left behind a briefing paper at a summit meeting indicating that the NIO thought the IRA was breaching the ceasefire by actively engaging in training, targeting and recruiting, which if true would require that IRA prisoners who had been released on licence be put back in prison. Michael Collins, the Taoiseach's Northern Ireland adviser, was shamefaced about the slip when he spoke to me the next day, but Trimble phoned me jubilant rather than angry.

Given the difficulty we were having getting the two sides to engage,

I spent my Christmas working up a new plan, instead of eating mince pies with my family. I thought there should be a joint declaration by the two governments setting out what we believed to be the acts of completion required by all sides, which we could put to the parties and challenge them to implement. The format of a joint declaration had always been preferred by the British government because it allowed a single text negotiation which could group together all of the parties' concerns. It would say that the IRA had to give up all paramilitary and criminal activity and accept that implementation of all the outstanding issues would remove the causes of conflict; an international body would monitor the ceasefire to give unionists confidence; we would address the issues in the 57-page paper of demands that Sinn Féin had sent us on Christmas Eve on everything from OTRs to human rights; there would be measures to reassure the unionists about what would happen if republicans reverted to violence once the institutions were set up; we would, if possible, agree on devolution of policing and Sinn Féin joining the policing board; and, finally, there would be a two-year programme for demilitarisation. I thought we could sell this to Adams and McGuinness, although a discussion was going on in the movement with significant opposition to their direction. The big problem was David Trimble. As he had lost touch with his party, it was questionable whether he could sell a deal on his side, and this time it looked terminal. And he had already ruled out devolution of policing, which was crucial to getting Sinn Féin into a position where they would join the police. We devised a Plan B: if the Unionists were to blame for failure this time, we should press ahead and implement as much of the Agreement as we could by ourselves. If Sinn Féin were to blame we should cancel the Northern Ireland Assembly elections in May. This was something we and the Irish kept promising ourselves we would do – attribute blame to one side or the other for a breakdown – but it never worked out that way. Either the parties manoeuvred at the last moment to avoid the blame or we decided it was not sensible to create a villain if we wanted to continue with the process. Since this time both sides were heading away from the common ground as fast as they could, it was clear we would have to lasso them and get them back into the ring.

After the new year I discussed the plan with Adams and McGuinness. Adams indicated he could agree to such an approach but they would probably have to have the special Army Convention they had been avoiding to get the deal through, and the army executive would need winning over. He said there was little confidence among republicans that we would be able to deliver our side of the deal. They believed implementation of our promises would be frustrated by 'old mind-sets further down the system'. McGuinness added that if they tried to join the policing board now, they would split the republican move-ment. He was not talking about a mere strengthening of the RIRA but the rise of a new and more effective republican physical force movement.

On Thursday 23 January 2003 we invited Bertie Ahern to No. 10 to discuss the plan over lunch. Unusually we had a guest chef come in, this time Jamie Oliver. The food was extraordinarily good but compli-cated. Michael Collins told me sotto voce as we were sitting down that Bertie didn't really like fancy food. He was much happier with bangers and mash. Even so, Bertie managed to choke down the pome-granate and rocket salad and be charm itself when meeting Jamie Oliver afterwards, thanking him profusely for the meal. And we managed to get the Irish to agree to our outline plan, with only a few caveats. They were much encouraged by the fact that McGuinness would be in charge of implementing the agreement this time. They always believed that McGuinness was much more representative than Adams of the IRA itself and therefore better able to deliver. I always thought Adams and McGuinness operated in lockstep in a highly disciplined fashion, although they were not above playing out 'good cop, bad cop' routines.

As agreed, I spent two days in Ireland with the Irish team working up the Joint Declaration at Farmleigh, the old Guinness mansion in Phoenix Park, now an official Irish government residence. The govern-ment had originally been offered the mansion by Lord Iveagh's family and turned it down, but later changed their minds and had to fork out £20 million to buy it, plus another £20 million on returning it to its original splendour. It is a quite remarkable place, with blazing fires and wonderful eighteenth-century rooms. Our two days were more like a house party than a negotiation and I was lucky enough to be given Lord Iveagh's bedroom, complete with a nineteenth-century bath you could disappear into. It made a change from the more usual venues for talks on housing estates in west Belfast. We managed to agree most of the Joint Declaration and its annexes fairly easily now the Irish accepted the idea of an independent monitoring commission (IMC) based on Trimble's original concept. They suggested it have one British, one Irish and one American member, and we agreed it should monitor both what we did in terms of demilitarisation as well as what the IRA and Loyalists did in giving up paramilitarism. They also accepted the idea of sanctions on those parties found to be in breach and we agreed a clear list of the paramilitary activities the IRA had to give up in paragraph 13 of the Joint Declaration. We had built up a real relationship of trust with the talented team of Irish officials working for Bertie led by Michael Collins. They were from a new generation and there was no edge to our discussions. Negotiations between British and Irish officials had not always been so smooth.

The difficult part of the negotiation was the paper on demilitarisation. The Irish objected to our conditional approach to demilitarisation, which still indicated the measures would only go ahead if the dissident threat was reduced, and I had no authority to change it further. The police and army said that what I had was the bottom line. But the Irish rejected it and said we would get nothing from the IRA in return for something so paltry. Tony refused to see the GOC and Chief Constable again so I had to negotiate a text I thought was acceptable with the aim of going back to sell it to the military afterwards. In return, we got from the Irish a good draft IRA statement committing them to standing down and completing decommissioning. Now all we had to do was get it past Sinn Féin and the UUP.

My driver to the airport for the plane back had worked for Lord Iveagh at Farmleigh when it was still a family home and had some wonderful stories about the place. He had also been Christopher Ewart-Biggs's driver when, in 1976, as British Ambassador in Dublin, he was killed by an IRA bomb. The huge old car had been blown right over and Ewart-Biggs died, but because of where they had put the bomb just beyond the gates of the ambassador's residence, it had impacted on the back of the car more, and even though the driver was wounded he had survived.

Having agreed the Joint Declaration with the Irish I went to Northern Ireland to see if I could sell it to the others. I didn't give the document to David Trimble but I ran through it with him orally. He was relaxed, which always worried me. He focused on verification and sanctions but did not raise any major problems. He said he saw this as the last hump in the road and he really thought we could make it work this time. The problem was he was not telling his colleagues what I told him, and this characteristic failure to communicate was to come back and haunt us yet again further down the line.

I went on to the Clonard monastery to see Adams and McGuinness. Predictably they rejected our text altogether with their usual bucket of cold water, and said it was very disappointing. McGuinness wanted to know where *our* 'big bang' was. In particular, they didn't like the Independent Monitoring Commission, partly because it was Trimble's idea but mainly because it would focus on reality rather than words. Their nervousness about the commission was a mirror image of the worries of the NIO, who were concerned it would undermine the role of the Chief Constable, and the Security Service, who were not sure they could share their intelligence with such a body.

Nor did I have much luck when I talked to the security forces about the changes I had been forced to make at Farmleigh to the section on demilitarisation. They made it clear they were not happy with the way I had abandoned conditions based on the end of the dissident threat, and they didn't like the way I had speeded up and front loaded the programme of demilitarisation so the Republicans would have something to show their supporters straight away. On 10 February we held a summit to try to resolve the issue. The military decided to over-whelm us with numbers, turning up with one admiral and two generals as well as Geoff Hoon and the head of the Security Service. In fact, despite all their huffing and puffing beforehand, we were able to agree fairly amicably on a revised annexe on demilitarisation, with the help of the Chief Constable, Hugh Orde, appointed in 2002, who was, as always, the most reasonable person in the room.

Tony and Bertie went to Northern Ireland two days later to launch the idea of a joint declaration formally with the parties. The weather was too bad to take a helicopter from the airport to Hillsborough, and instead we travelled in a motorcade, which unfortunately missed the back gate of Hillsborough, causing the embarrassing sight of twenty cars and motorbikes trying to back up a small country lane to return to the correct entrance. Even more embarrassingly, the car with the Irish officials in it had a puncture and got left behind. They were convinced we did it deliberately to keep them out of the negotiations. We gave the parties our new paper on demilitarisation and they seemed fairly satisfied with it although Adams was less so. Tony and I were clear with Sinn Féin that, this time, they couldn't lead us down the garden path and then deliver 10 per cent less than was necessary at the last moment, as they had done up to now. If they did, the deal would collapse. The only way to rebuild unionist confidence was by the IRA making a historic leap forward in deed as well as word. We had asked the Irish to crack down hard on dissident republicans so that we could feel more secure in going ahead with demilitarisation on an unconditional basis. Michael McDowell, the Irish Justice Minister, had drawn up draconian steps to deal with dissidents, using every-thing short of internment, but then the Irish backed off under Sinn Féin pressure, arguing that such severe steps would be counter-productive, alienating the republican population. We concluded the meeting by deciding we would enter into intensive negotiations with the aim of reaching agreement in time for the May Assembly elections.

On the way back to London, our RAF plane detected a heat-seeking missile targeting us as we came in to land at Northolt. The RAF told the security authorities but forgot to tell us and we only found out about it later by accident. I was glad to have been kept in ignorance, particularly since I would have worried unnecessarily: subsequent investigations showed the signal to have been given off by a train spark rather than a terrorist with a shoulder-launched surface-to-air missile. I found the best way to deal with security threats was generally not to think about them. Ignorance is a great release.

On Tuesday 18 February I went back to Belfast to begin the intensive negotiations. My first meeting was with Sinn Féin to go through their 57-page wish list. We met at Windsor House, the home of the Anglo-Irish secretariat, and one of the few skyscrapers in Belfast. It had a lovely view over the city, but the view didn't compensate for the amount of time we were forced to spend there. Sinn Féin decided to extract their pound of flesh by making us work for a straight fourteen hours as we went through their document line by line with our experts, covering policing, criminal justice reform, human rights, the Irish language and a series of other highly technical subjects. At about two in the morning, as Bairbre de Brún, not the lightest and most charming of human beings at the best of times, started going through ten pages on human rights, I decided the treatment we were getting from Sinn Féin was, as I wrote in my diary, 'their revenge for all those years of Special Branch men being impolite to them in the interrogation rooms at Castlereagh'. At four in the morning, after we had been through all the documents, Adams said it was probably better not to have an IRA statement after all. The IRA were expected to do everything upfront while we wouldn't demilitarise till after three years. The Irish were terribly depressed, but I wrote, 'I have seen Adams do this too often to think this is the end of the process.' Adams took Michael Collins and me into an adjoining room and asked us for a series of compromises on policing, particularly on banning the use of plastic bullets. I explained that if we withdrew plastic bullets, the police and army would have to resort to live rounds which would lead to many more deaths.

The next day we showed the Joint Declaration to David Trimble and Michael McGimpsey, a moderate in the party and increasingly in Trimble's inner circle, and they reacted very badly indeed even though it had his IMC in it. As I wrote in my diary, 'All they ever do is say no, and focus on the irrelevant details, like the Irish parliamentary committee to consider Northern Ireland matters in one of the annexes, instead of the main issues at hand.' Trimble insisted on the sanctions being set out in detail, wanting them as a way of punishing Sinn Féin if the IRA returned to violence. But since we hadn't been able to agree what the sanctions should be – just fines or expulsion from the executive – we had proposed to refer the issue to George Mitchell to decide.

As agreed in February, the two prime ministers came back to Hillsborough for a two-day negotiating session on Monday 3 March. It was at the height of our efforts to secure a second UN Security Council Resolution authorising the use of force in Iraq. We spent the first part of the morning at Downing Street in our daily meeting with the military, diplomats and intelligence experts on Iraq, and only then headed off for Northern Ireland. But Tony's mind was on Iraq the whole time. He was trying to find a way for Chile and Mexico, the key swing votes in the UN Security Council, to climb down from their previous opposition so they could support our resolution.

At Hillsborough, Adams and McGuinness demanded their conces-sions on plastic bullets, demilitarisation, criminal justice and policing. Tony ummed and ahhed and failed even to raise the date of the Assembly elections with them, on which the Unionists wanted a post-ponement. Luckily Bertie was more focused. The Unionists completely flipped when we told them we could not put off the election date, and threatened to walk out of the talks altogether. We went back to Sinn Féin, who would not agree to put off the elections, but said they would not make a huge fuss if *we* did so, as long as everything else was right. They were in too weak a position to make much fuss anyway, since they were demanding four weeks to clear the ideas with the IRA, and the holding of an Army Convention. It was looking very rocky until Adams and McGuinness met Trimble and Empey in the evening and told them they would get the IRA to disband and have a large act of decommissioning before the UUC were required to approve the deal. They followed up by repeating the commitment to the Unionists in front of Tony and Bertie and it changed the mood.

Tony spent most of the next morning working the phones to Pres-ident Lagos of Chile and other key members of the Security Council. We were unable to get hold of President Fox of Mexico because he had retired to hospital to avoid any more calls about Iraq. Meanwhile Sinn Féin talked direct to the UUP while Des Browne and Jane Kennedy, the political and security junior ministers, went through the detailed issues on policing and human rights with the parties. We thought we were making progress but in the early evening, when Tony was on the phone to Goran Perrson, the Swedish Prime Minister, discussing the Security Council Resolution, Trimble burst into the Lady Gray room, where Tony was based, and told us he was leaving. Tony carried on listening to Perrson with his hand over the receiver trying to persuade Trimble not to leave, but Trimble slipped out of the room anyway. I chased after him, pleading with him not to go, but to no avail. We assumed that meant there were problems in the negotia-tions but in fact it was just that he wanted to fly back to London for Prime Minister's Questions in the Commons the next day.

Sinn Féin kept us going all evening with a series of demands on policing and sanctions, only to tell us at 11 p.m. that there was no deal. Bertie went to see them in the office set aside for them and offered to make the issue of sanctions a separate free-standing agreement in which they did not have to acquiesce. We had an agreement by midnight and postponed the May elections until the autumn.

Notwithstanding all the time they had already used up, Adams and McGuinness still insisted on coming to see us again in Downing Street on 25 March. They said there was a huge problem with the choreography of the different steps. The IRA wouldn't re-engage with de Chastelain and begin on decommissioning until the institutions were back up and running, but the Unionists required decommissioning before they would go back into government. We said we would try to find a solution. Adams floated the idea of Volunteers dumping arms as they had at the end of the 1950s campaign. The IRA would remain as a skeletal structure with no weapons and no paramilitary activity. Tony said there needed to be complete decommissioning. Adams said this was an either/or – either they dumped arms unilaterally or they decommissioned through the IICD. Adams also suggested that policing was a very difficult issue for them and they might need to postpone dealing with it. For good measure they finished off by giving us a lecture about the Iraq War.

The two issues came together again when, on 7 April, President Bush came to stay at Hillsborough. It had been my idea to hold our talks in Northern Ireland, and we had floated the notion when we went to Camp David in early February. With the war in Iraq now under way, we wanted somewhere for a quiet summit to discuss the aftermath, where we would not face a big anti-war demonstration and where the President could relax. I also hoped we could use the visit to give the Northern Ireland peace process a boost. The idea did not meet with universal approval on our side but we did it anyway.

We helicoptered in on the Monday afternoon and the Bush armada arrived shortly afterwards. Tony and President Bush stood for an hour in the sunshine at the gate to the flower garden at Hillsborough talking about the parallels between the Middle East and Northern Ireland and Bush said he wanted to go beyond the road map. He was going to use his political capital to move the Middle East peace process forward by appointing a special envoy and summoning a new Madrid Conference. We were delighted, having been arguing for a focus on Middle East peace since the President had been elected. After the meetings we had a joint press conference but, in the preparations, Bush got irritated with his National Security Adviser, Condoleezza Rice, when she tried to change his statement to the press to tone down the Middle East section. I thought he performed extremely well. He went out on a limb saying the UN would have a vital role in Iraq, as we had asked him to do, and that he would spend as much time on the Middle East as Tony had on the Northern Ireland peace process. Rice was furious afterwards and they huddled with Colin Powell in the big drawing room as she tore him off a strip. But Bush was not having any of it, and said he didn't care if the Pentagon would be upset about what he had said about a UN role in Iraq. In one of their long walks in the grounds that afternoon, Bush told Tony he intended to make Condi Rice Secretary of State after the election.

In the afternoon Bush met the Northern Ireland parties. Most of them had announced to the media in advance that they were going to give Bush a hard time on Iraq, but predictably they were overwhelmed by the occasion and just asked for his autograph or a signed photograph. It didn't stop many of them going out afterwards and announcing they had lectured him on the subject and I was glad I had vetoed the idea of allowing them to sit down and make set-piece speeches.

The visit failed, however, to make progress on Northern Ireland and for the next two weeks we were stuck in a prolonged wrangle about the wording of the IRA statement.

A couple of days after the Bush visit, Adams and McGuinness summoned me and Tim Dalton to Belfast to give us the IRA statement. As soon as we saw it, it was obvious to both of us that it was inadequate, and Adams didn't make much of an effort to sell it. Adams and McGuinness left Windsor House, where we were meeting, to go and see Reg Empey at the Clonard monastery. I called Empey after they had met and he had found the text hopeless too. It had some obscure IRA-style language that might hint in the right direction but was of no use with the public. Adams went back to the IRA overnight but what they came back with was no better.

The next day Adams called Tony asking him to come over to publish the Joint Declaration as he had promised. Tony said there was no point as the IRA statement was at best ambiguous. It did not say the war was over, it did not say paramilitary activity would cease and it did not commit them to complete decommissioning. There would be no deal without a clear statement. Adams complained that Tony wasn't coming because Trimble had told him not to. We agreed amendments with Trimble that would make it acceptable and sent them to Adams.

At this point the Irish got more involved. Bertie called Tony on Saturday 12 April saying he had Adams and McGuinness still with him in his office. He wouldn't be able to secure the amendments to the IRA statement we had agreed with Trimble but they could get something that said the same thing. Adams and McGuinness were going away to consult a 'wider group' and would come back to hand over the revised words in Dublin the next afternoon. He asked if I would go to Dublin to join him in seeing them at his constituency office in Drumcondra in north Dublin.

Before I left, I went to see my mother who was in a home near Salisbury. Suffering from Alzheimer's, for the past week she had been in a coma and was now close to death. It had been difficult to find opportunities to see her in the preceding weeks and now I had to cut short saying my last goodbyes to her in order to leave for Dublin. It was a sad occasion for me. When she died a few weeks later, Adams and McGuinness sent me condolence cards and I thought there was a certain irony. My mother came from an Anglo-Irish family and her view of Ireland was formed by the *Irish RM* books, with their description of the life of the ascendancy and their fox hunts and grand balls in the Irish countryside. Fenians were not her cup of tea and whenever I told her I was off to see Sinn Féin she would say, 'I am so sorry for you, darling.' What she would have thought of two of them marking her death I do not know.

To make matters worse, I had been struck down with some ghastly intestinal illness and spent most of my flight to Dublin doubled up in pain. So when Adams and McGuinness made us wait four hours for them without any word whatsoever my mood did not improve. Bertie's constituency office in an old house on the main road into north Dublin was fascinating. The walls were lined with pictures of world leaders he had met, even obscure ones like Victor Klima, a former Chancellor of Austria. I passed the time with Brian Cowen, Michael McDowell and Irish officials, much of it over the road in a well-known pub opposite Bertie's office. When Adams and McGuinness eventually turned up, Bertie and I saw them in an upstairs room alone. They handed over the scrappy piece of paper and Bertie and I read it. Bertie turned to me and asked me what I thought. I said it was no good; it was unclear. Tony had a theory that Sinn Féin were at root ultra-leftists and like other ultra-leftists deliberately refused to use language that was clear. Bertie agreed. Adams started getting angry. He said the problem was not a shortage of thesauruses or dictionaries but that the IRA did not *want* to say what we wanted them to say. I remember thinking to myself that eight stubborn middle-aged men in South Armagh were stopping Northern Ireland moving in the direction most of its people wanted it to.

The next day Northern Ireland Secretary Paul Murphy, who had waited all Sunday at Hillsborough for the IRA text with Richard Haass the US envoy, made a statement in the House saying that we were seeking clarification from the IRA of what their real intentions were. Adams, who was getting increasingly desperate, contacted us to suggest that he clarify Republicans' intentions himself instead of leaving it to the IRA. Tony and Bertie discussed the approach in the margins of the EU summit in Athens two days later. Tony said Trimble would be eaten alive on the basis of the existing statement which failed to address the crucial three questions properly. The IRA needed to be clear that: a) this was the end of the conflict; b) they would cease to engage in paramilitary activities; and c) they would put all their arms beyond use. He said Adams was trying to split the two governments and we must avoid any daylight between us. Bertie admitted that the 'clarification' Republicans had now offered was 'one step beyond Jesuitical'.

Tony decided to call a press conference with the Northern Ireland media the next day to pose the three questions publicly. The pressure this applied discomfited Sinn Féin no end. Tony and Adams had a fractious phone conversation in the afternoon, in which Tony said elections to a non-existent Assembly made no sense. Adams said the IRA constitution forbade it to cease to be an army. He said again that he didn't believe the problem was a lack of clarity, 'but the fact that the IRA statement did not go as far as the government would like'. IRA Volunteers had been waiting around all Easter to put weapons beyond use and it was bizarre *we* were now putting decommissioning off. Adams also complained about the 'Alice in Wonderland' world in which Unionists insisted Sinn Féin and the IRA were one and the same but would only accept clarification from the IRA rather than from

Sinn Féin. Tony said he would consider a statement by Adams rather than the IRA.

The Irish showed us Adams's words on Saturday and it was clear they were not good enough. But when Tony called Adams on Sunday to suggest some amendments, Adams said he was 'flying solo and risked running out of fuel'. On Monday 28 April, when Tony called him again and said his words still did not answer the questions clearly, Adams said he was at the end of his tether. Tony said he had to make it clear that paramilitary activity *would* rather than *should* end. For the first time Adams got flustered and said he and the Prime Minister could fall out over this. Someone else would have to pick up the pieces. He was clearly under intense pressure not to move further. That afternoon Adams went ahead with his statement as it was and we made a show of welcoming it (even though it failed to be as clear as we wanted), but Trimble called in a terrible state. He said the UUP would refuse to put anyone up for the job of First Minister if we went ahead on this basis and would vote against anyone who stood. What was more, he would be out of a job within a week anyway if we went ahead. Tony said we had to accept the answer 'yes' from Adams to our three questions and he shouldn't worry: we could use the verification and sanctions mechanisms to hold Republicans to their commitments. Tony promised not to leave Trimble high and dry but he urged him to handle the situation cannily.

Adams called Tony two days later and asked whether, if he answered Tony's third question on the end of paramilitary activity, we would publish the Joint Declaration. Tony said we would if he did so clearly, and I faxed him some appropriate wording. Adams called me at twelve, just as Tony was going into the Chamber for Prime Minister's Questions, with language that did not meet the point at all. He said he was holding a press conference at one. I said that was fine but he still hadn't answered the question. Afterwards, Bertie called Tony to try and persuade him that Adams's language was sufficient, but Tony made clear it wouldn't work. Adams's spin worked at first with the press, but it rapidly became apparent to journalists that he couldn't actually answer the key questions we had put.

On 1 May Adams held yet another press conference to ask 'What part of "no activities" do the Brits not understand?' But he didn't do well under press questioning. We told Trimble we had decided to postpone the elections. Bertie said he would have to disagree with our decision in public although he understood the reasons. He asked Tony if he would come to Dublin to kiss and make up. Before we had got off the phone, Michael McDowell, who as a leader of the small Progressive Democrats Party in the Irish coalition government was crucial to keeping Bertie in office, announced that we were cancelling elections and welcomed the decision.

On 6 May we went to Farmleigh to publish the Joint Declaration with Bertie. The Irish Cabinet was meeting there and again the place was full of blazing fires and liveried staff. Tony and Bertie held a joint press conference that evening. The IRA put out a statement denouncing us for our failure to go ahead as they wanted, but without much steam behind it. We had made a decision to push forward with implementing as much as we could of the Joint Declaration ourselves and started removing two of the towers in South Armagh that day. After the press conference Tony met the Irish Cabinet in the huge conservatory attached to the house and they started the meeting by singing him happy birthday and serving him champagne. Tony and Bertie discussed Northern Ireland politics and Tony said to Bertie that the DUP would be impossible to deal with and would reject all North/South cooperation. However frustrating David Trimble was, he was better than the DUP.

That week the *Sunday Times* Northern Ireland correspondent published a series of transcripts of phone calls he had reportedly been given by a disgruntled former policeman. They included records of conversations between Mo Mowlam and Martin McGuinness, and of a conversation between me and Martin McGuinness in which I poked fun at one of the UUP MPs who had rebelled against Trimble. The Security Service were embarrassed and called me to say Special Branch had been told years ago not to transcribe such conversations. And Trimble called me up to say, amiably, he thought my criticisms of the MP in question were understated.

But despite Tony's view that Trimble was the best leader of unionism we were likely to have, it was becoming clear he was on the way out. When we invited Adams and McGuinness to lunch at Chequers on 27 May to talk about a way forward, Adams said most republicans saw Trimble as the road to nowhere and thought we should see what happened to unionism after an election. It was evident that Sinn Féin had no ideas of their own about how to progress, and rejected ours. McGuinness said the IRA thought we had set the bar too high. One day all activities would simply cease. He and Adams had been trying to get it all to fade away gradually. I asked if they were still thinking of calling an Army Convention. Adams said it would be unwise. Tony proposed again that he should meet the IRA leadership. It was a request he had repeatedly put to Adams over the years. And Tony had been pressed two years before to propose such a meeting both by President Clinton, and by Ahtisaari and Ramaphosa after their inspection visit. But Adams had always said no. This time, after a minute's reflection, Adams said yes and it seemed he might be serious because he rang me from the airport to ask me not to mention the idea to others. A week or so later he told me the IRA were prepared to meet Tony. They weren't very keen but they had some things they wanted to say to him. They thought he had a one-dimensional view of them as criminals. But, as before, the offer never came to anything.

Donaldson finally attempted to mount a coup against Trimble by calling a UUC to reject the Joint Declaration. I asked Trimble what we could do to help. He told me 'he hoped he lost'. In fact, Donaldson overplayed his hand by threatening to leave the party: Trimble survived with 54 per cent of the vote and Donaldson was on the road out of the UUP. Despite Trimble's survival, however, there was a sense in Northern Ireland that he was a goner. In the words of the NIO there was a 'deep and developing crisis' within the UUP. Trimble appealed to us to put off elections in order to give him time to stabilise the party and set out his policy. He said he thought the familiar elements of the equation, like the insistence on decommissioning, would no longer do the trick. We would have to surprise unionists into feeling things had changed. A quiet summer would help. He suggested the IRA should become transparent. If they weren't engaged in illegal activity why not de-proscribe them and treat them as any other organisation? He argued for a Northern Ireland member of the Independent Monitoring Commission to give it greater credibility, and we agreed to appoint John Alderdice.

I met the Irish and Sinn Féin on 9 July to try and agree a package for the autumn. I said we required five things: a statement by the IRA, or by Adams, making it clear that paramilitary activity was over; an act of decommissioning; a statement by the UUP agreeing to set up the Executive after the elections; a report from the IMC on a quiet summer; and agreement on policing if possible. Adams said the atmosphere was poisoned. The British government had lost all credibility among republicans. He would not even ask the IRA for a statement on paramilitarism until we had agreed a certain date for elections. At the final meeting before the summer break, McGuinness said the IRA would not be able to improve on its April language. Adams contradicted him and said Sinn Féin would seek to improve it. The problem was that the IRA could not admit it was engaged in the paramilitary-style activities described in paragraph 13 of the Joint Declaration so they could not say they were going to refrain from them. We needed some other way for them to say what they were not going to do.

Republicans managed to deliver a quiet summer in Northern Ireland with minimal street violence and when we saw them again at the beginning of September, Adams and McGuinness said the IRA leadership was prepared to call it a day, but not while unionism was so unstable and there was a threat to them from republican dissidents. Who would protect them from the RIRA, McGuinness asked, if not the IRA? Adams said in any case he couldn't sell anything to the IRA without a date for an election. Tony said he was 95 per cent certain he would have elections in November. Adams said that 95 per cent certainty wasn't enough. I said we would need 100 per cent on the other side if we were going to be 100 per cent clear about elections. At a meeting a few days later in Belfast, Adams said to me he would not show us the new draft IRA statement until he got an unqualified commitment to an election date. I said we had got into 'a ridiculous "you show me yours first" impasse'. We had to get an IRA statement ending paramilitarism and an act of decommissioning before we could call elections.

We arranged a meeting with Sinn Féin and Bertie Ahern at Chequers on Sunday 14 September to try to cut through the impasse. Since we made it a rule never to stand on our dignity in such a situation, I had agreed with Tony in advance that we would give Adams a letter with a date for elections. We had decided to go ahead and hold them anyway so it was no skin off our nose to give them the commitment they wanted. I got to Chequers late but managed to slip in just before Bertie's motorcade. Michael Collins, Bertie, Tony, Adams, McGuinness and I had dinner in the dining room overlooking the rose garden, and I handed over the letter. It said we would hold Assembly elections on or before 4 December 2003. Once called, the date of elections would not be changed. Even then Adams initially refused to show us his statement, although he did, eventually, later in the evening. Predictably, it was hopeless. Tony wrote out an alternative on a scrap of paper on the spot and told them to just do it: it was up to them whether they got Trimble or Paisley as their partner; if they wanted the former, they had to take a step forward. They hinted that they might consider issuing an instruction to Volunteers to lay down arms and to have a moratorium on activity. We were not sure that would do the trick, particularly if it was time-limited rather than once and for all.

When Tony called Adams on 24 September, Adams said he could get the IRA to 'do the desired action' but his problem was getting them to 'say it'. I came back early from the Labour Party conference to meet Sinn Féin, the Irish and Trimble and Michael McGimpsey at Downing Street in early October. Adams gave us another draft of the statement in manuscript. I said it was not clear about the end to para-militarism and it still made the closure of the conflict conditional. McGuinness said rather theatrically that, if the two governments insisted on Sinn Féin clarifying how 'the IRA would fold up its tent and go away [. . .] there would be a change of leadership'. Trimble was in a bouncy mood, wanting a deal, and was more focused on getting transparency and visibility for the act of decommissioning than on the actual wording of Adams's statement. I told both of them that, if they could agree wording between them, we could live with what they decided. Adams ended the meeting by giving me a signed copy of his latest autobiography and disappearing on a book tour for three days.

Tony was getting completely fed up with the messing around, and when he met Bertie in Rome at an EU meeting, they agreed a joint letter to Adams trying to pin him down. The letter, which referred to his agreement to give instructions to Volunteers on the ground to end paramilitarism, caused a furious reaction from Adams who sent back a stiffly worded reply talking about the misrepresentation of Sinn Féin's position by the two governments. He rang me to complain bitterly and say he suspected we had written the letter in order to leak it. It would cause him real difficulty with the IRA. He realised after a few days that it was not a trap we had set for him but it expressed the frustration on the part of the two prime ministers at the slowness of progress.

That October, Adams and Trimble met a number of times to negotiate between themselves. We attached great importance to these face-to-face meetings between them and, in my diary, I noted having seen Adams and Trimble sitting next to each other on the sofa in Tony's den in actual bodily contact. I saw it as a sign of hope, but sadly I was wrong.

Adams called me in triumph on 16 October, saying he had got a deal with the IRA and was taking it to Trimble. But shortly afterwards I got a call from Trimble saying he was losing Michael McGimpsey, his one remaining supporter in the party, who was demanding a date for the standing down of the IRA and an end date for decommissioning. I spoke to Adams and tried to get the deal back on the tracks, but as I commented in my diary at the time: 'It is like herding cats. I have no idea if I will be able to corral them by next week.'

The package was this: elections on 26 November, after an Adams statement endorsed by the IRA; an act of decommissioning; a Trimble statement calling a UUC; and a statement by the two governments. We kept getting a deal, only for it to slip away from us. Then Tony was rushed in to hospital with a heart problem, and I was left juggling Northern Ireland and a raft of other issues.

For a moment, it looked good. Adams asked for a conference call at ten on Sunday 19 October with himself, Trimble, Michael Collins and me. He said they would go ahead with the act of decommissioning on Monday and that Trimble had promised him he would go ahead with the deal on Tuesday. But we still had a major problem. De Chastelain called me on Sunday evening: 'P. O'Neill' had made it clear that de Chastelain wouldn't be allowed to say more about what he had witnessed than he had been able to say after the last act of decommissioning. He was going to go ahead and observe the decommissioning anyway but he could see it would be a problem with the Unionists. I called Adams and McGuinness to warn them what would happen if this condition held. It would be ridiculous to have a major act of decommissioning and yet lose the whole process simply because they wouldn't allow de Chastelain to talk about it.

On Sunday morning Trimble had been cheerful because he had Reg

Empey back on board, but by the evening he was discombobulated because it became clear Empey had only come back on board in order to denounce the whole deal. On Monday Trimble called repeatedly, one moment on a high, the next in a panic, at one stage asking for a conference call with Adams to discuss the choreography of announcements. In the evening the Republicans briefed the media that Tuesday was a historic day. Adams called me to say that Trimble should be boosting the event too. But unless de Chastelain could say the right thing about the act of decommissioning on Tuesday, the whole deal would collapse. We tried to set up a conference call between Tony, who had come back into the office on Monday, Bertie and de Chastelain but we could not get hold of de Chastelain. Trimble called me late on Monday night to say he must have something convincing from de Chastelain tomorrow or he was sunk.

Monday night was incredibly tense. We spent until dawn trying to find de Chastelain by all the means at our disposal. Only later did we discover that he had been held incommunicado in the south by the IRA overnight. They had been instructed not to start decommissioning until the elections were called and for some reason had thought we would announce the date of the election on Monday, and it was only once we had made the announcement on Tuesday morning that the IRA actually started the decommissioning.

On Tuesday Bertie said he wasn't sure we should go to Belfast for the launch until we got the de Chastelain report back. In retrospect he was probably right to try and avoid yet another embarrassing failure for the two prime ministers, but Tony wanted to get on with it. We finally managed to track de Chastelain down once he had been released by the IRA and was able to respond to the messages on his mobile phone. We were about to land in Belfast and I spoke to him on the phone in the front cabin of the RAF plane. I told him to get up to Hillsborough as fast as he could. Once de Chastelain and his colleague, Andy Sens, arrived at Hillsborough, looking a little crumpled after their night inspecting, we rushed them into a meeting with Tony and Bertie in the Lady Gray room. We urged them to say the maximum possible but they refused, citing their confidentiality agreement with the IRA. We repeated this exercise a number of times and asked them to go away and prepare the best statement they could. Tony drafted elements for them to use but they were reluctant. Eventually we had to let de Chastelain go and talk to the waiting press and it was a disaster. We had probably made it worse by trying to coach him. He was completely tongue-tied and, even under questioning, could not indicate what sort of weaponry he was talking about, apart from at one stage saying, ludicrously, he wasn't talking about tanks. When it was over de Chastelain was excruciatingly embarrassed by the event. He had been put in an impossible position. But the damage was done.

I phoned Trimble in advance to warn him what to expect, but as we were watching the press conference on television, first David Campbell and then David Trimble called me to say rather hysterically that this was nothing like enough. Trimble was bouncing off the walls and said de Chastelain had blown it. I asked if he was issuing his statement and going ahead according to the agreed choreography. He said probably but he needed to consult his colleagues. When I called him back a few minutes later he said he was going to do a press conference saying the whole process was on hold. Tony tried talking to Trimble and to Adams. Trimble asked for a list of headings of the sorts of weapons we were talking about and a timescale for completion of decommissioning. Adams said no. Soon afterwards, Adams and McGuinness turned up at Hillsborough. We urged them to agree to greater transparency but again they said no.

The debacle illustrated the continuing gap between unionists and republicans. The IRA thought what they had done was historic, and it was. But the unionists thought 'seeing was believing', and given the history of delay and deception they were right too.

Tony was furious and blamed me for not preparing the event properly. With the benefit of hindsight, we should have stopped the sequence when de Chastelain called me on Sunday night to tell me how restricted he would be in what he could say. After de Chastelain's call, I had spoken to Tony just after his heart operation, and he had said we should let the act go ahead but ask de Chastelain to tell the IRA that he would be giving more detail to the press. I had repeated Tony's injunction to de Chastelain but of course he was unable to deliver. I apologised to Bertie about having gone ahead with the visit despite his qualms, but the alternative would have been a counsel of despair because the whole process would have ground to a halt. Tony carried on blaming me all the way back on the plane.

De Chastelain, who was a thoroughly decent man, offered to resign.

We said that of course he should not. The next day Tony said to Adams that the problem was not the Unionists but the failure of the IRA to move definitively. Bertie called Tony and said that Republicans had delivered and the problem was de Chastelain and Trimble. Mark Durkan called Tony and said, rather smugly, that he 'didn't need to say "I told you so"', having told us we would have nothing but trouble trying to cook up a deal with just Sinn Féin and the UUP and excluding the other parties.

In a desperate attempt to save something from the wreck, the two sides met at Hillsborough the following weekend by themselves. My daughter's sixth birthday party on the Saturday was disrupted by phone calls from both Trimble and Adams asking for advice, and soon they turned into pleas to come over. I jumped on a plane and on Sunday morning I managed to get the negotiations on to a sensible track. To my surprise, McGuinness indicated that the IRA could agree to saying that a certain percentage of their weapons had been decommissioned, but the Unionists switched their demand to a timetable for decommissioning. Trimble's mood shifted dramatically at a certain point in the day. In the morning and early afternoon of Sunday he wanted a deal, but under the influence of his negotiating team he suddenly changed and then nothing would do for him.

Eventually the Unionists convinced themselves they couldn't get a deal through the UUC and it was better to fight the election, if we were going to insist on having one, without a deal than with a bad one. Sinn Féin, for whom negotiation was a way of life, thought they were just playing hardball. In the end the Republicans offered both a timetable of twenty-four months for decommissioning and a percentage of arms decommissioned together with an annexe listing the types of weapons, an incredibly good deal, but still the Unionists turned it down.

Trimble took me aside at one stage towards the end of the day to say to me rather tearfully that he was finished one way or the other. Either he would go down at the UUC on the deal – even Sylvia Hermon, Jack Hermon's wife and the most moderate and sensible of the UUP MPs, wouldn't support it – or he would go down after the election because the UUP would lose seats. I urged him to go for the deal. Better to go down in flames trying to achieve something if he was going to go down anyway.

Tony called Trimble the next morning to see if he could talk him into accepting the deal but did not try very hard. He then called Adams and tried to persuade him to pull his punches with Trimble so we could put the thing up again after the election. Both Tony and Adams thought Trimble was still likely to beat the DUP in the coming elections. The IRA put out a statement on 29 October saying they had fulfilled their commitments but others had not fulfilled theirs: 'When we give our word we keep it.'

We were then into the election campaign. We carried out a private opinion poll which seemed to show the situation static and Trimble safe. But Trimble was in the wrong place fighting a defensive campaign with a divided party and a record of failure, he managed to lose the election. The DUP fought a tight, disciplined campaign and won. Although he remained as leader of the UUP, Trimble's political career was effectively over.

I was sorry to see David Trimble go. He had often been frustrating, but having been elected leader of the UUP as a hardliner, he had shown real statesmanship as the leader of unionism. He had been haunted by the fate of Brian Faulkner, whose downfall he had helped bring about, and in the end he went the same way, but unlike Faulkner his legacy was a lasting one. He had persevered in trying to bring about a deal with nationalists, and although he failed, it was essentially his deal that was eventually delivered by the DUP four years later. He had shown the ultimate political bravery by sacrificing his political career and his party for a greater cause, which was the future of the people of Northern Ireland as a whole. He will be remembered kindly by history.

II

'Sackcloth and Ashes':
November 2003 – December 2004

All our hopes of building agreement out from the centre in Northern Ireland were dashed by the election of 26 November 2003. The DUP and Sinn Féin came out of it as decisively the largest parties on either side and we now had to make peace between the two extremes.

On the day of the election results we met Bertie Ahern and his team in an odd little museum in Wales for a session of the British-Irish Council. Tony was depressed and extremely sceptical that Ian Paisley would ever do a deal. He proposed that our strategy should be to give the DUP enough rope either to reach an agreement or to hang themselves politically by obstructing one. If they said they wanted to renegotiate the Good Friday Agreement, we should say go ahead. If they said they could not talk to Sinn Féin face to face, we should offer to shuttle between the two of them carrying messages. At the same time, Sinn Féin should negotiate an agreement with the UUP. If the DUP were totally recalcitrant, we could then run d'Hondt, and if they refused to go into government, call new elections which the UUP might then be able to win.

I saw David Trimble a few days later. He was bitter, and blamed us for calling elections at all. He asked me why we did it. I said because we had an agreement to do so. He suggested we should have changed our minds, but I said that would have been too perfidious even for us. Trimble accepted our strategy of allowing the DUP to show themselves to be wreckers while he tried to reach an agreement with Sinn Féin. He wanted new elections soon, by Easter 2004 if possible.

Unfortunately, the flaw in Tony's plan was soon apparent. We could all see that it would be impossible for the UUP to win the elections unless the DUP were demonstrably unreasonable and intransigent, and the DUP were determined to avoid that trap. I wrote a note to

Tony at the beginning of December suggesting a refinement to his 'give them enough rope' strategy. Northern Ireland had had its quietest summer for thirty years and the economy was booming. Unionist voters were not much bothered by the political stalemate and had voted for the DUP as the stronger defender of their interests. New elections would only give us a bigger DUP majority. Our aim should be to accustom the DUP to negotiating, as we had the UUP in 1997, through proximity talks with Sinn Féin, something Paul Murphy and the NIO had already started working on. Regardless of whether we thought the DUP would do a deal (as the NIO did), or wouldn't (as David Trimble believed), our strategy should be the same. Their principal aim was to gain hegemony in the unionist community and they did not want to put that at risk by being presented as wreckers. So we should play the negotiations long, patiently working for an agreement and never giving the DUP an excuse to blame us for frustrating progress.

One problem we had to confront straight away, however, was the Sinn Féin demand that we deliver the promises we had offered them in the context of the October deal. Adams was on the phone to me the day after the election threatening to publish the private letters we had sent him promising to sort out the problem of Rita O'Hare and other OTRs. I explained that if we moved on these issues now we could kiss goodbye to any chance of getting the DUP to engage with them.

When Adams and McGuinness came to see Tony in No. 10 on 17 December, they were in a sour mood. McGuinness said in his opinion there was 'no chance of the DUP moving before Ian Paisley died'. Adams pressed us to deliver on our promises. Tony began suggesting we would, but I intervened to say the price of a deal had gone up since the election: we could not be expected to deliver our part of the agreement if they didn't implement theirs. I then went through with Adams a catalogue of recent IRA activities, including punishment beatings which had begun again after the elections. Adams reacted aggressively, challenging me to a debate on television. He was sure he would wipe the floor with me. I said that was not really the point. We were talking about reality not debating points. Tony said we had to remove the IRA as an excuse for the DUP refusing to make an agreement.

★   ★   ★

Early in January 2004, I wrote another note to Tony, this time arguing passionately that we should confront Adams and McGuinness about the continuing IRA activity. I said it had become a bit like the old Soviet joke – 'we'll pretend to work and you pretend to pay us'. We now had to face up to the reality of what was going on. I commissioned a dossier from the Security Service that we could use with Adams and McGuinness. It contained details of what the IRA were up to in intelligence work, targeting members of the security forces, recruitment and training. Meanwhile, Eliza Manningham-Buller arranged for Tony and me to come over to see first-hand some of the intelligence material. It was very convincing, and I drafted a speaking note for Tony to use with Adams, not covering specific cases, but saying 'this is not a matter of securocrats now. It is clear the IRA is still engaged in paramilitary activity. Unless you stop I will not be able to deliver on our side of the agreement and the Independent Monitoring Commission will expose you.'

When Adams and McGuinness came in on 16 January, Tony delivered the script although he pulled his punches a little. Adams was in conciliatory mode and, instead of trying to rebut the charges, said he didn't think the IRA were fighting fit after so many years of cease-fire, they were simply carrying out housekeeping. McGuinness added it would take time to wind down after twenty-five years of war. They asked where we should go from here. I mentioned the idea of the Republican leadership issuing an instruction to Volunteers to cease activity plus a motion at an Army Convention and suggested they come back soon for a brainstorming session.

But then, on 20 February, the IRA were caught red-handed as they tried to abduct Robert Tohill, a dissident republican, from Kelly's Cellar bar in central Belfast, with the intention of killing him. The police came to show me the graphic closed-circuit television footage of the event a few days later. It showed four men running into the pub in white forensic boiler suits and gloves and then appearing again dragging a man and beating him with iron bars, blood streaming down his face. The video then cut to a police car stopping the getaway van and the four abductors tumbling out along with their victim.

The attack led to an immediate outcry, in which the Irish government was particularly outspoken, in part because the IRA had also recently been involved in criminal activity in the Dublin docks. Michael

McDowell, the Irish Minister of Justice, accused Adams of knowing all about the activities at the docks and called him a fascist. Eventually, in April, the IMC recommended fines on both Sinn Féin and the Loyalist PUP, the latter because of an outbreak of UVF attacks at the same time.

Despite Tony's best efforts to keep them in the game, the UUP managed to render themselves irrelevant in this period. In late February, John Taylor and David Burnside tried to mount a leadership coup against David Trimble in favour of Reg Empey, but failed, leaving a wounded Trimble still in place. And Trimble responded by trying to 'out-Paisley' Ian Paisley by walking out of the talks after the Tohill abduction. The DUP cannily remained at the table.

The DUP had adopted a new persona after the election, good-humoured and moderate when they came to see us rather than hectoring and extreme. On 5 February, Ian Paisley led a delegation to Downing Street, where Peter Robinson gave a PowerPoint presentation of their position in the state dining room, a first for the peace process. They said they would be prepared to share power with Sinn Féin if the IRA met what they called the 'Blair necessities', the steps to end paramilitarism and criminality that had been assembled from Tony's Belfast Harbour speech and paragraph 13 of the Joint Declaration of 2003.

At a meeting on 3 March between myself and Jonathan Phillips, the NIO political director, and Peter Robinson and Nigel Dodds, the two most senior members of the DUP after Paisley, Robinson set out their strategy. They were confident they could hang on to the right-wing unionist vote and their aim was to win over the centre ground, so they were open to making progress. They still hoped they could find a way of forming a government with the moderate nationalist SDLP in a voluntary coalition. We were sceptical. Mark Durkan, the leader of the SDLP, said to us a week later that he was prepared to move ahead without Sinn Féin if the IRA failed to stand down and if the two governments stuck with his party in doing so. But we never thought the SDLP really meant it, and even if they did, it seemed extremely unlikely the Irish government would give up on Sinn Féin after all those years of trying to find an inclusive settlement.

At the 3 March meeting, Dodds and Robinson were clear that they would go into government with Sinn Féin once the IMC confirmed, over six months, that paramilitarism and criminality had ended, decommissioning was complete and if the Republicans accepted changes they were proposing to Strands 1 and 2 of the Good Friday Agreement. And they wanted us to open channels for them to Sinn Féin.

Tony flew to Dublin on 10 March to see Bertie Ahern. On the way over he phoned Aznar, the Spanish Prime Minister, to express his sympathy about the Madrid terrorist attack. Aznar sounded shell-shocked and emotional. He said it was a massacre and they didn't know if it had been carried out by ETA or some other group. Terrorism expert Tim Dalton guessed the bombs in Madrid had been set off by mobile phones and he was proved right later that day. Tim was by far the best person at second-guessing republican thinking, probably from his time looking after so many of them in Irish jails, and he was clear that the IRA would not stand down on the basis of a bilateral deal with the British government. They would only do so if it were part of an agreement with the DUP. And he was proved right again. A few days later, at Hillsborough, Tony put three choices to Adams and McGuinness: 1) a deal with the DUP that would require minor changes to the Good Friday Agreement, IMC verification of the end to IRA paramilitarism and criminality and complete decommissioning; 2) a deal with the UUP followed by elections; or 3) a bilateral deal with the government. They opted for a deal with the DUP and asked us to put in place a negotiating structure to explore the DUP position. They said, rather pettishly, they had received more attention as terrorists than they got now they had a big electoral majority. We flew on from Hillsborough to Madrid for the funerals of the victims of the train bombs, and then on to Libya for talks in the desert with a reformed terrorist who had in the past armed the IRA – Gaddafi – as a reward for his renunciation of weapons of mass destruction.

On our return I had a meeting with Robinson and Dodds who were retreating fast, saying they were having trouble carrying Ian Paisley with them. I wrote in my diary, 'They are a reflection of Sinn Féin. They want to move together in one body and not risk losing people through splits, so they will take no risks.' They were nervous about the idea of proximity talks with the two parties in adjacent buildings and said they would not be bounced or badgered into a bad deal as the UUP had been. When I saw them again a few weeks later they said they had now sold their ideas to Ian Paisley in a three-hour meeting and he hadn't objected. They said they could accept the implementation of the unpopular undertakings we had made under the Joint Declaration on OTRs as long as Tony wrote to Paisley making it clear that these concessions had been agreed during David Trimble's watch not theirs. We sent the letter and they later used it as an effective political weapon against Trimble.

We began a series of meetings with Sinn Féin and the Irish in Dublin to try and smoke out the Republican position so that we could start exploring it with the DUP. But as always Sinn Féin strung us along, refusing to reveal what the IRA would say until they knew what the whole deal was. On 23 April, Adams and McGuinness came to see Tony at Chequers. The staff were about to serve them champagne, as they would to any distinguished guest, but I thought it would give the wrong impression in current circumstances and I had to jump in and veto it. McGuinness said he had changed his mind and now believed Ian Paisley did want to be First Minister of Northern Ireland before he retired. Tony was quite firm with them, saying there could be no more transitional steps and they had to move straight to ending paramilitarism and joining the police.

Adams and McGuinness asked me to come to a private meeting without the Irish at the Clonard monastery the next week, prior to their internal brainstorming with their leadership team. They said a deal was possible but the IRA would only do it if everything was agreed, including the changes the DUP wanted in the Good Friday Agreement, because they wanted to be certain the DUP would go into government and would not erect new hurdles after an agreement. They accepted it was essential to include policing in the deal so that an end could be brought to punishment beatings, but that would require the DUP to agree to a date for the devolution of policing. They added that they needed to know there was at least the possibility of a Sinn Féin justice minister.

They said that no one was going to stand against progress for reasons of personal enrichment or for reasons of status in local communities. The discipline of the movement would see to that. But, they warned, calling an Army Convention now would be a disaster. There was a possibility of one or two younger leaders trying to take over the movement in the way Mickey McKevitt had tried earlier. There was huge

cynicism in the IRA about the Agreement and the only way to overcome it was with a renewed sense of momentum. This chimed with
an earlier comment they had made to Bertie Ahern, saying they were
now both in their fifties and were watching the twenty-year-olds very
carefully.

At one point in the meeting Adams said he needed to go to the
toilet and McGuinness followed him out of the room. When they
came back they said they had decided to tell me that they were already
in contact with the DUP through an intermediary. I was very dubious
that this contact, which passed through a journalist and which we
already knew about, would lead anywhere, but since it was our aim
to get the DUP and Sinn Féin to talk directly to each other I welcomed
it. Backchannels can be useful to feel out positions on both sides but
they are not usually strong enough to take the full weight of a negotiation because they are by definition deniable, and if anything goes
wrong people just walk away from the positions they have taken.

Jonathan Phillips and I then embarked on two months of shuttle
diplomacy at an ever increasing pace. Robinson and Dodds impressed
me with their professionalism and sophistication as negotiators. In the
view of the NIO, Robinson had been the most creative and imaginative negotiator on the unionist side right back to the early 1990s. He
and Dodds were capable of making tactical concessions and showing
hints of flexibility as well as being firm. They knew what their bottom
line was and, unlike Trimble, carried their party with them through
regular briefing meetings with the party officers. They said that Paisley
was now on board for proximity talks after the European elections in
June, and asked us to produce papers setting out the positions of both
sides. We went on to Dublin to pass on this news to Sinn Féin and
the Irish. Adams demanded to see Jonathan's note of our meeting
with the DUP, but we couldn't hand it over because it contained some
of our comments as well as reportage. Jonathan laboriously tippexed
out the offending passages and McGuinness joked he had a solvent
for Tippex. That was why, I said, they would be getting a photocopy
of the tippexed document rather than the original.

On 19 May the shuttling moved to London, with Sinn Féin ensconced
at the Irish Embassy and the DUP in the House of Commons. The
DUP stressed the importance of transparency in decommissioning and
said they wanted film or photographs of the weapons being destroyed.

They were not prepared to agree to a timescale for the devolution of policing. It would only happen when the conditions were right. McGuinness said there could be no filming of decommissioning, but Tim Dalton told me he thought photographs might be possible. I had a sneaking feeling that Sinn Féin were just trying to resuscitate the previous year's failed agreement with Trimble, but that was not going to work with the DUP. They would not settle for anything less than the 'Blair necessities'. Adams gave me more details about their backchannel to the DUP, which had resulted in several face-to-face meetings.

At the beginning of June we were in Belfast for private talks with the DUP and Sinn Féin, meeting Robinson and Dodds in Stormont House, and then moving up the hill to the Parliament buildings a short walk away to see Sinn Féin. Robinson came to meetings dressed like a mafioso in black shirt and black tie. The DUP were businesslike and not particularly yielding, insisting especially on a six-month decontamination period after the IMC had declared paramilitarism over and decommissioning was complete before they would go into government with Sinn Féin. In response, Sinn Féin proposed that a shadow First and Deputy First Minister should be in place in the testing period after the end of paramilitarism and before the Executive was established, to give Republicans some comfort. Hurtling back down the hill to Stormont House, we decided not to show the Sinn Féin paper on timing that we had been given to the DUP, for fear it would put everything back in the melting pot. It was clear to me that both sides wanted a deal, but only on their own terms and in their own timescales. Unfortunately, I was spotted in Stormont and on my return to London the leaders of the other parties phoned me to complain that I was excluding them from the negotiations. Trimble was the worst. I wasn't very sympathetic, given all the times we had spoken to the UUP to the exclusion of the other parties.

In the midst of all this, I was distracted from Northern Ireland by a problem in the press. I was waiting at Heathrow Terminal 1 for the flight to Belfast with Jonathan Phillips, his deputy David Cooke and Michael Collins on Thursday 3 June when Tom Kelly, the press secretary at No. 10, called me to say that the *Spectator* was running a story alleging I had told Boris Johnson, its editor, that Gordon Brown would never be prime minister and that the situation was a Shakespearean tragedy. I said he should dismiss the story as comic nonsense. I had indeed stopped my bicycle at the traffic lights on the Mall alongside the large, unruly mass of Johnson balanced on his bicycle. And I had engaged in banter about Shakespearean tragedies, before riding off fast from the lights and leaving him in a cloud of dust. But, as so often with journalists, Johnson had attributed his own comments to me. It didn't seem to me to be worth taking seriously. But my attempts to dismiss it were not entirely successful and the quote about a Shakespearean tragedy was hung around my neck from then on.

Inch by inch, the shuttling made progress, although it was clear Adams was more sceptical than McGuinness about the prospects of things working out with the DUP. Robinson and Dodds continued, meanwhile, to be firm, calm and rational negotiatiors. McGuinness had a lot invested in the process, not least because he was the point man in Sinn Féin for the private backchannel. Discussion turned increasingly to ensuring a quiet summer on the streets of Northern Ireland. The Irish in particular were keen to keep negotiations going into the autumn, to make sure both sides had an incentive to ensure their supporters were on their best behaviour through the 'white nights'. It was an approach that worked. In July, Republican leaders would show some courage in trying to keep the mob under control during the marching season. Gerry Kelly more or less single-handedly held back trouble during the Whiterock parade in north Belfast and was, we were told, shot at by dissident republicans for his pains.

On 25 June Tony and Bertie Ahern held a formal session of talks with all the parties in Lancaster House. As usually happens in formal sessions, people stuck to their formal positions and we made little progress, other than agreeing that the outstanding issues to be resolved were paramilitarism, decommissioning, reviving the power-sharing government, policing and the changes to the Good Friday Agreement sought by the DUP. There was however one important development. At the end of the day Ian Paisley asked for a private session with Tony and Bertie Ahern and said that 'if Republicans did indeed give up paramilitarism everything would be possible. He would then be prepared to go into government with them.' His undertaking made a big impression on Tony, who told Sinn Féin later that he had been very sceptical that the DUP would really go into power-sharing, but now he thought there was 'an opportunity to show they could seal the deal that Trimble had failed to do'. We announced there would be intensive talks through the rest of the summer leading up to another hothouse session in the autumn, and we embarked on yet another search for a suitable stately home, eventually opting for Leeds Castle.

It was at this time that Adams and McGuiness started down a path which appeared at the time to be a distraction leading nowhere, but turned out later to be the beginning of the end. On 23 June Adams had, very unusually, asked to see Tony and me by himself, and had sketched out a plan for a unilateral standing down of the IRA. He said he had not discussed the idea with anyone, not even Martin McGuinness. He had looked at the statements made by the IRA at the end of previous stages of the conflict. In 1923, de Valera had given the order to dump arms and disperse once the IRA had been beaten by Free State forces, and after the border campaign in the 1950s, the IRA had given the order to dump arms and move back. Perhaps this time too the IRA could just announce the war was over and instruct Volunteers to dump arms; but he did not know how to do it in a way that would prevent unionists from simply discounting it and asking for more. Tony agreed it might be less humiliating for the IRA to act unilaterally than to grind on in negotiations with the DUP. Adams said the IRA was worried we would just take republicans for granted if they gave up paramilitarism. They did not expect a united Ireland tomorrow, but they did want to be sure that the unionist veto on change would not just be reimposed. Tony said that, if the IRA acted unilaterally, unionists would come round, even if it took them time to do so, as long as the IRA action was real and clear and carried credibility. I said that, as Ariel Sharon had demonstrated in Gaza in the previous few months by his plan for unilateral withdrawal, it was only worth undertaking a unilateral approach if it were bold. Adams said the government would have to fill the gap till the unionists came round. He would discuss the idea with McGuinness and use the summer to work it up. He wanted to persuade the entire republican movement to take this step together.

After the Lancaster House talks, Adams came back to see us, this time with McGuinness. He said the IRA would not sign up to paragraph 13 of the Joint Declaration requiring an end to all paramilitary activity and would not accept the conditions on decommissioning imposed by de Chastelain, so he was considering the path he had suggested: a unilateral instruction to Volunteers to dump arms. But, if we went down this route, we would need to get rid of the IMC and the IICD. Tony said those two bodies were essential for credibility with the unionists. I said we could work with him to find technical answers to their problems. McGuinness asked how we would deal with the fact that the estimate in *Jane's Defence Weekly*, the only published source, grossly exaggerated the amount of weaponry in the hands of the IRA. Adams said we should remember who had been responsible for the weapons in the 1980s when they received the Libyan shipments – an allusion to Mickey McKevitt who had subsequently left to found the RIRA – implying they would not be able to recover all the weapons listed in *Jane's*.

Adams and McGuinness came back to see me on 15 July and appeared to have abandoned the unilateral approach and reverted to the nego-tiated route. They gave no explanation why, but were still interested in discussing the practicalities of decommissioning. They said that de Chastelain was only prepared to say that they had decommissioned 'all the weapons the IRA said they had'. I suggested we could give de Chastelain our assessment of the IRA holdings so he could say, accu-rately, all IRA weapons had been decommissioned. Adams said the IRA could not get weapons back from individuals and could only decommission those weapons held centrally. If they approached indi-viduals they would be told to get lost. His aim was to get decom-missioning completed by Christmas. Adams wanted to know how they should deal with the DUP request for transparency. I said I assumed the problem with a photographic record was that it smacked of surrender but there needed to be something in addition to the de Chastelain procedures to convince the DUP. Adams asked if an instruc-tion to Volunteers that became public was better than an IRA state-ment. I said a clear IRA statement coupled with an instruction to Volunteers would be best but what was important was the reality. If they carried on trying to run IRA activities in secret they would be found out.

There seemed to be corroborating evidence that, this time, the IRA were really thinking of standing down and Adams and McGuin-ness had general support for a dramatic move. The brightest people were being moved out of the IRA and into political activity in Sinn

Féin. I commissioned work from the Security Service on an assessment of the IRA's weapons holdings and discussed the approach with Tim Dalton, who had already asked the Garda to work up a similar assessment. We agreed it should reflect the figures given by *Jane's Defence Weekly*, but should have a discount for the weapons taken by McKevitt and lost through pilfering. Tim said he had discussed the approach with de Chastelain who was content and we agreed to share lists.

Tim and I saw Adams and McGuinness at the Clonard monastery on 29 July. Adams said it was the end of the IRA as we knew it. There would be an instruction to Volunteers and a statement. I said the key was what the Volunteers were instructed to do, or rather not do. Any statement should be clear, short and unambiguous. And it was essential the inventory included prestige weapons like Semtex. There was an interesting difference of emphasis between the two men. Adams was more reluctant to go down the IICD route, while McGuinness was clear it was right and inevitable. At one stage in the meeting Adams passed me a folded piece of paper saying it contained something about parades, but when I opened it up, it in fact said he had inadvertently hinted at their contacts with the DUP in conversation with Tim and he hoped I would not raise the subject in front of him. Sinn Féin were still being very coy about their channel to the DUP. At the end of the meeting he asked for the note back. Immediately afterwards Tim and I met de Chastelain and Andy Sens who had arrived at Clonard to meet Adams. They were worried about how they would inspect explosives, for which they needed an expert, and about the transparency of decommissioning, a problem which of course had bitten de Chastelain before.

We reverted to shuttle diplomacy in September in the run-up to the Leeds Castle meeting. I went over to Northern Ireland on 1 September and was spotted en route, as I feared I would be, after which the BBC started running a story about my presence. Ian Paisley had just returned from hospital where he had come near to death, and at an impromptu press conference outside Stormont he was asked if his party was meeting me. Not having been briefed about any meeting, he replied 'no', after which Peter Robinson called up, apologetically cancelling our meeting. Instead, I saw

Adams and McGuinness in Stormont House. Michael Collins was there with an Irish delegation, but Adams and McGuinness claimed they hadn't expected the Irish. They were always suspicious that the Irish Department of Foreign Affairs staff, whom Gerry Kelly called Freestaters, would leak titbits to the press and often treated Irish officials appallingly in the hope of terrifying them into submission, but to their credit Collins and his colleagues never allowed themselves to be browbeaten. Adams insisted on seeing Tim Dalton and me alone.

They assured us that they would be discussing decommissioning with the IRA that weekend, but warned that the vast bulk of the weapons were now held by Volunteers and could not be recovered. I said that might be true of revolvers but couldn't possibly be true of Semtex. Adams reported that the IRA had agreed to issue instructions to Volunteers to desist if there were a satisfactory agreement, and they would call a special party conference on joining the policing board if the DUP agreed a date for the devolution of policing. He claimed to be in trouble with republicans after his comments that week in the *Irish News* about the IRA being used as an excuse for inaction by unionists, and now regretted having made them.

Adams, McGuinness and Gerry Kelly came to Downing Street to see Tony on 6 September and Adams said he was 'authorised to say that the IRA would complete the process of putting all its arms beyond use as part of an acceptable agreement'. He said they had difficulty in judging whether the DUP were serious in reaching an agreement and the manner of Paisley's return from hospital made them doubt it. Tony had to break off to take a call from President Putin and when he returned said we needed to see the IRA statement. Adams said it would not be possible to get an IRA statement till they had seen the outlines of an agreement.

Tim Dalton and I went on to see the three of them again that afternoon at the Irish embassy. McGuinness said we had to understand they could not deal with those weapons held by the Volunteers rather than held centrally. I said it was a matter of credibility. If they came in below the level de Chastelain set, the securocrats would denounce it as a sham and the whole deal would collapse.

Tim returned to the idea of photographs and they did not rule them out.

In early September, Tony invited Bertie Ahern to lunch at 'Myro-bella', his house in his Trimdon Colliery constituency, to prepare for the Leeds Castle talks. The house had been stormed that morning by pro-hunt protestors and the police had been unable to cope. The garden was littered with eggshells and debris. Bertie was dubious about the chances of success at Leeds Castle, but seemed content to go ahead. He said the IRA were collecting up weapons across the Republic ready for a major act of decommissioning. We were in the same place as the Irish on pretty much everything except some details of the changes to Strands 1 and 2 of the Good Friday Agreement, and we agreed the outline of a deal to give to Sinn Féin and the DUP in advance. Tony and Bertie swapped stories on reshuffles. We had just had a rather bloody one and Bertie's was still to come.

At the weekend I went over to Dublin with Jonathan Phillips to see Sinn Féin and the Irish. Adams gave Tim Dalton and me a handwritten version of what the IRA would say in its statement. I said it was fine on decommissioning but, as I had predicted, it missed out the crucial point of what the instruction to IRA Volunteers would actually be. We needed to know that the IRA was ceasing paramilitary activity for good. I rushed off to get the last plane back to London and, as I settled in my seat to read my official papers, Bernard Donoughue came and tapped me on the back. Bernard had been Harold Wilson's domestic policy adviser and was one of our ministers in the Lords. He was close to the Unionists and earlier in the process had sent us a paper on their behalf suggesting a way forward. He had come over to Dublin for a day's racing and tea with the Aga Khan and now Aer Lingus security were trying to throw him off the plane. He had checked in as Bernard Lord Donoughue, but someone called Bernard Lord had later checked into the same seat. Since the airline had no record of a reservation in his name, because, as it later turned out, he was in fact booked on a flight the next day, the rules meant he had to leave. I interceded on his behalf and they allowed him to stay. He regaled me all the way back with hysterical stories about his times with Wilson and his kitchen cabinet. He told how Wilson, who late in his premiership became paranoid about the security services, had summoned Bernard into his study and put a finger to his lips to indicate he should remain silent. He had then beckoned him to follow him across the room and lifted up a large oil painting of Gladstone to show a small hole in the wall behind. It looked to Bernard like a hole for a bolt to hold up the painting, but Wilson then ushered him into the lavatory at the end of the room, shut the door, and said, 'Well, what do you think of that?' Bernard looked quizzical, but it was clear Wilson thought it was a bug, and later had a private security firm sweep the room for listening devices.

We had a bug problem of our own. Republicans had uncovered a listening device in the house of one of Adams's assistants and were trying to make great public play of it. Adams and McGuinness brought it to Leeds Castle and presented it to Tony. It was embarrassingly large, about a metre long, and looked extremely antiquated. They did it all with great good humour, and simultaneously presented Tim Dalton, who was about to retire from the Department of Justice, with what they claimed was its aerial wrapped in a canvas bag. When Tim eventually opened it, it turned out to be a fly-fishing rod for him to enjoy in his retirement.

On Monday 13 September I went over to the Clonard monastery for one last meeting before Leeds Castle. The Catholic priests were very kind and even gave us dinner in the refectory. It was a bit odd sitting there with Adams, McGuinness and their team eating monastic food. McGuinness noticed that I was worrying away at my watch. The minute hand had come loose and I was afraid I would miss my flight back. He said there was a watchmaker at the end of his street in Derry who could fix it. I tried to resist, saying it would be too much trouble, but he insisted and I took the watch off and gave it to him, having visions of getting it back with a listening device or a beacon in it. He brought it back to me at Leeds Castle and promised, on his word of honour, that it had not been bugged. I gave it the next day to the security people and they dismantled it but could find nothing untoward. Unfortunately, they succeeded in loosening the minute hand again and I had to take the watch to a very expensive watch shop in London to be repaired again.

Ian Paisley, who was still weak from his operation in the summer, was under doctor's instructions not to fly, and instead had to come by ferry and car for the three days of negotiations at Leeds Castle. He seemed a new man. He had always been charming and humorous in person, in contrast to his harsh, negative public persona; but now all negativism had switched to a driving desire to conclude the Northern Ireland question before he died. This was not to say he couldn't still be intransigent, but it was a bizarrely constructive intransigence. It was the only way, he believed, of squeezing the last concessions he needed from the IRA on policing and criminality, which would convince the unionist people that the settlement was lasting – but a lasting settlement was what he wanted. At one stage at Leeds Castle he said to Tony, 'If Sinn Féin were serious, it was clear then the DUP could do a deal. He wanted to see a peaceful Ulster before he passed on.'

Going into the negotiations I saw no prospect of ending up with a public agreement. At the very best we might get to a package on which the two sides would go away and consult their parties, and I worried about our credibility, poised as we were to go crashing through yet another deadline. As always happened going into a hothouse negotiation, the two sides, who had seemed quite close before they got there, started pulling away from each other under pressure from their constituencies as the spotlight fell on them.

We started by meeting Ian Paisley and six of his DUP colleagues. It took ages. It seemed to me that they had never before had to negotiate in this way. The party was, as its name suggested, too democratic, and every member of the party executive had a say. We then saw Sinn Féin who demanded a series of concessions on their wish list before they would discuss anything else. This worried me, but when we made some steps towards them, they came back saying they wanted to do a deal. I had a sense they were leaning over backwards to look reasonable and demonstrate it was the DUP that was the unreasonable party. The DUP raised the stakes on decommissioning by asking for a Protestant clergyman to observe decommissioning alongside de Chastelain, with the unrestricted right to take photographs. Paisley said he had a suitable person in mind. He said 'no one in Northern Ireland would be convinced that the IRA had gone away until they saw it for themselves'. Adams said the idea of third-party observers in addition to de Chastelain was a step too far but a photograph should be sufficient. On that basis Tony said to Paisley photos would be possible. We were fierce with Sinn Féin on the wording of the IRA statement, with Michael McDowell being particularly hard-line, and agreed a text they said they would go away and put to the IRA. We did not show it to the DUP at that stage.

The DUP were divided. Robinson and Dodds clearly wanted a deal and told us Paisley had been arguing strongly for one in the party meetings, against the fundamentalists. The problem was, we couldn't make progress on the changes the DUP wanted to Strands 1 and 2 of the Good Friday Agreement relating to the Assembly and the power-sharing Executive, and that was holding everything else up. When Tony summoned Paisley on Friday night to tell him they were not going to get to a deal, Paisley refused to sit down and told Tony a deal had been within our reach but he had frittered it away. He said it was 'a dark day'. Nevertheless, Leeds Castle saw the establishment of a new closeness between Paisley and Tony which was crucial in the process leading up to the final settlement. Before the negotiation Robinson and Dodds had told us that the only way we would achieve a breakthrough was through cultivating Ian Paisley in private conversations, and this is exactly what Tony did, although Paisley insisted on bringing his son, Ian Paisley Jr, with him to the first meetings at Leeds Castle.

Robinson and Dodds were under strict orders from the party not to meet with us alone, so the only way Tony or I could speak to them was to try and catch them in the corridors of the castle to find out what the real DUP position was and get imaginative suggestions on how to move forward. On Saturday morning we persuaded them to talk to Tony sitting on the four-poster bed in Paul Murphy's bedroom and they showed some signs of flexibility, but it was by then too late.

It seems ridiculous that the deal was lost largely on technical points. The Nationalists thought what the DUP were asking for on Strands 1 and 2 smacked of majority rule and the DUP insisted they needed ministers to be accountable to the Executive and the Assembly rather than going off and doing their own thing. They were seeking what was described as 'mutually assured obstruction' – whereby either tradition in the Executive could stop something happening they did not like. Tony blamed me for having given insufficient attention to these issues in advance, but I had been certain these more minor aspects would fall into place if we could agree on what the IRA should do. The Irish, under Foreign Minister Brian Cowen, were unyielding, and they were supported by the SDLP and the UUP. On Saturday morning the Irish came up with compromise language on the issue of account-ability that interested the DUP, but it was too late to swing things.

I had proposed on Friday evening splitting the difference between the two sides and tabling a government proposal for them to consider, but we kept putting it off and then it never happened. It was clear to me by mid-morning on Saturday that Tony just wanted to get away from the place. There was no chance of agreement. Tony and I spent a good deal of the time striding round the grounds waiting for the parties to make progress on the detailed negotiations on the Strands, with Tony worrying away about the hunting ban that was just then coming to a head. We were confronted too by a logistical problem. Leeds Castle had been booked for a wedding at lunchtime on Saturday and the staff, and presumably the couple getting married, were anxious we would just stay on negotiating and refuse to leave. We felt in good conscience we had to clear out and not risk disrupting their nuptials when our attempt at a shotgun wedding between the DUP and Sinn Féin was clearly not going to succeed. We ended Leeds just before lunch on Saturday with a joint statement by the two governments saying we believed we could solve the issues of paramilitarism and decommissioning but we needed more time to resolve the issues in Strands 1 and 2.

After Leeds Castle, Tim Dalton and I went into a period of intense negotiation with Sinn Féin. McGuinness came to see me at the Labour Party conference in Brighton the following week. Unbeknown to me, one of the 'Garden Room girls', the elite corps of PAs at No. 10, hadn't been back to Brighton since the Tory Party conference in 1984 – she had been staying at the Grand Hotel when it was blown up by the IRA bomb. Despite the shock she suffered she had bravely decided to come this year to try to overcome her phobia. In my ignorance, I asked her to arrange for Martin McGuinness to get through security and come to our hotel for a meeting without being seen. It was only after the event I realised what I must have put her through. Even the Special Branch men on the corridor outside our rooms looked at me oddly after I took McGuinness into my bedroom, the only place we could meet privately. A few weeks later I had to give him a lecture on criminality. The IRA had been responsible for a major cigarette heist, as well as two other fund-raising criminal acts in the previous week. I told him it had to stop. If they thought we would turn a blind eye, they were greatly mistaken. Criminal activities such as this would show up in the next IMC report and, if they continued, blow the process out of the water.

Adams and McGuinness came to see Tim Dalton and me in Downing Street on 30 September carrying the IRA statement as approved by the Army Council. They had taken out the three crucial elements we had inserted at Leeds Castle and we told them it was unacceptable. They had no good explanation of why the elements had been removed other than that including them would require an Army Convention. One of the strange things that became clear through the years of negotiations about IRA statements was that the Army Council was made up of barrack-room lawyers. They took great pride in their obfuscatory language and their refusal to accept the clarifications we put forward. Adams said the IRA could agree to two independent observers but not to photographs. I said the DUP would insist on photos. In case the DUP did not agree they wanted us to work up a 'Plan B' which built up North/South cooperation to give the Republic a greater say in the affairs of the North. I said they should be realistic. We were not going to make Northern Ireland ungovernable by provoking the unionists too far.

McGuinness continued to attach importance to his backchannel contacts with the DUP and he dropped into No. 10 after one meeting and told me he had shown them some potential IRA language for the statement and they had responded that it was in the ballpark. I said I would believe that when I heard it from the DUP myself. McGuinness rang me later to say they were sorting all the remaining issues out with the DUP direct and did not need my services. I recorded at the time that 'given how many times I have been disappointed I ought to know better, but I do feel that this time the ground may have shifted and a deal may be possible in the next ten days'.

It wasn't, however, quite that smooth and Ian Paisley phoned me late on Friday 15 October to ask me to come over on Monday and shuttle between Sinn Féin and the DUP. I went by Flybe from Gatwick to avoid being spotted. We started with Sinn Féin at Hillsborough. They turned up late because they had been meeting with the DUP backchannel. When they arrived they handed us a draft IRA statement and told us that if we showed it to the DUP they would welcome it. They did not want us to table a paper on Strands 1 and 2 because they were close to agreement with the DUP on that as well and finally they said policing was too hard for their community to swallow at the same time as the IRA disappearing, so they had given up on that. I urged them to reconsider.

Jonathan Phillips and I got in our car and headed to Jeffrey Donaldson's constituency office which was in the old Lisburn Council Chambers, a large wood-panelled hall with a gallery. Rather than the small delegation we had been promised, Ian Paisley was there with all their MPs, some of their MLAs and their MEP, plus tens of observers. I gave them the IRA text and they asked us to withdraw while they considered it. When we came back they gave us a series of amendments to it and Paisley treated us to a lecture about the need for photographs of decommissioning and the complete freedom for the photographer to take pictures of anything he wanted. Finally they totally rejected the timetable for setting up the Executive in January, which Sinn Féin had told us had been agreed.

We went back to Sinn Féin in Hillsborough and they were discombobulated, but they checked on the backchannel and came back reassured that things were still going according to plan. They agreed to accept a couple of the DUP amendments to the IRA statement and Adams undertook that they would go back to the IRA to try and secure photos, but he doubted they would succeed. With that, they sent us back to the DUP, where we arrived at ten in the evening. They were beginning to get tired. They demanded a further series of changes to the IRA statement and sent us back again. Before we left we spoke to Peter Robinson who said Ian Paisley was trying to lead his delegation in the right direction but his MPs kept heading off elsewhere. He suggested I propose a smaller delegation, but when I rang Paisley later in the evening he said no.

Back at Hillsborough, Adams reacted with fury. Sinn Féin sent people off to talk to their contacts on the backchannel who told them it had been very difficult to keep things on track with so many other people in the room, particularly Jim Allister, the DUP's maverick MEP. We kept going until midnight on Monday and carried on through Tuesday but it became clear to me that, far from making progress, we were actually making things worse, so I persuaded Sinn Féin we should pull stumps. The DUP were a bit taken aback. But by then the backchannel had gone dead and nothing the Republicans could do would bring it back to life. Adams was worried about how many people had seen the draft IRA statement and I got the DUP to destroy the copies we had given them.

When I got back to London I proposed to Tony that we should have one more go at proximity talks and then the two governments should draw up what they thought to be a fair agreement and send it to both sides privately, giving them a week to think about it and then publish it so the world would know what they had rejected. Tim Dalton told me he thought the IRA could agree to photos at the end of the day, and Adams said they would go back to the IRA on the issue if everything else was resolved. I spoke to Paisley on the phone on Friday and told him we were organising proximity talks in London for the following Tuesday and he agreed to come. Both he and McGuinness told me that they thought they could get agreement. The only problem, as I pointed out to them, was that their terms were different.

The proximity talks took place in Downing Street. Since the DUP were not prepared to sit in the same room or even the same building as Sinn Féin, we installed Ian Paisley in Conference Room A in the Cabinet Office, which is graced with a throne and portraits of the Georgian kings, and Sinn Féin in Margaret Thatcher's old study on the first floor of No. 10. They were separated by the green baize door made famous in *Yes, Prime Minister*, making the two technically belong to separate buildings. I and my NIO colleagues shuttled backwards and forwards through the door taking propositions from one side to the other, each time making them a little more palatable to the other before presenting them.

This time the DUP were a small, well-organised delegation, negotiating seriously with Robinson in charge. Sinn Féin, in contrast, were sulky, difficult and unprepared. McGuinness was more cooperative because he had invested so much personally in his backchannel, and spent the afternoon wandering around on the Embankment looking forlornly for his interlocutor. On Wednesday things started going backwards fast. Paisley even complained about having been brought into the building the long way round. I discovered later that he had in fact arrived at the wrong door and had to be escorted all the way through the basement of Downing Street to get to the Cabinet Office. He then went on to complain that Sinn Féin weren't moving, which was true, because Sinn Féin were pinning their hopes on the backchannel. We went back in to Downing Street and got Sinn Féin to table their position on Strands 1 and 2, but the DUP gave us nothing back. Robinson suggested privately to us that we stop the talks to allow a period of reflection, and we did. Paisley gave us an emotional ending saying it was 'a lost opportunity'.

We spent the October and November of 2004 working with Irish officials led by Michael Collins on the draft agreement the two governments would give to the parties. I wrote a note to Tony saying we needed to persuade the Irish to position the paper so that it would be hard for the DUP to say no, because a large part of the party wanted to put off any deal till after the Westminster elections in the following year, which would lose Sinn Féin. I thought a way of getting the DUP on board would be to accept their proposal that the starting date for the devolved government be March 2005, rather than the Sinn Féin date of December 2004, but give Sinn Féin a shadow Assembly starting in January for balance. On 10 November, I and an NIO team met with the Irish to finalise the draft agreement and gave it to Ian Paisley and Gerry Adams, allowing them a week to respond informally to the draft. Tony saw the DUP and Sinn Féin at the end of the week and initial responses from both were positive, although Adams asked for a series of further concessions from us. I warned Adams 'that of course the whole agreement might collapse if the IRA were caught red-handed in either paramilitary activity or in criminality in the intervening period'. Adams and McGuinness said they understood that.

As the deadline expired for a response to the draft, both sides got increasingly fractious and came back with long lists of questions. The Irish and our team drafted answers and gave them to each side. In the middle of it all, David Trimble and Reg Empey came in to complain about not being told anything, and the SDLP and Alliance parties phoned to complain about not being invited in to Downing Street at all. On the evening of Wednesday 24 November we went to the Irish Embassy so Sinn Féin could put us through a lengthy and painful session of detailed negotiation, and then went back to the House of Commons to go through the same process with Robinson and

Donaldson. We met again with the Irish team at midnight in Downing Street to finalise the agreement and send it out to the parties for their formal response. I was worried that we had leaned too far in the direction of the DUP because it was so much easier for them to walk away from a deal. I didn't get to bed until after two, and then woke up with pins and needles in my left leg and arm, convinced I was having a heart attack. I woke my wife who told me to look up the symptoms on the Internet. The next day Tony had me call his heart specialist who told me, to my relief, that all I had was a trapped nerve, with a strong implication I was a malingerer.

On 25 November I wrote a note to Tony saying 'my biggest fear is that Sinn Féin say they are going off to see the IRA but come back on Monday saying the IRA has changed the statement or said no to photos'. Adams and McGuinness came in the next morning to have one last go at Tony. They were very keen to meet Nelson Mandela who was having breakfast upstairs with Tony, so I took them up to the small dining room to shake his hand. Their meeting with Tony lasted two hours, the whole of which they spent bullying him. Then they spent another hour bullying me. Tony made concessions on plastic bullets and on demilitarisation, which he then asked me to sell to Chief Constable Hugh Orde. We also persuaded President Bush to phone Ian Paisley to urge him to accept the agreement, which obviously rather pleased Paisley, although he told Bush the issue would 'be decided by Ulstermen'.

In the hope of getting the issues of plastic bullets and demilitarisation resolved quickly, I arranged a meeting for Gerry Adams, Martin McGuinness and Gerry Kelly with Hugh Orde. Orde was a bit worried about how he would sell the meeting to the 'Continuity RUC', the vestiges of the old order in the Police Service of Northern Ireland, but decided to do it anyway. He brought one of his senior Catholic officers Peter Sheridan, who had grown up not far from Martin McGuinness. Tony chaired the meeting to start with but then left and I carried it on. The two sides had a lot in common. We managed to agree at least some progress on all the points, including on the need for republicans to cooperate with the police in areas like South Armagh.

Paisley came in to see Tony again the next day. He was clearly flattered by Tony's attention, and as I was greeting him said he hoped there would be no civil servants in the meeting. I reassured him. He told me how Jacques Chirac had had him thrown out of the European Parliament years before and had accused him of being the most foul-mouthed politician he had ever met. Paisley had been outraged. I found the mental picture of 'le Bulldozer' and 'the Big Man of Ulster' clashing irresistible. He told me he couldn't conclude the negotiation on Friday as we had requested, because he had a wedding and a funeral that day but he could finish it by the following Tuesday, which was more or less acceptable. He had an hour alone with Tony. Tony suggested to him that he agree to Peter Robinson being able to meet Martin McGuinness during the shadow period of the administration in January. Paisley ruled this out, saying it would finish off Robinson in the party. Informal contacts were all right, although every time they happened Sinn Féin leaked them.

Then, on 27 November, after things had been looking so promising, the whole deal fell apart. Ian Paisley said in a speech at a rally in his constituency that Sinn Féin needed to wear 'sackcloth and ashes' in penitence for their past behaviour. Trimble called me to say Ian Paisley Jr had set the event up because his father was worried at having been accused of selling out and wanted him to say things that would spook the IRA. I relayed the analysis to Adams, who was getting desperate. He said the trouble was, the tactic was working. Paisley's comments enraged the IRA, who made it absolutely clear they would not agree to a photograph of decommissioning if it was being presented in the context of humiliation and surrender. Tony told Adams and McGuinness that refusal to agree to a photograph would be a deal-breaker and we tried every compromise we could think of on the timing and form of the publication of the photos, but they said there was nothing they could do. On the other hand, Adams assured me that there would be no problem over the weapons which the IRA would, we hoped, eventually give de Chastelain: he could say authoritatively that they would be complete.

I went to the Clonard monastery at the weekend for one last attempt to resurrect the deal. We didn't get far. Adams asked for a quarter of an hour alone with me at the end, and we went for a walk in the gloomy garden-cum-graveyard. He was agitated and said he did not think there was any way he could persuade the IRA to agree to published photos after Ian Paisley's comments. He understood, therefore, that there would not be an agreement. But he'd had it with the negotiations. They had to bring this thing to an end and get it on a political track. His notion, instead, was to agree an instruction to the IRA to dump arms, issue an IRA statement and to call an urgent Army Convention. They would take the decision once and for all. He thought a unilateral act by the IRA might be more sustainable than an agreement with the DUP anyway. The latter would entail them losing too much of the army in the process. I said if an agreement was not possible Tony would favour acting unilaterally. He said that some individual republicans would remain mixed up in criminality but the movement needed a divorce from all that so they could carry on with politics. I told him about a comment Tony had made to me. He'd said McGuinness and Adams had outgrown the IRA but other people had been left behind.

On Tuesday we got a formal 'no' from Sinn Féin via Tim Dalton, who had met Adams and McGuinness in Dundalk. They had told him the IRA would not agree to photographs. I had a number of long conversations with Adams who was exhausted and bitter. I felt very low myself. Ironically, Stephen Wall, our European adviser, who had handled Northern Ireland for John Major many years before, congratulated me on having sorted out the issue when we had our morning meeting the next day. All the papers were reporting that there was agreement but I knew there was not.

We had originally fixed the day of publication for a different date but Paisley had pointed out to us it was the annual Lundy's day celebration and he would be accused of being a 'Lundy' if he signed the agreement then, so we had moved it to Wednesday 8 December. Tony and I flew over after Prime Minister's Questions to publish the 'Comprehensive Proposals' so the world could see what the two sides had thrown away, and to try to bank the progress we had made. Tony called Ian Paisley on the way over to tell him that the answer from the Republicans was no. He sounded genuinely disappointed. The press conference at the Waterfront Hall, with prosperous modern Belfast as the backdrop, went well, although both sides made a fuss about which documents we had chosen to publish and which we had omitted. In the following days we tried to see if we could rescue anything from the wreck by looking for alternatives to photographs, but neither side was interested, taking solace in the fact that there was support for their obduracy from their own communities.

We had come quite close to an agreement between the DUP and Sinn Féin that would have put the power-sharing Executive back in place, but the disagreement about the photographs of decommissioning and Ian Paisley's comments about 'sackcloth and ashes' derailed it at the last moment. As succeeding events were to show, in fact it was too early for a sustainable agreement. The two parties were not really ready to say goodbye to the past and if we had succeeded then we might well have been back into the stop–start political crises we experienced with Trimble in the late 1990s, particularly in light of what was about to happen.

12

The IRA Goes Away:
December 2004–April 2006

If things looked bad at the beginning of December 2004, at the end of the month they suddenly got a lot worse.

On the morning of 21 December I had flown into Belfast City airport to meet Adams and McGuinness at the Clonard monastery. We were due to discuss a possible bilateral approach, whereby the British government and Sinn Féin could move forward together without the Unionists. We had gone out on a limb to keep things going after the failure of the peace deal and the Irish government, who disagreed with this approach, were not participating. I was met at the airport by Jonathan Phillips who was already in Belfast. Once the car had pulled out of the airport, Jonathan asked it to stop and ushered me out on to a grass verge at the side of the road. He told me the police had just informed him that there had been a huge robbery at the Northern Bank's headquarters in Donegal Square. Initial estimates were that up to £30 million had been stolen, and 'the dogs on the street know that the IRA carried out the crime'.

I was dumbstruck. It was a huge betrayal of trust, and I felt like a complete idiot coming over for talks with Adams and McGuinness when the IRA had been planning a major crime like this. I contemplated cancelling the meeting and heading straight back to London. But the one rule I had stuck to throughout the peace process was to keep the talking going whatever the political pain. The alternative was to let that dangerous vacuum develop which was so easily filled by violence. At crucial moments like this I had to separate the anger I felt personally from my role as a negotiator, which required me to remain cool and rational and focused on the strategic goal. But I really felt like kicking something.

When we met Adams and McGuinness I could not mention the

robbery because the police had still not announced it, but I decided to open the meeting with a discussion on criminality, referring to a punishment beating on the previous Friday. Adams and McGuinness had little to say, other than pressing again for a joint North/South body to administer the police in Northern Ireland and the Republic which I dismissed as unrealistic. I returned to London and agreed with Tony we could hardly overlook the biggest ever robbery in the history of the United Kingdom. This was the end of the bilateral route, and since there was no immediate chance of an agreement with the DUP after a crime like this, the only way forward was the unilateral route, where the IRA put itself out of business. We had reached another pivotal point. We had to use the crime to drive the process into the endgame.

The Chief Constable, Hugh Orde, came in to brief me on the robbery on 5 January with Sam Kincaid, an old-time RUC officer and then head of CID. They took me through the detail of the raid and there was no doubt that it was the IRA. I met the Irish who were relieved we were giving up on the bilateral route. And then I called Adams. For the first time ever, I left him speechless. I expected him to argue back, but the starkness of the decision to end the bilateral route and the clarity of the position on the robbery caught him by surprise. I wondered to myself if Republicans in fact ever intended to deliver an end to the IRA at all or if the whole thing for them was just an unending negotiation.

On Friday 7 January Hugh Orde announced to the public that the robbery had been carried out by the IRA, and we and the Irish put out the tough statements we had agreed. All hell broke loose. Trimble called me from Mount Kilimanjaro, where he was on holiday, saying he had heard we were being weak on the IRA. I said he had got the wrong end of the stick. Adams started calling up, demanding a meeting with Tony, but I said it would be inappropriate. He threatened to publish the letters we had sent containing private undertakings in the run-up to the December near miss. I said he should go ahead, but if he did it would mean a conclusive end to this phase of the negotiations since we couldn't then return to those undertakings. I said they couldn't just hunker down and ride this crisis out in the hope of finding

things all the same once the storm had passed. They had lost all credibility with unionists. The only option was the unilateral route and
for the Provisional IRA to disappear the way the 'stickies' (the slang
for the Official IRA) had.

On 21 January I went once again to the Clonard monastery for a
meeting with Adams and McGuinness. They were weary and taken
aback by the tough message I'd delivered. They didn't make much of
an effort to pretend the IRA had not carried out the robbery, but
McGuinness made a histrionic attempt to persuade me that he and
Adams had not known about it in advance, and asked rhetorically how
we could work with him if we didn't trust him. I said I hadn't believed
their denials of IRA membership down the years, but had carried on
working with them. The time had come when they could no longer
carry on riding two horses. Adams asked if we had given up on our
aspiration to keep the IRA united and now wanted them to move
forward without a large section of the movement. I said we had to
move forward one way or another, and if that was the price, so be
it. He said we did not understand how serious it would be if we left
a vestige of the IRA in place. I said that, if the vestige remained
obdurate, the pressure to move ahead without them would become
irresistible.

   Tony saw Ian Paisley on 26 January. Paisley told him that 'some had
said that the robbery had saved the DUP's bacon by blocking a bad
deal but he was not of that view. He was disappointed that a great
opportunity had been lost.' We eventually agreed that Tony should
meet Adams and McGuinness, but at Chequers rather than Downing
Street, so there would be no pictures.

   In the car on the way down to Chequers, Tony and I discussed the
forthcoming general-election campaign and the need to get an operation in place in advance. He was just back from Davos and not much
focused on Northern Ireland, but we both felt let down by Adams and
McGuinness. They were there before we arrived and were in emollient form. They denied again that they had known about the robbery
and, this time, were adamant that the IRA weren't the perpetrators.
They said there would be a row between them and the IRA if it turned
out they were. McGuinness asked if they could see the evidence but
Tony said that would be quite inappropriate. Adams said there were

question marks over his leadership in the community and if the Prime Minister had no confidence in him he was perfectly happy to walk into the sunset. McGuinness said he had been horrified by what I had said about splitting the IRA. That would be a disaster. Tony reiterated the point that the IRA was a lifeline for rejectionist unionists. It should be wrapped up.

At the beginning of February, the IRA put out a statement designed to make our flesh creep by hinting at a return to violence, and when we downplayed the statement, put out another, even more menacing. Michael Collins called me to check whether we thought they were about to go back to war. I didn't think they were. There was intelligence that the IRA were involved in unusual activity, the police were worried, and there was a feeling of uncertainty in the air. But on the other hand Gerry Adams had told Tim Dalton that the IRA would not go back to violence because their own community would not allow them to do so. Bertie Ahern was worried that all the worst elements who had left the IRA as it followed the peaceful path were rallying back to it in its moment of difficulty. I thought these were probably the last death throes of an organisation that had lost its rationale.

In parallel we had been trying to make progress with the loyalists, the ugly sisters of paramilitarism in Northern Ireland. Over the past few years, we in No. 10 had been encouraging the NIO to reach out to the UDA and the UVF to help them follow the IRA into oblivion. It was harder in the case of the loyalists than the republicans. While they had a handful of impressive political leaders like David Ervine, the mass of them were pretty poorly educated and politically unsophisticated. There was something to the old saw that, in prison, the republicans turned the gyms into libraries and the loyalists turned the libraries into gyms. There had been a series of loyalist feuds; criminality, particularly the drugs trade, was deeply embedded in the loyalist paramilitary organisations; and the UDP, the party representing the UDA, had lost its elected seat. But the community they represented suffered the same sort of ingrained deprivation as those republicans represented and the underlying problems needed to be addressed.

The Irish government, through the work of the husband of President Mary McAleese, herself from the North, had managed to start a dialogue with the loyalist groups and find money to help community projects in the deprived Protestant areas of Belfast. After several abortive attempts, the NIO had started a political dialogue of sorts with the Loyalists. We had offered a meeting with Tony as an incentive for renouncing violence, with earlier meetings with Paul Murphy and myself as half-steps along the way.

My meeting with the leadership of the UDA finally happened on 18 January in Stormont House, in the first-floor dining room where the London-based officials of the NIO usually had dinner together when staying in Belfast. There were two political representatives of the umbrella organisation called the UPRG, Ulster Political Research Group, but the figures in the room that carried weight were the brigadiers of the UDA. All six of them were there and they made an odd collection. As I wrote in my diary rather starkly some of them lived up to their reputation. Jim Gray was a thug with diamond stud earrings, a coke habit and more tattoos than brains. But some of them were different and articulate, wanting to find a way out. One of them was dead a year later and others in prison, but Jackie McDonald was quiet and determined and struck me as a serious leader. They were very suspicious at the start of the meeting but gradually warmed up. I said if they ended criminality then a meeting with the Prime Minister was possible, and that we would engage with them in funding projects in loyalist neighbourhoods. Jim Gray suggested finding jobs for their members in the security industry. I wasn't sure about that. The NIO followed up the meeting and made money available for projects in their areas, but it was much harder to make progress with them than with republicans because, in the end, they lacked a political agenda.

Our main focus remained the Republicans, and things got worse still for them with the murder of Robert McCartney on 14 February. McCartney had come to the rescue of a friend in a bar-room argument and appears to have been stabbed by IRA members on the order of a local IRA capo. Local republicans had subsequently gone about a detailed clearing up of all forensic evidence. His murder might have been forgotten, like many others within the community, if it had not been for his brave fiancée and sisters continuing to insist on justice. The problem it posed for the IRA was that the family were typical republicans, living in a republican community, but they weren't prepared to put up with the continuation of the mafia-style rule of local IRA bosses, driving around in four-wheel-drive cars, able to terrorise anyone into doing what they wanted. The family's campaign took off quickly and they met President Bush on 17 March. Tony and I didn't get to meet them until 10 October when Tony presented them with an award at the Pride of Britain ceremony. I found it extremely moving. They were articulate and very determined. They asked us to persuade Adams and McGuinness to get people to cooperate with the police. Adams had publicly called for such cooperation on 4 April and introduced the family to the Sinn Féin Ard Fheis in an attempt to co-opt them, and keep the row within the republican community. But no one, including the family, was convinced that his pleas were genuine. From among the dozens in the bar that evening not one person had come forward to give evidence.

The IRA illustrated their complete incomprehension of how obsolete their methods had become when they put out a statement on 8 March saying they planned to shoot Robert McCartney's killers. They were trying to demonstrate they were serious about revenge, but instead they let everyone see that they still lived in the mafia twilight of arbitrary killing and counter-killing, rather than a civilised world with the rule of law and justice. In this sense the McCartney killing was a bigger crisis for the IRA than the bank robbery because it affected their base.

The combination of the Northern Bank robbery and the McCartney murder meant Republicans had no choice but to dissolve the IRA unilaterally if they wanted to pursue a political future. Adams and McGuinness came to see Tony privately on 23 February and we brought them in by the side door at No. 10 so they wouldn't be noticed. Adams said the whole thing was a big mess. He seemed to Tony and me to be physically shrunken. Tony tried to give him some cause for hope. Adams said Sinn Féin was trapped in a downward spiral and had to find a way out. He needed to be given the space to turn the movement round. While he understood that the international climate had changed since 9/11, that wasn't an argument he could use in the internal debate within republicanism. Tony asked why the IRA had carried out the robbery, and Adams, without conceding that they had, said there was a problem with tunnel vision among some people. It might, however, be possible to turn the current difficulties into an opportunity.

On the one hand, the bank robbery set us back more than a year by finally destroying any remaining unionist confidence in republicans. But on the other, paradoxically, the shock of the reaction made it clear to the meanest intelligence in republican ranks that the dual strategy could no longer work and strengthened the hands of those who wanted to opt for the purely political path. Clever tactical dodges would no longer allow them to avoid that fundamental choice.

After the meeting, Tony wrote an internal note on the way forward. He said there was a complete misunderstanding between the two sides. The IRA believed they had made huge gestures and that the demand for photographs of decommissioning had been deliberate spoiling. They didn't think they could be expected to give up until they had seen the good faith of unionists in practice. Continuing criminal activity was a necessary consequence of operating in an unfair political state. The other parties, however, were watching apprehensively as Sinn Féin's political strength grew. They didn't believe the IRA were serious about giving up, and they thought Sinn Féin were trying to have their cake and eat it too. Tony thought it was impossible to go back to a big deal and instead we should, again, try to rebuild step by step. I wrote back to him saying our big opportunity now was that we had finally got the focus exclusively on the IRA. We had to use the moment to force them to choose finally between the political route and descending into a purely mafia-style organisation. The IRA needed to decide to give up unilaterally.

On the weekend of 5/6 March, Adams and McGuinness asked me to come and see them privately in Dublin. I tagged it on to another meeting I had with Tony Ryan, the founder of Ryanair, so no one would know the real reason I was there. I arrived at a seedy airport hotel and was met by a guy with a shaven head lurking by reception. He took me up to a room where Adams and McGuinness were working on their speeches for the Ard Fheis. I gave them the note Tony had prepared and my proposal on the way forward. They said they couldn't get the IRA to do anything under pressure; they needed to be given space, but the idea of a step-by-step approach appealed to them. McGuinness said they had decided the IRA was not going to give up to the government or the unionists. The only person the IRA would give up to was Adams, so they were going to start with an appeal from Adams, followed by an IRA response in which they announced an end to all activity as well as decommissioning and only then action by the British government. The IRA would disappear and the British government should respond by demilitarisation. Adams reverted to the idea of the IRA dumping weapons, but I said they should stick to the de Chastelain route and McGuinness agreed. They said they would not agree to photographs and I suggested they think of other ways of achieving transparency, including the idea of independent observers. McGuinness said they needed to move on policing too. I gave them a draft of a section of a speech I had written on the future of the IRA. Adams said it was too late to put it into his speech but gave it to his speechwriter who was working in the hotel. It was an odd sensation to hear it coming out of Martin McGuinness's mouth later that evening at the Sinn Féin Ard Fheis.

Adams called me on my Easter holiday and asked me to cut it short and come over again. I set off at five in the morning on Sunday 3 April and met him at the same airport hotel in Dublin. This time Adams was by himself waiting in the foyer. Martin McGuinness was away talking to the IRA. He seemed recovered, no longer the shell-shocked man I had seen in February and March, and he showed me a statement he said he had first started work on over a year before. I could look at it but not keep it. He had not shown it to anyone else other than McGuinness. The statement was an appeal to the IRA to give up the military route and choose the exclusively peaceful and democratic path. It accepted the IRA had become an excuse for Unionists to refuse to make progress and said that 'the struggle can now be taken forward by other means [. . .] In the past I have defended the right of the IRA to engage in armed struggle. I did so because there was no alternative for those who would not bend the knee or for those who wanted a national republic. Now there is an alternative. That alternative is Sinn Féin.' He was not intending to wind the IRA up but to put it out of business. I was slightly shocked by the ice-cold clarity of the language. I thought to myself, so this is how it is going to end, finally, with a stark appeal from Adams and the IRA folding their tents.

I suggested some improvements but said the key issue would be how the IRA responded to the appeal and what they did in reality. He read me what the IRA would say in response, and it struck me as rather dismissive. He said this was the holding reply and they planned to put a common leadership position to an Army Convention in the summer.

Adams asked what the government response would be to his appeal. I said we would say it was a significant and welcome statement, but everything would depend on what the IRA did in practice. We would of course have to refer back to what we had said before on criminality and paramilitarism. He said he wasn't going to tell the Irish about the appeal till Wednesday because he was afraid they would leak it. But he wanted us to persuade the Irish government, and Michael McDowell in particular, to give a positive response – the Republicans and the Irish had been snarling at each other since the previous December. I said that was not in our gift. I asked about policing and decommissioning and he said he wanted to get back into a negotiation on those issues after the general election. We worked away on the various statements for a couple of hours. On the way out Adams said he had been stopped in the hotel foyer that morning by a retired Northern Ireland prison officer who had asked after various IRA prisoners. He had replied that most of them wouldn't speak to him now.

Adams made his appeal on 6 April and the reaction was more or less as we expected. Tony's response was enthusiastic and the Irish, SDLP and Unionists were more restrained. The IRA put out a holding response saying they would consult Volunteers. Adams had positioned Sinn Féin where he wanted them to be before the anticipated general election.

During the election campaign I went out to Heathrow to meet Martin McGuinness at Terminal 4. As I was working for the party rather than the government during the campaign I no longer had access to VIP suites etc., so we were reduced to agreeing to meet at the Starbucks in arrivals. But when I got there I discovered it was right in the public gaze and recced the terminal for somewhere quieter. The only place I could find was on the mezzanine level right next to immigration, and I escorted McGuinness and Aidan McAteer up there once they came through arrivals. McGuinness said there would be another forward statement by Adams during the election campaign and the subsequent IRA response would cover decommissioning as well as standing down. They had decided against an Army Convention and the much smaller Army Council would decide by itself. When

I suggested it would be better if the decision were wider than just a leadership position, he said, rather tartly, that was a matter for the IRA itself.

The 2005 election campaign once more distracted us from Northern Ireland. The DUP and Sinn Féin improved their electoral positions yet again, and David Trimble lost his seat. In fact, the UUP were left with only one MP, the moderate Sylvia Hermon. We reshuffled the Cabinet, replacing Paul Murphy with Peter Hain. Paul's inexhaustible patience and deep understanding of Northern Ireland had helped salve the wounds opened by all the preceding failed negotiations.

Tony's meetings with Adams and Paisley after the election results set the scene for the next stage of the process. Tony said to Adams that by acting unilaterally the IRA would put the DUP to the test. Adams said the IRA would act by the end of June but he needed to know the timescale we proposed for restoring devolved government after that. The nine months that had been mentioned previously was far too long. Tony said he couldn't give them a timetable because it depended on unionist opinion. Pressure on Paisley would only be effective if the DUP were seen to be unreasonable by the majority of unionist opinion. That would take time. We didn't know how much time. Adams said, 'The aim here was to make the IRA give up, in order to get the DUP into government before Ian Paisley died.' I gave him our suggested words for the IRA statement. Meanwhile, Paisley was in a positive frame of mind. The DUP were sitting pretty and didn't need to do anything till the IRA did. Nigel Dodds said time was needed to convince the unionist community that the IRA had really gone away. Paisley said we shouldn't get hung up on particular words. The key was what actually happened.

After the meetings Tony wrote a note suggesting that the British government should move forward on demilitarisation and OTRs in response to the IRA statement and the completion of decommissioning. Once there was an IMC report putting Republicans in the clear, we should call all-party talks. From then on the timescale would depend on Sinn Féin. The bolder Republicans were, the more pressure there would be on the DUP to move. Sinn Féin should join the policing board. If after two more clean IMC reports the DUP still refused to move, we should consider turning to a Plan B: going ahead with as much as we could of the Agreement, particularly North/South co-operation, or fresh Assembly elections. The Irish continually suggested using the existence of a 'Plan B' and more Irish involvement in Northern Irish affairs as a threat to persuade the DUP to move. We were reluctant, recalling the impact of Harold Wilson's ill-judged 'spongers' speech.

I went with Robert Hannigan, who was about to replace Jonathan Phillips as the NIO political director, to see Adams and McGuinness at Stormont on 22 June. We spent most of the meeting wrangling about Sean Kelly, an IRA prisoner whose release on licence from prison had been revoked. Adams said he was extremely popular and must be released. They said they were having great difficulty controlling the crowds at flashpoints between the two communities in North Belfast. Six hundred youngsters had been chanting 'Hey, Provos, leave them kids alone' at Gerry Kelly the previous weekend to the tune of Pink Floyd's 'Another Brick in the Wall' as he tried to hold them back. Adams told us the date for the IRA statement. I said it was important that activity cease. If the IRA was caught out again the whole process would collapse. Adams said he didn't care. He had made his best effort. If it fell over, he would not try again.

When Adams and I talked again on the phone about the statement, it was in the midst of the second wave of attempted London tube bombings by radical Islamist terrorists. This time the predictable Republican chiselling was not very convincing. The IRA had to make the announcement anyway and had nothing to negotiate with. Besides, by comparison with the new school of bombers, they looked pretty irrelevant. Adams and McGuinness came to Downing Street on 25 July to hand over the IRA statement. They demanded a series of further concessions and wanted the Executive up and running again by Christmas. Adams asked Tony to get President Bush to call Ian Paisley after the IRA statement and again in the autumn, which we did. But on the day of the statement Adams and Michael McDowell got into a stand-off. McDowell would not produce the letter on Irish government undertakings Adams wanted and Adams would not authorise the IRA statement without it. Adams went to Hillsborough to show Peter Hain the IRA statement. Jonathan Phillips had to copy it out and send it to me. It was clear and unambiguous. Using the words 'the end' was something they should have done a long time before.

We finished up with the ridiculous situation of Adams sitting at Hillsborough with Peter Hain, calling me and asking me to call the Irish as we approached the deadline to get the statements out. Eventually we got it done. My mind, however, was more focused on the tube bombings and I wrote in my diary, 'One chapter closes just as another begins.'

After the summer break, the IRA moved on to decommissioning, also on a unilateral basis. At the beginning of September, McGuinness told me they would deal with decommissioning by the end of the month but they needed time before de Chastelain announced that decommissioning was finished, because they wanted to check what the IRA and de Chastelain statements said. Neither of them was very good at public relations. They would appoint two independent observers to witness the decommissioning. I went by myself to see Adams and McGuinness at the Clonard monastery later in September, prior to decommissioning taking place, and on the plane ran into Jonathan Phillips, about to become the permanent secretary in the NIO, and had to tell him what I was up to. At our meeting, Adams wrote down the names of the independent observers they had chosen on a piece of paper and handed it to me. They were Harold Good, a Methodist pastor, and Adams's friend Father Alec Reid. He did not want me to say their names out loud there in the monastery or repeat them to anyone else. I told him we already knew them. McGuinness said that de Chastelain would be able to say that the estimates he had been given by the security authorities had been met or exceeded.

Tony spoke to Ian Paisley the next day. We were worried he would make a fuss about the absence of photographs or the choice of independent observers and try and discount decommissioning. But he accepted the approach and recognised there was no point in making a fuss about it. On 26 September de Chastelain announced that all IRA weapons had been put beyond use. The DUP reacted in a predictably curmudgeonly way but did not rule anything out.

We had expected jubilation at the demise of the IRA and the decommissioning of all its weapons, but instead a strange thing happened. The unionist community fell into a gloom. Tony's first reaction was to get irritated with them: they had peace, they had the Union, the

IRA had now gone out of business, and yet still they weren't happy. But gradually in October we began to understand what had happened. As Tony put it, 'unionism felt flattened rather than encouraged by the IRA move.' The middle ground felt disenfranchised now the extremes had taken over. Tony thought he ought to make a speech reassuring that middle-ground unionism by saying peace was not enough; we needed a change of heart from Republicans, not just a change of practice. Tony told Bertie Ahern when he came to see us on 11 October that he had been struck when the McCartney family had said to him the day before that the culture in their community had not changed despite the end of the IRA and decommissioning. That culture had to change.

Adams and Paisley came into Downing Street on 6 October one after another and we got in a tangle to avoid them running into each other in front of the TV cameras outside the front door. We brought Paisley in through the back door to avoid this clash and he made a terrible fuss about being relegated to a lesser entrance. In private Paisley told Tony that he wanted to do a deal, but in the bigger meeting with the DUP delegation there was no hint of flexibility. Adams just accused us of lacking a strategy.

We decided to put off Tony's speech till after a further IMC report to give unionist opinion time to settle down. When Peter Robinson and Nigel Dodds came in to see Robert Hannigan and me in early December they said their ability to move depended on the right mood in the unionist community. Our strategy was to try, during this interregnum, to push through the legislation allowing the devolution of policing and justice wanted by Sinn Féin, and the OTR legislation, and then try to make progress after a second IMC report in April 2006 by pushing the DUP into talks.

By January 2006, Adams was getting desperate at the DUP's continued refusal to move. He came with McGuinness and Gerry Kelly, increasingly part of the team, to see Tony at Chequers and said their leadership would be finished by the summer if we had not set up the Executive by then. We had backed away from our promises on OTRs and we were still spying on them. Tony agreed we had to put things like Stormontgate behind us. They said they did not like the OTR legislation as it stood because it covered the security forces as well as the IRA and Tony said if they were asking us to withdraw it then we would. I wrote in my diary that quite a lot of what we were doing was simply to convince Adams we had not got bored with the process and that we were still paying attention to them even though the IRA had gone away. Tony pressed them to move on policing – it was the only way to deal with the sense of gangsterism on the streets. They needed to move out of the no-man's-land they had got themselves into: the IRA couldn't police the community any more, yet they wouldn't let the police do so either, and people like the unfortunate fifteen-year-old girl raped in west Belfast a couple of weeks before were the losers. Adams reacted angrily, saying we were setting another precondition. The DUP would not move unless the government pushed them. Tony said he was not setting a new precondition, but the DUP would only move if they felt under pressure from their own community to do so. Adams said Sinn Féin might have to pull out of the Assembly and asked if Tony would undertake to run d'Hondt by the end of May. Tony replied he would do so before the summer.

In early January we held a strategy session at Chequers with Peter Hain and his team where we agreed we had to set a deadline to begin putting pressure on the DUP. Ian Paisley came to see Tony on 25 January for one of his increasingly frequent one-on-one meetings. There would be lots of laughter from behind the closed door to the den and when I went in I would often find little religious tracts left behind for Leo. On this occasion I asked Tony for a summary of the meeting and he said 'no'. I thought he was saying he wouldn't tell me what Paisley had said and so I asked again and he listed all the things Paisley had said 'no' to. I later discovered that Paisley had given Tony a DUP pamphlet which set out the party's position on an interim Assembly, an idea that was gathering support from the UUP and SDLP as well as the DUP, but Tony had forgotten to mention it to me so it was thrown away when his room was cleared out. Embarrassingly, we had to go back to the DUP to ask for another copy.

Shortly after the Paisley meeting, Tony and I went to Farmleigh to see Bertie Ahern. The Irish, who had also just seen Paisley, had been knocked back by his relaxed demeanour in saying no to any progress. The DUP were just not under any pressure to move. Bertie said we had to get the institutions up and running that year. The DUP were just playing it long. And the risk we faced was another generation of republicans going back to violence. Tony said we needed to shake the

DUP out of their complacency, but when we'd talked about elections to Paisley, he'd simply said fine: he knew he would get an even bigger majority. We needed something to convince the DUP we would go ahead without them. Policing would help reassure unionists but Sinn Féin just said that was a new precondition. Bertie sort of signed up to our approach of applying increasing pressure on the DUP and making the autumn the break point, and he and Tony agreed to take the reference to needing to 'achieve certainty by the summer' out of their joint statement, which I correctly warned would cause heartburn for Sinn Féin because it implied we would not be putting a devolved government in place by then.

I started working on a plan. We would establish an interim assembly with a firm end date in the autumn and run d'Hondt in November after a further clean IMC report. If that failed to result in a government, we would suspend the Assembly, cancel elections and move to a Plan B of greater Anglo-Irish cooperation.

Sinn Féin were at first completely opposed to the idea of an interim Assembly. They thought it would just give the DUP what they had always wanted, a corporate Assembly without an Executive, and there would be no pressure on them for further movement. Republicans needed a devolved power-sharing Executive. My argument was that we had to get the DUP on to the conveyor belt somehow. Once on, it would be very hard for them to get off. Robinson indicated to us privately he could agree to a transitional Assembly and to a sunset clause. Unfortunately, Peter Hain chose that moment to brief the press about the idea and Sinn Féin came down on it publicly like a ton of bricks.

When Bertie Ahern came over to London on 8 March, we had to adapt the proposal in light of the leak. Tony said the DUP were still under no pressure, while Sinn Féin were despairing and floundering around for ideas. He proposed to Bertie that we run d'Hondt in May, and if the DUP refused to participate, leave the Assembly in place till November and then run d'Hondt again for a last time before closing the whole process down. Bertie said no one in the Republic believed the DUP would do a deal but accepted our proposal anyway. I put the idea to McGuinness and Gerry Kelly on 23 March – Gerry Adams had two slipped discs and could not travel. They objected to the DUP being given two bites at running d'Hondt and said we would be a laughing stock, since it was clear the first attempt would fail because the DUP would obviously not participate. But they did not reject the idea out of hand.

Together with the Irish team headed by Michael Collins we worked the idea up into a joint statement to be launched by the two prime ministers in a pair of matching speeches. Adams and McGuinness were nervous and made threatening noises, but Paisley came in the day before the speech and Tony said it was the most positive meeting he'd ever had with him. His tone was quite different. Paisley said the 'atmosphere had changed in Northern Ireland'. The public wanted politicians to move on, and if the IMC gave Sinn Féin the all-clear in October, the DUP would be able to do a deal. Then I got a call from Michael Collins reporting that Denis Donaldson, a Sinn Féin employee who had been caught up in the Stormontgate affair, had been found dead at a cottage in Donegal, according to first reports shot in the head and with his hand chopped off. I spoke to Adams who put out a statement immediately condemning the murder and so did the IRA. It didn't look like an authorised operation, and the furore died down quite quickly, with everyone apparently determined not to allow the murder to knock the peace process off track.

On 6 April we helicoptered down to an Iron Age fort in Navan in County Armagh that had once been the seat of the High Kings of Ulster. In his speech Tony said the moment had arrived for the ultimate decision. The problem since the Good Friday Agreement had been that each side had believed in its own good faith but doubted that of the other. After eight years this was the last chance to make politics work. We couldn't force people to share power but we couldn't have a prolonged period of paralysis either. There were serious political issues facing the people of Northern Ireland, like water charges and education reform, and decisions on these issues should be taken by Northern Ireland politicians not by Westminster. Tony set 24 November as the deadline for re-establishing the Executive. The endgame had begun.

13

Endgame:
April 2006–May 2007

We had set deadlines before. This time we tied our hands by putting the deadline in legislation so that the Assembly automatically closed on 24 November if we didn't get a deal. But in April 2006 as we started trudging forwards in negotiations there was no way of knowing whether this was the final ascent or just another false summit. There were certainly enough bigots in the DUP who didn't want to go into government with Catholics at all. And although the ending of punishment beatings and other paramilitary activity on the republican side was so complete as to be almost miraculous, there was no reason to be certain that this time it was for good any more than it had been all the other times the IRA had switched off the violence. I asked Robert Hannigan, political director at the NIO, to start the search for a Scottish castle to host another attempt at hothouse negotiations. I had decided on Scotland, rather whimsically, partly to ring the changes and partly because it was nearer to Northern Ireland both physically and spiritually than England. He eventually came back with a golfing hotel in St Andrews. We booked it for Wednesday 11 October, letting the leaders know the location and the date of the final negotiations well in advance.

In the run-up to the summer we were engaged mainly in a waiting game as the parties danced around each other in the Assembly, which we had reconvened. It was clear to us that the DUP, or major elements within it, wanted delay and if possible to put off any agreement till 2007. But Ian Paisley, when he came in to see Tony in June, was still positive and said if the IMC report in October was as good as it had been in April, then he would go ahead. He said he was not just an old man determined to say no. If it could be done, it should be done. Sinn Féin were more anxious, complaining that the DUP were not engaging in the Assembly and urging us to draw up a 'Plan B' in case the DUP said no. 'The key,' McGuinness told us, 'was for the PM to face down the Taliban in the DUP.'

At the end of June, Tony and I visited Northern Ireland to put the DUP on warning that we were serious about the November deadline (although Tony told Bertie privately that if the DUP accepted the deal but asked for more time, then we would probably have to concede). Pressure continued to build on the DUP when Peter Hain announced the end of the eleven-plus in Northern Ireland, as well as the reorganisation of local government to reduce the number of local councils (and therefore the number of local councillors). He also started the process that would lead to people in Northern Ireland having to pay water charges. The motivation was probably more to impress a Labour Party audience in Britain in the context of the deputy leadership race, but the consequence in Northern Ireland was to make it clear to even the least politically sophisticated in the DUP that a devolved government might be the only way of avoiding a series of policies that they found distasteful and their electorate hated. It was a very effective form of political blackmail.

We in No. 10 had to waste a good deal of time in the summer with the beginnings of John Yates's investigations into the 'cash for peerages' drama. To add some light relief, Gerry Adams called me up in mid-July on the day after Michael Levy's arrest to express his solidarity and ask if Tony and I would seek political status if we went to prison. He recommended that we not recognise the court. The picture of Tony and me 'on the blanket' helped me temporarily see the funny side of the police investigations and associated press briefing.

What time we had, we spent working with Sinn Féin on policing. It was clear the vacuum left in Catholic working-class areas by the end of punishment beatings was serious. Crimes were going undeterred and the community was getting increasingly restive. The IRA had to bring off the difficult trick of frightening the dissident republicans out of filling the vacuum themselves without being able to use violence. McGuinness had for some time been complaining about dissident graffiti on his street in Derry and the lack of discipline. Every so often he would raise his worry about dissidents trying to kill either him or Adams. We had been working on ideas with Hugh Orde for over a year to see if we could come up with half-steps that Republicans could take to cooperating with the police and, at one stage, Orde had introduced us to a group of his officers responsible for policing South Armagh. They were a remarkably positive bunch and full of ideas on how we could get greater cooperation, for example by removing the ban the IRA had traditionally imposed on any police officer entering schools in South Armagh on pain of death for the headmaster.

We discussed these ideas in some of the meetings we arranged between Orde and Sinn Féin leaders including Gerry Kelly and Conor Murphy, their representative in South Armagh. But Kelly and McGuinness were clear when they saw me on 15 September they would have to get over the hurdle of policing in one leap, not in a series of little steps, and that in many ways it would be the hardest decision for Republicans to make, given the history of enmity between them and the police force in all its guises – be it the Royal Irish Constabulary, the Black and Tans, the B Specials or the RUC. Bertie Ahern had always been clear that policing would be Sinn Féin's last card and they would be loath to play it.

We carried out some polling in Northern Ireland in September and it showed unionist opinion gradually recovering from the Northern Bank robbery, and even DUP voters seeing no alternative to power-sharing. Interestingly, Sinn Féin voters had also shifted decisively in favour of policing. We held two sessions with the Irish and the parties in September to get them to focus on the endgame. In a major move, Sinn Féin indicated they would join the policing board in December if the DUP agreed to set up the Executive, and if they gave them a timetable for the devolution of policing and justice. This latter step had become their talismanic demand on policing. Most of the reforms and limitations to the police that nationalists and republicans had wanted had been secured through SDLP pressure, so Sinn Féin needed to ask for something else. And devolution of policing would allow them to claim that the security forces were no longer under the Brits, but were devolved to Irishmen.

Paisley, too, seemed to us to be limbering up to do a deal. In late September there was a rumour that the DUP would refuse to come to St Andrews and I was nervous when Paisley asked to speak to me on the phone. But in fact his call was simply to say that he was happy to come to talks but had to be back in Northern Ireland by the Friday evening for his fiftieth wedding anniversary. He had friends and relatives coming from all over the world.

The IMC report in early October was very good for the IRA. As I wrote in my diary, 'The truth in the change of the Republican position is hard to disguise.' We'd had one final pre-St Andrews meeting with Adams and McGuinness at Chequers in late September. To get some publicity in the run-up to the Irish elections in the following spring, they'd brought with them the Sinn Féin candidate standing in Bertie Ahern's constituency, Mary Lou McDonald, a new sort of republican educated at private school and thoroughly middle class. They confirmed they could join the policing board if their conditions were met. Adams was ready to call a special Ard Fheis to decide the matter if they got a date for devolution of policing, and he wanted us to move on their demands on MI5 as well. This was a new issue for them, although the SDLP had been campaigning on it for some time. As part of the normalisation process, we were giving the lead responsibility for national security issues in Northern Ireland to MI5 instead of the local police, in order to bring it into line with the rest of the UK. Nationalists were worried that in some way this might lead to the creation of a 'force within a force', which they believed Special Branch had been in the 1970s and 80s, responsible for collusion in the death of numerous Catholics. Sinn Féin weren't about to be outflanked by the SDLP on such a visceral issue and started making demands of their own. I suggested Adams and his colleagues meet the Security Service, but the idea of senior Republicans meeting MI5 privately was a step too far for them.

On 6 October we met Michael Collins and the Irish team to agree the text of the agreement for St Andrews. Slightly disconcertingly, Ian Paisley was being very optimistic and hinting strongly that a deal was doable. The IMC report and a successful meeting with the Catholic archbishop had put him in a good mood. The private channel between the DUP and Sinn Féin had reopened. The DUP were insisting that Sinn Féin accept the legitimacy of the police and, slightly more problematically, that the IRA hand back all the assets they had stolen over the years, a totally impractical idea which they quickly dropped. I wrote in my diary that 'the omens are good. As in December 2004 an agreement is within reach but, as then, some silly issue like photographs can take it all away from us. In the end it is a matter of political will.' Tony had announced he would be standing down as prime minister and all sides realised it was their last chance to do a deal with a Prime Minister in place who was prepared to devote significant time and attention to Northern Ireland. The trade-off we were seeking this time was policing against re-establishing the institutions. And as always the problem would be who would go first.

Tony and I flew up to St Andrews on 11 October with Tom Kelly and the rest of the team. The weather was appalling and we couldn't land at the airbase and had to reroute to Dundee and drive down. When we finally got to the hotel, all the parties had been there for some time.

It was the most luxurious location we had chosen for the talks so far, and everyone was clearly making the most of it, despite the lashing rain and cloud which made it impossible to see the sea, even though it was only a few hundred yards away across the golf course. It was a bit odd to have tartan-clad American tourists with their golf clubs mixing with former terrorists, but neither side seemed to mind. The mood was terrific, with everyone congratulating us on such a fabulous success. I pointed out to anyone who would listen that it was exactly when things looked good on Northern Ireland that they all went terribly wrong. And, indeed, wrong they went.

As soon as Adams and Paisley began negotiating, they started back-pedalling like mad. In the first bilateral meeting of the talks, Sinn Féin took a different position to the one they had expressed at Chequers only a week before, saying that their Ard Fheis on policing could only take place *once* the power-sharing Executive was in place. Tony pointed out the obvious problem of sequencing: Paisley had told him he needed Sinn Féin to hold their Ard Fheis on policing before he could agree to re-establish the Executive. Adams started to get irritated that the DUP were such experts on internal Sinn Féin procedures. He doubted Paisley could even pronounce Ard Fheis. McGuinness then went out from the meeting to propagate this new hard-line position to the waiting TV cameras, deliberately making it clear Sinn Féin would not shift.

During the meeting a note was handed to me saying that Ian Paisley wanted to see Tony alone. I agreed to it. But it was clearly a misunderstanding, because the whole DUP delegation came down and made a terrible fuss; they clearly thought we were trying to split Paisley off from his party and that became a running theme throughout the

negotiation. The DUP refused to allow any group smaller than six to
negotiate and seemed to need an internal session to agree the delegation for each and every meeting, reflecting internal divisions in the
party. Robinson set out seven DUP demands: 1) practical cooperation
with the police rather than more words; 2) the disbandment of all
remaining IRA structures; 3) the reversal of the Hain reforms on education and water charges; 4) the changes they wanted to Strands 1 and 2;
5) a financial package for Northern Ireland; 6) a long list of confidence-
building measures for the unionist community; and 7) a promise there
would be no side deals with Sinn Féin. Tony said he thought that
looked more like twenty-six issues than seven but was prepared to
consider them. It was clear that Nigel Dodds, a potential leadership
rival to Robinson, had set himself up as the spokesman for the most
recalcitrant group.

Afterwards Tony saw Paisley alone. Paisley was in a benign mood.
He sensed that his community was ready to move, and if Republicans
could do what was needed on policing, his instinct was to come to a
deal quickly before things unravelled, and then hold an election in
January. He said the only thing that was necessary was for Sinn Féin
to hold an Ard Fheis on policing before the Executive was set up –
the one thing Adams and McGuinness had now made clear we could
not deliver. But when Paisley went back to his party there was serious
opposition, particularly from Dodds, to such a short timescale.
Robinson told us the DUP were in turmoil and had virtually thrown
out Paisley as leader – something we took with a pinch of salt.

The two prime ministers, meanwhile, were seeing the other parties.
Sean Neeson of the Alliance, whom I had known when dealing with
Northern Ireland in Washington, wondered whether he should
compare their partnership, which had been sustained for so long
through such trying circumstances, to Gladstone and Parnell. Tony
and Bertie were touched by the sentiment, but thought not, although
actually in my view it was in some ways a more remarkable partnership and certainly a more successful one.

It was agreed that Robert Hannigan (whom the DUP trusted) and
I (whom they seemed to regard as a devil incarnate who might talk
them into something they did not want to do) should meet with
Robinson and Dodds early on Thursday morning to relay our account
of Tony's meeting with Paisley, and agree a sequence which would

get us round the problem of both sides wanting the other to go first. But they failed to turn up at the appointed time and we had to have a lengthy negotiation to get them to appear at all. When they did, they were visibly jittery. I tried to reassure them that this was not a negotiating meeting but just an information-sharing one. Having listened to the sequence I outlined, they said it was impossible. Dodds complained they were being rushed into an agreement on sequencing without knowing the substance on policing. I assured them we were exploring their ideas with Sinn Féin but one way or another the governments would be publishing their proposals at the end of the talks the next day. They went away rather shocked.

Bertie and Tony then saw Sinn Féin in Tony's hotel suite which still reeked of kippers from his breakfast with Bertie. Adams continued to insist he could only carry out the Ard Fheis on policing after the institutions were up and running. He described the community's hostile reaction to the speech he had made earlier in the week, urging Sinn Féin to move forward on policing. And he demanded that we move on their entire wish list, from plastic bullets to MI5, before they would agree to anything.

When the DUP then came back to see Tony later in the morning Paisley was no longer so benign. For the benefit of his colleagues, he delivered a message with a much harder line, frequently referring to how tough he'd been with the Prime Minister the night before. They said they wanted to test whether Republicans were really cooperating with the police to be sure that they had indeed changed, and that therefore a short timescale to devolution was impossible if they were to carry the community with them. As Paisley spoke, it became clear that they had dropped their demand for an Ard Fheis before an election, but replaced it with a long period of seeing Republican cooperation with the police on the ground before they would go into government. Of course, time was precisely what Sinn Féin and the Irish, because of the anticipated Irish elections in 2007, did not have.

The weather had improved by then and we could see the sea from the hotel as well as hear the roar of the Tornado engines from the airbase across the bay. We and the Irish team decided to walk down to the clubhouse overlooking the sea for lunch. Bertie Ahern was distracted. He had been having a terrible time politically at home and kept getting calls on his mobile. He was determined to stay close to Michael McDowell, on whom his political survival at that moment depended and who, in the peace process, had tended towards a hard-line on Sinn Féin. In fact, McDowell was extremely constructive and, over lunch, came up with a proposal on sequencing that helped resolve the problem. He scribbled his plan on a scrap of paper, suggesting we propose the nomination of the First and Deputy First Minister for 24 November followed by Sinn Féin endorsement of the police and then elections. He gave the scrap to me and I passed it to Tony who scribbled further on it. Conveying this new idea to the Republicans proved simple. While we'd been eating, Adams and McGuinness and a large number of other members of their group had gathered outside the window of the clubhouse to look at the sea. Bertie, Tony and Michael McDowell went outside to put the change in plan to them and they did not object. We then sent Robert Hannigan off to meet Peter Robinson to see if he might accept the compromise, while we divided the other parties up into working groups to discuss the outstanding issues.

I had a sense of foreboding, however, when, in the afternoon, Paisley and Robinson asked to come and see Tony. I tried to find out from Robert what it was they wanted, but he didn't know, saying only that he thought they wanted to make a compromise proposal – if true, a novel approach from the DUP. When they came up to Tony's suite, Paisley and Robinson settled on the sofa with the rest of their delegation spread out around the room and set out, in the most reasonable manner, a proposal that I knew would bring everything crashing down. Instead of symbolically nominating the First and Deputy First Minister, they suggested that the existing Preparation for Government Committee of the Assembly be chaired alternately by Paisley and McGuinness during the 'testing period'. Tony looked rather nonplussed and it seemed he might even welcome the idea. He asked me what I thought. I said it was like asking someone for an orange and being presented with a raspberry. The existing Preparation for Government Committee was a joke. Paisley was taken with the image of an orange, but he was getting tired and it was clear that any further pressure on him that evening would be counterproductive.

We then met the Irish who rejected the committee proposal out of hand, and we agreed to start preparing for failure. Both Sinn Féin and the DUP could smell our anxiety for a deal and we needed to convince them that this was their last chance and we would chase after them no longer. They both needed to be shocked into agreeing to move. Michael Collins and I and our teams spent Thursday night until 3 a.m. preparing the text of a draft agreement the two governments could put out on Friday morning in the hope the two sides would see sense. We tried to make it as tempting as possible to the DUP. Meanwhile, McDowell went down to the bar to give Robinson the Irish government's gloomy assessment that we were heading for failure, and to repeat the gist of his compromise formula on sequencing. It was clear the DUP were aware of the abyss ahead of them and were starting to look for a way out. The DUP reactivated their backchannel to Sinn Féin to see if they could find a solution overnight.

In the middle of all this, we had a call from the No. 10 press office making us aware of comments by General Dannatt, the Chief of the General Staff, apparently calling for a withdrawal from Iraq, criticising the government and making other disparaging remarks in an interview with the *Daily Mail* that was to go out on Friday morning. For over an hour I couldn't get hold of anyone senior from the MoD. The Chief of the Defence Staff was in Australia. The Vice Chief of the Defence Staff was giving a lecture on a ship and couldn't be disturbed. Dannatt was refusing to return calls. And Des Browne, the Defence Secretary, was on a plane to Glasgow. It was lucky we were not under nuclear attack and trying to decide whether to loose off Tridents in response.

We eventually got hold of the Chief of the Defence Staff in Australia and Des Browne in Glasgow and they agreed to speak to Dannatt. We were getting pressure from Labour politicians to dismiss him, but to do that would turn him into a martyr. At six on Friday morning Des called me back to say that Dannatt had agreed to go on the morning shows to eat his words. It turned out to be difficult to ascertain what he had actually said, since neither he nor his press officer had bothered to record the interview. Nor did they think he had said anything remarkable. So we were kept guessing until we saw the *Mail* on Friday morning. To prevent the same thing happening again, I arranged a meeting between Tony and all the service chiefs for a few weeks hence, so he could make the point that if commanders behaved in this political way they could guarantee that prime ministers in future would not put British troops in harm's way. It would not be worth the political pain to risk deploying them, which would be a tragedy given they were one of the few effective fighting forces in Europe.

I went back to Tony's suite at seven on Friday morning exhausted. I stood at the window looking out to sea. Both of us had hardly slept. As I recorded in my diary, Tony, who was sitting on the sofa in his pyjamas, was in a deep gloom about both Dannatt and the talks. He said, 'It's hopeless, isn't it?' and criticised me for not having prepared the talks properly. I told him not to be so stupid. My diary goes on: 'The situation was grave. Both sides had pulled well back from their opening positions and were now too far apart to allow us to close the gap. A fitful sleep had been disturbed by the thought that the agreement would be rejected not just by the DUP but also by Sinn Féin and even by the other smaller parties. On the other hand the key prize was to get the DUP on board, just as in earlier stages of the talks the key aim had been to get the Republicans on board. And I said to Tony we had to remain patient. Patience was just about the only virtue required in the Northern Ireland negotiations.'

As usual, the clock was ticking. We had to conclude the talks by lunchtime because Paisley had made it clear he would leave then to go back to Belfast for the long-planned celebration of his golden wedding anniversary. We would not be able to delay his departure unless we provided him with a private plane – which we later did – and even that would only buy us a few hours, until four in the afternoon.

There was a gleam of hope when, at 7.30 a.m., Robinson called Robert Hannigan to say that they had reconsidered and were prepared to look at the idea of the nomination of the First and Deputy First Minister on 24 November. By nine, Robinson had sold the idea to the rest of the DUP. Paisley and his team came to see Tony at ten. Paisley was in jovial form, asking when 'the hanging' would be. He said he could agree to a symbolic step on 24 November but no content or trappings of office could be taken on then. Before that could take place, there must be an Ard Chomhairle (the Sinn Féin Executive) on policing, which was necessary to prepare for the bigger Sinn Féin Ard Fheis later. He waved at Tony their proposed new wording of the pledge of office they had presented to the NIO the previous day, and stressed the importance of getting that too. Having cleared this barrier,

the negotiation moved on to the date on which the devolved government would be restored. Robinson and Dodds said February was
impossible and it had to be April. Bertie Ahern would not agree to
shift beyond February. He said the paraphernalia of setting up the
Executive would mean that April translated into a May start to effective government, which had always been Dodds's aim. It was clear
Bertie wanted visible progress before the traditional Irish visit to
Washington for St Patrick's Day. Robert shuttled back and forth
between the different sides and finally got an agreement that the parties
would nominate their ministerial teams on 14 March and actually take
power on 26 March. Paisley, who was having lunch with his wife, told
Robert this was his final offer and he shouldn't come back unless the
answer was yes. The date was finally agreed at two in the afternoon,
and we started to print the agreement. Alan Ewart, the general secretary of the DUP, asked for a photograph with Tony. It turned out he
was a cousin, connected with Tony's Orange antecedents from
Donegal, and he presented Tony with a picture of his grandfather in
his Orange sash.

But we were not out of the woods. At the very last minute, as we
were printing the document and had called the plenary of all the
parties for 3 p.m., Adams and McGuinness insisted on seeing Bertie
and Tony to go through a series of final demands. Their aim appeared
to be to run out the clock so that Paisley would be the one who
walked out. I got angry and tried to get Tony to end the session. The
DUP were just outside the door and were getting increasingly restless. I explained that we could not change the document – which had
been printed – at this stage, but Adams kept pushing. Tony decided
to keep going until he had addressed all their points. The most serious
issue was the role of MI5 and we negotiated on that as Tony walked
the quarter of a mile back to his suite to change. The NIO security
expert briefed Tony while he got dressed in the bedroom and we
concluded the conversation with Adams on the walk back to the
plenary.

Finally it looked as though we had a breakthrough. Tom Kelly,
the No. 10 press secretary, rushed off to the press centre to change the
backdrop for the press conference from 'St Andrews Talks' to 'St
Andrews Agreement'. We gathered all the party leaders in the main
conference room and presented the agreement to them. There was

no discussion. Apart from Paisley and Adams, they were all a bit stunned. Then Tony got up to make a little speech to Ian Paisley and his wife, sitting in the front row of the DUP delegation, about their golden wedding anniversary and presented them with a leather photo album. Bertie Ahern topped us by presenting them with a bowl made of wood recovered from the site of the Battle of the Boyne. Paisley shook the Taoiseach's hand, the first time he had shaken the hand of an Irish Prime Minister, and made a gracious speech. He said this was a 'great day for peace' and a 'great day for all Ireland and those who loved democracy'. Gerry Adams, to whom Paisley would still not speak, surprised us all by jumping to his feet and leading the applause to the couple. The psychological barrier of Ian Paisley agreeing to be First Minister to Martin McGuinness's Deputy First Minister had been crossed.

We hustled them all off back to Northern Ireland before they could change their minds. It was not the end of the negotiation, but at least the framework had been set and we would never have to gather everyone together in a castle for forcing talks again. The journey round the stately homes of Britain was finished.

Predictably, it wasn't long before the St Andrews Agreement started to come apart at the seams. Paisley managed to go to church on the Sunday after St Andrews with no one complaining to him, but, nevertheless, on Tuesday he refused to attend the first of the new meetings of the Preparation for Government Committee with Adams, on the basis that McGuinness was saying that, when they were nominated as First and Deputy First Ministers on 24 November, he would refuse to take the new pledge of office proposed by the DUP because it referred to the police. This was one of the unfinished bits of business from St Andrews. It is true that Paisley had waved his new version of the oath at us at St Andrews and Tony had promised to look at it. But, equally, it was difficult to ask McGuinness to swear an oath to the police force before Sinn Féin had met to agree to join the policing board. We soon got into a classic stand-off. Sinn Féin were refusing to hold an Ard Chomhairle on policing before the nominations on 24 November and the DUP were saying they wouldn't allow the First Minister and Deputy First Minister to be nominated unless that happened.

Meanwhile, Adams and McGuinness were demanding movement on plastic bullets, on OTRs and, most seriously, on MI5. Eliza Manningham-Buller called me to ensure we weren't going to give in, but Tony wanted to offer Sinn Féin more on local political oversight of the Security Service. Nor had we resolved at St Andrews the issue of whether to hold a referendum on the agreement or hold an election. The DUP had made it clear they insisted on an election and Sinn Féin said they would prefer an election to a referendum. But the parties that stood to do badly, notably the UUP and SDLP, were against elections.

In the run-up to 24 November we made repeated efforts to resolve the policing and MI5 issues. On the weekend of 4/5 November I managed to satisfy most of Sinn Féin's niggles, but they got hung up on a particular paragraph in the changed Strand 1 paper that unintentionally had the effect of meaning that only a unionist could be First Minister. They had a good point in logic but this particular paragraph had been agreed by everyone in 2004 and was very hard to reopen now without encouraging the DUP to reopen the whole agreement. Robert came up with a clever fix that satisfied them. I managed to get Eliza to sign up to some more compromises on the role of MI5, but she could not agree to the statutory right to access intelligence material that Sinn Féin were seeking for the police ombudsman in Northern Ireland.

We resorted to proximity talks again on 16 November, in the hope of resolving the pledge of office disagreement. I couldn't help remembering that last time we'd held such talks in Downing Street they had ended in failure. We started off with Sinn Féin in Conference Room A where the DUP had been last time. Robert and I concocted a compromise that meant watering down the events of 24 November so they were purely symbolic and removing the new pledge of office from the legislation so it could be agreed privately between Sinn Féin and the DUP. I tried this out on Adams and he indicated he could live with it. Tony saw Paisley alone and told us afterwards that he had accepted it too and wanted us to go over to the House of Commons and brief his MPs. But when we rushed over, Paisley was with Peter Robinson and Paisley Jr, who denounced our scheme completely: they would do nothing till McGuinness took the pledge on policing. Paisley made no effort to defend the compromise proposal, nor did he volunteer he'd told Tony he could accept it.

We went back to explain the situation to Sinn Féin, who had moved into the old Thatcher study in No. 10 by then. They were unimpressed and said they needed the nomination of First and Deputy First Ministers on 24 November if they were to call an Ard Fheis on policing. So we went back to the DUP in the House of Commons but they were completely unyielding. I told them I thought it was going to be a bust. That got their attention but they still conceded very little. They said they would not be 'Trimbled' by jumping first; Sinn Féin would have to take the first step. When we went back to No. 10, Adams completely reversed track. He said they were now ready to acquiesce in the new pledge of office as long as they got a more substantive event on 24 November. After some time huddling by themselves, they offered us a new wording for the pledge, which kept the same words proposed by the DUP but reversed their order.

It was getting late by now so I asked Vera the messenger to go out and get them a Chinese takeaway. Food had been important to Sinn Féin throughout the process, particularly to Adams, whose first demand in any negotiation was normally to be fed, and who complained regularly about the quality of the food we provided for them. They gobbled the sweet-and-sour pork in the small dining room while the Speaker was addressing the annual gathering of the Cabinet in the next room on the eve of the Queen's Speech. I guess this was the nearest they got to ending abstentionism to the Westminster Parliament. We left Sinn Féin in a happy state in No. 10 and went back to see the DUP in the House of Commons.

This was a mistake, as I knew it would be. The first plan had been for Robert to go and see Peter Robinson alone, but at the last minute Paisley had asked that I come too, and that we see all of them. We showed them Sinn Féin's revised language for the pledge and Paisley said immediately it was completely unacceptable. I pointed out it was the language they had first given us, simply in a different order, but decided to bring the meeting to an end without any conclusion because I feared doing anything else would lead to disaster.

The next day, Queen's Speech day, Paisley came to see Tony in his office in the House of Commons where we were based. Nigel Dodds and others were kept away because they were too negative, but they had written to Paisley telling him he had made a mistake and begging him not to go on with the negotiations, which spooked him. However, we made some progress on the pledge, accepting an addition that Robinson had asked for earlier. But at the last moment Paisley suddenly said he couldn't accept the pledge as worded at all because it didn't use the term the 'police' rather than 'policing'. The whole agreement disintegrated in front of our eyes. Luckily Robinson was able to take Paisley outside and to get him to change his mind.

Adams and McGuinness came down to see us but got tangled up in the procession for the Queen's Speech on their way to the Prime Minister's office from their eyrie in one of the towers above the St Stephen's entrance. One of the Speaker's flunkeys told them they could join in, but they couldn't go beyond the line in the floor in the Lords since they hadn't taken the MP's oath. They tried to explain they had no desire to do so. We didn't get far in our meeting in the morning and later in the afternoon we went up to see them in their offices. There was no natural light and there were bars on any windows there were. I said the authorities must have put them there to remind them of prison. They said two police snipers had jumped through the skylight earlier in the day after watching the Queen's procession from the tower above them. McGuinness said that one of the beefeaters had told him he had been in Derry fighting the IRA.

We managed to meet most of their points – Robert had tried to clear one of them with Peter Robinson who was on the M25 on the way to buy a new car, but only got a holding reply. Adams was becoming angry, hectoring to get his way, one element of his nego- tiating repertoire that I found particularly tiresome. Later we got them to come down to Tony's office and went through the last few points, but had to shuffle them into Gordon Brown's office next door when the Labour Party Parliamentary Committee started arriving. We thought it was all sorted, but they came back again at 7 p.m. absolutely insisting on a change to the legislation removing the requirement that Ministers agree all measures with the full Executive. They said it was a deal-breaker, because it would stop Sinn Féin ministers being able to do anything. I said there was nothing we could do about it because the bill had already gone to press. I called the Parliamentary Counsel to see if he could stop it, but he said it had already been handed to the parliamentary clerks and was no longer in the possession of the government. The House of Commons was now the owner of the bill. I had to call the Clerks and beg them to change it, which they kindly did. The amendment was in reality totally irrelevant, but it was a way for the Republicans to demand one last ounce of flesh and demonstrate that they could get us to change something. We were able to let them leave happy, the key aim of a sensible negotiator, which was rather remarkable given all that they'd had to concede to the DUP in the course of the previous two days. The happiness was short-lived, though. Adams called me on Friday to say he was going off to see 'senior colleagues' over the weekend and he thought the whole package might be too difficult for them. He himself thought they should soldier on but he could not guarantee he would carry the day.

Nor was Paisley having success at selling the package to his party. He and Peter Robinson came to see Tony after Prime Minister's Questions on 22 November to say that the party was terribly split, with the Dodds and church wings blocking everything. The events of 24 November were crucial to Sinn Féin but Paisley said he could not indicate then that he accepted the nomination to be First Minister. Tony suggested that instead of saying anything new he repeat language he had already used before so that nobody could criticise him. When they left I cobbled together a draft statement for Paisley, drawing on what he had said in the House of Commons the previous day, and sent it to them. The next day Paisley sent us his speech and it was hopeless, negative, and failed to indicate that he was to be First Minister at all. Tony called him with amendments but he kept resisting, saying God would decide. He was obviously in a bit of a state having been criticised by members of his own church. The phone cut off, but when we got him back he agreed to include our key sentence: that 'if the St Andrews Agreement was adhered to and implemented by all the parties then he would be prepared to take the office of First Minister'. Adams called and tried to get us to change the script of what the Speaker of the Assembly would say during the ceremony. But we knew if we did we would lose the DUP. We cancelled Tony's visit to Scotland the next day so he could go to Northern Ireland on the 24th, as requested by Paisley, but in the evening Paisley called saying he did not want him to come after all.

This was a bad sign, and things looked even more ominous when, at ten the next morning, we rang Paisley, as agreed the night before, and he failed to answer. We kept trying but he wouldn't take the calls and I started to get very suspicious. Finally, at 10.28, he answered as he was walking into the Chamber in Stormont. He told Tony it would be OK, but it was obvious he had dropped the sentence that Tony had asked him to add the night before. It turned out that he had had a very difficult party executive meeting that morning, from which half his team had walked out, and in the face of that opposition, he had decided not to say the key sentence.

Tony couldn't bear to watch the ceremony on television but I did. Adams made a warm and positive statement, Paisley waffled and the Speaker read out the statement we had drafted for her saying that Paisley had indicated his intention to be First Minister, although he patently hadn't. Paisley tried to raise a point of order but at that moment the Chamber had to be evacuated because of a bomb scare. The scare was, in fact, an attack on the building by Michael Stone, the mad loyalist infamous for opening fire on a republican funeral at Milltown cemetery in west Belfast. He had rushed the front door of Stormont with a pipe bomb, a knife and a gun, and was stopped by some brave security guards. The contrast between democracy and sectarian terrorism could hardly have been better made.

While all the Assembly members were milling around outside, we engaged in some frantic telephone diplomacy, calling Adams and Paisley and persuading the latter that he should not raise a point of order when the session resumed. But Adams then demanded that Paisley clarify his position or he would boycott the Preparation for Government meeting, the very body he had been complaining about the DUP boycotting. Eventually, Peter Hain managed to get Paisley to clarify his position by issuing a press statement with the crucial sentence in it; he told Paisley the Prime Minister felt personally let down by his failure to deploy the sentence as promised. But, by then, Adams was demanding the Assembly be recalled at a later date so Paisley could be forced to repeat the sentence there. To my relief, when we spoke to them both later that night they had calmed down. We had got through, but only just.

Adams, McGuinness and Kelly came to Chequers the following Friday to discuss the devolution of policing and justice and MI5. Tony had decided to throw away the carefully constructed text on MI5 I had prepared with Hugh Orde and the Security Service and gave them a much vaguer one. I protested afterwards, but Tony said Adams *needed* to be able to tell the IRA he had sorted it all out. Adams said he could only call an Ard Fheis if the DUP agreed to a timetable for devolution of policing. A few days earlier I had noticed Robinson saying the problem for the DUP was the notion of Gerry Kelly as Minister for Justice. That was just too much for them. So I suggested we have an understanding between the two sides that neither would take the position once it was devolved, and that we require a 70 per cent vote for the Minister of Justice to ensure both sides had a veto on the position. Adams thought that might work.

The following Monday, Bertie Ahern came to dinner at No. 10. We had agreed to host the final of the TV cookery competition *MasterChef*, in which amateur cooks had to demonstrate that they were good enough to cook for a state dinner. As we had discovered at Jamie Oliver's dinner, Bertie was no gourmet, but he was extremely tolerant and agreed to come nevertheless. It was difficult to have a serious conversation when, after every course, the TV cameras would come in and the two prime ministers would be expected to comment on the food. We were told the chef who prepared the main course, a venison Wellington, had burned the bottom of it and was in tears at the end. Bertie pressed us to agree to an apology on the various acts of collusion by British security forces over the years of the Troubles. We were sympathetic, but of course it could not be one-sided. People on all sides had been hurt and deserved apologies.

A few days afterwards, Paisley and Robinson came in with Nigel Dodds and Maurice Morrow, two of the most recalcitrant DUP leaders. It was evident that they still wanted more time before going into government, but we were adamant this was not on offer. Paisley was clearly of the view they should go for it, but Dodds and Morrow asked some difficult questions. We managed to set up the conversation on the devolution of policing so that Dodds stipulated that the crucial point was that they could not accept Gerry Kelly as Minister for Justice, a problem we already had an answer to.

But we still had not made enough progress to allow Adams to call an Ard Fheis on policing, and time was ticking away. As a result it turned into the Christmas from hell. For nearly three weeks, every day was taken up with endless phone calls, with the exception only of Christmas Day and part of New Year's Eve. My children kept asking me who the Gerry and Ian and Martin were who we appeared to have taken on holiday with us. It led to me having to join in conference calls in some extraordinary situations: standing, coatless, outside the Apple computer shop on Regent Street, where I had been buying Christmas presents, on a freezing evening with snow falling, until I could stand it no longer; in a clothes shop in west London where I had to hand the phone to my wife Sarah each time I tried on a pair of trousers and she would then give me a summary of the discussion I had missed when I came out of the changing booth; and, most perilously, while cycling through the marshes near Walberswick on the Suffolk coast with my children (I put the mobile on loudspeaker so I could hear Tony talking to Ian Paisley Jr). Robert Hannigan's wife took a dimmer view of such disruptions to family life. After one particularly long phone call between Tony and Gerry Adams on Christmas Eve, the No. 10 switchboard just couldn't get him back. It turned out his wife had finally had enough, snatching his mobile from him and flinging it away.

From 15 to 20 December, Tony was on a tour of the Middle East. He called Paisley from the King David Hotel in Jerusalem, looking out at the Mount of Olives, and after a discussion of the biblical scene, Tony suggested some language Paisley could use to indicate that he was sympathetic to the Sinn Féin wish for a conditional timetable for the devolution of justice. He urged Paisley to look at what Sinn Féin were offering: it was clear that Adams wanted to move forward on policing. Tony said he was worried that Morrow and Dodds were being unnecessarily negative. Paisley agreed that Morrow could be abrasive, but said that both men would follow him in the end.

On 19 December Peter Hain got the two sides in to Stormont and, on the backchannel, Sinn Féin showed the DUP their draft motion on policing for the Ard Chomhairle. Tony, now in Dubai, called Paisley. Together they agreed to exchange correspondence so that Paisley could put in writing to Tony that 'of course it was possible that conditions could develop in which it would be possible to envisage devolution on the timescale Sinn Féin wanted'. But the letter Paisley faxed from his home bore no relation to what we thought we had agreed. Every time Tony called him, Paisley would agree with the logic of what he said, but he resolutely refused to say so in cold print.

Meanwhile, Sinn Féin desperately needed Paisley to commit to the timetable for the devolution of policing in his new year's message.

Adams called Tony on the day before Christmas Eve and said he had been told the draft Paisley statement he had seen from No. 10 was the best he was going to get and asked if Paisley would really say it, but added rapidly, 'Don't tell me if the answer is no.' Tony didn't disabuse him. I was uncomfortable about us getting so far away from the truth, and spoke to Tony about it afterwards. But he said that Adams did not want to be handed the wrong answers to give his supporters. He had no choice but to press on and we were trying to make it easier for him.

On that basis, we got Sinn Féin to call their Ard Chomhairle on 29 December and approve the motion on policing which had been amended by the DUP. But then, of course, Paisley refused to deliver the response the Republicans had expected and Adams started talking about having to resign as leader of Sinn Féin, saying his position was untenable. Paisley told us he wasn't issuing his new year's message till Monday 1 January, although the DUP had told Sinn Féin on the backchannel that it would come out on Friday in advance of the new year's holiday. What's more, when Paisley sent the draft of his message, it did not contain the words of comfort he had promised us. All our negotiations were complicated by the fact that Paisley's wife was acting as secretary, and quite often sent us the wrong texts. In one conversation Paisley appeared to be considering changes to a draft statement proposed by Tony, even though he knew very well it had already gone out.

Having failed with the father, Tony started calling Ian Paisley Jr, but had no luck there either. Paisley Jr clearly could not envisage devolution of policing taking place on the timescale proposed, and there seemed little chance of persuading him. Meanwhile, the text of the Ard Fheis motion had not been published, but we knew it referred to an agreement on the time frame for devolution of policing and justice to which Paisley had still not assented.

So it was that the beginning of 2007 found the peace process once more on the brink of collapse. I was feeling desperate, willing the calls to end but not wanting to give up on the process. Tony was on holiday in Florida, getting up at five every morning, because of the time difference, to make urgent phone calls to Adams and Paisley from the room where he told me President Kennedy had wooed Marilyn Monroe. At first it seemed that Paisley Sr and Jr had gone to ground.

They wouldn't return any calls and it was only when we got a message to them that the whole process was about to implode that we got their attention. They agreed that if Tony made a statement interpreting their position, Paisley would confirm it. But when we put out such a statement, Paisley issued something that seemed only vaguely like an endorsement, and Adams said he couldn't call an Ard Fheis on this basis. He asked us to get more out of Paisley. Tony said we had been trying for two weeks and it was the best we could do: Adams would be making a catastrophic mistake if he put off the Ard Fheis. At this, Adams became quite emotional and said he was going away to walk on the shores of the Atlantic in Donegal to think about whether there was an alternative basis on which he could sell the proposition to Sinn Féin

In the end, the inspiration that Adams managed to find on the beaches of Donegal was of dubious help. He decided to inject a conditionality of his own into the proceedings, by making it clear that Sinn Féin would only join the police if the DUP went into government and if there was devolution of policing. Tony, who had come back early from Florida to avoid disrupting the family holiday any further, told Adams this approach would not work unless there were concrete signs of Republican cooperation with the police in the meantime.

On Friday 12 January I was an hour into my interview with the police about cash for peerages when the principal private secretary, Olly Robbins, put his head round the door of Tony's office where the interview was taking place and interrupted with the words, 'The Northern Ireland peace process is collapsing. Can you take a break?' The police agreed and I spoke to Adams who said he was putting out a press release revealing that the DUP had agreed the original Ard Chomhairle motion in advance and yet had failed to deliver on their part of the deal in return. He was therefore announcing that the outcome of the Ard Fheis on policing would be conditional on the DUP agreeing to a date for the devolution of policing. I said he could issue his statement if he wanted but he should not announce that the outcome of the Ard Fheis was conditional or the whole process was dead. He immediately backtracked and dropped that part of the statement. I returned to Tony's den and continued my police interview.

Tony asked me to call Adams before his appearance on the Sunday TV programmes the following week to urge him to be careful, but he refused to return my call, saying he was at Mass. I felt a certain resentment, given that we had been available at all times over Christmas and new year at the drop of a hat. We managed to get Paisley to put out a statement saying he was going ahead with a power-sharing Executive, which we tried to boost. But, as a result, Adams called me saying we were making ourselves look ridiculous by spinning. He said he was going to open a 'Paisley interpretation centre'. I retorted that Paisley had learned the art of ambiguity from previous IRA statements. Still, it looked as if we might be making progress. In the course of the week Paisley Jr told us his father was preparing for government, and Adams said he would call for cooperation with the police immediately after the Ard Fheis on policing.

The Ard Fheis was held on 28 January and was preceded by an IRA Army Convention. Both went well for Adams. McGuinness came out of the Ard Fheis around teatime to call me: he said it was difficult but they would succeed. Unfortunately Paisley watched much of the proceedings on TV and reacted badly to the Republican rhetoric, particularly an earlier comment from Adams about 'putting manners on the police'. When we heard that Paisley was preparing to put out a negative statement calling the whole thing a 'confidence trick', Tony immediately phoned to try and stop him, but Paisley said he was just about to preach a sermon and had already put out the statement. Fortunately, since we knew that the statement had not, in fact, gone out, we managed to put some spokes in the wheels to stop it damaging what was otherwise a momentous day. We then held our breath, wondering whether the DUP hardliners would notice the conditionality in the Sinn Féin motion. It took them until Monday 29 January to do so, when some inexperienced Sinn Féin politicians fluffed their lines in interviews, but even then it was not too difficult to smooth things over. I called Adams to point out the problem and he publicly announced that Republicans would cooperate with the police and urged young republicans to join the police force.

With these hurdles cleared, all eyes were now on the deadline for the establishment of the Executive on 26 March. When we met Bertie Ahern at Downing Street, shortly after Sinn Féin's Ard Fheis, he was sceptical that Paisley would really go into a power-sharing Executive in March and was worried that, if the DUP did not, he would look foolish in the run-up to his own elections. Yet, despite his anxieties, we agreed to call Northern Ireland elections on 7 March anyway. In the following weeks, Adams went out of his way to be amenable, finally demonstrating that he had learned how to occupy the moral high ground, even when being set impossible tests by unionists. Paisley said that Sinn Féin should cooperate with the police in solving the McCartney murder and so Adams made a public appeal for anyone who knew anything about the murder to go to the police. There would still be a problem, of course, if the dissidents succeeded in killing someone because, in such circumstances, it would not be safe for republicans to cooperate with the police. And we knew that the dissidents were desperately trying to kill someone.

To our relief, however, there was no violence during the election campaign, which was dominated by prosaic internal issues like the water charges, rather than by different versions of the constitutional question as elections had been in the past. On 7 March Sinn Féin and the DUP did even better than expected, and we hoped that there might, after all, be an easy glide from there into government at the end of March. We were particularly encouraged by the private exit polls which showed that an overwhelming majority of DUP voters wanted the two sides to go into government on 26 March. We took further encouragement when Ian Paisley moved into the offices provided for the new First Minister shortly after the elections. Perhaps, we thought, the move was not just physical, but psychological. To provide a further incentive for him to go ahead, we arranged for President Bush to phone him nearer the deadline for forming the Executive. (We'd initially suggested a visit to Washington, but Paisley said he was too busy to go.)

But it was not long before our fears about the 26 March deadline began to look well founded. When, on the Wednesday after the election, Tony saw Paisley in his office in the House of Commons after Prime Minister's Questions, Paisley was friendly and positive about the future but would not commit to going into government on 26 March. In the evening, we heard from other leaders in the party that forces were gathering that would stop Paisley entering government by the deadline and that, instead, we would have to have a two-month period in which there was a shadow Executive rather than a real one. Just in case we didn't get the message on the usual channels, they also told John Reid, the former Northern Ireland Secretary, so that he would pass it on to me. We couldn't easily back down on the deadline we had set at St Andrews without losing the Irish government and Sinn Féin off the other side. But Peter Hain came up with a compromise: the Executive would be established but would hold just one meeting to agree to stop the bills for water charges going out, a key issue in the election, and then be put on hold for two months while the ministers read themselves into their new briefs. He said he had put the idea to the DUP and Sinn Féin, and that they seemed willing to accept such an arrangement.

When Ian Paisley came to a meeting with Tony on Wednesday 21 March, instead of coming alone as usual, he brought Paisley Jr, Peter Robinson and Nigel Dodds with him. It was clear to us that Paisley wanted Tony to tell Robinson and Dodds himself that he was serious about the deadline of 26 March. Dodds, Robinson and Paisley Jr put up an impassioned resistance, saying it would split the party while Paisley watched mutely. They said we were always doing things to help Republicans and now we should do something to help them. After all that had gone before, delay was essential so that unionists could have a period in which to test Sinn Féin's bona fides on policing and criminality. But Tony was firm in making it clear that we were not prepared to introduce emergency legislation to suspend the Executive, although we would be happy to work for a reading-in period after the Executive was established. They went away a bit chastened, but we were struck by the yawning chasm between them and Paisley. Paisley kept saying that the people of Ulster had spoken, and that it was the will of the people 'to do it now', while the other three were demanding a reprieve.

Nor were Sinn Féin up for the compromise. When we saw Adams and McGuinness the next day to propose a reading-in period to them, they rejected the idea, even though Peter Hain had told us they had indicated they would accept it. Tony was in despair. He couldn't believe we were going to lose the whole peace process after ten years of trying. Everything depended on the DUP party meetings scheduled for 23 and 24 March.

Meanwhile we were actually making some progress on the economic package for Northern Ireland demanded by both Sinn Féin and the

DUP. They had a summit with Gordon Brown on 22 March, at which Adams and McGuinness sensibly deferred to Paisley, making him the chief spokesman and chair of the pre-meeting between the Northern Ireland parties. They had been amused when, at one stage, Paisley had walked out of the meeting saying loudly he had to take a call from President Bush. The parties pressed Gordon hard and secured a review of corporation tax, which is higher in the UK than in Ireland, and where all the Northern Ireland parties favour a lower rate, and new money to fund the suspension of water charges.

I had always known the crisis would come just as we approached the deadline because it always did in Northern Ireland. At half past midnight on the morning of Friday 23 March I was woken by a phone call from Ian Paisley, who had just come out of a late-night meeting of the DUP. He wanted to speak to Tony, but I explained it was impossible to wake him up for a call at that time of night. Paisley said the party officers had gone against him and he had to come and see the Prime Minister later that day. I agreed and asked Robert Hannigan to find out what had happened. Some time after 1 a.m., Robert phoned back to say that, during the meeting, the DUP had coalesced around a position that they would only go into government in May. It was unanimous: even moderates like Peter Robinson and Jeffrey Donaldson had rallied to this position. Robinson had told Robert that, to keep the party together, they had to delay. To try and force entry into government now would split the party irrevocably, and it was far better for everyone, including us, if they could bring the DUP into government united.

Paisley came into Downing Street at five the next afternoon with Robinson, Dodds and Paisley Jr. The Prime Minister ushered them into his den and they handed over their party motion. It was phrased cleverly, saying they would set a date in May to go into the Executive, provided everything else remained the same, and that we put off water charges and the abolition of the eleven plus. Tony, having read their motion, said that we could not go ahead on this basis and we would have to collapse the process.

It was a blow. We had deliberately tried to set up events so that, if the DUP refused to form the Executive, they would pay a political price by getting the blame for the water-charge bills going out the next day, and the implementation of reforms to the education system that were very unpopular with the unionist middle class. It was to have been a sword of Damocles over their heads: agreement, or an indefinite future as a socialist republic presided over by Peter Hain. Robinson was saying that they'd be happy to collapse the process and then pick things up again in May, as long as we didn't send out the water bills, when we were interrupted by a convenient knock at the door.

It was the day the Iranians had kidnapped fifteen British sailors and marines. Before the meeting, Tony had asked me to arrange for a note about the kidnap to be brought in halfway through, to give him an excuse to leave the room. It was useful that the No. 10 duty clerk came in at this particular moment with the note. I handed it to Tony, explained what it was, and said he needed to go out and speak to the Admiral in charge of negotiations with the Iranians. He jumped to his feet, excused himself and headed for the private office with me in his trail.

Up until that point I had kept Tony focused on not, yet again, dumping the deadline. My reasoning was that, if the DUP would not go into government in March after the election, we couldn't count on them going into government later. But as we walked up and down between the jumble of desks in the private office, Tony said he thought the offer of a date in May for going into government was irresistible. There was no way the DUP were going to back down from a unanimous motion, and why throw the whole thing away for six weeks? I said the problem would be convincing the Irish and Sinn Féin that we had not just given in to the Unionist veto yet again. If the Nationalist side walked away we had lost everything. I suggested linking acceptance of the postponement to an agreement to a face-to-face meeting between Adams and Paisley. The two had never met and I knew the symbolism of such a meeting was so important to Republicans that it might just be sufficient bait to tempt them to agree to further delay. It would be the DUP's job to sell the new date to Sinn Féin at the meeting.

We went back into Tony's den, and he settled back in his armchair, apologising for the interruption and giving a diversionary description of the Iranian crisis, before putting forward the proposal we had agreed outside. If the DUP could persuade Sinn Féin to accept postponement in a face-to-face meeting, then we were happy to go along with it. Ian Paisley Jr was the first to speak. He tried to redefine the meeting as a round table of all the parties chaired by the Prime Minister. Tony said firmly that would not fly. Paisley Sr looked thoughtful, and Robinson whispered to Dodds on the sofa. Robinson asked a few questions, but essentially it was clear they accepted the idea. They said they would go away and consult, and come back to us the next morning. By the time they got back to Belfast, Paisley had agreed.

On Saturday morning I phoned Tony early and told him he had to make it clear to Adams that we were simply putting forward a DUP position and that if it were rejected by Republicans we would just go ahead on Monday, the 26 March deadline, and pull the whole show down. But when Tony called Adams at eight o'clock as agreed, Adams did not react with horror. As I had surmised, the possibility of a face-to-face meeting was sufficient to make him hesitate before rejecting the further delay. He said he wanted to speak to Martin McGuinness and would come back to us. He called me a few minutes later and asked a series of detailed questions about the proposal. He wanted to squeeze further concessions out of us on legislation going through the House of Lords on trials of terrorist offences before a judge without a jury (which we had promised to abolish earlier), and on an Irish Language Act. And he wanted us to persuade Paisley to agree to a private two-minute conversation with him one-to-one in the margins of the meeting, and to shake his hand. I asked Robert Hannigan to call Peter Robinson before he went into the DUP Executive and Party Officer meetings at ten o'clock to say a deal was on. And I got Tony to call Bertie Ahern, who was getting ready to give his speech at his last party conference before the planned Irish elections. Bertie said it was fine with him as long as the 'Shinners' could go along with it. He said he had never thought the DUP would accept the deadline of 26 March anyway.

By lunchtime we heard back from Robinson that he, Dodds and Paisley Jr were prepared to meet McGuinness secretly later in the day to agree on the arrangements for the face-to-face meeting. The meeting took place at Stormont while I was in London. Both sides called me repeatedly to complain about the other and I had to juggle the calls on my mobile while taking my daughters to swimming lessons and showing my wife's relatives round No. 10 Downing Street. Both sides were apprehensive at first. McGuinness asked Robinson if he would shake hands, but Robinson said he would do so only when the deal was done. Once they actually got into a room together, however, they made rapid progress on what both sides would say in their prepared statements and on what would happen in the intervening period until the Executive was established in May. The discussion went on late into the night and the sticking points narrowed to whether the two party leaders would sit next to each other on one side of the table or opposite each other across the table. And they couldn't agree whether the Executive should be established on 1 May or 8 May. Each time McGuinness went away to consult Adams in west Belfast he would come back more hard-line and with more demands. The problem of the table was that the DUP wanted the two parties to sit opposite each other so they looked like adversaries rather than friends, while Sinn Féin wanted Adams and Paisley to sit next to each other like partners. Then Robert Hannigan had the inspired idea of a special, diamond-shaped table so that Paisley and Adams could sit at its apex, thereby being both opposite each other and next to each other. There was no end to the ingenuity we were prepared to resort to in order to make the last steps to peace, but it was worth it because these face-to-face meetings between the two sides were crucial to building the trust that we had been seeking all these years.

The DUP infuriated Sinn Féin by refusing to meet on Sunday for religious reasons. But they did agree to negotiate by phone. By Monday morning, they hadn't quite resolved everything because Adams called Tony still asking for a handshake and for an earlier date in May. I established that Paisley was getting nervous and if they asked for anything more we might push him over the edge. As we knew all too well by now, the Republicans were always inclined to over-negotiate. I got Tony to call Adams back and say that he must stop now or we would lose the whole thing. Adams concluded their conversation by saying to Tony, 'If we pull it off, then ten years of your life will have been well spent.'

In the meantime, I had promised Adams I would get Tony to sign a letter laying out our undertakings on the Irish Language Act and on juryless trials, without which Sinn Féin wouldn't start the meeting, which was scheduled for eleven o'clock. By this time Tony, having called Paisley to tell him the deal was concluded, was in the Cabinet

Room holding a big office meeting. Not realising that this meeting was being filmed for a TV documentary, I took the letter into the room and walked up behind Tony at the Cabinet table to get him to sign it. 'Do I have to do this now?' he hissed at me from the side of his mouth. 'Actually, I'm just doing this for fun,' I said, and stuck the letter in front of him. He signed it without looking, and as I walked away I said, 'At last you have signed up for a united Ireland.' The whole room collapsed in laughter, and it was only then that I spotted the camera in the corner of the room.

The picture of Adams and Paisley sitting next to each other reading out their statements was indeed worth a thousand words. The media had been deeply sceptical that anything would happen. They were so inured to a decade of near misses that they thought this would be just another disappointment. But now they went into overkill, pronouncing the peace process complete and broadcasting lengthy retrospectives back to the Good Friday Agreement and even before, with pictures of the young Paisley and the young Adams in their ranting phases. I had expected an impact but not quite such an over-whelming one. In the past, for example after the conclusion of the Good Friday Agreement, or in December 2004, colleagues had come up to me to congratulate me on achieving peace and I had said, correctly, that it was premature. This time when they said well done, I did not feel the need to enter the same caveat. After ten years of effort and disappointment I couldn't quite believe it was over. I felt a bit like you might feel when you have been pushing against a closed door for a long time and suddenly someone opens it. There is a relief you can stop pushing but you miss the comforting certainty of the closed door you had got used to.

Still, it was difficult to believe that the thing wouldn't start to unravel, as it had so many times before. Gerry Adams called me twice the next day, and I delayed getting back to him, convinced he would be wanting to reopen some issue or lobby on some concession we had failed to deliver. But when I eventually returned his call and began to say we were working on the sunset clause on juryless trials, he interrupted my excuses to thank me for all I had done. I was quite taken aback.

Tony had the same experience. Ian Paisley asked to come and see him after Prime Minister's Questions on 18 April, and we were anxious it was connected with something he had said publicly about making an announcement on security that would 'make people's hair curl'. Adams, too, was concerned and called me to find out whether it was something that might blow the whole agreement out of the water. In the event there was no security announcement and Paisley was full of bonhomie. At Prime Minister's Questions prior to the meeting he publicly invited Tony to come to the swearing-in session at Stormont in May, and in the meeting he simply repeated the invitation and agreed that Bertie Ahern should come as well.

The 8th of May was an extraordinary day. Tony and I flew over to Belfast with John Reid. On the plane, he told us he was announcing that he would stand down as Home Secretary when Tony stood down as Prime Minister. At the airport we met up with Bertie Ahern and drove to Stormont in a motorcade. Outside the parliament building there was a protest on Iraq and one of the protestors threw himself in front of the cars and was dragged away by the police. I thought to myself it was nice to see ordinary politics rather than sectarianism.

Before the swearing-in, Tony did a series of interviews with all the Northern Ireland TV correspondents with whom we had sparred over the years and they all wanted their photos taken with him. After that, we went to meet the new First and Deputy First Ministers in Paisley's office, with their junior ministers Ian Paisley Jr and Gerry Kelly, as unlikely a combination as you could ever expect to find. Ian Paisley and Martin McGuinness were competing with each other to tell jokes, and you would never have thought that they had been blood enemies leading two warring communities for three decades. Then the moment came. They filed in to the open atrium of the Assembly and delivered their speeches. Paisley's was subtle and clever. It was an occasion well adapted to a preacher. Martin's was straight and clear and full of hope. When Tony spoke, he said it was time for Northern Ireland 'to escape the chains of history', in a conscious echo of his 'hand of history' sound bite. They all shook hands as they received the audience's applause and the agreement was sealed. Two days later Tony announced his resignation as Prime Minister and leader of the Labour Party. For him and me, the story was over.

But, of course, the story is not over for Northern Ireland. So far it has gone remarkably well. When, a few weeks into the new government, I got a call from a civil servant telling me Ian Paisley was tired because he had been up late the night before Scottish-Irish dancing with Martin McGuinness, it dawned on me quite how much things had changed.

Assuming the politicians can get past the hurdle of devolving police and justice, there is no reason why Northern Ireland shouldn't remain at peace and enjoy even greater prosperity. But the burden of history remains, and before the two sides become truly reconciled they need to find a way to deal with the past. If a truth and reconciliation process of the sort that helped heal the wounds in South Africa is not quite right, then it will be necessary to find something similar. The trauma of IRA murders, security-force collusion and loyalist sectarian violence needs to be exorcised. If it is left to the police and the courts and yet more inquiries, there is a danger that everyone will simply be dragged back into the morass from which they are trying to escape. So, if I have one wish, it is that the people of Northern Ireland find an acceptable way to lay the past to rest.

Epilogue

By giving a detailed account of the negotiations leading up to May 2007, this book has attempted to show how, after so many failed attempts by others, we were finally able to bring about peace in Northern Ireland. But the questions remain: why were we able to conclude it then and could it have happened earlier? Was the agreement of May 2007 just 'Sunningdale for slow learners', the question posed by Seamus Mallon, the former SDLP Deputy First Minster, after the Good Friday Agreement?

My answer is no. There were underlying factors necessary for peace which were not present in the 1970s.

Most importantly there had clearly been a generational change in Northern Ireland in the late 1980s and early 1990s. By then, Adams and McGuinness, who had joined the Provisional movement in their early twenties, were well past fighting-age and saw another generation being arrested or killed. They appreciated all too easily how the cycle of blood could repeat itself for another generation and, having tried the short, sharp shock and the long campaign and then the tactical use of armed struggle they knew that neither side could win, that it was possible the stalemate might continue indefinitely. To their credit, they had the courage to start seeking a political settlement. So often those confined to a ghetto, who talk only to people on their own side, contract tunnel vision, but Adams and McGuinness managed to break out of the blinkers, becoming, over time, increasingly sophisticated politicians.

They were fortunate in finding leaders in the Irish and British governments who also came from a new generation. Bertie Ahern was from a Republican family and led Fianna Fáil, the Republican party of Ireland, but he did not carry the complexes of the past as his predecessors had. He was prepared to override his system by rejecting traditional Irish positions and to take political risks in order to achieve peace. And Tony came from a new breed of British politicians, one that did not bear the resentments of the past about Ireland or about the terrorist campaign that the British people had suffered for a quarter-of-a-century. The two of them complemented each other and worked together as a team, rather than competing.

Moreover, the much maligned 'securocrats' had changed too. After a disastrous start in the 1970s, the British Army had been one of the first participants in Northern Ireland to realise the campaign could not be won militarily: all they could do was contain the terrorists. By the early 1990s, they, the leadership of the police and the Security Service were absolutely clear about the need for a negotiated settlement, even if they were sceptical about how easy it would be to achieve or how quickly it could be done.

Ireland too was going through a period of transition. During the 1980s and 90s, it transformed itself into the Celtic Tiger – a process so well chronicled by Roy Foster in his book *Luck and the Irish* – becoming a modern, European state with a thriving economy. Although this went almost unnoticed by many unionists (as late as 1998, John Taylor was still talking of Ireland as a priest-ridden, backward, impoverished country), it enabled Ireland to throw off its inferiority complex about its big neighbour, and left the unionists without a bogeyman or threat.

And then there was 9/11. Despite Gerry Adams's repeated protestations to the contrary, the attack on the World Trade Center made it easier to bring about the end of the IRA. Nationalist terrorism of the sort carried out by the IRA was simply out of date. They could not compete with Islamic terrorists who were prepared to kill themselves, and as many other people as possible. Terror is relative and if another group is more terrifying than yours, you have less impact. The attack also changed the thinking of the IRA's American supporters, political and financial, and added to the pressure on them to choose the exclusively political route.

But even prior to 9/11, American attitudes to the IRA had altered. Although during the nineteenth century, American presidents had been happy to weigh in on Irish matters for electoral advantage at home, the twentieth century was characterised by a reluctance to become

EPILOGUE   311

involved in the internal matters of a close ally, even under the presidency of Jack Kennedy. Bill Clinton changed all that, however, by becoming the first modern US president to make a sustained effort to work for peace in Northern Ireland. Sometimes that effort entailed taking risks. His relationship with John Major had never been good, but granting a visa to Adams made it much worse. Nevertheless, it is hard now to say he was wrong, given that the visa allowed Gerry Adams to show the IRA that politics could achieve more than the bomb. Clinton's willingness to pick up the phone to offer advice or chivvy Northern Ireland politicians from all sides at any time of day or night for many years was extraordinary for the leader of the Free World, even one who doesn't sleep.

And there were two other, mould-breaking political leaders whose willingness to take risks made an agreement possible. John Hume and David Trimble deserved their Nobel Peace Prizes for the sacrifices they made in achieving peace. Hume was the first Northern Irish politician to see that the only solution lay in talking. He was reviled for his contacts with Gerry Adams in the 1980s, while terrorism was still continuing, but he did not stop them. It was he who came up with the concept of the joint declaration and he was clear that he wanted an inclusive peace, with Sinn Féin as part of it, even though that meant the eclipse of his own party, the SDLP, which gradually and inexorably slipped into second place in Catholic Northern Ireland, just as the Nationalist party of Redmond did in Ireland after 1916. Nor would there have been peace if the UUP had still been led by the cautious and traditional James Molyneaux rather than the outsider David Trimble. In the 80s and early 90s the Unionists were comfortable just blocking any progress rather than facing up to making concessions. Trimble was the most unlikely of heroes and one of the hardest questions to answer, on the basis of his background, is why he was willing to risk everything to secure a lasting agreement. He was all too conscious of the fate that had befallen his predecessor, Brian Faulkner, not least since he contributed personally to bringing about Faulkner's downfall, and yet Trimble demonstrated great political courage when confronted by the really difficult choices. He felt cheated by the failure of Republican leaders to reciprocate by taking the risks he took with his party, which in the end proved terminal, but he can feel proud of what he achieved by his persistence.

At first we tried to build from the centre, working with the UUP and the SDLP. But in the end perhaps it was inevitable that peace could only be made by the DUP and Sinn Féin on the principle of 'Nixon goes to China' – it is only the extremes who can build a durable peace because there is no one left to outflank them. After his close encounter with death, and even more so once elected as the leader of unionism, Ian Paisley was determined to try to bring about a lasting peace in Northern Ireland, often leaving himself isolated. He paid a price in his party and in his church for doing so. I will never forget seeing him sitting in Tony's office saying that the people of Ulster had spoken and insisting that a power-sharing government should be formed, while the party colleagues around him did everything they could to frustrate an agreement.

But perhaps the most important change of all was in the attitude of the British government, which became prepared, after many years of trying to ignore the problem of Northern Ireland, to devote considerable time and attention to it. This process began with John Major, who was the first Prime Minister since Lloyd George to make a serious effort to find a solution. But although Major was able to open the door to agreement, he was not able to step through it. For that, Northern Ireland had to wait for Tony Blair, who from his first day in office made the search for peace his priority, and just wouldn't let go of the problem until he had resolved it.

Tony said as early as 1994 that 'I believe the most sensible role for us is to be facilitators, not persuaders in this, not trying to pressure or push people towards a particular objective'. He said he was 'easy either way' as to what the people of Northern Ireland decided. Although neither the unionists nor the republicans would ever quite believe it, the British government were clear that they were a neutral facilitator, content with any outcome as long as the two sides could live with it. But they were also a powerful mediator with many of the cards in their hands, economically and in security terms.

It was in developing the opportunities provided by this position as facilitator that we managed to broker the Good Friday Agreement. But what we failed, initially, to realise was that we would need to mediate in a much longer process: the building of trust between the two communities. Even after the Good Friday Agreement, the unionists and republicans were still unreconciled peoples. With all the history that had gone before, they simply could not make the necessary leap of faith in the other side after such a short period of time. It took nine years to build that trust, step by painful step; nine years of allowing the history to work itself out of the system on both sides so that the war could be formally ended and true power-sharing happen. It was never inevitable we would succeed, and right up until the last minute, every breakthrough was followed by a setback.

So, even if it is true the elements that made up the May 2007 agreement would, in large part, have been familiar to negotiators at Sunningdale in 1973, fundamental forces had to shift, and a certain configuration of leaders needed to be in place before a lasting agreement could be achieved. The other thing that was new was that the British government were this time active rather than passive. We were buffeted by events from the Omagh bomb to the Northern Bank robbery, but at the same time we were driving the process forward. And it is these proactive steps that we took to bring about a settlement that might well be worth taking into account in other peace processes.

One of the lessons that comes most starkly out of the Northern Ireland experience is the importance of maintaining contact. It is very difficult for governments in democracies to be seen to be talking to terrorists who are killing their people unjustifiably. But it is precisely your enemies, rather than your friends, you should talk to if you want to resolve a conflict. Moreover, talking should not be seen as a reward to be held out or withdrawn. Without contact there is no way of making the first steps towards peace. And if the government have to make this contact secretly it is unlikely that, when discovered, they will be punished by the electorate. Far from being censored by the House of Commons when he had to admit to the government's secret contacts with the IRA in 1994, an apprehensive Paddy Mayhew was praised by MPs from both the opposition and the government. Indeed, it is often essential to keep these initial communications secret, and people will understand the necessity for that.

Sometimes, however, a certain amount of political pain is unavoidable to keep the process going. Whether to continue to release terrorist prisoners even when the IRA were failing to decommission their weapons was a very difficult question; our decision to carry on led to criticism from both the Unionists and the Tories. But if we had stopped prisoner release we can be fairly certain that violence would have started again. We carried on because we understood the battle that Adams and McGuinness were facing in their attempts to win over the Republican movement. Having come to understand that the Unionists were not just a surrogate for the British government, and that their views had to be taken into account, they had the challenge of persuading their fellow Republicans to settle for something less than a united Ireland. This was an extremely difficult task and, if they were to carry the whole movement with them, they had to move crablike towards their goal, in cautious and gradual steps, never revealing in full to the movement their eventual destination. To do so would have been to invite either an instant rebuff or a serious split. Others have criticised them for not being bold enough, but it was a remarkable act of leadership by Gerry Adams and Martin McGuinness to talk the IRA into peace, and to persuade them to settle for something far less than they had demanded in 1993, let alone when the Provisionals were formed in 1969.

We were determined to aid them in this, even if it entailed making politically risky moves to do so. Previous British governments had tried to split the IRA in order to defeat it and had enjoyed some success. But we wanted to make peace only once, rather than many times, and above all we wanted to keep the Provisional IRA together rather than letting it be replaced by yet another capable republican terrorist group. It was the same when, at the end of the process, there were rifts in the DUP: at some political risk to ourselves, we agreed to a delay in the forming of the Executive so that they would come in as a united party rather than allowing a more extreme unionist party to develop ready to outflank them at any time, as Paisley had done with Trimble. By keeping our eyes on the long-term goal of resolving the conflict, rather than letting ourselves be distracted by the tactical games that all sides play, we maintained a strategic focus throughout. This was helped by at least the appearance of bipartisanship from the Tories. It is far more difficult for a government to negotiate when faced with criticism of their efforts by the Opposition, as the Socialist government in Spain have found, where any contacts with ETA have been subject to a full-frontal attack by the opposition Partido Popular.

The part played by ambiguity in a negotiation is complicated and needs careful handling. In the initial stages, ambiguity is often an essential tool to bridge the gap between irreconcilable positions. The only way we could get over decommissioning at the time of the Good Friday Agreement was to make its terms ambiguous so that each side was able to interpret the Agreement as endorsing their position. If we had tried to force Sinn Féin to accept that decommissioning would happen at a specific given point, there would have been no deal. And if we had told the UUP we were giving up on decommissioning, there would, likewise, have been no deal. So constructive ambiguity took the strain. But later in the process, ambiguity ceased to be constructive and became the enemy of progress. Each side began to distrust the other because it had not implemented the Agreement in accordance with their own interpretation of it. So for unionists the failure to decommission meant republicans were not prepared to end violence for good, and for republicans the failure of unionists to maintain a power-sharing Executive illustrated the deep-rooted unwillingness of unionists to accept that Catholics should have an equal voice. The ambiguity that had been essential at the beginning began to undermine the Agreement and discredit the government – the referee for its implementation. We then had to drive ambiguity out of the process, starting with the Belfast Harbour speech of October 2002, and insist on deeds rather than words. This process of squeezing out the ambiguity and building trust was painful and it took time, but a durable peace cannot rest on an ambiguous understanding.

Most of the blockages we ran into from 1998 to 2007 were questions of sequencing. Neither side wanted to go first because they doubted the other side would deliver the reciprocal gesture they had promised. Our job, as facilitator, was to come up with a choreography that broke the process down into small steps and then to gain agreement in advance about who would take which partial step. This created a sense that neither side was going first, but that, instead, both were moving together in a harmonious if rather clodhopping ballet. Making such a choreography work, however, requires both sides to fulfil what they have agreed, or the whole thing breaks down. Both Sinn Féin and the UUP repeatedly failed to deliver on their promises, most notably when Trimble refused to go into government as he had promised to do after the IRA decommissioned in October 2003. Likewise, the IRA failed to decommission after the agreement with Mitchell in 1999.

Nor were the government entirely blameless in this regard. From time to time, we too were forced to break our promises, particularly over our undertaking to deal with the issue of IRA terrorists on the run, where we just could not get the Attorney General of the day to move, or get the legislation through. An Irish official told me that they had a saying that summed it up: the Irish always asked for more than they hoped to get and the British always promised far more than they truly expected to deliver. We were lucky that such failures to deliver didn't cause a breakdown in the process, as they have else-where. In Spain, it is clear that both the government and ETA thought the other side had reneged on crucial promises made before the cease-fire, and these perceived betrayals brought the whole edifice of peace crashing down. Similarly, in Sri Lanka, the Tamil Tigers thought they had been given clear undertakings of what would happen after the ceasefire, and when they were not delivered the ceasefire crumbled back into violence on both sides.

We used deadlines as a tool because they were often the only way to force the two sides to choose. If left to their own devices, the parties would go on talking indefinitely rather than face up to hard decisions. It worked well with the Good Friday Agreement, where the rush imposed by the Easter deadline gave us the momentum to achieve an agreement that would not otherwise have been possible. But if you set deadlines too often and then go through them, as we did repeat-edly, you lose credibility with the parties and they will call your bluff. You then need to find some other way of demonstrating that you are serious about driving at the wall, as we did by legislating for the end of the Northern Ireland Assembly in November 2006. Forcing-house negotiations also helped us to reach agreement at crucial stages. The Unionists were always chary of such gatherings after their tribal memory of Faulkner being stampeded into an unsatisfactory agree-ment at Sunningdale, but sometimes it was necessary to take the party leaders away from their constituencies and the daily pressures of poli-tics, as Richard Holbrooke did at Dayton in order to bring the war in Bosnia to a conclusion, and as we did at countless country houses. Again, there were diminishing returns the more we did it, but even at the end of the nine years, the meeting in St Andrews was crucial to bringing the Agreement to fruition when it was in danger of being frittered away yet again.

It is always an error to set a precondition to a negotiation. A public precondition forces the other side to reject it and dig in. You are left with a choice: either climb down yourself, as Major had to on the issue of clarification in 1994, or face indefinite stalemate. The Major government made a mistake in making decommissioning a precondition in 1994, and we spent nine years trying to work a way through that. By the time decommissioning itself actually happened, it had almost ceased to be an issue. There is, in any case, no need for a precondition as long as everyone's position is protected by the rule that in the negotiation nothing is agreed until everything is agreed. The issue should be resolved in the negotiation itself rather than made into a prior test.

Nor is public pressure by itself likely to produce the result you want. Of course it is important to set the trap by allowing the build-up of pressure for action, but it is also crucial to provide the parties with a way out. We wanted the IRA to end violence, but if we had just carried on demanding it and applying pressure nothing would have happened. We had to combine the pressure with a sufficiently attractive political alternative to tempt them out of violence. This is just as true in Sri Lanka: although the Tamil Tigers have tacitly accepted that they will not get an independent homeland, unless the Sinhalese majority makes a convincing constitutional offer on federalism, no amount of military pressure will bring their campaign to the end. In those circumstances, the sensible peacemaker takes pain on their own side to make an offer that is so generous that the other side looks unreasonable in maintaining its violent campaign rather than opting for the political path.

Many of the other bloody and ancient conflicts in the world have reached the stage of a breakthrough agreement as we did with the Good Friday Agreement. In Sri Lanka it was the ceasefire agreement in 2002; in Spain, the ETA ceasefire in 2006; and in the Middle East, the Oslo Accords of 1993. But, in each case, the process collapsed back into violence. With the Oslo Accords, it was in part because no one tried to sell the agreement to the Israeli public. The government weren't prepared to take the political pain necessary to implement the agreement and the Palestinian people, who had at first been enthusiastic, lost faith in it. It is essential not to give up at the stage of the breakthrough agreement; that is exactly the moment to redouble efforts in trying to get it implemented and in selling it to both sides.

Politics can be a zero-sum game, particularly in a small place like Northern Ireland. If one side comes out of negotiations smiling, the other side thinks it has lost. In the first ceasefire in 1994, it was the republicans who were celebrating and the unionists who were down in the dumps, even though an end to violence was what the unionists had been demanding since 1968. Again, when the IRA decommissioned and declared the war over in 2005, it was the unionists who felt deflated. An intelligent facilitator always wants to avoid any hint of surrender and wants to reach an agreement that allows both sides to feel they have won, even if that involves absorbing a bit of criticism yourself.

But sometimes we reached an absolute impasse where neither side could move. The only answer then was to widen the focus. John Major gave an unsuccessful example of this when, having failed to get the IRA to confirm the ceasefire was permanent, he switched his demand to decommissioning as a practical manifestation of permanence. It made things worse. But when we faced complete blockage on decommissioning in 1999, we found a way round by suggesting that arms be kept in sealed dumps and inspected regularly by credible international inspectors, as had happened in Bosnia. Republicans then adopted this idea, as if it were their own, and it provided an effective solution. It wasn't decommissioning but it offered a way forward which the unionists found acceptable.

So often during the peace process, my role was one of interpreter. If the two sides wouldn't meet face to face, I had to shuttle back and forth between them explaining to each side what the other really meant. The republicans and unionists were, in Bernard Shaw's words, divided by a common language. The Republicans were florid, wordy and ambiguous, the Unionists blunt, rude and unyielding. My job was to explain to Adams what the Unionists meant by a particular stance, and untangle for Trimble what the parameters were within which the Republicans could move. Sometimes it is necessary for a facilitator to temper the message rather than pass it on too literally, or to bend it a little in order to point out the opportunities it presents and so move the negotiation along. But it is crucial not to distort that message too far or you will find the two sides negotiating on false premises. To carry off the role of 'interpreter', you must build personal trust with the two sides and maintain it by straight dealing. My biggest fear, the fear which would wake me up at night, was of failing to deliver on a promise or being caught out in some apparent lie. If you lose your reputation for being straight, you are of no further use.

Sometimes even being straight is not enough. You need to bring in an outside mediator who is regarded by both camps as fair in a way that the government, as one of the parties to the dispute, cannot be. Many governments spend huge amounts of political capital ensuring their conflict is not internationalised, for example the Indian government over Kashmir. Generally this is a waste of effort. No outside government can force you to do what you don't want to do, and international involvement can be helpful. John Major took the first step by inviting Sir Ninian Stephen, the former Governor General of Australia, to chair the talks in 1991, and followed this up by involving George Mitchell and his team. We found it useful to have independent bodies to referee particularly difficult aspects of the process, from the International Independent Commission on Decommissioning under John de Chastelain to the Independent Monitoring Commission with representatives from the US, Ireland and Britain, as well as Northern Ireland.

But much of the effort has to go into events outside the negotiations themselves. In the words of Mao, the 'water they swim in' is essential to terrorist groups and you have to address the reasons they enjoy support in their community. The British government rapidly came to realise that the conflict could not just be resolved by security measures, but needed a hearts-and-minds component addressing the causes of the alienation among the Catholic population, particularly the discrimination in housing and jobs. In the late 1970s and 80s they brought in a new independent housing administration to improve the standards of housing and to ensure it was fairly allotted to Catholics and Protestants, and implemented new fair employment legislation to tackle the differential unemployment rates. The reforms were not enough in themselves to resolve the conflict but they did reduce the pressure.

During the negotiations themselves it was also necessary to develop confidence-building measures for both sides. Sometimes these were trivial, like the support offered to Unionists for the Scottish-Irish dialect 'Ullans', to balance the help for the Irish language; sometimes they

were more substantial, such as the raft of public inquiries into allegations of security-force collusion in the murder of Catholics, necessary to get the SDLP on board for policing after Weston Park. At times
it felt as if we were rushing up and down the see-saw to offer a sop
to one side and then a sop to the other. And it is possible to go too
far, as we did by offering comfort to Trimble on policing symbols, a
move that alienated the Republicans and possibly put off the date at
which they would join the police force by years. But such concessions
on small issues can help the leaders demonstrate to their constituencies that they can deliver, so that when it comes to bigger issues later,
it is easier for them to move. We certainly made mistakes in this regard
and, if feasible, it is best to retain transparency for the bilateral steps
so that both sides know what has been offered to the other. Similarly
we learned, through our mistakes, to avoid one-sided negotiations
where the whole deal is sewn up with one party before talks start
with the other. Sinn Féin were forever trying to inveigle us into agreeing
everything with them first before we approached the Unionists, and
then wanting us to implement what we had agreed with them regardless of what the Unionists later said and did.

As far as possible it is best to leave the issue of weapons to the end
of a peace process, as in the case of the Lancaster House Agreement
on Zimbabwe concluded by the Thatcher government in 1979, where
arms were dumped but not required to be handed over till the end
of the process. There is no real security or political gain in getting rid
of them early since the terrorists can always acquire new weapons if
they want to. But when you do get rid of them it is best to do it with
some form of independent verification that contributes to confidence
that they have really been put beyond use, especially if you are dealing
with high-tech weapons like surface-to-air missiles and Semtex.

Criminality is among the hardest issues to deal with in a peace
process because it is cultural and therefore not so easily eradicated
once the causes of conflict have gone. It grows up in part because the
terrorists do not accept the legitimacy of the state and feel no compunc-
tion about robbery and extortion to fund their efforts. But once they
and their followers have acquired a taste for it, it is then difficult to
persuade them to give it up or to find other means of livelihood; it
is a problem the Nigerian government have faced in an acute form in
the Delta where young men are unwilling to abandon the lifestyles

they can afford through kidnapping and oil bunkering and return to poverty. And once the foot soldiers have killed someone, it has a profound effect on them. Going back to a normal life is not easy. In the end, the only way to deal with a culture of criminality is to force a divorce between those who want to stay engaged in crime and those who want to opt for a political path, as has happened gradually with the Loyalists in Northern Ireland. It was far harder to engage with the Loyalists in the peace process, in part because they were not as coherent an entity as the IRA, but also because they lacked a true political agenda. Their violence was largely reactive and, as IRA violence declined, they focused most of their firepower on internal feuds. But now even they are disappearing from the scene.

Lastly, the issue of self-determination itself. There is no cast-iron rule about the unit that should be entitled to self-determination. Should it be Chechnya or Russia? Should it be the Basque country or the whole of Spain? Should it be the Tamil territories or the whole of Sri Lanka? But in the end the question is immaterial, because it is not possible to rule a unit, however small, for a long period without the consent of the people ruled. So the real issue is how you gain that consent through power-sharing arrangements or protection for the rights of minorities. Simply to deny the aspirations of either side indefinitely is a recipe for continuing conflict.

There is therefore no blueprint for making peace to be derived from our experience in Northern Ireland and no magic to rub off from the negotiators themselves. The burden of history is different in every conflict and requires different measures in different places. Crucially, attempts at conflict resolution will only succeed where both sides have come to realise they cannot win. If either side still believes that victory is possible, as in Sri Lanka at the moment, then the cycle of blood will go on. Nevertheless, it is possible to reach a settlement between two sides who disagree on substance. In Northern Ireland, the two traditions still do not agree. Republicans want to be part of a united Ireland while unionists want to stay in the United Kingdom. But they have agreed to settle their differences by political means rather than violently.

As I read back through the official files on Northern Ireland to write this book, there was one thing more than any other that kept jumping out at me, and that was the importance of having a functioning process

GREAT HATRED, LITTLE ROOM

and keeping it going regardless of the difficulties. Shimon Peres observed about the absence of process in the Middle East that 'the good news is there is light at the end of the tunnel. The bad news is there is no tunnel.' And that is what makes me believe so strongly in my bicycle theory. You have to keep the process moving forward, however slowly. Never let it fall over.

So if there is one lesson to be drawn from the Northern Ireland negotiations, it is that there is no reason to believe that efforts to find peace will fail just because they have failed before. You have to keep the wheels turning. The road to success in Northern Ireland was littered with failures. And there is every reason to think that the search for peace can succeed in other places where the process has encountered problems – in Spain, in Turkey, in Sri Lanka, in the Middle East, in Afghanistan and even, in the longer term, with Islamic terrorism, if people are prepared to talk.

List of Illustrations

Gerry Adams, Martin McGuinness, Tony Blair and Jonathan Powell in the Prime Minister's Office in the House of Commons © Stephan Rousseau/PA Photos; Kitty O'Shea © Hulton Archive/Hulton Archive/Getty Images; Wolfe Tone © Topfoto; Siege of Londonderry © Topfoto; Edward Carson © Topfoto; Gerry Adams on the Falls Road © Sipa Press/Rex Features; Ian Paisley addressing rally © Rex Features; Brendan Duddy © John Thynne, BBC; Gerry Adams and Martin McGuinness outside 10 Downing Street © Jils Norgensen/Rex Features; David Trimble and UUP members announcing their acceptance of the Belfast Agreement © Alan Lewis; Tony Blair, John Hume and David Trimble awaiting results of the Referendum © Lewis Alan/Corbis Sygma; Tony Blair and Bertie Ahern © PA Photos; David Trimble slipping through police lines © PA Archive/PA Photos; The Orange march approaching blockade © John Giles/PA Archive/PA Photos; Drumcree riots © Lewis Alan/Corbis Sygma; Aftermath of Omagh bomb © Lewis Alan/Corbis Sygma; Bill Clinton in Omagh © PA/Topfoto; Hillsborough Castle © PA Archive/PA Photos; Stormont Parliament Buildings © Cathy McArthur/epa/Corbis; Mo Mowlam at Labour Party Conference © Ian Waldie/Reuters/Corbis; David Trimble and Seamus Mallon © Crispin Rodwell/Reuters/Corbis; IRA weapons © PA/Topfoto; George Mitchell, John de Chastelain and Harri Holkeri © PA/Topfoto; Tony Blair and George Bush at Hillsborough © Reuters/Corbis; Ian Paisley giving press conference © Haydn West/PA Archive/PA Photos; Tony Blair and Jonathan Powell in 2004 © *The Times*; Gerry Kelly during intercommunity violence © Jeff J. Mitchell/Reuters/Corbis; Ian Paisley, Peter Robinson and Jeffrey Donaldson meeting Tony Blair in Downing Street © PA/Topfoto; The Clonard monastery © Harrison Photography; The fiancée and sisters of Robert McCartney © Ian McIlgorn/Rex Features; Gerry Adams and Martin McGuinness carrying Siobhan O'Hanlon's coffin © Peter Morrison/AP/PA Photos; Gerry Adams and Ian Paisley at the apex of the diamond-shaped table © AFP/AFP/ Getty Images; Martin McGuinness, Bertie Ahern, Tony Blair and Peter Hain laughing at Ian Paisley's joke © Paul Faith/AP/PA Photos.

Index

BA – Bertie Ahern; DT – David Trimble; GA – Gerry Adams; IP – Ian Paisley;
JP – Jonathan Powell; M – Martin McGuinness; TB – Tony Blair

Adams, Gerry 16, 24
1969–2001
joins Provisional IRA (1969) 44; on
Bloody Sunday (1972) 45, 46; on
internment 46; talks with Frank Steele
67; meeting with Whitelaw 46–7; on
campaign against the British 47;
unofficial contacts with Hume (1980s)
63, 167, 196, 311; and Brooke's remarks
64; writes to Major 65; and the Link 73;
and Downing Street Declaration (1993)
74, 75, 76–7; US visa blocked 77–9, 311;
and IRA decommissioning (1995) 82, 83,
84; invited by Clinton to White House
85; confident of IRA ceasefire (1997) 13;
US view of 19; advances dismissed by
DT 21; first meeting with TB 15–16; at
Downing St meeting 22, 23–5; complaints
regarding 'Heads of Agreement' 28; and
expulsion of Sinn Féin from talks (1998)
30–31; and Good Friday Agreement 97,
98–102, 104, 106; wins vote in Ard Fheis
111–12; and McKevitt and formation of
Real IRA 112–13; and parole of Balcombe
Street Gang 115–16; and Drumcree
march 123, 124, 126, 130, 133; pushes for
meeting with DT 133; condemns
Omagh bombing 139, 140; and Clinton's
visit to Northern Ireland 140; and
decommissioning 142, 144, 146, 149, 150,
151, 153, 155; first meeting with DT 143;
meeting with JP 144; skateboarding
at No. 10 151; meeting with TB 156; and
arrest of republican gun-runners in
USA 157–8; and Mitchell talks 162, 164,
165, 167; demands more concessions
from JP 163; discovers bug 166;
complains of TB's failure to deliver
promises 166; bumps into CDS Guthrie
166; on IRA refusal to decommission
167–9; gets nowhere with DT 169; and

suspension of Executive and Assembly
169–70, 171; clandestine meetings with
JP on dumping of weapons 172–4;
requests demilitarisation 176, 181, 184;
floats idea of third-party inspection of
weapons 177; shakes hands with DT 178;
complains of British concessions to
Unionists 179; meets weapons dump
inspectors 179–80; demands meeting
with JP, TB and Mandelson 180; demands
action on OTRs 180; flummoxed at
Chequers meeting 185; storms out of
meeting with JP and Jeffrey 185–6; refuses
deal on policing and Patten report (2001)
191, 192, 193; and creation of contact
group with DT 194; post-election
cockiness 195; meeting with JP at
Clonard monastery 196–7; on need for
'bigger statement' 197–8; hugs trees at
Weston Park 199; further postponement
of decommissioning 200–1
2001–2007
and 9/11 202, 310; appeals to IRA to
decommission 203; and disbandment of
IRA 205, 206–7, 210; and arrest of
republicans in Colombia 205, 206;
disappears after 'Stormontgate' 209;
responds to TB's 'Belfast Harbour'
speech (2002) 212–13; and discussions over
Joint Declaration 215–16, 218, 219, 220,
221, 222, 223–9; sends JP condolences for
mother's death 224; and government
commitment to Assembly elections
229–30; his problem with IRA 230; gives
JP signed autobiography and goes on
book tour 230; furious at TB/BA joint
letter 230–31; meetings with DT 231;
further negotiations on decommissioning
231–2, 233, 234, 235; threatens to publish
private letters 237; presses TB to deliver
on promises 237; challenges JP to

with Sinn Féin (1987) 63; refuses to join all-party talks without Sinn Féin (1997) 14, 17, 20; critical of Irish for conceding to DT 27; proposes d'Hondt method for Executive (1998) 98; comes top in Assembly elections 117–18; and Orange Order 122, 127; and policing (2001) 192, 194; presses for inquiries into murder cases 199; supports Irish at Leeds Castle talks 253; complains of being excluded 257; against elections (2006) 290; *see also* Durkan, Mark; Hume, John; Mallon, Seamus
Society of United Irishmen 37–8
Soderberg, Nancy 77, 78, 79, 141
Spectator, The 243–4
Sri Lanka *see* Tamil Tigers
Steele, Frank 66–7
Steele, John 101, 105
Steinberg, Jim 182, 183–4, 191
Stephen, Sir Ninian 64, 319
Stone, Michael 116, 294
Stowe, Ken 70
Straw, Jack 187, 188
Sunday Telegraph 26, 172
Sunday Times 227
Sunningdale Agreement (1973) 13, 47, 50, 56, 59, 93, 106, 110, 316
Swift, Jonathan 37

Tamil Tigers 4, 316, 317, 321
Taylor, John: leads campaign against Faulkner (1974) 56, 110; at meetings with TB (1997) 17; on Ireland 310; and 'Heads of Agreement' (1998) 25, 27, 28, 32; and Good Friday Agreement 91, 96, 105, 106; introduces debate at UUC 110; and negotiations over IRA decommissioning 144, 150, 151, 152, 154; and 'Way Forward' document (1999) 154; as 'the key' to agreement 164; not called in support of DT 165; and further negotiations on decommissioning (2000) 178; given secret assurances on policing by Mandelson 179; flown back from Taiwan to vote at UUC meeting 179; attempted coup against DT 239
Teahon, Paddy: criticises TB's Balmoral speech (1997) 11; and Good Friday Agreement 90, 94, 96, 102, 103; and McKee 130; and decommissioning negotiations (1999) 150, 154; negotiates with Sinn Féin over IRA disbandment (2000) 170; and publication of de Chastelain's report 171, 172; retirement imminent 173, 177; farewell dinner 190

Thatcher, Margaret 4, 48, 59–61, 62–3, 64, 65, 70, 76, 208, 320
Thesiger, Wilfred 66
Thomas, Quentin 13, 14, 82, 83–4, 86
Thomson, David 125
Times, The 152
Tohill, Robert 238
Tone, Wolfe 36, 38
Trimble, David: on Partition 53; joins Vanguard 56; presses Molyneaux to be more hard-line (1993) 76; and IRA decommissioning (1994) 82; becomes leader of UUP 121, 311; proposes elections to negotiating body 86; good relationship with TB 9, 88; and TB's 'Balmoral' speech 11, 13; criticises TB's strategy towards Sinn Féin 17; and IRA ceasefire 18; new relationship with No. 10 and TB 18–19, 20; visits USA 19; advised on IRA thinking 19; stays in talks process (1997) 20–21; tells GA to grow up 21; and 'Heads of Agreement' negotiations (1998) 25–6, 27; clashes with Mo Mowlam 26; sees UDA prisoners 28; and Sinn Féin's expulsion from talks 30; difficult meetings with TB 32; demands decommissioning 33; and Good Friday Agreement 90–91, 92, 93, 95, 97, 98, 99, 103, 104, 105–6, 109; difficulties with party members 109–10; challenged by Donaldson 110–11; poor people skills 111; has makeover in USA 114; and referendum campaign 114–15, 116–17; and Assembly elections 117, 118, 119; becomes First Minister designate 118; and Mallon 118, 146; and Drumcree march (1998) 119, 121, 123, 124, 125, 127–8, 130, 132–3, 136; awarded Nobel Peace Prize 53, 141, 311; addresses Labour Party conference 142; first meeting with GA 143; worried about UUP plots 144; optimistic about IRA decommissioning (1999) 147; and negotiations on decommissioning 148, 149, 150, 151–2; attacks government in press 152; fails to gain UUP support 154, 155; more optimistic 156; denounces IRA to media 156; denounces Patten report on RUC 157; in gloomy mood 158; amends draft IRA statement 164; narrow victory in UUC election 164–5; post-dates resignation letter over decommissioning 165, 166–7, 171; supported by TB 169; and new IRA position 171; meeting with MM 171; and publication of de Chastelain report 172; obsessed with Patten report 177;

relationship with Mandelson 177–8; and inspection of IRA weapons dumps 178; shakes hands with GA 178; and IRA refusal to re-engage with de Chastelain 181–2; walks out of Clinton's speech 184; and John Reid 190–91; 'worn down and resentful' 194; bad election results (2001) 195; decides to resign 195, 196; and Weston Park talks 198, 199; loses UUP support 201; sees TB with Durkan 203–4; attacks Reid in press 204; and further IRA paramilitarism 205, 206, 207–8; proposes independent assessor of ceasefire 208, 217, 218; at 'turning-point' 208; and TB's support 209--10; his future role 210; suspects TB of deal with Sinn Féin 214; walks out of multi-party talks 214; out of touch with UUP (2003) 215; and Joint Declaration 217–18, 220; meeting with GA and MM 221; walks out of Hillsborough talks 221; and publication of Joint Statement 225, 226; and *Sunday Times* transcript of JP's phone calls 227; 'as the road to nowhere' 227–8; survives leadership coup 228; focuses on decommissioning at Downing St meeting 230; and Empey 231–2; and de Chastelain debacle 232, 233; at negotiations to save deal 234–5, 315; political career effectively over 235; bitter about UUP defeat 236; survives another coup 239; walks out of talks with DUP 239; complains of being excluded from negotiations 243, 257; on IP's 'sackcloth and ashes' speech 259; calls JP from Mt Kilimanjaro 263; loses seat (2005) 271
Tyrconnel, Earl of 50
Tyrone, Hugh O'Neill, Earl of 37, 50

UDA *see* Ulster Defence Association
UDP *see* Ulster Democratic Party
UKUP *see* United Kingdom Unionist Party
Ulster Defence Association (UDA) 28, 29, 265, 266
Ulster Defence Regiment 48
Ulster Democratic Party (UDP) 21, 28, 29, 265
Ulster Freedom Fighters (UFF) 28, 29
Ulster Political Research Group (UPRG) 266
Ulster Unionist Council (UUC) 52, 56, 110, 144, 164, 165, 179, 182, 201, 207, 221, 228, 234
Ulster Unionist Party (UUP) 9; and Anglo-Irish Agreement 62, 63, 74; and talks with government 73; accepts Downing St Declaration (1993) 76; Major's dependence on 85, 88; and 'Frameworks' document 86, 89; and TB 31; and Good Friday Agreement 94, 95, 96, 97, 98–9, 102–4, 105–6, 109; and referendum campaign 110–11, 114; and Assembly elections 117; opposes establishment of Executive without IRA decommissioning 142; and 'Hillsborough Declaration' (1999) 148, 149; and Downing St talks 150, 151; further talks and 'Way Forward' document 153–6; in Assembly (1999) 165; and Mandelson 172; and IRA decommissioning 178, 181–2, 194, 195; leadership coups 228, 239; against elections (2006) 290; *see also* Molyneaux, James; Trimble, David
Ulster Volunteer Force (UVF) 40, 42, 52–3. 239. 265
Ulster Workers Council 57
United Kingdom Unionist Party (UKUP) 18, 21, 87, 118
United States of America 11, 19, 65–6, 76, 77–8, 84–5, 202, 310–11; *see also* Bush, George W.; Clinton, Bill; Mitchell, George
U2 concert (1998) 114
UUC *see* Ulster Unionist Council
UUP *see* Ulster Unionist Party
UVF *see* Ulster Volunteer Force

Vanguard (party) 56
Volunteers *see* IRA

Wall, Stephen 260
Warrington bombing (1993) 72
'Washington Three' 82
Watson, Dennis 124, 125, 127, 128, 131
Wesley, Joshua 50
Weston Park talks (2001) 196, 198–200
Wheeler, General Roger 173, 175
Whitelaw, William (Willie) 46–7, 48–9, 55, 56, 67
William III, King 37, 51
Williams, Gareth 180, 181
Wilson, Harold 4, 47, 55, 57, 68, 249–50
Wilson, Padraig 116
Wilson, Richard 188
Worthington, Tony 95
Wright, Billy 28, 199
Wright, Oliver 66

Yates, John 279
'Young Ireland' movement 38